The
Irish
Garden

The Irish Garden

A Cultural History

Peter Dale
Illustrated by Brian Lalor

The History Press Ireland

In memory of my gardening parents

*Brian Lalor's illustrations do not represent particular gardens,
but rather the spirit of all Irish gardens. They are generic,
not specific.*

First published 2018

The History Press Ireland
6-9 Trinity Street
Dublin 2
D02 EY47
www.thehistorypress.ie

British Library Cataloguing in Publication Data.
A catalogue record for this book is available from the British Library.

ISBN 978 0 7509 8809 4

Typesetting and origination by The History Press
Printed in Turkey by Imak

The sunlight on the garden
Hardens and grows cold,
We cannot cage the minute
Within its nets of gold,
When all is told
We cannot beg for pardon ...

The earth compels,
We are dying, Egypt, dying

And not expecting pardon,
Hardened in heart anew,
But glad to have sat under
Thunder and rain with you,
And grateful too
For Sunlight on the garden.

Louis MacNeice

Tá súil le Dia agam go bhfaighidh sí fhéin agus m'athair a luach insa Ríocht Bheannaithe agus go mbuailfeadsa agus gach n-aon do léifidh an leabhar so im dhiaidh leo ann in Oileán Parthais.

Tomás Ó Criomhthain, *An tOileánach*

My mother was carrying the turf so that she could send me to school when I was eight years old. I hope in God that herself and my father will inherit the Blessed Kingdom; and that I and every reader of this book after me will meet them in the Island of Paradise.

Tomás Ó Crohan, *The Islandman*

The gardens of Buckingham Palace
Were strewn once with Irish loam
So those English moles that knew their place
Would have no sense of home.

Paul Muldoon

Contents

Acknowledgements

This book has benefitted incalculably from being read, in part or in whole, by Peter Chadwick, Brian Lalor, Brandon Yen, Martin Ventris-Field, Jonathan Blaney and Alexander Mattei. Similarly, conversations with Nigel Everett and Seamus O'Driscoll have, in equal measure, refined often and corrected occasionally what I have written. David Wheeler, in whose journal *Hortus* many of these chapters were first published, had the idea of collecting them into a book – something I'd never have dared to think. Again and again, he has encouraged the long gestation.

Pat Hennessy – always the best touchstone of Irishness, for me – is laid in Milltown Cemetery now, in Dingle, but he's here quite often in these pages, his quizzical eye, his Irish eye.

To Hal Robinson, a man who thinks and does, I owe a lot of the physical fact of this book.

Ruth brooded over the years of this book's writing, carefully, caringly.

To my father – whose gentle ghost haunts all of this book – I owe the simple but central idea that gardens matter.

Introduction

And Grateful Too For Sunlight

What – if anything – makes a garden Irish? On the face of it, there isn't a lot in the reckoning. A west-facing Scottish garden will likely be, at least superficially, quite similar to an Irish garden twenty, forty, one hundred miles away. Likewise many a Cornish or Devonian or Welsh garden. Mount Congreve in County Waterford, at least in some respects, is manifestly a scion of Exbury in England's Hampshire. But if the question were slightly shifted, slightly refocused – What goes into the making of an Irish garden? – it becomes both more answerable and, perhaps, more interesting.

In the first place, gardens, in Ireland or anywhere else, though not entirely determined by climate and geology, are certainly conditional upon them. A garden in Ireland is different from a garden in Iraklion or Islamabad in the first place because of climate. In one rough and ready sense, Ireland itself is popularly defined by precisely that. Because it is damp, because sun or wind rarely scorch, because there is so little frost generally, Ireland is green – the Emerald Isle. Geology too is a shaping factor. Ireland has perhaps the most famous limestone landscape, and then limestone flora and fauna, in the world – the Burren in north County Clare – but liberally spread all over Ireland are also miles and miles of poorly drained bogland, intensely acidic. At a stroke, Ireland can provide places for both acid-loving and lime-loving plants to thrive. It is no accident that probably more primulas and gentians – acid soil-lovers, all of them – have been bred in Ireland than anywhere else in the world; nor that harebells or toadflax ('Killarney Ivy' indeed) or maidenhair spleenworts – lime-lovers – are almost as emblematic of Ireland as maples are of Canada or pæonies of China.

But soil, and soil conditions, can be figurative as well as literal, just as cultural conditions can embrace not only climate and soil but also the culture of human intercourse, the arts, politics, even religion. And such is certainly the case in Ireland, not uniquely to be sure, but with a defining bite. If the rose is emblematic of England and English gardens, that is certainly not the case for Irish gardens. There is, not uncommonly, clay heavy enough for roses to thrive if people wish to grow them, and indeed some are grown, but not really all that many. Two of the world's great rose breeders did their work in Ireland, the McGredys and the Dicksons. But that was in Ulster, what is now Northern Ireland, part of Britain's putatively United Kingdom, where not only the cultural conditions, in the conventional horticultural sense, but also the cultural climate in the broader, figurative sense were propitious. Roses are grown measurably less in the Republic of Ireland. You are considerably more likely to encounter a rose in the lyrics of an Irish song than on the walls or in the beds of a typical Irish garden. Conventional wisdom sometimes has it that the summer rains spoil the blooms, so people don't try to grow them much, but the soft rain doesn't prevent the same people growing (say) asters (which are notoriously prone to mildew) or pæonies (whose flowers are also easily ruined by too much rain). Perhaps the challenge to grow them is sometimes a lure as well as a deterrent: twice at Mount Stewart – first in the 1920s, in response to a fiat from Edith, Lady Londonderry, and then again in the 1970s. On this latter occasion it was on the instructions of Graham Stuart Thomas (but, though he was hugely respected as garden advisor to the National Trust in Great Britain, was he really the person best placed to be alert to the nuances of nationalist iconography in Ulster?). The roses failed there in the Italian Garden in the 1920s (wrong soil, they said then, but there *are* some roses there now), and they failed again in the Mairi Garden in the 1970s despite, I'm sure, their having changed the soil and made it bespoke before planting even a single bush. The really interesting question is why they should have been so persistent in trying to settle a lot of (essentially English) roses into an Irish garden in the first place. The defining factor here is culture in the figurative sense – a deep brew of history and loyalties and affections and disaffections. Indeed, the very frequency of roses in those ballads and songs from the sixteenth to the nineteenth centuries reflects not just a love of a singularly beautiful flower, nor are they working simply as symbol and shorthand for pretty girls. Those songs are also a covert process – no doubt sometimes unconscious, but frequent enough to constitute a national habit – by which the flower is repossessed for Ireland, by which it is detached from its adhesively sticky English cultural soils.

Beyond climate and soil, what goes into the making of a garden becomes progressively less visible and incrementally more interesting. Money – such a very visible component in the making of so many English and American gardens – is only occasionally important in the Irish context. In the Republic, Powerscourt, in County Wicklow, is the only example of such a place that springs obviously to mind, though there are several in Ulster (which is perhaps what you would expect). On the other hand, the absence of money – on a moving scale from genteel poverty to breadline subsistence – is a major contributing factor, as it is, not entirely coincidentally, in the English cottage garden style, the other side of the moneyed coin of the grand manner of a Chatsworth or a Blenheim Palace, or indeed of a Powerscourt.

At the furthest extremes of money, or its absence – I mean the poverty and privation and punishment of famine – the Irish landscape and the Irish garden have both been shaped, subtly but indelibly, either by wealth, or by its lack. And the way poverty carves a national consciousness as surely as a glacier carves a landscape is not to be overlooked, even when, centuries later, that landscape appears to be different, seems to have been recovered, because now it is tree-bearing or pastured, ploughed or built on. History, Irish history, the nebulous but shaping paradox of a very old, mature culture in a very young, sometimes volatile nationhood, is a part of the Irish Mind, passed on and reflected in the Irish garden – physically, sometimes, as in the remarkable number of follies (and lovely walls, and excavated lakes – in other words, the products of charitable Famine Works from the 1840s), and psychologically in the deep craving in the Irish psyche for a place of its own, somewhere safe, in the face of a centuries-old history of deracination, depopulation, dispossession, eviction and emigration. It is no accident that the boom years of the Celtic Tiger were driven frequently by property lust, speculative and foolish though so much of it was. The frenzy was at least partly fuelled by an ancient, chthonic yearning for security. Irish gardens – their walls and sense of enclosure and safety, keeping some things (people) in, and others out – quietly but powerfully reflect an Irish history. Trollope, in 1848, has his Widow Kelly (in *The Kellys and the O'Kellys*) consider herself not 'at all fit company for people who lived in grand houses, and had their own demesnes, and gardens, and the rest'. She is voicing a kind of inverted snobbery: 'she had always lived where money was to be made' (she runs an inn and sells pennyworths of tobacco over the counter of a small shop) rather than in 'a place where the only work would be how to spend it'. She thinks she is claiming a species of moral and fiscal superiority. But she is also self-parodying; there is a comic irony within her words deprecating gardens and their like, because subconsciously she would love to have access to what a garden means even if she would happily jettison all the social and political entailments of the same. A comic irony indeed. But there is, perhaps, a tragic irony too, if and when essentially that same attitude can be worked into the weft of national consciousness.

The first-time visitor to Ireland – the person who, because their eyes are fresh, sees both more and less than the rest of us – quickly spots, of course, what they think they have come to see (what Bord Fáilte, the Tourist Board, has led them to expect): the sober dignity of Dublin's eighteenth-century streets and the liveliness of some of the others – Temple Bar, Grafton Street, Henry Street, and so on; the undemonstrative softness of the countryside, the laziness of rivers, of the weeds along the roadside, of the drinkers in country bars who seem immune to the tiresomeness of time. And these visitors love it. All being well, they're even inducted into that most Irish of mysteries: how it is that rain – steady, almost daily rain – can sometimes invest a landscape not with less but with more charm and character, can supply more, not less, of a moodily atmospheric beauty. But they also notice things the Irish themselves are apt to overlook, things Bord Fáilte don't mention, things that are significantly less likely to attract visitors in the first place. In the countryside they spot the ruins of farmhouses and sometimes these ruins are really rather pretty, but very close by there will be characterless new buildings, and these have been erected in preference to restoring the old. Then they notice the frequency of cemeteries, those proprietorial, eye-claiming, space-colonising forests of Celtic crosses, and they notice the respect afforded them. They're not marginalised as they so often are in other countries, with the telling Irish exception to this of Famine Graveyards or of those out-of-the-way places – in Irish, *cillín* (the 'church beyond the pale') where unbaptised children, suicides, mothers who died in childbirth, vagrants – outcasts all – are laid to rest, out of mind and out of sight. The regular cemeteries you cannot miss, and – as if just to make sure of this – there are commonly road signs telling you that one is nearby. And the third thing visitors notice? It's the hideous new bungalows – ranch-style, Mexican *casita*-style, American West-Wing style – the unmissable concrete, brick and glass litter on hillsides that were previously unspoilt and beautiful. The contention that these three things – picturesque but spurned ruins; the cities of the dead (the ubiquitous cemetery, the necropolis); and the unregulated new housing that effectively destroys a place – amount to a defining characteristic of modern Ireland is one of the quiet theses of this book: the places themselves – so often versions, or paraphrases or parodies of gardens actually – and then the reasons for their presence, for why they have happened or have been tolerated, the way they reflect a nation historically habituated to dispossession, people whose claim to a place of their own could never have extended – for hundreds of years – beyond a grave plot, people to whom the conventional idea (in other cultures) that a beautiful landscape is an unpopulated one seems to aggravate an invisible sore in the collective memory which not even sensible planning laws are allowed to modify; people for whom the picturesqueness of ruins could never compensate for the shame and pitifulness they had once entailed ... and perhaps still do.

Strangely, though, that very same craving – for home, for a home and a garden, for a safe place of your own, for a glimpse of a Paradise Recovered – leads to a paradox in the Irish Mind, and then in the Irish landscape: gardens and gardening in Ireland are indeed (almost) always associated with the Big House – the residence and lifestyle of the colonial overlord – and therefore something to be eschewed by a nationalist, as if there were something fundamentally un-Irish about having a garden ... unless, of course, it were prefaced by another word, one singularly resonant in an Irish context – *potato* garden. Put crudely, viscerally, in an Irish context gardens are Protestant, and Protestantism is alien. Austin Clarke, the poet, has it succinctly: 'the house of the planter [the usurper, in other words] is known by the trees'. To grow rhododendrons or Sweet Williams (say) is as un-Irish as spelling whiskey, 'whisky'. But, crude or not, it is essentially true. Not just true in the ghetto of some pinched, tribal, Paisleyite mentality, but true to historical experience: to grow rhododendrons or Sweet Williams requires at least a little bit of both money and leisure, and at least a little of the luxuries of space and time and superfluous energies denied to the poor, the rent-squeezed, the landless. Irish cabins, the stone and thatched cottages of the peasantry, had potato gardens; Irish demesnes had pleasure gardens. Even the name of a plant could fall foul of history. Sweet William – *Dianthus barbatus* – sounds innocent enough, but word-hygienists in nationalist Ireland would look askance once they had spotted a certain English flavour to the name, and nationalists in the Six Counties of that province of Ulster would home in on the covert resonances entailed in the name *Billy*, itself encoded in the innocent-seeming *William*: King Billy, William III of England, the Battle of the Boyne, the Relief of Derry, the Orange Order, and so on.

Perhaps even as fundamental and simple a word as *plant* carries with it the germ of language distressed. It would be hard to talk or think about gardens and gardening without using the word – like writing a travel book without ever using the word *journey* – and, on the surface, it seems neutral, value-free. But in an Irish context it isn't necessarily so – far from it. To *plant* is to *sup-plant*, to evict, and then to impose alien settlers upon lands ancestrally Irish. *Plant* and *plantation* are words, in an Irish context, that are actually deeply infected. They are the euphemisms, the corruptions of language, used by the colonist and conqueror to mask theft, dispossession, deracination … and they worked. They achieved those goals both in the mind and on the ground: by the end of the seventeenth century only fifteen per cent of Irish land remained in Irish hands, a larceny whose scale had no equal anywhere else in early modern Europe. I know of no explicit occasion in Irish discourse when the word *plant* is treated – in an agricultural or horticultural context – with caution (or worse), but equally it seems extremely unlikely that the word did not – does not – carry a subliminal freight of contaminated meaning even now.

The sum of all this is as if there has been an Irish abstinence – Catholic, nationalist Ireland, that is – from garden-making, as if what we encounter there (sometimes? often? almost always?) is a kind of conscientious objection, as if gardens and garden-making were a forbidden zone, even now, nearly a hundred years on from Ireland's independence. The word *boycott* springs to mind (as well it might: Captain Charles Cunningham Boycott was a Mayo landlord's agent, from whom cooperation was withdrawn early in the Land War, which began in 1879). It is as if there were a taboo – unspoken, unwritten often, though not always unconscious – yet powerful enough to compel observance, as if it were written into the collective Irish Mind. Damien

Enright, for example, author of two marvellous books about living for twenty years in West Cork, notices everything – flora, fauna, weather, birds, fish, rockpools, rabbits that go on eating the grass though the rain is pouring down. He notices *everything* about the natural world and the way humans interact with it. And not often does he mention a garden, but he does remember what Austin Clarke says about the 'poshness' of growing trees and then remembers to distance himself with a terse 'I am not a planter'. Of course, there have been, and are, exceptions: Catholic gardens and Catholic gardeners. Even in the 1840s, the years of the famine at its worst, there was a Catholic middle class. It was small but growing, and some of these people had gardens, even pleasure gardens. But they were exceptions then, and even now such gardens are not all that common. In his book *Irish Gardens* (1967), Edward Hyams was of the opinion that: 'The Irish householder is not by any means such an enthusiastic gardener as his English opposite number'. Irish readers might bridle at that. For their part, English readers – the natural citizens of what is not uncommonly dubbed 'a nation of gardeners' – might bridle at an Italian author observing that *his* countrymen garden more and better than the English. Both comparisons are more or less true, for all that local pride may have been offended. What Hyams saw in Ireland fifty years ago is only marginally less the case now: on the whole, the Irish do not garden all that much. To the innocent eye of the visitor (English? Italian? Japanese?) this is so conspicuous that he or she might be forgiven for wondering if there were some cultural disincentive, some invisible, unspoken, even unrecognised embargo at work. The absence of gardening in Ireland – relative though that is – is indeed quite striking. And yet, the Irish mind, eye, ear and soul seek satisfaction in beauty as much as do those of any other ethnic collective – indeed, more so, you could soberly argue. On the one hand, Irish music is probably unrivalled for a certain beautiful melancholy in its slow airs and, on the other, an irresistibly contagious liveliness in its jigs and reels; Irish literature – and poetry in particular – is a world-beater. The Irish aren't insensitive either to beautiful flowers or to beautiful landscapes, to wit – if we confine ourselves in the first case to just one flower (indeed, why not to that rose again!) – *The Last Rose of Summer*, the *Dark Rosaleen*, the *Roisin Dubh*, the *Rose of Tralee* (Irish all of them), and in the second case all those ballads lamenting the loss of those lovely places that the emigrant must leave. The rosary is the Irish devotion of choice, of course it is. There have been quite a few Mollys in Irish literature, history and folklore, and it is not surprising that they're quite often Dubliners. Molly Malone belongs to Dublin's 'streets broad and narrow', and she it is who catches the popular imagination. But it is surely no accident – and unusually for her maker, a certain Mr Joyce, not entirely ironic either – that the most imagined of them, the most celebrated (notorious, PhD-discussed, parodied, blushed over) Molly of them all *Blooms*. Jack Yeats is surely the greatest of Irish painters – another world-beater, in fact – but it is Paul Henry's Connemara landscapes which epitomise Ireland both to the Irish and to the rest of the world – achingly beautiful, melancholy, wistful. In the case of the rose – both flower and symbol – historians have sometimes noted the irony implicit in the Irish making so much in their songs of what is quintessentially an English icon, but, as we remarked earlier, that is really to miss the point: it is as if a willed repatriation of the rose were being enacted, and – given that the context of this plant is normally a *garden* – it is a repatriation into what is perhaps the most sensitive arena (sensitive culturally, politically) it is possible to imagine. The citizen of the world might smile at this point, might recall other roses from Iraklion or Islamabad, might think some special, selective pleading is being invoked. I almost wish it were so, but I have to doubt it. Here is a verse from a northern Irish song popular in the 1860s and for years after:

Rule Romania, Romania rules the taigs;
Poor Rosie's childer ever, ever, shall be slaves.

If these are the words, you have no difficulty in guessing the melody. Taig (Teague, Teigue) is an anglicised form of the Irish *Tadhg* – Timothy – but it also became the stock name of the stage Oirishman in Victorian popular dramas. From that it became shorthand for 'Catholic Oirishman', that is to say, 'nationalist bog-trotter'. This song was coined almost certainly in the 1860s or, just possibly, a little earlier. There's no doubt, however, about the period of its great vogue: those same 1860s. In 1886, Gladstone introduced his first Home Rule Bill. Songs like this helped to defeat it. The slogan 'Taigs Out!' (out of Ulster in particular, but out of Ireland in general too) was first slung then. Since then it has become a stock-in-trade of Unionist invective. And if Taig is the Irish *Man*, Rosie is the Irish *Woman*.

One argument periodically dusted off to address this strange paradox – this seeming reluctance to garden – is that Ireland is naturally a garden anyway. And so it is (though there are dreary, featureless rural parts to be sure, and there are mean, ugly towns too). The further west you go, the stone walls – or ditches, the Irish call them, the earth-walls and hedges – are replaced or just overgrown by hedges of massed fuchsia (*F. magellanica*, which looks as if it has been there forever but was actually introduced as recently as the late 1700s). The roadsides become ribbons of montbretia (*Crocosmia x crocosmiiflora*, a hybrid in fact, and raised in France in the 1870s). The telegraph poles become so smothered in swags of ivy that they look like clubbable yetis. Fields – particularly damp ones – have margins marked out by the yellow flags of iris (*I. pseudacorus*). Others are carpets – huge ones, sometimes – of purple loosestrife blended into meadowsweet with its cream-coloured breaths of those lovely vanilla-scented flowers in July and August. All the year round, hillsides are golden with the blossom of the furze, gorse, a weed in England, but almost actively cultivated once-upon-a-time in Ireland because its new growth, cut with leather-gloved hands and crushed in a mill, was fed to horses who enjoyed it and found it highly nutritious. Ireland is a garden indeed, and, the further west you go, the more that is the rule rather than the exception. After a day or two in West Cork, Kerry, Clare or maritime Galway, the visitor almost ceases to notice it, this gratuitous flowering everywhere. But it must never be forgotten that these are the very same districts where people were gnawing grass in the late 1840s to stay alive if they could. As Yeats put it, beauty can be terrible, terrifying in its implacable hardness.

Gardens reflect climate and geology. They reflect history and, if there is such a thing, they reflect national temperament. But garden-making is always, in some measure, autobiography – singly and individually, or collectively perhaps, or even the aggregate of an entire people. Gardens reflect the minds of the people who set aside time, space, money perhaps, to embark on the more or less gratuitous act of making them – almost certainly not a lucrative venture (though a bit of pomp and circumstance might impress the neighbours and prospective clients if you were in business or politics as, for example, were the Wingfields – viscounts in due course – at Powerscourt; their métiers were brewing, distilling whiskey, and politicking). The matter begs the fundamental question: *if gardens are not to make money, what are they for?* Worldwide, a certain consistency of answers emerges, but not necessarily comprehensively. Gardens are often meant to show off wealth, power, chic. Some gardens – and they tend to be the big, famous ones – are simply fantasies, ideal worlds peopled by ideal characters: worlds fit for the gods (albeit stone ones) if you are wealthy and classically educated and incline towards nudes (and you are not exercised by the absurdity of even the gods wearing nothing in a northern winter), or by nymphs and shepherds (if you are pastorally inclined and bashful about all that flesh). They are tableaux really, and then *tableaux vivants* – bits of theatre – once you yourself come out of the house, step into the garden and walk among the gods too. Better still if you are accompanied by your admiring guests. And then there's the working-class version of this tendency to fantasising in gardens: here it is a case of little chaps with shovels over their shoulders and peaky hats. Gnomes began as the fantasy of certain spiritualists in mid-Victorian Germany and Britain, but pretty rapidly became a craze among either the potty or the urban artisan class – a bizarrely prescient anticipation of twentieth-century Disneyfication really, and one that never caught on in Ireland, presumably because it would have seemed recklessly self-mocking in its blatant reification of the fabled Irish Little People, the *Sidhe*. Once again, in an Irish context it is an absence rather than a presence that has a tale to tell.

Sometimes (and much more interesting than the foregoing), gardens are ways of recovering lost Edens – another kind of fantasy perhaps, but much more adult, much closer to real ghosts. Fantasies possibly, metaphors certainly. Individually, that usually means a real or an imagined idyll of childhood, but some gardens are modelled on (say) memories of a holiday in Spain, or of a private myth of goals achieved (*Dunroamin*, *Thistledoe*, and so on). Collectively, it means something very deep indeed, something groping towards mythic, or even religious, meaning, some barely glimpsed and even less understood platonic recoveries – the sort of thing evinced (crudely, I know, but none the less really) in barbecues (atavistic memories of life on the savannah?), or (strangely, if not crudely) in that weird tendency we have, on the one hand, to try to make our gardens into outside rooms, as if they were (seasonal) extensions of the inside of our houses and, on the other, to make the rooms inside our houses into simulacra of the gardens outside, by covering the walls with flowery, leafy wallpaper, laying flower-patterned carpets under our feet, putting petal-shaped lampshades over electric light bulbs, covering sofas in flowery chintzes and – most strangely of all – displaying framed landscapes on the walls as if they were *trompe l'œil* windows onto the world outside. Whatever it is that is going on here in the way of striving to recover something – however crudely, strangely – it is evidently a kind of compulsive, primal nostalgia and it can assume quite a lot of different forms, but it is most acutely evident (and interesting) in the act of garden-making … which perhaps should be the subject of another book entirely, but it is certainly not out of place to mention it here either, and we shall indeed return to it.

Gardens are hobbies. Hobbies provide occasions for recreations and for stress relief, for asylum from all-too-busy, or boring, or intractably bootless lives. In Shakespeare, gardens are always places for amorous assignations – wooing, canoodling, cavorting. But cuddling in February would have to be driven more by the imperative to keep warm than by strategies of the heart, so it tends to be a rather seasonal occupation. Nevertheless, the proposition broadly invites our consent. Gardens are sometimes places where people set up their own inviolable little kingdoms – unilateral declarations of independence from an otherwise unsatisfactory world – places where the gardeners/

owners are in control and no one may gainsay them. As a matter of fact, there must be an element of that in *all* gardens really: it goes with the territory, both on the ground and in the mind. Sometimes gardens serve as places to exercise and express one's constructive – perhaps even creative – impulses. Or they can be the places where control freaks can manage, manipulate, manacle every blade of grass, every twig on wretchedly trussed bushes. They may serve as a last bastion for beleaguered blokiness to make a lot of noise and fumes with 'manly' machines such as chainsaws, power-washers and strimmers. More likeably, gardens – especially town gardens – are oases of peace and quiet. That can be as true of a shared, communal garden in a London square as of a private garden behind a private house. Some gardens are playgrounds for children. Some are places where collectors compile botanical showcases – zoos really, but for plant materials, not animals. These are intense versions of the garden-as-hobby.

There is a paradox here. The very best gardens – the ones that affect you most, then and there, and later in the recollected memory

– achieve that impression because they appear to be gratuitous, they appear to be above and beyond the exigencies of something as mechanical as purpose. They rank up there with playing football or chess, with listening to or performing Beethoven, with *Hamlet*. If these things were not to happen, life would go on without them, not much would change, but we would be demonstrably lesser human beings. In their gratuitousness, their economic pointlessness, lies their power, because we are never more human than when we are doing profoundly useless things, useless but not necessarily pointless: acts of kindness, altruism, acts of love, stopping to stare at a moment of fleetingly beautiful landscape, tottering through a Chopin nocturne, wrong notes and all, playing a game with your feet when it would have been so much easier to pick up the ball with your hands, running a race only to come back to where you began. Gardens – especially back gardens, and certainly not just *big* gardens – are all of a piece with that: very profoundly human events, because they are essentially useless, because they float free of function and purpose. In fact, of course, they probably don't. Or not entirely. But nevertheless, an *impression* of gratuitousness is achieved, and that's what matters. And that is actually what marks out a *great* garden: it is the impression made that is *great*, rather than the dimensions or even the contents. What it means is greater by far than what it is.

The foregoing fundamentally destabilises the question *What are gardens for?* in the first place. But – placing one's feet back upon the ground, and going along with the conditional proposition that, despite all this, they can and do serve at least some purposes, some functions – we must address the last, but not least, of the answers to that conditional question. It is the one most difficult to pin down at the same time as it is the most contemporarily relevant, indeed urgently pressing – in the sense some of us (a lot of us? but inarticulately? mistily?) have that gardens are, definitively, the liminal, transitional zones between Nature and Human Nature. But then that sense is coupled, first, with the growing apprehension that Nature is not necessarily on our side any more (if it ever was), and then that Human Nature, *homo sapiens* indeed – uniquely among animals, and actually anything but *sapient* –

is essentially self-destructing because we are already pretty far down the critical road towards the fouling of our own nest. Gardens – we begin dimly to perceive – mediate between the urge to control (that is to say, usually, to destroy) and the willingness to go with the flow, to learn from, to cooperate with, to accept a revision of received hierarchies vis à vis who is in control, a revision of the mandate we have traditionally believed ourselves to hold, to 'have dominion over the fish of the sea, and over the fowl of the air, and over every living thing that moveth upon the earth'. Never mind that that is a commission we exercise no less vigorously for probably not much heeding these days its source – the God in the Bible, in the Koran. I take it as axiomatic that the situation is serious, and also that not much is being done about it. Controversies about peat-based composts and chemical insecticides apart, gardeners are probably among those who are most particularly sensitive to this. At the very same confluence of Nature and Human Nature, Wordsworth could have been found two hundred years ago, and the profundity of his careful observations and psychologically acute, philosophically searching ruminations, is one of the great intellectual and emotionally compelling achievements of our forebears, but – by and large – we haven't seen fit to learn from his (and anyone else's) insights any more than we do from the incrementally obvious evidence of global environmental degradation. We gloss *breakdown* as *change*, we mock anxiety about change as feeble-mindedness, and we carry on with business as usual. Nevertheless, it would seem that a not inconsequential number of people now mistily perceive of gardens – theirs and the sum of gardens as a whole, and then co-opting the meta-gardens of allotments and wildlife reserves and municipal parks – as places where rapprochements can be made, wounds dressed, new treaties tentatively negotiated. Gardens are radically at odds with the zeitgeist: they reward husbandry but they – most of the good ones – more or less reprove management, and management is one of our contemporary gods. Gardens intimate – they always have done – who we are and where we stand in terms of the several time-schemes at work in a garden: the annual, the seasonal – the great life of a tree, the small life of an ephemeral blossom. They afford places where real repairs to the consequences of concrete, fumes, waste, over-population, under-education, can be embarked upon: a bird-feeder here, a CO_2-scrubbing tree there, water for frogs, shelter for beetles and hedgehogs, a plot for children to grow their own carrots and marigolds. Gardens are places of refuge for endangered plants. They are laboratories for wiser ways of living, penitentiaries for lapsed egos, for reformed control freaks. In short, though gardens may not make any money, though they don't generally make waves or friends for us, they do make sense, and therein lies possibly their most profound *raison d'être*. The pressure – global anxiety about the condition of the Earth – is at last gathering pace (I hope), but Ireland has space, a generous ratio of population to space that gives the country a rather special advantage. There is also a sense that there, gardening is something new – an adventure, for most people.

You learn quite a lot about a person from the books on their shelves (or even from whether they have books and shelves in the first place). You learn to read parts of people's characters from their gardens. The impersonality – the absence of a single originating mind – in a public garden is instantly recognisable; the presence of the same in a private garden is correspondingly revealing. Sometimes a garden – however horticulturally complex – is emotionally, psychologically simple. Stourhead, for example, is self-evidently someone's reconstruction of an Arcadia, but it also has the air of an Eden just out of reach, a paradise not exactly lost, but unachieved, an Arcadia reconstructed but not quite recovered. Henry Hoare, its maker, was driven to create it having gained the whole world (or at least the ownership of a very remunerative bank and the possession of vast sugar estates supplying sweet-toothed Georgian England), only to lose, one by one, those whom he loved. This garden is essentially about grief. Versailles is about a king's bloated ego, it's about hubris. Little Sparta, Ian Hamilton Finlay's garden in the Pentlands of Strathclyde, is not really horticultural at all. It is a place designed to frame a poet, and it's about poetry frustrated and refracted into a kind of barely sublimated embitterment: violence and the unleashing of violence are only just held in an uneasy abeyance by the artifice of the inscriptions you find there at almost every turn.

In the case of Ireland, Mount Stewart has a similarly simple (fairly simple) *raison d'être*, it seems to me. Originally conceived as a hobby for a very rich woman married to a philanderer, it became in the end an act of contrition, a gesture, a token of wished-for expiation, almost literally a deed of repatriation. But answers to the question *What is a garden for?* are generally muddier, more tentative – they are compounds rather than purities.

Just as there is occasionally an Irish garden which is simple and more or less singular in its sense, in the answer it offers to the question *What am I for?*, so there is at least one individual who rises out of and beyond the otherwise all-embracing and collective scope of national temperament in the way that he has influenced the character of Irish gardens. That person is William Robinson, and his ideas about wild gardening – transmitted in the first place through his own garden at Gravetye Manor (albeit in Sussex, where he latterly settled, rather than in Ireland where he was born and learned his craft), then through his book, the gardening classic *The Wild Garden* (1870), and finally through the discipleship of Gertrude Jekyll (and of many other people since) – have had an enormous influence upon gardens worldwide but especially in Ireland and Britain. Robinson represented – he still does – the opposite pole to everything exemplified by Chelsea, by the whole business of garden design, by the notion of style and styles, by the modern mantra of self-expression, and so on. A Robinsonian garden is kind to the earth but a bit harder to live with than many people's idea of what a garden should be, because it is always in process, never a product. Actually, that is true of *all* gardens, but frequently neither acknowledged nor respected. A Robinsonian garden tends towards deregulation (or some might call it, untidiness), so it may be harder to live with for people to whom order, regime, control is important. It is harder too in the sense that to husband it well is quite time-consuming, not least because the work must be relatively invisible. If you have a gardener, he or she must really know what they are doing, because the division between weed and plant is as fluid and contextual in a Robinsonian garden as the shoreline in a tidal estuary. Being time-consuming, it would also be expensive (if it were done well), and therefore it pays to do it yourself. It follows that in many an Irish garden – large as well as small – the work is often done by the owner. Elsewhere, however, owners – rich ones particularly – tend not to work but only to dabble, often to the irritation of the real gardener. But that is markedly less the case in Ireland than elsewhere. That might simply reflect a certain contraction of cash among the once affluent. I think that's quite likely, but it also reflects the type of a conscientious gardener, sensitive to the sort of care that a Robinsonian garden requires; and Robinson himself, quietly but significantly, reflects the national temperament anyway.

The alert reader will have noticed in all this a similarity between the English cottage garden on the one hand and, on the other, the received idea of the Irish national character – easy-going, un-ostentatious, convivial – and those two things coinciding, or overlapping, we have noticed already elsewhere. Most Irish gardens are more or less Robinsonian, some out of conscience and principle, some out of indigence, all out of consent to the climate and geography. Robinson's other important, hugely influential book, *The English Flower Garden* (1883), would seem, by its title, to run counter to the idea of Irish character in a Robinsonian garden; but, title apart, more or less the opposite is really the case because this second book (and its numerous subsequent editions – well over forty at the last count) is the *locus classicus* of precisely that very (English) thing idiomatically paralleled so closely in the character of so much of Irish gardening: the English cottage garden style. But even here, surfaces and appearances and common forms of words can be deceptive. In England, the term *cottage garden* denotes (now) a style, in origins humble but evolved into what is seen now as virtually the vernacular of English gardening, however modest – or indeed plutocratic – the premises. It defines the Englishness of a particular manner – informal, artless, abundant, generous and somehow natural. In Ireland, though, the cottage garden was almost never that at all. Even the sense of the words slips away: there is no word in Irish for *cottage* but only the diminutive of the word for *house*. All that prettiness and cosiness entailed in the word *cottage* in England vanishes at a stroke. And the word *garden* – as we shall see

– means something very different from the English usage. In Ireland, a cottage garden was the acre or so growing potatoes, a few oats, a cow and a pig, attached to the cabin where a farm labourer and his family struggled to live and to feed themselves. They lived on the potatoes, and the pig paid the rent if all went well. If there were flowers – woodbine perhaps, bindweed, wild garlic, wild roses, flag iris where it was wet, meadowsweet too – they would not have been actively cultivated. They would have been the pleasant incidents of country life. Accidents, but they must have been at least passively enjoyed.

There is quite an extensive literature pertaining to cottage gardens within the Irish complexion of the term, or simply as *gardens* as they were more generally spoken and written of there. These writings are to be found in official or private reports of rural poverty, in the pages of philanthropic schemes to make those famous 'improvements': the radical cooperative at Ralahine in the early 1830s, for example; the proceedings of bodies such as the Labourer's Friend Society and of the Cummer Society, the latter set up to improve techniques of husbandry; and then of the Vacant Land Society, established in 1909 to encourage allotments, especially but not exclusively, in Dublin. Occasionally there is a survival of a non-literary kind: the vast Gortahook cabbage, for example, which can reach a metre or more in girth, and then there is the famous Lumper, the potato most widely cultivated in the famine years of the later 1840s. What the written texts describe is probably broadly similar to what would have been found in England through the later eighteenth century and for most of the nineteenth, though minor differences of classification may imply larger differences of social character as, for instance, in the interesting incidence of the names of gentry and even nobility in the membership of Irish Florists' Societies in precisely this period – clubs that grew and competitively exhibited not so much vegetables (as now) but tulips, auriculas, violas and, as the nineteenth century wore on, dahlias and chrysanthemums. In mainland Britain, Florists' Societies were definingly a working-class phenomenon. At some point there must have occurred a bifurcation of English and Irish meanings in the term *cottage garden*. In Ireland, it remained, as it always had been, an expression denoting the vegetable patch (and perhaps a little livestock too) attached to a farm-worker's dwelling. In England, it became that blend of the edible and the ornamental – something for the eye, something for the pot – that we think of now as one of the two national styles associated with horticulture in England (the other being the English Landscape Garden of the eighteenth century). At what moment the two islands parted company in their understanding of what was meant by a cottage garden we do not precisely know, but I would hazard a guess that William Robinson had something to do with its final (modern) canonical form, even though its origins are probably several decades earlier. In the 1830s, J.C. Loudon rhapsodises (fantasises?) about the (English) rural labourer's garden and tries to employ it – or what he imagines of it – as a model for the gardens of English suburban villas. Fifty years later, Richard Jefferies – in *Hodge and his Masters* – is much more realistic, but by the end of the century, in the sentimental paintings of people such as Helen Allingham, it had become a vision of a sort of Merrie England. It must have had *some* basis in fact – look at Samuel Palmer's *In a Shoreham Garden* of 1829 – but in the absence of photographic records there is no certain telling of how much.

In Ireland, the author T.P. Gill, in a manual published in 1911 by the Department of Agriculture and Technical Instruction for Ireland, includes that rare thing, a paragraph about flowers – or, at least, about the possibility of flowers – in 'narrow borders' along the edges of your garden. These are neither literally nor metaphorically at the heart of gardening, but at the peripheries. You might have 'simple and inexpensive' nasturtiums, roses, sweet peas, lupins, wallflowers, and so on. You could be 'more adventurous' and sow candytuft and godetias, staples indeed of the cottage style now. But really this is in the nature of an afterthought, an appendix, a brief indulgent holiday away from the proper industries of cabbage growing and manuring the potato beds. It doesn't sound very Irish either. This is, I think, someone looking over his shoulder at the contemporary Garden City Movement in England.

In origin, the English cottage garden was a construct of (some) reality, quite a lot of idyllising and idealising, and a very great deal of nostalgia – especially formative, I think, where it is least visible.

That – the blending of these three elements – is very rare in Ireland. You catch a glimpse of it – but that is all – in the 'Swiss Cottage' near Cahir in Co. Tipperary. It's a *cottage orné*, a fantasy, a toy … and it was probably built by the Englishman John Nash for the Anglo-Irish land-owner Richard, Lord Caher, the Earl of Glengall. It's a gingerbread house bred out of memories of an arrested childhood, Alpine holidays and a vision of distilled Englishness. Not Irish at all. But there are/were, in fact, at least two other such 'Swiss' cottages in Ireland: Glena Cottage at Muckross, Co. Kerry, and Lord Bantry's Lodge at Glengarriff in Co. Cork. Exceptions that, more or less, prove a rule.

Gertrude Jekyll was not exactly a romantic escapist, but there is no more favourite word in her writing than 'old'. If a plant has a pedigree that is old, it is straightaway desirable. And yet … though its origins squelched no end with sentimentality, the cottage garden style did come to have a real identity, a real character. So much so that we need not blush to recognise it as indeed a defining character in English gardening, in some respects the envy of the rest of the world. As so often – in this book, as in life – it is language itself, rather than the material things which language denotes, which is the critical and pro-tean factor. You might take, for example, the cabbage rose. In some respects, it is the epitomous plant of the cottage garden style. Its very name fuses the utilitarian, the workaday and kitchenesque, with the gratuitously beautiful. But which came first, the rose or its name? Botanically it is *Rosa centifolia*, and it is an ancient plant. But when did it become the cabbage rose? *Mawe's Gardener* – a Dublin publi-cation which was in its nineteenth edition by 1808, the edition I am consulting – doesn't ever use the term. Jekyll, seventy years later, does, and those intervening years are precisely those in which the expression 'cottage gardening' shifted its meaning. Is our perception being led by the forms of the words we use, or is it the thing itself that shapes our seeing? Is this, in fact, yet another piece of image-manu-facture, usefully representative in this context as a miniature of the whole idea/ideal of the cottage garden? At the risk of courting hilarity and bathos, it is not entirely unrelated either to notice that that is certainly what is going on in that very English habit of making the public lavatory in the park masquerade as a Tudor cottage – the coy style much preferred for these buildings for some of the nineteenth and much of the twentieth centuries: an exemplary piece, if ever there were one, of fantasy and euphemising and play-acting not all that far removed from cottage gardens themselves and, of course, from the *cottage orné* these places often so much resembled. Indeed, *cottage* used to be the very name used by people whose breeding prevented them from using the words *public lavatory*.

In any case – and murky though the whole nomenclature of the cottage garden is – cottage gardening, as the term is now generally understood, is rarely found in Ireland. And perhaps this reflects simply that Irish labourers were poorer than even their English counterparts. But given that, latterly, cottage gardening has been in any case very much less to do with the gardens of the working class (be they Irish or English), and very much more to do with the romantic nostalgia of the middle classes, it may also reflect a frame of mind: to epitomise England or – even more potently – a vision of Englishness, you would plant and grow a cottage garden. To avoid precisely that – to conscientiously depart from a sense of Englishness – you would *not*. You would strike out for something more Irish – even perhaps if that meant not having a garden at all … which actually is what quite often happens in Ireland.

Go to Glasnevin in Dublin or to Altamont in County Carlow and you encounter another kind of Irish inflection in their respective gardens. There you will find plant labels in three languages, not just the usual unitary, botanical Latin or a grudging binary (Latin, plus English common names). The third language here is that of the Irish local name. Every little bit (of cultural appropriation, I suppose) helps, and I hope the habit becomes widespread. Irish gardens deserve Irish plants, as it were, and there is – as always, wherever you are, whatever the language – a wonderful realm of meaning in local names, local plant lore, and local genealogies in which *history* begins to fray into just *story*, and is none the worse at all for it. For example, *Hyacinthoides non scripta* we familiarly translate as bluebells, but in an Irish garden such as Altamont they are also *Coinnle corra*

... which slips rather nicely off the tongue, as it happens. It means 'Candle-taper', and candle-tapers do, indeed, lean a little out of the perpendicular just like the bluebell (the 'English bluebell', not the wicked, invading Spaniard which is, of course, bolt upright). Cowslip (*Primula veris*) is *Bainne bó bleachtáin* – a lovely lilting alliterative name (and it means 'Milk of the milch cow'). The maidenhair spleen-wort (*Asplenium trichomanes*) – one of the most beautiful and most common of Irish ferns – comes into Irish as *Lus na seilge*, a name probably so ancient that its sense is now misty but nevertheless suggestive, 'Herb of our quest' or, possibly, 'Herb of the chase'.

Gardens can – and often should – be enjoyed without reference to any botanical, historical or biographical baggage at all, either one's own or that of the person who made the place. That's what children do and – at least before they are of an age to be infected by the obligation to be bored – children are the most infallible of all critics in their responses to and evaluations of gardens, in their capacity to understand a garden by entering into and sharing its spirit. Without the impedimenta of education, you get just the beauty and, if you're lucky, a bit of magic. In the end, beauty transcends. But indispensable to the serious study of Irish gardens, if you are that way inclined, is E. Charles Nelson's *A Heritage of Beauty: The Garden Plants of Ireland* (2000). The first thing that impresses about the book is its sheer size: *thousands* of 'plants of Irish origin' (albeit that that's an elastic expression covering everything from plants discovered in Ireland, or bred in Ireland, or introduced – from China, or wherever – through Ireland). As with the number of Nobel Prizes Ireland has won (in relation to its small population), or the number of world-class writers it has spawned (in relation, again, to its relatively miniscule population), for a long time Ireland has boxed far, far above its weight in terms of plants. You look up particular genera. You notice particular gardeners' names cropping up again and again, ditto particular gardens; particular plants – heathers, ferns, ivies – occur frequently as varieties of native Irish plants. And then you get to the Annexes. There are twelve, and they cover Irish historical peculiarities and particularities (the legendary auriculas at Kilruddery; potatoes, of course; daffodils; Irish-bred roses, etc.). Then comes Annexe XII, *Augustine Henry's Plants*. It is essentially just a pair of lists, the first descriptive and detailed (Henry's own plant discoveries in China), and the second, all the plants – some three hundred or so – named after Henry by other botanists. If you didn't know already about Augustine Henry, you would be astonished by the number of plants he introduced, and then red-faced that while most of them (hundreds and hundreds) are fairly obscure, fairly specialised plants, so many others turn out to be indispensible plants, staples of any self-respecting garden: the handkerchief tree *Davidia involucrata*, the winter box *Sarcococca humilis*, the tasselled *Itea*, his lily *Lilium henryi*, and so on. Only occasionally do they carry his name; he was an inveterately modest man, and so many of the plants named by others after him have the name differently encrypted – *henryii, augustinii, henryana, augustiniana, henrianum, augustinei* – that it is quite easy to see why, for all these years and all those hushed references to Reginald Farrer, Frank Kingdon-Ward, Joseph Hooker, Ernest Wilson, etc., Henry has been overlooked. That is not the end of it, though: there is yet another category of his plants, those that are not at all well known but should be, and yet (because of their Irish backwater provenance, is it?) are almost completely overlooked. I mean, for example, *Emmenopterys henryi*. Ernest Wilson thought it was 'the most beautiful tree ever to have come out of China'. See for yourself – if you can; it is very rarely planted – and you'll likely agree, I think. In fact, whether visibly or more or less invisibly, Henry's contribution to occidental gardens has been colossal, easily the equal of those of the vaunted 'great plant-hunters'. And he, in the form of his plants, is another factor in what makes a garden Irish.

Then there are (were) the great Irish nurseries, two of them in particular: Daisy Hill in Newry, and Slieve Donard in Newcastle, both in County Down. Between them these nurseries must have been responsible for a very significant number of the good plants in Irish gardens. These would all have been propagated on the premises but a lot of them were also bred there too. Having accessible nurseries run by really skilled, really committed plantsmen, impinged upon the character and quality of the gardens they served. These were remarkable places by any standards. Daisy Hill originated four hundred and eighty-seven different plants of their own (the number of plants in their catalogues, however, of whatever source, ran into thousands). Their specialities were bergenias and asters, dianthus and berberis, hepaticas and delphiniums, hebes, lupins, kniphofias, primulas, trollius and lobelia. Slieve Donard was (is) famous especially for dieramas and for escallonias. They bred fifty-seven of the former and twenty of the latter. Then there were the rhododendrons (twenty-seven), eucryphias (two), leptospermums (five), daffodils (thirty-six) and pittosporum (four), etc., etc. All in all, Slieve Donard introduced or bred three hundred and forty-one new plants. It is probably not an accident that both nurseries were situated in Ulster. It is a crying shame that Slieve Donard closed in 1976 and Daisy Hill in 1996. A third nursery – interestingly breaking the mould by not being a Northern Ireland business – was Watsons of Killiney, outside Dublin (but absorbed into Dublin's suburbia and concrete now). Watsons specialised in breeding brooms – thirteen altogether – and quite a lot of them, still in commerce, have the word 'Killiney' in their name. There were also hebes and berberis, Lawson cypresses, eucryphias and three new buddleias.

It is in the nature of gardens to be temporary. Perhaps the (usual) shortness of their lives is a component in what we perceive of as their beauty: the ephemeral claims a different and deeper part of our attention from the perennial. The briefness of the life of a garden touches upon our own, a fundamental, elemental, point of contact that feeds into whatever of sense it is that gardens mysteriously make. Garden-making is a defining badge of our species: *homo topiarius* (where the Latin for gardener is that second word, which tells us a lot about Roman gardens, of course). One of the gardens in this book – Butterstream – is now under concrete, and another – Fernhill – at least threatened with the same, though we hope it will survive. Yet another – The Dillon Garden in Dublin – has been sold (house and garden) to a private individual; probably it won't be seen again, the new owners (from October 2016) being wise to make it their own rather than try to perpetuate it as

The Dillon Garden. One of the most formative of all Irish gardens – Creagh, near Baltimore in West Cork – was a lovely, much admired place, but it closed several years ago now and the word is that it is much decayed. But to be willing to consider carefully a garden that no longer exists is, it seems to me, as it should be, even though this book is in no sense a chronological history of Irish gardens (though, in almost every other sense, it is most certainly a history of Eden, the idea that underpins *all* gardens). Time – the much vaunted fourth dimension that those who argue for gardens as a species of art are wont to draw our attention to – is *the* fact of life, and gardens are treatises in that very thing, Irish gardens no less than any other. There is, though, in a good garden a fifth dimension. Over and above climate, soil and style(s), we sense the sum of elusive but necessary things: purpose (that question again: *What is a garden for?*), culture and context (everything from the sort of books that conscientious parents read to their children at bedtime to the big issues of history, national character, even diet, and so on) – nebulous but profoundly shaping things, all of them. Every garden in every clime has at least something of these, this fifth dimension. Call it *resonance*. Every good garden has at least a bit of it. In a Taoist garden, almost no horticulture, but mountains and seas of Thought. In an Islamic garden – places born out of a faith conceived in a desert – green means that God is nearby, and water is the simplest, deepest metaphor of all. A Brazilian garden thrums with life on the brink of vegetable anarchy, and it thrills. A Renaissance Italian garden is, at heart, a trope on (local) ancient myths of a perfect world peopled by mighty beings, which nobody really believes in any more but – playfully – conspire and collude in pretending as if they did. Irish gardens have no monopoly of resonance, but they do tend to have a little bit more than most – resonances that run deeply, run laterally too, and run in unusually fascinating ways. That's one of the ubiquitous themes of this book.

But the central contention – and here it is in summary – is that, beyond climate and geology, topography and economy, there are still three more rather special things which shape and characterise the gardens of Ireland. Individually they are interesting – more than usually penetrating, more than usually formative – but in combination they amount to something – more than an ethos, much more than merely atmosphere – that is peculiarly Irish, a spirit indeed, an indelible watermark.

Two have been sketched out already, but are briefly revisited again here now. The third, and possibly the most formative of them all, at the same time as it is the hardest to pin down and materialise – as if it were indeed a watermark, invisible until you know where and how to look for it – is introduced here too, but not in the very sharpest focus possible. That is reserved until the last chapter, the *Envoi*, to be read when the book as a whole, and its sequence of ruminative visits to twenty Irish gardens, has been completed. Sketched now, it will work prospectively, but much, much more it will work retrospectively once the whole book has been negotiated. It will throw light backwards upon the intellectual territory as well as the turf that has been covered.

The claim that there *is* something special about Irish gardens is bold, and if – even only in essence – it is correct, it deserves a special place. It will depend upon the cumulative, collective impact of these three factors, but especially upon the third. The assertion – that there really is something, as special as it is important, about Irish gardens – has been made before (by Edward Malins and The Knight of Glin in their 1976 book *Lost Demesnes: Irish Landscape Gardening, 1660–1845*): 'The Irish union of man-made landscape with innumerable natural loughs, rivers, mountains and sheltered harbours is an achievement unique in European art', and that is probably true notwithstanding the fact that it is very similar indeed to the assertion about English (eighteenth-century) landscape gardens made by Nikolaus Pevsner in his 1956 classic *The Englishness of English Art*. The overlap does not disqualify or diminish the justice of the claim(s), nor does the circumstance that the one was speaking of classic Irish gardens and the other of their English contemporaries. In some respects, the spirit of the two is essentially the same (which is what you would expect anyway, given that Irish grandees with their grand gardens were often one and the same as the equivalent English grandees), but the contexts are not: the contextual Irish landscapes are subtly, or sometimes boldly, different from those English contemporaries, different materially (geologically,

horticulturally, topographically) and different – radically different –
in terms of social, historical and cultural context. Nevertheless, these
earlier claims to special status and character are not at all the same
as that which is being tentatively explored in *this* book. Pevsner was
writing about eighteenth-century landscape gardens in England. Quite
a number of them have survived, unlike almost all the equivalent Irish
landscapes, which are indeed 'lost demesnes'. This book is not about
historical sites, no matter how beautiful they are said to have been.
It is about Irish gardens and their spirit now. And it is not necessarily a claim to their status as works of art. It is about what makes them
peculiarly – and interestingly – Irish … rather than just West-British or
European or occidental.

In summary, then, the first of the factors that make Irish gardens
different is the ambivalent sense in which gardens and gardening are
perceived in Ireland: on the one hand they are treasured, but on the
other – for deep historical and cultural reasons – there is something
about the whole enterprise that is seen as tainted.

The second devolves upon the fact that there is no plant, no vegetable, anywhere in the world – not even the opium poppy – that carries
such a freight of meaning, resonance, misgivings, symbolisms and
memories as *Solanum tuberosum*, the potato. This plant is at the heart
of Ireland's consciousness and identity as a nation, not in a decorative
or emblematic sense (like the shamrock, like the fuchsia in the Kerry
hedgerows) but etched by the acid of history into its soul. In a sense
this book hinges upon the difference – simple enough on the ground,
but complex and vast in its cultural ramifications – between the potato
garden of the Irish vernacular and the pleasure grounds of the Big
House. In another sense, the history of Ireland (since 1606, the date
of the first mention of potato cultivation there) revolves around the
fact that since the name of this vegetable is not to be found in the
Bible, Protestants – the religionists of the Book – would not eat it (but
would feed it to their pigs or their horses, these beasts being without
souls to preserve). Catholics, on the other hand, took their instruction
not so much from the source text, the Bible, as from their priests, and
their priests offered no opinion on the subject of whether the potato

was a food fit for human consumption. Being cheap to produce in bulk and rich in belly-filling carbohydrates, it became the staple of Protestant pigs and the Catholic poor – that is, the majority population – supplemented on good days by some milk, and on best days by some milk and herrings. And upon that curious bifurcated reading of scripture hangs, eventually, the worst, globally the biggest, man-made disaster of the entire nineteenth century: The Great Famine.

Having said that, though, this disaster was not historically inevitable in the first place any more than, in the second place, it was not humanly remediable once it had begun. It wasn't necessarily culturally entailed in the genes of Ireland's past, Ireland's sorrows. It looks like it – particularly to nationalist historians – but it might just as well have been the case that it was this vegetable, rather than this place, that was jinxed. Something about the very plant attracted hysteria. In eighteenth-century France, for example, it was almost a taboo plant,

anathematised in law as a source of leprosy, and popularly perceived as poisonous. If you ate the potato raw it would, in fact, be quite likely to trigger eczema, and that was reckoned to be a form of leprosy. There was thought to be a similarity between the potato's tubers and the roots of the deadly nightshade. I can't quite see it myself, but it's not fact or truth that counts. It is perception. And then somebody must have eaten a green potato ... and vomited. Somebody must have ingested one of the potato's fruits, those tomato-like balls that sometimes occur ... and vomited. Even without the knowledge that this plant belonged to the *solanaceae*, a large genus of plants which includes the tomato, the *brugmansia* – indeed the solanum itself, that choice climbing plant usually grown in its form *S*. 'Glasnevin' – all of which contain poisonous parts, the potato was reckoned devilish. Perhaps – in the Irish context – that was at least part of the point: the perception of it was not just that it was unpalatable but also that it was devilish, diabolical, stigmatised not just comestibly but morally too.

The third, and the last, of our peculiarly Irish contexts – the one that *in*forms Irish gardens above all others, in the opinion of this book – is this: not so much a thing, or even an idea, as a way of seeing, and not of Ireland itself, but of the way both the country and its distillation into its gardens are perceived by the vast number of people who identify themselves as Irish, who identify Ireland as *Home*, but who do not live there. At the last count they numbered something like eighty million. Statistically, the situation is this (and numerically it is impressive, to say the least): the current population of Ireland itself is about five million; the number of people calling themselves Irish the world over is around eighty million. That means that the Irish diaspora is almost ten times larger than its nearest modern equivalent, the globally scattered Jews (who currently number something like nine million, with about four million living now in Israel itself). Historically, the largest diaspora of all is that of black Americans, but by and large they see themselves as Americans now rather than displaced Africans, so the comparison is historically academic (thank goodness!). There are expatriate Italians, Greeks, Somalis, British, Nigerians, and so on, everywhere, all over the globe, but none of them remotely approach the number reached by the Irish. The Irish – once upon a time 'the Blacks of Europe' – live with the consequence of that geopolitical fact: a huge monopoly of displacement and all that that entails for the cast of their minds.

For these eighty million people, Ireland is a place in the mind, and – if that place were distilled to its very essence – it would of course, indeed, take the classical form of an emerald-green island, somewhere fertile, with a kind climate, somewhere whose acres would easily sustain you, but whose fields would be small and homely – more like gardens than agribusiness. They muse – these people – they reminisce, and they dream … in colour. To these displaced people – dis-placed but not really imaginatively re-placed, re-settled – the remembered hills back home are *blue*, the fields are not starved, or ill-drained, or bleeding thistles and ragwort, but *green*: the Green Fields of Home; the Emerald Isle.

It follows that this place – *Home* – is not somewhere you'd ever find on a map. 'True places', as that connoisseur of homelessness Herman Melville noticed, 'never are'. Recorded in the index of no atlas yet devised by Man, *Home* nevertheless stands as by far the most important place in the world, the place where you don't have to explain your-self, justify yourself. The place where – no matter what – you belong. Of course, that image of home – as Emerald Isle, the old country – is capable of myriad inflections depending on who you are, where you are, how many generations removed from Ireland you are. Essentially, however, it is of a green, welcoming place. It is also essentially unachiev-able, somewhere that was home once but is unlikely ever to be so again. These people see 'dirty, darlin' Dublin' and they picture smoky bars and streets whose architecture has been brought to a pitch of perfection of shabby gentility no other city can even approach. They've read their *Dubliners*, they can quote Brendan Behan's blue jokes, they've seen the film of *Strumpet City*, they can sing along with 'Mustang Sally' in *The Commitments*. And their souls ache a bit every time they're reminded of what they've lost. Their feet itch too when someone mentions Aer Lingus or Ryanair. And this – a vision of Dublin – is one form of Ireland that the aching yearns for. It's the form catered for by themed Irish pubs –

O'Neil's, O'Shea's, Malone's – in every city of the world. Dublin is indeed the *omphalos* – the belly-button of Ireland, the magnetic north of every Irish exile's imagination. Joyce called it that and he would have known, exile as he was. Nevertheless, almost all of Ireland is not Dublin, and that fact accounts for the other complementary image in the exile's mind: those small farms, the hills and the mountains, the bogland, the narrow lane – the *boreen* – that leads to the little house by the lazy stream. They've seen it for themselves, or it's the world they know from *The Quiet Man*. They picture small towns, townlands smaller still, places with wonderful names – Mooncoin, Ballybofey, Killibegs, Dingle. They remember the names of those mystical offshore islands – Skellig Michael, Valentia, Cape Clear, Achill, Aran, Tory, Inishvickillaun, Ireland's Eye at Howth – and the word *island* blurs into *Ireland*, some place in the mind offshore from a mainland which, being set apart, is special, betokens safety and home, and represents everything that a land of heart's desire should. Being so green and being so unachievable it is Eden, a garden, a paradise, of course, but by the same token a paradise probably lost. Irish folk songs are brimming full of images of this place. Irish mantelpieces scattered the world over will bear a clock, a vase perhaps … and postcards, photos of this lost place. Atlases don't record it; songs and letters and poetry and novels do – over and over again:

> 'Growing up,' Beth said, 'I used to think this bog and Laban Lake were strange and beautiful. A kind of paradise.'
> 'Try living here. You'd have the same life as that rat [the rodent in the kitchen of his cabin that he has just stamped upon]; and who'd choose to slave and be beggared in a bog?'
> 'Mr Parnell's changing all that.'
> 'He can't change the weather, stop blight or beggary …'

[says Liam Ward in Eugene McCabe's fine 1988 novel *Death and Nightingales*.]

For most people the world over, lost paradises are metaphysical – childhood, their mother's lap, their father's smile, the intense nostalgia for certainties, lost forever, that catches up with you, when you go to church on Christmas Eve – that sort of thing. But for the Irish there is a Paradise Lost that is also physical, terrestrial. That peculiarly Irish perception of Ireland as an Eden, the place where you belong but where you cannot stay, profoundly shapes the way Ireland reproduces Eden in its gardens, perhaps even *why* it gardens in the first place and, when a garden does occur, what it means. Exile – a condition of mind even in those who actually live in Ireland – has radically formed the spirit of the Irish garden in a way and to a degree no other nation can equal. If you'd grown up reminded, day after day, that, the world over, opportunities galore lay waiting to be taken up, with the proviso that 'No Blacks or Irish Need Apply', you'd need no other cue to sigh and remember what you'd left behind: even if Ireland couldn't fill your belly, it never would, never did, slam the door in your face.

Exile, emigration, diaspora – all the textbooks tell us – are a fact of Irish life, Irish history, Irish destiny. Historically it was 'economic necessity', racially it was 'ethnic inevitability'. Since the Great Famine of the later 1840s, it has indeed been a cultural norm, so much so that what would, of course, be wept over, but ultimately conceded to by any other impoverished (or persecuted or overpopulated) nation, has quite often become to the Irish something more: not just a capitulation to the iron laws of economic gravity, but a vocation. Only for the few short chimerical years of prosperity, the years of the Celtic Tiger, has Ireland not sent away its children. Briefly the tide was stemmed then, but then (since 2008), the pattern of exile has begun to creep back once again into Irish life. Roughly but readily reckoned today, something like a seventh of Americans and Canadians, a third of Australians and a sixth of New Zealanders are of Irish extraction. And then there's the rest of the world. Of course, since the 1840s that world – as they say – has shrunk. Even in the early twentieth century, Blasket Islanders, off the west coast of Kerry – inured to watching their children leave – would gaze out over the Atlantic and say 'next parish America', and it probably comforted them a bit, both the leavers and those left behind. Certainly, there's some truth in it now – the idea of living in a global village – but the heart-wrench of deracination and parting remains.

How to make it bearable? How to draw, or at least assuage, its sting? The answer lies – as proverbial wisdom has always told us – in making of necessity a virtue. A virtue … or a vocation. Take the cases of two famous Irishmen. In 1904, James Joyce, aged twenty-two, left Ireland more or less for good. He excoriated his homeland, his home city, Dublin, as 'a sow that eats its own farrow'. It would have made it easier to go if you believed that, and he had quite a lot of reason to do so: clerical narrow-mindedness, intellectual cowardice, sexual hypocrisy, lack of educational opportunity, artistic pigmyism, and just downright poverty. 'Paralysis', Joyce sums it up as. In the very opening paragraph, the very first reductive, monosyllabic sentence of *Dubliners*, the boy, learning of Father Flynn's third stroke, says: 'There was no hope for him this time.' Indeed, there was not, he was dead, a corpse, laid out in his coffin: 'As I gazed up at the window I said softly to myself the word "paralysis".' In Joyce's eyes, of course, the priest is not just victim but also instrument of Ireland's morbid condition, yet this paralysis embraces not just the body, but the mind too, the will, the spirit not just of truth and the arts and of intellectual inquiry, but also of enterprise. Joyce's final commercial venture in Ireland – setting up and running a cinema, actually – had failed like all his others, but in the end it was not really economic necessity so much as conscience that drove him to leave, and to invoke 'for my defence the only arms I allow myself to use – silence, exile, and cunning'.

Joyce didn't win the Nobel Prize (though it was almost tailored for achievements such as his) but in 1969, Samuel Beckett did. And he too left Ireland, a self-willed exile. But he redoubled the voca-tion of absence thereafter by not even writing in the language he had been born into. After 1953, almost everything he did was written in French, and only later (sometimes, and then grudgingly) translated into English. Take the case of his most famous work: *En Attendant Godot* is what he wrote first, and probably what he really meant.

In so many ways, linguistically, geographically, religiously, eco-nomically, culturally – from the anonymous *Voyage of St Brendan* in the eighth century to *Brooklyn* (Colm Tóibín's novel of 2009) – exile has shaped the Irish mind and stained the Irish soul. And this – the way Irish people see Ireland through the lens of exile – is the third of the elements which, while not necessarily materially changing the presence of an Irish garden, changes the way it is perceived. What is perhaps a constant of the human mind the world over – a blurred idea of paradise in the form of a garden, a memory of the world before the world began – is, in the Irish mind, a peculiarly strong, peculiarly intensified, sometimes even volatile atavism. Ireland-in-the-head shapes the meaning of Ireland-on-the-ground.

This, the most elusive but most penetrating element in *What Makes an Irish Garden Irish*, is the aesthetic, cultural watermark, invisible (until you know how to see it) at the same time as it is indelible, that makes Irish gardens, in the end, such engrossing places, such moving places sometimes, such strangely homecoming places – not utopias at all (impossible places, *no-places*), but xenotopias certainly, *strange-places* where the heart belongs for sure but the feet dither, the mind cannot quite commit. You'd want your ashes scattered here ... in the end. You'd settle that matter once and for all – in the end – but in the meantime, you've a career in Toronto, your children are naturalised at their schools in London, Melbourne and Cape Town, the address of your bank is in Springfield, Massachusetts.

The final chapter of the present book, the *Envoi*, is given over to using precisely this perception – the bitter-sweet treasure of the exile – to locate and configure what this might mean on the ground, in the gardens, in the place – rural or urban – we call Ireland, but the places and territories discussed are not by any means entirely terrestrial. In the first instance, and perhaps in the last too, they are places in the mind.

This is not a compendium of all the important Irish gardens. Glasnevin, the National Botanical Garden in Dublin, is mentioned often but does not have a chapter to itself. Powerscourt – the epitome of the garden built to clinch contracts – is on all the tourist itineraries, but not here.

Were there world enough and time, there should have been chapters on brave, beautiful gardens like the Bay Garden and Coolaught Garden, neighbours in the vicinity of Enniscorthy, and the new, immature but groundbreaking garden at Kells in County Kerry, the new and the fashionable such as the Duignan Garden in Shankill, or old and unfashionable but heart-winning gardens such as Kilruddery at Bray. There would have been the Heywood Garden deep in County Laois, surely the most un-Irish (but very English) garden in the whole island ... except that it has as curious a collection of (quintessentially Irish) follies as you could ever wish for. Glenveagh Castle in Co. Donegal, of all Irish gardens, has the most hard-won treaty with the landscape it is settled in: a *hortus conclusus* indeed in the surrounding wilderness. Kilmacurragh – Glasnevin's country cousin in County Wicklow – is a pretty marvellous place too, and getting better and better as the years pass, its trees young, cocky and anxious, or old and time-carved and very, very satisfying, its sumptuous double herbaceous border, its lovely windows onto the ambient countryside. There's Kylemore with its Victorian confections setting up the strangest of discontinuities with those Connemara mountains all around it. Fota, on the shores of the vast natural harbour of Cork, has a lovely collection of well over one hundred Irish-bred daffodils, and some glorious trees too. Perhaps it has also a crisis of identity – especially since its long-running restoration: is this a park? Or is this a garden? And are the two quite so glibly interchangeable as Fota seems to be trying to demonstrate? This remains to be seen. These are not the only gardens which do not receive individual attention here; and it would be invidious to go on. But insofar as this book is about the *spirit* of Irish gardens, and about what it is that makes them in their various ways Irish, it does not need to be compendious. And anyway, there are plenty of *Best Gardens of Ireland* books already, some of them good.

Nevertheless, if you do not know all the gardens written about here, I hope that you will feel moved to make good the deficiency. None will disappoint, and it may be that to carry this book with you will amplify your enjoyment, will swell your appreciation. I hope so.

Annes Grove

COUNTY CORK

No one is more accomplished, more committed, more vocational at navel-gazing than the Irish. There is a vast library of books available to fuel the process and more are published all the time. Here is a short list of that sort of book published in just one month (March 2013, and listed in *Books Ireland*): *The Country of The Young: Interpretations of Youth and Childhood in Irish Culture*; *Race and Immigration in the New Ireland*; *The Great Blasket: A Photographic Portrait*; *Plassey's Gaels*; *Temples of Stone – Exploring the Megalithic Tombs of Ireland*; *The Irish Edge: How Enterprises Compete on Authenticity and Place*; *Landscape and Society in Contemporary Ireland*; *Ireland Through European Eyes*; *Pilgrim Paths in Ireland*; *Geology of Ireland: A Field Guide*;

Melancholy Witness: Images of the Troubles; and that, I think it fair to say, was a lean month. Irish identity – for so long a thing in crisis, a thing contested, a thing caricatured abroad (especially, but by no means exclusively, in the pages of the nineteenth-century *Punch*), a thing physically menaced in the pubs of east London or the streets of New York – this thing mattered historically: the Irish were 'the Blacks of Europe'; they were 'the Jews of the post-Napoleonic world'. Identity – knowing yourself, and knowing your place (but emphatically not in the old British sense; this is place in a physical sense) – is a national vocation.

One of the impediments even now to Anglo-Irish relations is certainly this: the English regard it as bad form, bad mental health, bad social relations, to think or talk about what *being English* means. The Irish do it – they talk about *being Irish* – all the time, and more and more – thank goodness – they do it not with diffidence but pride.

Gardening and football are just about the last remaining topics of conversation where it is still permissible to talk about England and Englishness without either causing embarrassment or committing an offence against canons, or even laws, of race relations. In the case of football, the Thought Police probably wouldn't dare to intervene (and anyway, the Englishness of the team in question would probably be a bit notional, at least something of a fiction, a significant number of the players having been imported). In the matter of gardens, the case is probably simpler still: it is unlikely that the Thought Police have even noticed the breach of discipline, but, if they have, they probably aren't fussed, so insignificant do they deem the cultural and political constituency of gardening.

Style apart, and national temperament notwithstanding, what in the first place makes an English garden English is the soil – the soil and then the climate. It is nature, and not nurture, which makes the difference in the first place. Style, attitude, character, national temperament, and so on; they follow after, if they follow at all.

The English (and that includes me, in this instance) are always congratulating themselves on having – along with Japan – the kindest climate in the world (but there, of course, they also have earthquakes).

It has become a central tenet of national gardening discourse but, actually, it is not quite true, or it is not quite as true as it once was. These days East Anglia isn't getting anything like enough rainfall to sustain its herbaceous borders. And drought-stressed trees have become an almost endemic feature of the landscape everywhere.

Nevertheless, as an idea it lives on. In fact, it seems to enjoy as much, or even more, currency than ever, as if – forbidden any kind of nationalistic navel-gazing elsewhere – we still lay claim to a climatologically special place, an Isle of the Blest, without the religious or ethnic overtones, but reinstated with wellingtons, brollies and occasional sunglasses. Long may it continue, but …

If it is true of England – a uniquely favourable climate, that is – how much more is it true of Ireland? The rainfall there still comes up to scratch, on the whole. Summer there remains an idyll of soft warm days – wet sometimes, it's true, but not the sort of scorching solar acupuncture that England quite often receives now, or else deluginal rainfall intensified into hectic half hours. And the moderating, mitigating Gulf Stream flows past *all* of Ireland's coasts and not just the western littoral, as is the case of Britain.

As a fleeting visitor to Ireland, you could be forgiven for thinking that gardens and gardening have failed, so far, to bring out the best in the Irish. There are the big set-pieces, of course: Powerscourt, Birr Castle, Malahide, Fota, Mount Congreve, and so on. But away from these hotspots, what you tend to get is less a sense of gardening as an absorbing national passion, and more an abiding impression of *Acer platanoides v.* planted in every third front garden throughout the land. Though statistically unfair, impressionistically this would still be pretty faithful, and you'd have to wonder about what became of the real genius of the place. Jekyll worked a little in Ireland (Lambay Island, Co. Dublin and, with Lutyens, at Heywood, County Laois, that most un-Irish of Irish gardens, but very fine with it); Harold Peto translated the spirit of Italy to the island of Ilnacullin in Bantry Bay, Capability Brown was at Emo Court in County Laois and, sprinklingly, other English gardening luminaries have made their marks too, but you'd be forgiven (again) for thinking that latterly the traffic of talent had been flowing mostly in the other direction. To wit, at least one contemporary figure: like him or not, Darmuid Gavin, complete with his Irish brogue and caprices of crazy aerial gardens, has featured large in England – larger still at Chelsea. The odd thing is that his presence and impact in Ireland seem pretty minimal.

You'd be forgiven, too, for overlooking the enormous treasury we all enjoy, knowingly or not, of plants first bred in, or first introduced through, Ireland. All those fabled dieramas and libertias (from Slieve Donard once upon a time, and now from Ballyrogan). All those escallonias. All those yellow, gold, old-gold, tawny-bronze crocosmias. All those plants from the National Botanical Gardens: *Solanum crispum* 'Glasnevin'; *Cortaderia selloana*, the Pampas Grass; the ubiquitous *Olearia semidentata* with its daisy flowers and silver leaves; *Parthenocissus henryana*, the most characterful of all wall-hangings; *Zauschneria garrettii* 'Glasnevin'; *Tweedia caerulea* (though it is sometimes now *Oxypetalum caerulea*) and so on. Or the less than common and far more than ordinarily beautiful *Crinum moorei*, *Cymbidium mooreanum*, and so on. And forgiven also for not connecting those plant-specific names with those of the (Irish) plant hunters and/or directors of Glasnevin responsible for them: John Tweedie, Augustine Henry, David Moore, C.F. Ball.

Harder to forgive and indulge, but probably the most common oversight of all, is the fact that good old William Robinson – and the style he espoused (which, as the dust settles on the twentieth century, seems to be emerging as the most enduringly influential of them all, doesn't it?) – he was not English at all, but Irish. Once you appreciate that overlooked matter, does it follow that an informed approach to his famous Gravetye Manor in leafy Sussex would see it not so much as a distillation of Englishness and England, but as an outpost of Ireland? If so, there is a cat sprung up among the pigeons of our perceptions and misconceptions.

Gardens in Ireland are still not quite the widely visited, often discussed places that they are in England, or indeed in North America – staples of journalism, natural focuses of design concepts both trendy and traditional, places to lavish money on. Green space in Ireland is not the vanishing thing it is in England, not yet deemed so precious because it is not yet so threatened. The Irish are more realistic about their climate than the English, so they don't go in much for the fiction of the outdoor room so beloved of English design gurus (and particularly those further reaches of credibility which take the form of the outdoor kitchen and dining room: the barbecue, the savannah on your doorstep). The Irish are still quite ambivalent about all the cultural baggage that comes with their centuries of endeavour to sever the colonial connection with Britain. That baggage includes so much: above all language, of course, but there are also attitudes (to Europe, to America), and material things such as Dublin's eighteenth-century

streetscapes, attitudes and loyalties to place names, Georgian plastering, glass and furniture. Turn a stone in Ireland's history, in its self-consciousness, and it may well turn out to be a contested territory. Because they remain residually as symbols of alien occupation, some beautiful eighteenth-century houses are still being left to rack, ruin and rot down there in the country. Because gardens and gardening belong, in the associative imagination, with that same colonial way of life – immensely cultured as it was sometimes, but also alien, not vernacular, and therefore somehow tainted – because of this, gardens have yet to be 'forgiven' and absorbed into the perception – popular, scholarly and ethnographic alike – of what is legitimately Irish. Things – attitudes, mores, prejudices, memories – are changing though, and some of them very rapidly, as it happens. Some of them – some of the glue of social cohesion that oozed from the Church, for example, and this by no means attributable to British colonial legacies – are not necessarily losses that you could unequivocally welcome. But be that as it may, sooner rather than later, the national consciousness will recover and rediscover things about Ireland, and about gardens in Ireland, that predate by far the English centuries. I mean the whole panoply of mythic paradises rooted so far back in prehistory as to be historically invisible: the Garden of Fand, Hy Brasil, Tír na nÓg, and so on – or else the still palpable fact of the whole place, the entire island almost, being a natural garden at certain times of the year. These things will legitimate gardens and gardening in the end, and Ireland will no longer fight shy of its cultivated beauty any more than it does now of its natural beauty. Something in the Irish Mind prefers abstraction (or sublimation, or fantasy, or delusion, or escapism, or call it what you will, even 'clarification') – 'We Irish were intrigued ... by stories with a degree of unreality in them,' says Mr Quinton in William Trevor's *Fools of Fortune* – but then there's also a compulsion towards place, to emplacement, towards locating, connecting, reifying, whereby the abstraction fuses with the real. In a nutshell – that is to say, the recovering of Eden – that's exactly what gardens are about, the abstraction made real, and the Irish will take their place as masters of it in the fullness of time.

Like England in late spring, the lanes of (Irish) Queen Anne's Lace are fabulous: *Anthriscus sylvestris*, cow parsley, keeshions (one of its Irish names), it looks wonderful. But what happens after that, after April and May ...? Well, in June and July, consider this, for example:

> the road verges are golden with tall buttercups, and flag irises still wave their yellow banners from bogs and ditches by the West Cork roads. They stand tall amongst the deep green verdure of the damp places where they grow. Towering over them are the last of the fox-gloves, thirty and more fingers and no thumbs ... navelwort, that round-leaved plant of stone walls, seems sometimes to be almost com-peting with foxgloves, which it resembles in small scale. Some years, it flowers to unprecedented heights, a metre from root to tip, covered in creamy bell-like flowers ... Throughout July the procession of wild flowers goes on and on; it is a great month for a hedge scholar ...
> (Damien Enright, *A Place Near Heaven: A Year in West Cork.*)

That's one kind of Ireland-as-a-garden. Another, but much simpler and more beautiful even than that in my opinion, would be those still dampish but also sunny places a month later when meadowsweet – *Filipendula ulmaria*, white with the faintest blush of creamy yellow – and purple loosestrife – *Lythrum salicaria* – simultaneously come into flower. Seeing it, the effect of this artless juxtaposing and blending of the two colours, you would impulsively and quite unselfconsciously call it 'drifts' and 'drifting' – to borrow the Jekyllian expression – because so right, so natural and so stunning is the naturally massed combination of these two plants. A third instance of Ireland-as-a-garden – and this is the really famous one – is the western seaboard all summer long, where hundreds of miles of lanes are literally (and naturally) hedged by fuchsia (*F. magellanica*) and then, in late summer, hedged and edged by canary-yellow, berry-red montbretia. And if that were not enough to settle the matter once and for all, for the connoisseur of Lusitanian/alpine flowers in spring, there is the exquisite flora of the limestone trenches of the Burren in north County Clare. In early autumn, the heathers on the mountainsides of Connemara have to be seen to be believed. And so it goes on.

In that case, you might say: Why bother to garden at all, when you've got all that, free on the doorstep? I sometimes wonder that myself, but not for long. Nature is a great landscaper but only an accidental gardener. Or rather, it is our perception of these events as 'gardens' which is actually the accident. The plants are there all right – at their numerical peak, five hundred and ninety-two different species recorded on the islands of Roaring Water Bay off the farthest south-western coast, the richest concentration of flora in Ireland – but not, except occasionally by accident, the associative contexts you find and expect *in a garden*. Gardeners cultivate not just plants but also the mind – its constructs and artifices of form, aesthetic associations and patternings; its thoughtful settlements of the competing claims of variety, on the one hand, and unity, on the other; its invisible blurring of the edges between nature and nurture; literary, mythic, cultural, even philosophical associations, and so on; all these quietly but adamantly exercising criteria for inclusion and exclusion which are radically different from those found in nature. Garden-like accidents do occur in nature – I like to think that Jekyll would have given her eye teeth for that combination in natural drifts of loosestrife and meadowsweet – and very happy accidents they are too, but that is why we notice them in the first place and then go on to remember them – as serendipities.

Had I to choose one single garden which epitomised the idea and the ideal of an Irish garden, just one place which qualified as such, both because of its quality and because of its character, then – despite choosing from a wide field – I wouldn't have to ponder for all that long. Great gardens in Ireland spring readily to mind but, curiously enough, they are not yet all that numerous and not necessarily by any means *Irish*. There's Ilnacullin, of course, but it (the view of it that you see on the tourist posters) is explicitly Italian both in style and in spirit. There is Powerscourt, to be sure, but that's Versailles, plus elements of the Italian Veneto, plus a bit of Potsdam – and all refracted through a reactionary late nineteenth-century Englishesque, and then superimposed upon the milieu of an eighteenth-century house. There was until recently Butterstream – the darling of the pack, I thought – but, even on its own terms, Butterstream was modelled as 'the Irish Sissinghurst'. Mount Stewart – some would say, the flagship garden in Ireland these days – is actually a consummate performance in eclecticism: a Spanish garden here, an Italian garden there, an English Lutyens-like garden beyond … for all that it has also, and very prominently too, a harp in topiary for good Irish measure. And so it goes on. These high-profile, often admired places are situated in Ireland, but by no means could you argue that they are idiomatically Irish gardens or that they set the tone for any *true* vernacular. And now that one begins to think of it, a national differentiation between 'gardens in Ireland' and 'Irish gardens' begins to take on the character of a very clear and virtually categorical distinction.

So where would I go to enjoy an Irish garden on its own Irish terms, marrying Irish weather, soil and climate with a truly indigenous Irish frame of gardening-mind? The answer is Annes Grove, near Mallow in County Cork.

Not a lapse of the apostrophe, as it happens. The name came about as a playful (?) cross-pollination of surnames when, in 1776, one Mary Grove became wife of a new member of the Irish peerage, the first Earl Annesley. His estate was at Castlewellan in County Down. The garden there is now the Northern Ireland National Arboretum. There are some very fine trees indeed there, though none is probably quite as old or as early as Mary Grove and this first ennobled Annesley. (Some very, very fine trees, but at least one that also ranks as contentious, some would say notorious, namely *Cupressus x leylandii* 'Castlewellan', which was bred from a seedling found there.)

Gardening was more than usually literally in the blood of these early Annesleys. Towards the end of that long eighteenth century, the second Earl happened to be visiting his brother, Richard, who lived on an estate of his own just north of Dublin and had lately taken on a new gardener. And to whom should it fall to open the gates but the gardener's wife, Sophie! Whereupon Annesley took quite a shine to her. So much so that, on his way out, the noble gentleman prevailed upon Sophie to elope with him, there and then. They sped away to Castlewellan and were married a few days later. The match was happy and fruitful, but it wasn't until she had borne Annesley two children that Sophie owned up to having neglected to inform him of the fact that she was already the wife of Mr Kelly, his brother's gardener. The matter – bigamy among the upper classes – became one of the causes célèbres of the time. Kelly, the injured husband, was breathing sulphur and lawsuits and enjoying the sport of levelling the aristocracy. But it was patched up, after a fashion, by the expediency of parcelling Sophie and children off to Paris, where they lived in some style at Annesley's expense and to the greater glory of the city's reputation for tolerating louche behaviour.

By way of flagrant digression, I want to relate the story of another member of the family: James, born in 1715. It is the sort of story that used to be described – in the manner of a broadside ballad, I suppose – as 'famous'. And its fame has lapsed somewhat, but deserves nevertheless to be perpetuated, so here it is.

James was born (possibly) on the wrong side of the sheets. That wasn't a problem for the first ten years of his life: his father owned him and loved him, but something went wrong and they fell out. The boy was no longer welcome at home; the best he could do for a surrogate father, in his now-peripatetic life, was a butcher named Purcell. The real father died in 1727. James did not inherit. Instead, everything went to his uncle, Richard. But rumours persisted, to the effect that James was the rightful heir. They were, it seems, both widespread enough and substantial enough to have caused the new earl sleepless nights, so he took steps to deal with them. These took the form of having his twelve-year-old nephew kidnapped and sold as an indentured labourer to an American plantation owner. He escaped, was recaptured, escaped again and, after thirteen years of de facto slavery, he reached Jamaica, enlisting on 11 August 1740 as able seaman on HMS *Falmouth*. One of the ship's officers rumbled who he was and recognised the character of the plot: his own cousin Anne being currently at the disposal of Lord Altham (Richard Annesley), but without enjoying the courtesy of an offer of marriage for services rendered. James was discharged when the *Falmouth* reached England, was taken under the wing of a Scottish adventurer named Daniel Mackercher (who possibly saw rich pickings, should they be successful) and set about challenging Altham's succession in the courts. Quite a number of people willing (if not necessarily qualified) to attest to James' legitimacy were lined up ready. The stakes were higher than ever: Altham had garnered, in the interval of James' absence, a new title and new wealth as the Earl of Anglesey. And, indignant at James' obstinately litigious resistance, he had him arraigned on a capital charge of murder (a squabble with a poacher at Staines in 1742 was the pretext and context of this, if not the substance), but he was acquitted, the jury being satisfied that the gun had gone off by accident. Under these trying circumstances, milord is said to have offered £10,000 to the lawyer – any lawyer – who could get James hanged. In the following year, at a race meeting at The Curragh, Anglesey spotted James and had his servants beat him up. James survived and filed a suit for common assault. The noble earl was convicted and fined. A much greater loss than a mere exiguous fine was, of course, the one incurred by milord's dignity and sweet sleep.

More so still when the case of the inheritance reached the courts later that year. The evidence was confused – and, no doubt, partisan too – but it did emerge during the fifteen-day trial that Joan Lundy (who may, or may not, have been James' illegitimate mother, as well as his father's maidservant) had been known in the family as Juggy. Juggy! I like to think that that's what tipped the jury towards a verdict in favour of James' point of view. How could anyone rejoicing in the name Juggy possibly be either more or less than she seemed: a virgin and an honest woman!

But Anglesey resorted to the clout that money and interest yield when you need it. He lodged an appeal, correctly anticipating that James would not have the funds to stay the course of a suit carefully

compiled to be long, complicated and protractively expensive
… during which, of course, and pending the result of the appeal,
he would naturally remain in possession of title, property, etc., etc.
He was right. James died, poor and unsatisfied, in 1760.

The case itself was widely noised, Georgian society's appetite for
scandal having been well tickled. But its afterlife was greater still:
James' kidnapping and sale into slavery supplied the gist of Tobias
Smollett's *Peregrine Pickle* (published in 1751). Still running fifty
years later, the story reappeared in Scott's *Guy Mannering* (1815),
went on to supply substance – blended with more contemporary
matter from the equally famous Tichbourne case, where a chap called
Arthur Orton impersonated (as the jury saw it) the rightful heir of
a big inheritance – for Charles Reade's *The Wandering Heir* (1872)
and then became both theme and plot for Robert Louis Stevenson's
Kidnapped (1886). Another book – *Memoirs of an Unfortunate Young
Nobleman* – was actually written (in the 1740s) by one Eliza Haywood
(taking time off from writing more important works such as *The History
of Miss Betsy Thoughtless* and *Jemmy and Jenny Jessamy*) but was
widely thought to have been James' own work.

There's life in it still, I should think, and we may reasonably look
forward in due course to further incarnations.

To return now to our proper task, that is to say, the *gardening*
Annesleys, it was the fifth Earl, Hugh, who was the great gardener
– in due course – at Castlewellan, but our concern is principally
with the other branch of the family who lived in County Cork. Mary
Grove's dowry included this very estate, and it is her name, fused with
that of her husband, which has come down to us in the name, Annes
Grove. That playfulness with language continues with some of the
place names within the garden itself (which are, I'm guessing, the
caprices of Richard Grove Annesley, the man who inherited the estate
in 1907 and who created most of what we see there now). There is,
for example, the *Parkeen*, where park is the English word, but 'een' is

the Irish diminutive. Following the course of the river at the bottom of the garden, you can cross and re-cross bridges to *Top Inch* and *Skinny Inch*, *Upper Inch* and *Island*, where the fun is that 'inch' comes from the Irish *inish*, the Irish noun for island, and 'island' doesn't.

The house at Annes Grove is a lovely, long-windowed, tall-roofed essay in Palladian simplicity and Wyattesque modesty, but the gardens – the original walled garden excepted – are later, so much later in fact that you can almost reach out and touch them as part of our own times and mindset, and that's part of the charm of the place: it doesn't stand upon ceremonies, eighteenth-century airs and graces, nineteenth-century affectations, or indeed upon anything pickled in the artificial aspic of the heritage industry. What we see now was begun in 1907 and was more or less complete by 1966, when Richard Grove Annesley died. It's all pretty mature by now, of course. What we can see now, in effect, when the garden is open, is an almost-period garden now at its probable apogee.

There are no architectural features, no sculpture. Such stone as you see is still growing in the earth. This is something else that makes this place essentially different and – though I think it's quite unconscious – contributes not a little to the striking but quite unforced beauty of the place. The house is stone and stucco. So is a pretty, Gothic lodge-gate cottage. And part of the garden is walled – the wrought-iron gate singularly unfussy, simple, Gothic, beautiful – but beyond that all the architecture is natural.

Essentially, the garden partakes of three forms, three moods. First the woodland, and then river – fine beetling old trees on the one hand, along the woodland walks which wind the length of the garden (half a mile or so; the garden itself covers something like thirty acres) and which mark, first, its elevation, and then a steeply falling valley bottom – in part a gorge really – which takes in most, but not all, of the rest. Together, these comprise two of the garden's three broad moods.

This is certainly not a garden of big views, but it doesn't by that token lack drama. Look up from the ground in the valley bottom (rodgersia, primula, hostas, lysichiton, gunnera, bamboos, all in riotous quantity and rude good health) and, over and over again, the eye will be lifted on and on upwards by carefully placed stands of coniferous trees – groups of green sky-scratchers, really. The sense of scale – vertical rather than horizontal; a Sibelian tone poem rather than Wagnerian blockbuster – is terrific. The same goes for the valley floor itself. On the garden side it is spacious and meadow-like, but the paths wander oozily along the riverbank, then over bridges, through groves of bamboo, under gunnera leaves, past promenades of stooled willows and, of course, allow the construction of a dialogue with the river itself. Its name – a lovely word – is the Awbeg, not a joke this time because the word is ancient, but *beg* means little, and it isn't, really, except in comparison with the Blackwater into which it flows in due course, another of Ireland's lovely rivers, which eventually meets the sea at Youghal, some miles east of Cork City. Here at Annes Grove the Awbeg runs sometimes so slowly and quietly that you could set your watch for Christmas by it. It's so clear too. Then it speeds up, fairly chuckles on its way, but then finally shouts over the weirs. A heron gracefully beats upstream. But on the other side, away from the path, the garden and the flat meadows, there is a limestone cliff, a wall of rock, sheer in parts and thirty feet high, dripping with wild plants and well-behaved water.

The genius of the place is Ireland itself and Ireland's own gardener, William Robinson. There's not a straight line anywhere, except upward in those perpendicular trees. There's almost no formal, geometrical orderliness either. There is only one lawn (in front of the house, and it is daffodil-strewn in spring), and there is not even a whisper of bedding. That's Robinson. Instead, there's a fantastically rich collection of woodlanders: rhododendrons, azaleas and magnolias punctuated from time to time by summer spots planted with hoherias, embothriums, myrtles, abutilons, azaras and – unlikely though it might seem, on these steep rocky banks – hydrangeas. The health and happiness of the plants here is infectious: the heart sings with it all. The symphonic scale of the place and the planting is pretty impressive too, but not overwhelming or bombastic or grandiloquent. Here a *Magnolia obovata* or there a *Cornus controversa variegata*, each of extraordinary size, shares its neighbourhood with mosses and ferns, wrens and voles.

Within what is essentially a limestone landscape, Richard Grove Annesly had found considerable and deep pockets of acid soil. Many of these trees began here as seeds introduced by Kingdon-Ward. Hence acid-loving *Rhododendron wardii*, and many more besides. The same is probably true of a race of primulas which appears shyly beneath trees and by the waterside – types of *P. pulverulenta*, they are probably a great deal more hybridised now than they were originally, when Kingdon-Ward would have passed on the seed. Annesley was a sponsor of his Burmese, Chinese and Tibetan expeditions. Some of the rheums may well have been his originally, too. Down in the damp river bottom are the club-like, clout-threatening efflorescences of their distant cousin, *Gunnera manicata* (and if this weren't Ireland, you'd want to call them – contrarily – vegetable *shillelaghs*, I suppose, but we could settle for *life-preservers*, or *knobkerries*?). They share the space with tiny water avens and some miniature equisetum, just as up in the woods, the very big crinodendrons don't necessarily steal the show in spring; they share it with *Anemone nemorosa* (at least some of it, the beautiful lilac-blue diminutive *Anemone nemorosa robinsoniana*, as it happens). It's all a question of balance and blend: the exotic and the native, the large and the small, the showy and the modest, and almost all of it within an essentially woodland context. That's classically Robinsonian. Much more modern – but so very congenial indeed – is the absence of those noisy, fume-spreading little trucks – endemic to so many gardens these days – in which image-challenged gardeners rush about (with suspiciously clean hands – as clean indeed as the mobile phones they are generally stroking). These are corporate spaces by any other name – with their functionaries moving from meeting … to tearoom … to crisis-management event … and all of them convened in warm offices. But the paths here at Annes Grove won't accommodate these vehicles: too narrow, too winding, too steep, branches too low above them. This is a human space: mind-enlarging, but ego-deflating. And yet there must be times when mechanical help would be welcome – so much to do, probably so few skilled hands to do it (where to do it *well* it is to prune, lop, control as invisibly as possible). That sort of work is not just skilful, but also expensive in terms of time and wages.

So far then, two distinct zones of gardening – the woodland and the riverine – the two connecting and melding along their shared margins. But Annes Grove has a third element. That wall mentioned earlier occurs only in one part of the garden, just beyond the house. The gate is small, Gothic and irresistible. Simple, surely locally made at the smithy down the road, it's a trigger to memories of gardens in nineteenth-century fiction: you can see through but – unless you've the necessary key, or password, or permission – you cannot enter. Gates such as these are the thresholds of forbidden places at the same time as they offer a glimpse of somewhere quite magical beyond. And they're a recurrent feature of Irish gardens: the ironwork a little homespun, black-painted when they aren't rusty, glassless Gothic windows. There is a beautiful one at Kilmacurragh (said to be eighteenth-century, an early example of its kind), several at Rowallane, a lovely luring one at Ardsallagh in County Tipperary, and others – when you know what you're looking for – up and down the country.

This one at Annes Grove leads you through the wall, out of the Wild Garden, into the Walled Garden, and then face to face with one of the finest double herbaceous borders you'd find anywhere in Ireland, or England, or anywhere. It is a gem. Like all of its kind, it is extremely labour intensive; but like only the best of its kind, the labour, as here, is invisible. At eye level, thalictrum, helianthus, acanthus, helenium, aruncus, veratrums and golden achillea. Above and behind them *Echium pininana*, then the silver-leaved, oaty-flowered *Macleaya cordata* (with its strange orange sap if you break it), and right at the back the brilliant *Tropaeolum speciosum* scrambling over the yew hedges which shut in the space. Further forward and nearer you, all sorts of poppies, geraniums and evening primroses – an amazingly skilful blend of colour, height, texture and flowering times, each successive phase replacing the earlier ones but still being supported by them and set off to their best advantage by them. This is gardening indeed!

Look back and you see the wall with the gate you came through. You see it, but only just, because it is conceding most of its presence to a tumbling tumult of *Actinidia kolomikta*, the leaves green, pink, white and dusky-hairy. Every walled garden needs at least a little of an impression of secrecy, and this vanishing wall is what achieves that here: the wall vanishes when you're inside, but when you're outside the secret is tighter, more exclusive, as all the best secrets should be. From the outside – a gloomy, pretty rough, fern-dripping wall – you'd never guess that behind it and inside it is a garden, with light and blossom everywhere. Look up and your vision climbs a towering eucryphia, an enviable genus of small trees – flowers quite like beautiful old single roses, but generally much denser – which do far, far better in south-western Ireland than they almost ever do in England, for all the cosseting they may get there (though there's a fine avenue of them coming on at Sizergh Castle in Cumbria).

Then – and still within these walls – there's a water garden, and a pair of beds rippling with ribbons of box hedges which just fall short of being tied in knots. Instead, they are crammed full, not with high-toned perennials such as penstemons, or well-bred salvias, or toffee-nosed kniphofias, but (the last time I saw them) with lupins! And when did you last see lupins massed, mixed and unmustered as plants worthy of attention in their own right? Lupins are only notionally perennial; they don't last. So changes are rung on what is effectively the only piece of (counter-Robinsonian) bedding in Annes Grove: sometimes it's lupins, sometimes antirrhinums, sometimes impatiens and lobelia. As a little vignette of period-piece gardening in its own right, it's delightful. These beds lie along what was originally the main axis of the Walled Garden, before the herbaceous border came about, that is. On your right is a low mount, and a Victorian summer house, too fragile to use now, but curiously and characteristi-cally twiggy in construction and decoration – a latter-day root-house hung over from the eighteenth century, it seems. On your left there are roses and wall plants. Behind you, when you return (in spring, if you can manage it) is a large plantation of *Helleborus* × *hybridus*. But only the careless would retrace their steps too soon because ahead of you, though hidden behind a hedge, lies the nursery.

It has to be said that nurseries are quite rare in Ireland, and good nurseries are rarer still. Here is one of the latter – small, quite specialised (in woodlanders, and therefore quite Robinsonian), and not to be missed on any account: *Uvularia* in several varieties, like-wise *Convallaria*, *Maianthemum* (three species), hostas (Robinson called them *Funkias*, which is a shame because it's such an ugly word, but that's not his fault), *Jeffersonia* both *diphylla* and *dubia* (a perfect complement to *Anemone nem. robinsoniana* as a matter of fact: *Jeffersonia diphylla* is white, but *J. dubia* – certainly among the most beautiful of all spring flowers – is that same lilac-blue as the anemone, its flowers goblet-shaped). Species and varieties of *disporum*, *disporopsis*, *polygonatum*, *epimedium*, and much more of the same, are grown here. But there are also plenty of sunny things: half-hardy salvias, hedychiums, and, special among them, some varieties of *Pæonia delavayi* (*P. moutan* to Robinson ... very strange!), one of them probably unique to Annes Grove – small, double flowers, intensely, velvety, dark red. Oh yes, and there's a really charming kniphofia called 'Toffee Nosed'.

A few miles upstream on the Awbeg, at Kilcolman Castle, Edmund Spenser lived and, of course, wrote (until the castle was burnt out around his ears in 1598, and – poetry apart – he deserved it really, but never mind that just now). We know for certain that the first three books of *The Faerie Queene* were completed at Kilcolman. And – whether written there or not – Book Four, which famously and quite fabulously celebrates Irish rivers, begs for attention. Tradition has Spenser associated with Annes Grove. Even allowing for a slight anachronism, it is possible, though he was never a gardener as such. He called this stream the Mulla, which seems a pity really, Awbeg seeming so much sweeter and vernacular. Be that as it may, he might indeed have been penning an epigraph to this very spot, Annes Grove, when in *The Faerie Queene* his characters resort to:

A shadie grove not far away ...
Whose loftie trees yclad with sommers pride,
Did spred so broad ...
And all within were pathes and alleies wide,
With footing worne, and leading inward farre;
Faire harbour that them seems; so in they entred arre ...

Birr Castle

COUNTY OFFALY

Birr is one of those places that make the expression 'small town' a term of affection and esteem rather than of contempt. It *is* small, but it is also a place to be reckoned with: dignified, orderly without being bossy, occasionally grand, never po-faced, a place of character. It stands on the banks of the Camcor River and its tributary the Little Brosna; indeed, the name Birr means 'watery place'. Geographically, but perhaps not quite culturally, it is in almost the very centre of Ireland. Apocryphally (and onomatopoeically, if you listen to yourself speaking the town's name ... or try to spell it in your head: *Burr*) it is said to have the lowest winter temperatures in Ireland. The castle demesne – more than one hundred and twenty acres, and the largest private garden in Ireland – embraces parcels of the three counties

Tipperary, Offaly and Roscommon. The little town – largely spared the ravages of progress – is a mixture of the modestly Georgian with occasional caprices of early nineteenth-century Gothic. Thackeray's Becky Sharp might live here, enjoying the society and excitement of the garrison, running up debts in the milliner's, and lamenting the infrequency of local balls and assemblies. At one end of the town is a stern, conspicuous, very classical obelisk of 1746 commemorating the Battle of Culloden (which, being interpreted into an Anglo-Irish context, means 'Yaboo to all Stuarts/Catholics/Nationalists') and, at the other end, stands a Hibernian Gothick memorial to the Manchester Martyrs (1867), the Birmingham Six of their time, as it were. Schematised like this, you might think the place was an ideological battleground and, in a sense, so it is (and Ireland, and Irish history in general), but there's no militancy about it now, nor indeed for the last eighty years (though Ulster has joined this tendency to peace only relatively recently): Ireland is unequalled for peacefulness while still yielding rich seams of contested meaning to the alert visitor.

What, for example, could one construe from this: spotted once parked up on the very street that connects those divergent foci of loyalties was a tractor. Like most tractors in those days prior to the uncaging of the Celtic Tiger, it had already done a lifetime's duty of work on an English farm, but then – and just ahead of the looming axe of terminal MOT failure – it had been shipped over to Ireland and sold on into another incarnation. There it was, wheezing, farting, coughing, tied up with bits of bull-wire and chewed pony reins, the door a piece of sacking, the glass – such as remained – fractured into creased maps to match the tobacco-cracked faces of the farmers in the bar outside of which it stood ... eventually to limp away down the street once the affairs of the world had been set to rights within. On the ledge between the wheel and the windscreen, a plastic image of the Virgin kept a watchful eye upon events, which, all things considered, was probably just as well, though the risk of the vehicle being stolen by any opportunistic thief seemed remote enough.

On top of the cab, however, was a window box, a glorious galli-maufry of pelargoniums and gaudy marigolds, blue lobelia to match

Our Lady's mantle and one cheeky dandelion, the whole watered regularly by the summer showers and guarded – but in a relaxed mode, to be sure – by the dog who dozed on top of the toolbox, his master otherwise engaged within.

What should we make of that?

Or of this? Not far away, a heron standing stock-still in the flood of the river running below one of those squint-eyed mill buildings left behind when Ireland tried valiantly but, through having almost no coal of its own, failed to join the Industrial Revolution, and now one of the most enjoyable components of the vernacular architecture. Everything else moves except for the heron – the reflection of the mill on the puckered water, the reeds parting like a curtain for an invisible otter, the water itself. Only the heron is still, and it's that perfection of immobility which gives it away to the human eye. There he stands, however, and, not like us whose eyes are all too easily beguiled by surfaces only, he stares down, down into the submarine depths. Fishing is hard because the river is deeper and fleeter and more tawny-peaty than ever, following a storm the night before.

It's that old trope about the eye either resting on the reflection on the surface of a pane of glass (or water), or else graduating into seeing through and beyond it. George Herbert wrote a hymn about it; it's the stuff of many a parable about short-sightedness, about sight and insight, and so on.

Then the heron stabs, swallows and beats off upstream towards the castle like a bit of tattered, windswept bunting, the illusion of art at last broken by his artless movements.

The entrance to the castle and its gardens is through a yard, a bailey, where tea, huge cakes, tickets and an induction to the atmosphere of the place may be had. Access used to be by way of the main gate further along the curtain wall, and that itself was approached via a beautifully quiet, spacious street of handsome but not boastful small-town houses, framed between a pretty Gothic church at one end and the castle gate at the other, set in the castellated wall. Something about the symmetry, however, gives it away (that mischief of perfection again) as more akin to toy soldiery and Gothic folly than to real siege machines and medieval militias bent on mayhem and pillage. The wall, after all, is only one storey high; the arrow slits are blind; the gate itself, though just about conceivably defensible, is framed by two arches for pedestrians – set on either side of the aperture like doors on a cuckoo clock – which clearly are not. Defensible or not, it's delightful, all of a piece with the Gothic of the castle itself, which the visitor will see almost as soon as they are inside. It is, in fact, a distinctively Irish matter, a style of sham Gothic we now call Toy Fort (but it probably had a much grander name when it first saw the light in the very late eighteenth century, the first architect and first patron so pleased with themselves). It has been very long-lived and pretty widespread. Birr is my favourite example of it, but a close second is the dam and all the outbuildings of the Poulaphouca Reservoir in County Wicklow, a whole suite of them rather than just the occasional isolated item in a street. At Birr, however, there is another bit of Irish history and sentiment quietly encoded into the building. The castle used to face outwards towards the town, making a statement, as we'd say now, about wealth and authority, property and power. But now – and, indeed, since the early nineteenth century, when the castle was remodelled and the gateway and curtain wall were built – the castle faces in upon the garden and the demesne. The reason? The Act of Union with Great Britain of 1801 so dismayed Sir Lawrence Parsons – the jobbery of it all, the sell-out, the rinsing out of the rags of prin-ciple – that he (said by Wolfe Tone, no less, to have been 'one of the very, very few honest men in the Irish House of Commons') lost heart, literally turned his house around to face the other way, and set about gardening instead.

The earliest Parsons were English adventurers in Ireland, really. They were in the mould of Sir Walter Raleigh (poet, courtier, bucca-neer and beneficiary of the largest gift by the Crown of commandeered land ever made in Munster); of Edmund Spenser (poet, courtier, mili-tary man, the first person actually to put on paper the Final Solution – genocide, in effect – to the 'Irish Question'. He was given estates around Kilcoman Castle in north County Cork.) Or of Sir Henry Sidney (father of the poet Philip Sidney and thrice Lord Deputy to the Queen in Ireland where his forcefulness and thoroughness achieved a tripling of the tax revenue in only three years, much to the satisfaction of the Crown, which held naturally that the cost of suppressing and dispos-sessing the Irish should be borne by the Irish themselves). These were not necessarily very principled people in the first place. The castle at Birr and its very large estates were wrested then by force from the real owners, the O'Carrolls; but they in their turn probably hadn't come by them all that honourably either, so perhaps there is some rough justice in the bigger schemes of history at work here. However that may be, at some point in the process of conquest and resettlement, County Offaly became King's County, Birr became Parsonstown, and the Parsons became knights, and then – through inheriting the title from an uncle – the Earls of Rosse. The dynasty latterly has certainly made its mark and, by and large, an estimably benevolent one it is too, but that first Earl of Rosse (not, it must be remembered, a member of the Birr branch of the family) made his mark also, and it's not necessarily one that the family might want to boast about, though it's not without its interest to the rest of us. He was founder and first member of The Hellfire Club, an assembly of the cream of eighteenth-century Irish rakes, gentlemen recreationally – perhaps even vocationally – committed to drink, debauchery and diabolism. A pioneer in this field he certainly was. The club he founded anticipated by twenty years the so-called Monks of Medmenham, the English version of The Hellfire Club, led stylishly and infamously by Sir Francis Dashwood, and further developed by him in his garden at West Wycombe into the form of erotic landscapes within whose anatomical/horticultural nether regions the rites of the society were sometimes conducted, weather permitting. Those flakey Irish prototypes, however, led by the first Earl of Rosse – though they were more conventionally depraved – are not entirely unworthy of our cautious attention. Having said that, the Parsons family, those with the Birr connection – the latter Earls of Rosse – settled down to other things. Sir William, the second of them, set a trend towards establishing a family – generation after generation – of remarkably useful people. They became celebrated – and still are – for achievements in science, in engineering, in photography, in astronomy and then in gardening.

That sensible decision to give up politics in favour of gardening having been made upon the Act of Union, the shaping of the demesne at Parsonstown/Birr began to gather pace, but its beginnings were in a rather formless set of prospects – vaguely Brownian, with a sort of dammed stream, a maze probably, and a bit of fortuitous natural landscape. From these, bit by bit, they evolved into what we see today, a palimpsest of three hundred years of gardening styles, a place with a premium on style, indeed, but with a virtual embargo on swank, a place where the views are now articulated by one of the very finest collections of trees in the world, variously rare, beautiful and beetling, a place where that very characteristically Victorian confluence of science and horticulture (in the persons elsewhere of Joseph Banks, Joseph Paxton, Bagshaw Ward, people like that) is reproduced with astonishing flair and abundance by the achievements, over successive generations, of the immensely talented Parsons family: telescopes, turbines, suspension bridges, pioneering photography, as well as an important botanical collection. Those two intellectual streams flowing together and in parallel are most evident in this instance in the person of William, the fourth Earl of Rosse: a scientist in the Irish tradition of, say, Robert Boyle, and a botanist in the Irish tradition of, say, David Moore or Augustine Henry. But he wasn't the only one; the whole family shared in this intellectual breadth and depth.

You could go to Birr and revel in these very (scientific) things, and never mind the gardens, if you so wished: there is a fine, small, absorbing exhibition of plans, models (*inter alia*, of the very first steam turbine, invented here to power Brunel's mighty ships and, indeed, the *Titanic*), drawings of the nebulae first seen through the telescope at Birr (so accurate, and earlier than any photographs!), etc. All this will reflect and explain what you see outside: the largest telescope in the Victorian world, attracting astronomers from all over the globe, which employed a speculum of thirty-six inches, then, in a second telescope, of an unprecedented six feet in diameter, cast in a furnace on the estate, etc., etc. Elsewhere within the demesne, you'll see a very early, very beautiful suspension bridge, and you'll see for yourself the river which was harnessed to drive the world's first turbines. The telescope is a bravura assemblage of coopering, and clanking chains and levers, ratchets and winches, and then of lens grinding and polishing, all built into the battlemented housing of another of those Gothic caprices in which Birr rejoices. From 1845 until the commissioning of the Mount Wilson Observatory in California in 1917, this was the world's largest reflecting telescope. The huge cylinder, being made only of coopered wood, seems so much at odds with our plastic and steel-bleached perceptions of what high-tech equipment should look like, and yet this place – above all, a vast essay and education in trees – reminds one powerfully of the intellectual, commercial and environmental pressures gathering momentum more and more at this very moment regarding those very same (mis) conceptions: the vast laminate-timber beams and all-through wooden construction of the new buildings at Homerton College, Cambridge, for example; the shibboleth-felling essay at the end of Colin Tudge's *The Secret Life of Trees,* where he spells out uses both sustainable *and* industrial for trees, to name but two of the gathering throng of other examples and arguments pressing for a radical revision in the way we perceive trees.

The suspension bridge at Birr – white, weightless and wire-spun – dates from 1826. It is reckoned to be the first, the parent of them all, and I can believe it. There's something about the fusion of courage and curiosity in all these projects that delights rather than merely dazzles, like so much later applied science. There might be a lesson in education too: all these curious, calculating Parsons were educated at home, and not just by tutors but also by their parents, and not out of necessity but from conscientious choice. In due course, Parsonstown would be supplied with electricity generated from the flow of the Camcor River by these ingenious people. Conscientious too were their efforts to mitigate the effects of the Famine in the later 1840s. Famine Works – such a familiar presence in so many Irish gardens – included, at Birr, the enlarging of the lake and the building of the star-shaped ramparts around the castle – follies, in effect … which always put me in mind of Uncle Toby's reconstructions, on the counterpane of his sickbed, of the Siege of Namur with its fosses, scarps, revelins, groynes, demilunes, terrepleins, cuvettes, bastions, trenches, salients and other sundry fortifications, partly because *Tristram Shandy* is incorrigibly an Irish book and partly because it is incomparably absurd to boot. Thus Toby's revisiting of the battle serves as his only solace for the pain of the wound in his groin (where else!) received there. Birr's need of defensive ramparts – as indeed of the moat, another Famine Work – is purely academic, but those 'star-forts' sound suspiciously like versions of Toby's demi-lunes, and the wonderful whiff of the spirit of Irish Folly is sharp in my nostrils when I visit both book and garden.

In fact, the star-forts are very considerable earthworks, and they are still there but modified later to allow of a series of gardens terraced down to the river on the steep south-west side of the castle. These are richly planted in irregularly sized but straight-edged beds – pattern-defying, though essentially trapezoidal more or less – and, in the abstract, they resemble nothing so much as the fractured facets of a cubist painting. The variety and character of the climbing plants are particularly interesting, but the sites are gifts to precisely those plants anyway. Here, though, you will see this vertical gardening both above you and below because the sightlines are so various. The mixed grouping of shrubs and herbaceous plants in beds on the ground tends towards the sun-loving, the silver-leaved and the sumptuous. The quality of the maintenance and husbandry is exemplary too.

Right at the bottom is a river garden, wild and Robinsonian, and cousin to those other great riverine Irish gardens at Mount Usher, Mount Congreve and Annes Grove. Sheets of *Omphalodes cappadocica* have settled themselves in under some very fine trees. *Magnolia officinalis* (an Irish tree because it was first introduced by Augustine Henry), Japanese maples and a cork oak. If you look closely in April, there's also a good deal of *Omphalodes cappadocica* 'Starry Eyes', an old Irish variety whose forget-me-not flowers blink in the strong new light of spring. Until the gale of February 2014, there stood here the tallest known specimen of the grey poplar, *Populus x canescens*. In the breeze it used to shiver – true to its timorous kind: aspens, willows, poplars – like a bashful child being tickled. The trembling was audible as well as visual – a dialogue with the gossiping water at its feet. Now it lies prone on the ground, but spared all the indignity of being 'cleared up' like so much rubbish. Here, though dead, for a few more years, you can still grasp something of what had been its stature, its living dignity.

In 1912, William, the fifth Earl, bought a large job lot of pioneering plants from Veitch's closing-down sale in London. Among them were introductions by E.H. Wilson: *Magnolia delavayi* would have been the original star (but for the fact that it didn't flower for years) but botanists then were particularly excited by a number of rare Chinese conifers. There was also *Carrierea calycina*, a beautiful plant which flowers in June with blossoms that seem hardly to open from buds twisted, like a clematis alpina, like the twists of salt in the old crisp packets, but they are not blue. Rather they are waxy white and green, like a hellebore. In due course, these original plants were supplemented by further rare introductions, particularly of Chinese plants again, and it is the sum of these today which has made Birr one of the most magnetic places for anyone interested in trees, whether the interest be botanical or aesthetic, or – best of all – both.

There is published, at Birr, the usual guidebook, and leaflets too if that's all you want, but also one or two other things besides: a booklet of botanical paintings by a variety of hands and in a correspondingly wide variety of styles. It's called (of course) *Flora Birrensis*. Then there is a modern facsimile of a much larger volume of designs – mostly for garden buildings – made in 1745 by one Samuel Chearnley, a young man from Waterford who died at the age of twenty-nine in 1746. This book may well represent the sum of his life's work. The original belongs in the library at Birr Castle because the third Earl, a previous William, seems to have commissioned it, indeed even to have had a hand in some of the designs. This Parsons was also a patron of Handel and, apparently, it was he who persuaded the composer to give the première of *Messiah* not in London but in the Music Hall of Fishamble Street, Dublin on 13 April 1742. If Handel had seen the title page of *Miscelanea Structura Curiosa*, Chearnley's book, he might have wondered what sort of company he was entering when he became numbered among the loose company of artists and musicians who enjoyed the patronage of Sir William Parsons. Loosely but idiomatically translated, that title means 'Wacky and Off-beat Buildings of All Sorts'. The title page lays out the wares contained within as:

ruins, grottoes, surprizes, cascades, fountains, bridges, obelisks & pyramids, columns, terminations for vistows, temples, triumphal arches, chimneys, monuments, sections of halls & gallerys together with plans and elevations.

Farther on here is a comprehensively disarming footnote that reads 'NB. The plans and scales of the fore going designs have been omitted as being to depend on the workmans fancy more than any rules.' Actually, the designs themselves – derivative sometimes, but always completely competent – are delightful, but not so much as buildings than as flights of fancy, as stage designs perhaps, as caprices. Almost certainly without knowing it, Chearnley's work is blood-brother to the early designs of William Kent, made not for gardens at all but for the theatre, though Kent went the whole hog and drew with a brush whereas Chearnley worked only with a pen and a ruler. Sadly, none of Chearnley's designs was carried out at Birr, but there is no lack of caprices by other hands, as we have already seen.

A third volume available in the bookshop is *Fifty Trees of Distinction in the Birr Castle Demesne*. In it, D.A. Webb of Trinity College identifies the best of the extremely rich collection in the garden and then describes them in terms acceptable to the dendrologist but accessible to the amateur too. You would almost certainly need this booklet to be able to put a name to *Ehretia dicksonii*, perhaps the rarest of all the trees here. It flowers in June with white trusses conceivably mistakable for a cherry out of season, though the tree itself is too large and the blossom too demurely modest. No fewer than fifty of Birr's trees are listed in another book, *Champion Trees in the British Isles*. And there are two more trees that are simply unique to Birr: *Fagus sylvatica* 'Birr Zebra' (a beech with striped leaves!) and a hawthorn, *Crataegus monogyna* 'Birr-bi-Rosea'.

In due course – say one hundred years – Birr will have yet another extraordinary claim: a 'grove' of giant sequoias – *Sequoiadendron giganteum* – and coastal redwoods, perhaps as many as three thousand trees, spread over an area of twenty acres. There are a few of these trees here and there in the demesne already, some of them grand old things, but this new 'grove' will allow us to sense what they can mean collectively, and that is important too when the word *forest* has become so debased, so damaged. Birr's redwood grove will be yet another world-beater, world-teacher.

Mention back there of the botanical Mr Dickson prompts the question of whether Birr shares the same sort of southern hemisphere and

Australasian plants associated with the name – dicksonias, phormiums, gunneras, pittosporums, and so on – that you'd find in so many
Irish gardens on the Atlantic coast. The answer, but qualified, is *yes*.
In fact, Birr is significantly both colder *and* drier than those favoured
places. It is also relatively alkaline, so rhododendrons – bountiful in
the classic Irish garden – are possible here only in acidic pockets
(though, strangely, County Offaly as a whole is almost covered in peat
bogs, and thus is acidic). You might think that alkalinity would rule
out magnolias too, but interestingly enough that is not necessarily the
case, at least not here. Indeed, it is magnolias that form perhaps the
largest part of Birr's spring display. They also exemplify an important connection not so much with other Irish gardens, as with a very
particular English one: Nymans. Anne Rosse, who married into the
family in 1935, was born Anne Messel, and she grew up at Nymans in
Sussex; hence the extensive planting at Birr of magnolias in general
and of *Magnolia* 'Leonard Messel' in particular. There are also beautiful cultivars named after Anne Rosse herself and after her husband,
Michael. Among the finest things in August in almost any Irish garden
will be the eucryphias and, among the best of them – as here – will
be *Eucryphia x nymansensis*. The flowers are simple, single and rose-
like, but the purple stamens and the sheer profusion of blossom make
it really special.

There is also a special honeysuckle at Birr, *Lonicera* 'Michael
Rosse', but the best of the family plants is a tree pæony, 'Anne Rosse'.
It's a beauty. Michael Rosse made it by crossing *P. delavayi* – red,
elegant, with taffeta-textured but small flowers – with the yellow
P. lutea ludlowii: the result, a large, golden flower edged and veined
a little on the backs of the petal with red, and with an opulent boss
of peppery red stamens. So beautiful is this flower – and so skilful is
the botanical artist Wendy Walsh – that the page devoted to it in that
fabled book *An Irish Florilegium* is probably the most satisfying in
what is, in any case, surely the most beautiful of all modern florilegia.

Another dimension of the Messel connection is that Oliver (of
that name) – the designer of legendary productions such as Tyrone
Guthrie's *Sleeping Beauty*, MGM's *Romeo and Juliet*, Covent Garden's

Queen of Spades – was Anne's brother. He was a visitor at Birr quite a lot where he painted a bit and probably had gothic dreams which fed into his characteristic stage designs. Lifelong, he made masks, and there are one or two fine ones in stone at Birr.

A lot of the Birr demesne is grass, mown sometimes, tree-planted often – trees planted singly or companionably, trees inflecting the movement of wind, reflecting the mood of the light, deflecting the cares of the world, trees looking nothing like the prevailing contemporary style which would have them first bred (or lopped) into dwarf sizes and then placed in small groups in the middle of a field like so many knots of exiled smokers chucked out into the fresh air to teach them a lesson. Here at Birr, one of the groups of new trees – *Tilia cordata* – is planted in a spiral, a reflection of one of William Parsons' discoveries in astronomy: the tendency of the nebulae to be grouped in spirals. Paths here are as likely to be mown swards – rides – rather than gravel. Near the lake there's a meadow of fritillaries, flowering in spring and mown only much later. There's something similar at Mount Congreve. Both look amazing, Elysian Fields indeed. The dominant impressions at Birr, regardless of the seasons, however, are of trees and space, water and space, grass, water and sky.

Because trees live so slowly, because they slow time down – and us with it – they make us think of ourselves and see ourselves in the contexts of longer, slower spans of time. And that must effect a readjustment of relative importances. Trees humble us (a bit) by revising our self-importance and the span of our influence, but of course they pay us back with connections: we plant trees, trees connect through time with bigger pictures of continuity over bigger spans of time, connections to climates and the threat to stable climates when we apply the axe, the chainsaw and the principles of international commodity markets to trees without regard to them as components in much bigger pictures than merely the making of money. And, of course, trees are evidences of natural beauty; and then we get a sense of well-being as the beneficiaries of that beauty. And we enjoy the ancient inscrutable puzzle: we can explain almost everything about trees – their functions, their material properties, their origins, their place in the great scheme of things – we can account for all these things, but not for the stubbornly resistant fact that they are beautiful to behold, and that there's no reason on earth why they should be, but they are. Then there's that really primitive sense of awe – even of fear, perhaps – that we get when we plunge into the wildwood and, as we must, lose our way so easily, so quickly. Roger Deakin likened it to the nightly revisiting of our own subconscious when we drift into sleep. Mysteries at the heart of trees make them as inscrutable and as wonderful as people, and make us, sometimes, as grateful for them as we are for people.

Birr must attract the equivalent, in the arboreal world, of twitchers in the avian – people who pursue the exotic and the rare just for the train-spottiness of it – but much more than that, and irrespective of their rarity, with age individual trees assume individual character. They can be forbidding or they can be clubbable, or patronising, or bashful, or extrovert ... especially in a wind. They can be charming and groomed, or wayward and wilful. As various, in fact, as human beings. Unlike us, however, on the whole they tend to age well. Whether we take the trouble to notice them or not, willy-nilly they supply so many of the metaphors by which we make sense of ourselves: we 'search for our roots' and we 'bend with the wind'; 'hearts of oak' are our men; we take risks and 'go out on a limb', we 'go with the grain', 'branch out' into new ventures, or even 'turn over a new leaf', and so on, and so on. Most contemporary of all, there's the primal, Darwinian metaphor of the evolutionary Tree of Life. Trees visibly frame the views in our landscapes and invisibly frame the way we speak and think about who we are. But, however we look at things, it's a measure of how far we have come (how far we have mistaken or lost our way?) that it is precisely the opposite of the old proverb about not seeing the wood for the trees that holds true now. We see – sometimes – the wood, but the trees, as individuals, hardly ever.

Between the trees at Birr, a lot of the vistas (sorry, *vistows*, of course they are!) lie across or along the big lake whose flat, horizontal surface is the best foil to their perpendiculars and the best mirror to the lazy Offaly clouds. But there are other parts more intensively gardened and more formally shaped. Towards the north-east of the demesne and well away from the castle are most of the formal gardens.

There is a box parterre: a palindrome of intertwined R's which is repeated in the white-painted benches behind it, a tour de force of jigsawed curlicues. Box plats work well only when the edges are kept sharp, and they are here, but the other condition for success is that the whole can be seen from above. Seen from the ground – and this is more and more true the larger the plat – the pattern is lost, and so it is here, though that bench, not being horizontal but vertical, helps a great deal to repair the gap in perception and to make the point of the Rosse R's. If there were one critical shortcoming of Birr as a whole, it is that the absence of rising ground in the demesne prevents big, comprehensive, Brownian views of the lake (though not of the castle, oddly enough). This is nature's fault mostly, but the short-sightedness reproduced in the box parterres is Man's.

Similarly formal is a square of hornbeam *allées*. Planted in the 1930s, and planted quite far apart, the trunks are now very mature, very nobbly and jiving, and very enjoyably gothic. Underplanted with snowdrops in spring, in all seasons you can see through 'windows' in them as through rusticated picture frames into other parts of this formal garden. There is a working kitchen garden. There is a children's play garden with the largest turreted tree house in Ireland. There are beds full, all summer, of masses of delphiniums in every hue; there's a formal orchard and a beautifully restored period greenhouse, in front of which stands another of Birr's big trees, *Sequoiadendron giganteum*, the giant redwood. And beyond that there is another of those oddities – or eccentricities, or follies, or Gothic caprices – which crop up here and there at Birr. This one is living. It is an alley lined by very tall box hedges, indeed the tallest in the world in all probability. They are clipped narrow and tight like flasks, up to a height of twenty or twenty-five feet or so, and then left to their own devices. So they froth out at the top like so much green champagne out of slim glass flutes. Only a killjoy would be compelled to ask: Why? Why let them grow so high? Why not clip them all the way up? What are they for anyway?

They've been here for perhaps three hundred years. They are the El Grecos of the plant world: etiolated, anxious, somehow ecstatic.

Behind them is a small, formal water garden – lovely powdery-grey Irish limestone, simple spare lines, minimal planting, but the music of tumbling water. A little gem.

Birr's rivers, the Camcor and the confluent Little Brosna, leave soon on their journey to join the Shannon miles and miles away and to lose themselves eventually into the western ocean, but not before they have flowed beneath the seven or eight bridges that span them within the bounds of the demesne. Actually, however, there are even more bridges here than meet the eye. Birr is a remarkable place for metaphysical bridges too, bridges between historical gardening styles, between the witty and the serious, between Irish and English manners, between the grand gesture and the intimate detail, between sciences and arts. Best of all, perhaps, is Birr's commitment to encouraging as much public access as possible without for a moment compromising the quality of the plants, of the stillness, of the dignity of trees and the beauty of a flower.

And then there's that lesson in the fascination with that which is imperfect. That perfect, classical stillness of the stilted heron; the shrill, gothic honk of its barking as it flies away again downstream.

Carraig Abhainn

COUNTY CORK

One of the strangest, funniest episodes in modern literature occurs in J.G. Farrell's *Troubles*, a novel set in 1919, and not for the faint-hearted, the impatient or the cat-loving but, if that doesn't count you out, read on. Imagine a once proud Edwardian hotel on the south-east coast of Ireland which, against the forces of time and history, will not surrender in the struggle to keep up standards, to maintain a stiff upper lip, and to carry on swelling to the imperial theme. There is no lift of course, but instead a grand staircase, an oak-panelled library and, naturally, an Imperial Bar. On the lawn outside there's an equestrian statue of Victoria Regina. Inside there's a population of tweedy, feisty but slightly indigent elderly ladies, fading conversationally into an imperial sunset. There are canines of course. 'My dogs,' said Edward with simplicity. 'Aren't they beauties? Mind where you walk.' Rover is the favourite, but a close runner-up is Haig – not necessarily a dependable name so soon after the Somme, but at least he's better behaved than Rover who has taken to worrying the poultry, and, though a savaged chicken – or its remains – has been tied to his neck, and though he has been driven close to distraction by the shame of it all, it seems doubtful whether he has actually learnt his lesson. An ancient retainer – Murphy by name – puts up his own struggle against time and dilapidation, but he's losing: the Majestic's top storey – damp here and there where slates are slipping from the roof – has been abandoned to an empire of feral cats. The 'j' of Majestic has fallen from the hotel's facade and has been swallowed by the now feral shrubberies which once graced the gardens in front of the hotel – muscular vegetable growth that not even Murphy can control. A crazed Welsh tutor (a graduate from Evelyn Waugh's 'Church and Gargoyle, scholastic agents' in *Decline and Fall*, I should think) can make no impression at all on Charity and Faith, the younger daughters of the owner, Edward Spencer. They've been sent home from school, and we never find out why, though it's not hard to imagine. They are as impervious to education as they are to the noxious fumes of the sheep's heads that Evans boils in the yard behind the hotel to feed the dogs. Daughters, dogs, felines, shrubberies, none of these are governable.

But worse is yet to come. Beyond the hotel's coroneted gates, out there in the countryside of County Wexford, there is another ungovernable world: crops are being burned in the landlords' fields before they can be harvested, there are sporadic attacks upon lonely outlying police barracks, there have been acts of sabotage on the railways. These are the Troubles of the title, the struggles of the Nationalists to force a forgetful Britannia to live up to her promise, made in 1914, to free Ireland from British Rule. The contract had been that if Ireland would only fight for king and empire on the Western Front, then Home Rule would be conceded at last. Gladstone's first Home Rule Bill had been introduced in 1886 … and defeated, as indeed was the second in 1893. The third, the 1914 Bill, had been passed, but suspended for the duration of the war. In the view of those Nationalists, however, Britain – so used to ruling the waves – had also been waiving the rules: the war had ended but Home Rule was still not forthcoming. After the Curragh Mutiny, when British officers served notice on Westminster that they would not enforce any new law which broke up the Union, Britain had effectively reneged on her promise.

Gradually, this larger world outside begins to bear down upon the little world of the hotel, itself a microcosm of all that is vulnerable in this outpost of empire, in Ireland, in the soft underbelly of British imperium. Small but disturbing inroads have been made into the dignity of the place. A pet rabbit, dead, 'its body … riddled with bullets', was discovered one day on the edge of the lawn in front of the building. Old and fat, it had nevertheless been a favourite and, thus far, the dogs had been content to leave it alone. Not so the Nationalists.

In its heyday, the hotel would have boasted the finest of amenities, furbishments, appointments and services. Plumbing was second to none. In summer, there was a regatta in the bay below. In winter, one can imagine the convenience of there being, perhaps, a resident pack of hounds and, no doubt, foxes thereabouts were cunning but obligingly plentiful in season. Now, however, all is in decline. There is no *thé dansant* these days at the Ma( )estic Hotel. Yachtsmen no longer anchor offshore and hail the boy in the dory to come and bring them off. Croquet and a *menu á la carte* are in abeyance. There is nothing now that is not a wasted shadow of its former self … unless you count the appalling fecundity of the feral cats. Cats, and the exotic plants in the conservatory, that most Edwardian of amenities: they were taking over.

Instead of emaciation, dissipation and decline, the semi-tropical plants in the conservatory were romping away. This, the Palm Court no less, was now quite difficult of access. Inside it were 'beds of oozing mould which supported banana and rubber plants, hairy ferns, elephant grass and creepers that dangled from above like emerald intestines'. Such was the riot of growth that light was at a premium, even at high noon, and not much promise of illumination was forthcoming from 'a standard lamp [which] had been throttled by a snake of greenery that had circled up its slender metal stem as far as the

black bulb that crowned it like a bulging eyeball … Whereas previously the majority of the chairs and tables had been available, here and there, in clearings joined by a network of trails, now all but a few of them had been engulfed by the advancing green tide.' The floor, pressed upwards by the rude energy of the roots creeping beneath it, had started to buckle and bulge. Even Rover, 'dozing with his chin on the Major's instep', was seduced into canine torpor by the sheer vegetable force of the place. He 'went over to inspect a pile of leaves, lifted a leg to sprinkle them … before, inertia overcoming him, he rolled over on to his side to doze off once more'.

In the midst of all this, and seated at one of the few remaining tables, is a girl, the older sister of Faith and Charity. She ought to be called Hope, but she isn't. In fact, she is Angela, and she is hopeless. She is dying, but keeping the fact from her fiancé newly arrived from England, Major Brendan Archer, veteran of the Western Front. In these preliminary moments of their meeting, the Major's feelings veer, quite understandably, between horror, suspension in a sort of surreal trance, and appalled hilarity. In the green gloom also is a very old gentleman, up from the village, one Doctor Ryan, whose professional mantra is, 'People, you know, they don't last'. The place as a whole is testimony to a complete disavowal of the Voltairean precept about cultivating one's own garden when all the rest of the world is mad. Here it is the garden which is maddest of all, and the rest of the world is just ungovernable. Whatever the case, Doctor Ryan inclines to the expediency of oblivion: he mostly sleeps it out. There is also an emphatically 'grim lady', reluctant wife of Boy O'Neill, local solicitor. And there's his daughter, Viola. None of the assembled company is the least bit disturbed by the fact that it has slipped the doctor's mind, before dozing off, to button up his trousers.

Note the name of the philandering Boy O'Neill's daughter. Though not exactly a blushing violet, nevertheless – poor girl – she doesn't stand a chance in this vegetable nightmare. However, everything else, no matter how bizarre, fits perfectly. There's a symmetry of opposites everywhere and a dreadful kinship – appalling and hilarious by turns – between all this ungovernable botany and this human decay. And underlying it all there is a huge botanical metaphor, savagely ironic, about empire, about colonising species taking over, about alien growth and historical alienation – a great covert parable about Britain and that part of its empire – so near but so far, so geographically accessible but so ungovernable, and so adamantly resistant to the entire imperial adventure: Ireland.

Troubles is a marvellous book. It was written by J.G. Farrell – Jim to his Irish mother and to those who knew him (and who, in the end, had a whip-round for funds to mark his Irish grave with a modest headstone in Durrus churchyard, of which more shortly). But he was James Gordon to his father, who, despite the Irish name 'Farrell' (or even actually *because* of it), grew up in a very deliberately English family. At the core was a first-generation immigrant grandmother whose efforts to smother her own origins included a deep disapproval of 'all things Irish, with Catholicism at the molten core' as Farrell's fine biographer, Lavinia Greacen puts it. Those two versions of his name – unaffected, demotic Jim, and James Gordon, with its coded hint of Omdurman and Empire – perfectly mirror the difference in how you see things, depending on which side of the Irish Sea you're on.

Farrell was gripped by the theme: empire, its foibles, its vanities, its good intentions, its missions. *Troubles*, his fourth novel, was written in 1970, but in 1973 Farrell was the Booker Prize Winner with *The Siege of Krishnapur*. Being half-Irish, and having grown up for the most part in Ireland, he knew about sharing a language with the English but not necessarily an identity. In 1979, he bought a two-hundred-and-fifty-year-old cottage looking out north over Bantry Bay, near the village of Kilcrohane, on the Sheep's Head Peninsula in West Cork. There was no electricity. The water was drawn from a well last used twenty years earlier when the place was inhabited. It was, and still is, reached down an unmade lane – a *boreen*. A quarter of a mile further on and you reach the sea. It stands snug in a hollow of the hillside and monastic behind a thick, unkempt hedge. It's an astonishing country thereabouts – very wild, huge acts of sky above the mountains, epics of sea and more sky, and then far out in the western ocean and almost out of sight, islands, afterthoughts of earth and stone, like codicils to an ancient will expressed in the elements of the landscape itself.

Settling there was to have been a homecoming, a commitment to a place and a way of life where the discipline of writing every day would come easily. But Farrell, a keen shore-angler, slipped from rocks into the sea at the bottom of his *boreen*, into the vast water of Bantry Bay. He had never walked well – he had had polio as a child, and now his balance let him down. The body was washed up a fortnight later and laid to rest nearby in the churchyard of St James in the village of Durrus at the head of Dunmanus Bay, the next water down on this west coast of peninsular fingers out into the Atlantic. That churchyard is as lovely a spot as you could wish to find to await the Last Trump, almost narcotically beautiful, especially in the rain when the edges of vision are softened and the boundaries of thought blurred – the shore dark and mysterious with oak woods, a derelict eighteenth-century mill shyly staring out over the water and blinking through empty, ivy-cluttered windows when the wind shuffles and spins the leaves. A pair of swans a quarter of a mile out.

Go round behind the pretty church and there's the noise of water. A deep rocky bed channels a steep stream on its last dash before losing its voice in the immensity of sea. Somebody gardens here with the lightest of touches, the greatest of skills. You'd swear the deep blue hydrangeas were naturalised, and the butter burrs and heliotropes were domesticated, their plate-like leaves governable, scaled-down gunneras. The sound of this water – giggling, gurgling, tickling the silence into ripples of sound and splashes of music – and the fact that we notice it and are charmed – is a measure of how estranged (or not) from the natural we probably are. It takes some patience and discipline to hear it now, to notice that it's there.

And that's not good. But other worlds, other times, were underwritten by senses of connection rather than estrangement: water was a living thing, it moved, it spoke, therefore it was alive. Water was a condition of life of course, but in other, more angry moods, it was also a dealer of death. Ergo, water is a god. Or, at the very least, one of the gods.

The word 'god' is infinitely difficult now, but – the word apart, perhaps – the logic and sense and wisdom of the idea are simple enough – now more than ever perhaps, now that water is a thing commodified, something bought and sold, rather than something natural and gratis like air and sunlight still are, now when it is just as likely to be associated with drains and drainage, ablutions and sewerage solvents as with the magic of that colossal collision of moisture with seed which triggers the miracle of germination, or with the sheer elan of a fountain, a fist of water raised against the levelling dullness of gravity and against the tedium of the merely earthbound. A *jeu d'esprit* indeed.

In matters of connection, of joined-up stewardship, Ireland has kept the faith better than most. A very small 'f', of course, but of impressive longevity and constancy – and the evidence of that is a species of out-of-the-way places known, quietly, as holy wells. An embarrassment to the Church for the most part (that's the big 'F', of course), they are almost ubiquitous, but they're rarely signposted. Peter Harbison, doyen of Irish historical topography, reckons that there were as many as three thousand of these places used for local pilgrimages during the nineteenth century. I would be surprised if a discreet modern search did not locate at least half of those even now. But when you do get there – and it's often hard to find them – you won't ever encounter anybody else, though always there will be evidences of someone having been there not long before: ribbons tied on the hawthorn, prophylactic images, coins wedged into the bark of a tree or dropped into the water, a footprint still warm. These secretive places are about as Christian as singing 'The Holly and the Ivy' (which is to say, not very much at all) but as spiritual as a Zen garden in Japan (which is to say, a great deal).

The respectable, licensed, public versions of this unregulated, atavistic faith are the grottoes you also find – but much more easily – everywhere in Ireland. Let into the natural hillsides, or against a man-made scarp, there's a niche, almost a cave, and a garden laid out in front. An image of the Virgin Mary will be standing in or just outside the niche, the trace of a smile on a lovely face. It's a version of that critical moment in the Christian story: the Garden, the Empty Tomb, the Risen Christ, the faith of the Mother vindicated. Or it's a version of Heaven itself, Elysian Fields spangled with flowers, overseen by the Queen of Heaven. In a country where private gardens are often still in their quite tentative, larval stages, where it is only in the last few years that gardening has begun to grow into an important national pastime, these places – far more frequent than public parks – actually represent the quintessential moment of Irish gardening. They function competitively like the rivalry evident in so much conventional gardening elsewhere. One parish, one village, vies with the next through the size, the scope of the bedded-out lobelias, the quality of the maintenance.

But those other places – the hidden, despised holy wells – they have their place in the national consciousness too, somewhat like Jack-in-the-Green in English folk literature or something akin to those mysterious leaf-masked faces peering through the stone walls and vaulting of the Chapter House at Southwell Minster. These places too are gardens of a kind. But they stand for the other pole: the minimum, not the maximum of grooming, the minimum, not the maximum of visibility, the minimum of estrangement from the completely natural, the closest it is possible to be to the elements, to the bare rock, the raw wind, the rain, the earth. Minimalist, in fact, like a Zen garden (that analogy again where the spirit – indeed, the spiritual – blends with the chthonic), but also a garden in the sense of a place – can you imagine it? – as it might be fifty years *before* the moment someone begins to make it into a highly groomed, conventional garden, or fifty years *after* it had been gardened and then abandoned. So much is this the case that it is difficult sometimes to see these places as 'gardens' at all, so uncultivated, uncultured, so wild do they seem. But look closely – or, better still, go with the mood of the place and surrender the preconceptions of what you expect a garden to be – and you begin to see signs of shaping, evidences of intention. There are too many hawthorns, too many hollies, for it to have been just chance, for example. The well (pool, spring) itself is free from fallen leaves where the litter around its margin is centuries deep. The suggestion of circularity – stones, tracks, the trees themselves – very faintly hint at *stations*, at doing the rounds of a sacred journey. Seamus Heaney broaches precisely the same mysterious, liminal regions when he approvingly quotes Ian Finlay, author of *Celtic Art: An Introduction*, remarking:

> that it was not until the Romans dominated Gaul and reduced it to a province that the Gaulish or Celtic gods were reduced to the likenesses of living men and women; before that, the deities remained shrouded in the living matrices of stones and trees, immanent in the natural world

and he goes on to remember the:

> taboos and awe surrounding the fairy thorn in the Irish countryside until very recently [and] the pilgrimages which still go on in places to the ancient holy wells.

Yes, indeed, but it is not even 'in the recent past' that that happened but only yesterday that – after public outcries, public enquiries and huge expenditure – the spanking new motorway from Shannon to Ennis in the County Clare had to be re-routed a matter of several metres out of its intended course in order to preserve 'nothing more than a modest enough hawthorn tree'. Or was it? Appearances – like a landscape garden; like a garden with a ha-ha – can be deceptive.

The elements of both these *ur*-gardens – the public Marian grottoes and the chthonic, secretive holy wells – are essentially the same: earth, air, plants and, though to very different degrees, a sense of apartness, a sense of enclosure, as of a classic *hortus conclusus*, in fact, unlikely though that might seem at first sight. These primal elements are the same, as it happens, as those that made up those first gardens, those *paradeisos*, those set-apart places in ancient literatures and cultures of the Middle East: And the Lord God planted a garden in Eden, in the east ... But in the case of the Irish grotto there is always the standing figure, whereas at the well there is always an emptiness. You fill the vacuum, the gaps, with your own imagination, even with your own act of faith perhaps. And at the well – unlike the grotto – there always is water, always this moving, living, elemental presence.

The Irish for water is *uisce*. The Irish for river is *abhainn* or *abhann*. The cognate word *ábhann* means 'strain of music, tune'. So, if you listen to *water* you'll hear not just a voice (because, of course, it's alive, it speaks) but a voice enhanced – *music*, the voice of a god. Somewhere far, far back in the mists of Celtic consciousness, the framing of water in a garden was not just an accident of aesthetics, as it is for us with our voguish 'water features'.

Carraig Abhainn means 'Place of the River and the Rocks'. It is the name of a remarkable garden in Durrus at the foot of that Sheep's Head Peninsula in West Cork. Durrus itself might one day be famous for the grave of Jim Farrel, but I hope not. Nor – except among connoisseurs – is Durrus cheese all that well known, though it deserves to be: mild flavoured (but not so mild smelling!), crusty, its flesh almost pink, like a conch. Cheese and novelist apart, however, it is the garden in Durrus (it's behind Wiseman's Hardware Store) that has made a name for itself.

As gardens go – those that claim a large space in one's mind – Carraig Abhainn is quite small. It is no more than two acres in extent, and seems somewhat less. That's because the ratio of grass to garden is a good deal smaller than in the conventional image of the Rolling Acres.

If you found a sheep here it would be a sculptural caprice, not a dim-witted, black-faced hillwalker or a member of that flock that Capability Brown ordered in as a design accessory to his artifice and to Milord's commissioned pastorale. And it would only be there on sufferance as a working turf-cropper. If you met a dog it would grin at you, make friends, shake its wet fur all over your legs (and you'll remember the river of the garden's name), and make a run for it. But if you met with a water-sprite or a dryad, it would be the real thing: Carraig Abhainn is indeed a Place of Rocks and Stone and through it runs the Durrus River, coming down not from the westerly mountains of the peninsula (like that stream which borders the churchyard a quarter of a mile away) but from the mountains to the east behind Bantry and Mount Kid. Even by the time it reaches Durrus it makes no grand gestures, neither does it paint lazy riverine idylls. It is not that sort of river. But it does make quite a good deal of noise as it tumbles through a succession of pools and waterfalls, pools and cascades, races and rapids, on its journey through these two acres of garden. Pictured in *House and Garden* you'd suspect that this garden's setting was too good to be true. You'd infer crafty photography or a fibreglass and JCB recreation of a Bayreuth opera set – the Rhine Maidens at the very least, or *Pearl Fishers* at a push … on a warm day, and if you're tired of Wagner. You'd never see the like of it at Chelsea either, partly because the steepness of the cascades couldn't be done even there, but mostly because it would look out of place. Not English at all. Almost exotically strange, in fact. Or – to those in the know – quintessentially Irish.

The river defines as well as confines the garden. Its irregular banks defy straight lines. Its rapid falls in level keep the water moving, of course, but also the eye. The shelves and pools of the river predicate the island beds of the garden, the pools of grass, the serpentine paths: they are a series of beads on green threads, or picturesque incidents strung along the filament of the stream itself. There are no long views, big gestures, articulated geometries and the like – those familiar stage-properties of the classic grand garden.

The water is coming down from the hills. It is white and curdled on the surface, but below it is tawny-golden and brown. You catch the colour as you see through it, see down into the wave thumping on to the flattened drum-heads of the rocks below. Son et Lumière. Colour and music. *Uisce* – that ordinary Irish word for water – comes into Hiberno-English as the ordinary word for a certain spirituous liquor. Listen carefully to *uisce* and you hear *whiskey*. Light, sound and a certain intoxication or enchantment.

A necklace of beads, and each bead is different. One of the island beds is largely of ferns – a bed or divan indeed, with lumpy green scatter cushions strewn around and that ineffable smell of musk and spores. Another is carefully graded to allow the textures of barks to be seen and enjoyed through an underplanting of phormium, foxgloves and the dewy shawls of spiders' webs. There's myrtle bark – cinnamon and rusty; eucalyptus bark – two-toned blue-green and milky moon-stone; there's *Arbutus x arachnoides*, a plant you'd grow for the peeling grated-chocolate bark alone, though the flowers and their scent are excellent too and, being an arbutus, it quietly marks the place as characteristically Irish. In the middle of the garden is a tall, narrow poplar, and by sighting it – now on your left, now to the right, now somewhere behind you – you can get your bearings, though you're never far from sight and sound of the river.

The garden was twenty years old in 2010. It must be one of the very first of a new Irish generation of ambitious but generally smaller gardens, whose origins lie not in a role as artfully contrived landscape for the better display and appreciation of a big house, but in the horticultural passions of ordinary people, people modest in every way except that their garden matters to them. It may be that there is a local concentration of exactly that sort of person (and garden) here in West Cork: every year there is published a *West Cork Garden Trail*. When it began several years ago, there were six or seven gardens. Now it numbers more like seventeen or twenty. Some two or three are grand and conform to the old conventions of what you'd expect from an old established garden which charges you entry, but most are quite small, or even very small. Some are very new indeed.

The Irish – rather than the Anglo-Irish – have been slow to take up gardening, perhaps because the very concept of it was associated with a class claiming social superiority, while the actual practice of it (those who actually did the work in the gardens of the Big Houses) was associated with a class of social inferiors. That's a state of affairs the English patrician class – the genetic parents and cousins of the Anglo-Irish ascendency, the people who lived in those Big Houses – have long seen fit to practise back in England: gardeners live in cottages, do dirty work and are paid peanuts, and never mind that they are often infinitely more highly skilled than many a manager in the bank or well-paid panjandrum in a local authority. The situation in England was/is dire, but in Ireland it is enormously further complicated because labourers (gardeners) and the proprietors of the Big House gardens where they worked, belonged not just to different social classes and different income brackets, but also to different tribal castes. Those men with dirty hands came from families who had once owned the land they now had to serve on. The dispossessed had no choice but to labour for the planters, the usurpers, the very people whose ancestors had dispossessed them. Somewhere along the line, the very concept of a garden must have become tainted by association. Indeed, the very word *garden* – and perhaps even the word *plant*, the base line of any horticultural endeavour – changed their meaning along a social and political fault-line: to the Anglo-Irish ascendency, a garden was the pleasure ground, the part of their demesne nearest their residence where flowers were grown for the house, where ladies might tread gravel paths with the minimum of inconvenience and damp feet, and lovers might canoodle and whisper in the shrubbery. Beyond the garden, the tennis courts; beyond them, the woods and fields of the demesne. To the cottier, however, the word meant the third of an acre allowed him by his landlord where he grew the *lumpers*, the high-yielding potatoes which supported him, his family and the pig which paid the rent in due course. This garden was always the striated patch of lazy beds, undemanding of labour perhaps but not of anxiety, given the spectre of famine. The Big House had its kitchen garden, of course, but even this was not the same because it imposed a leap of imagination – a cruel leap in bad times – to convince yourself that the *need* for nectarines, pineapples and blanched celery was of the same order as the *need* for potatoes. You'll still hear the word garden used in this specifically Irish sense of a diminutive potato field, and when you do it makes our own word seem miles and miles away. Even talk of a Kentish hop garden seems like Cockney whimsy in comparison.

Twenty years – and more – since the garden was begun at Carraig Abhainn there is now a process of thoughtful revision there. The aralia has outgrown its welcome. They usually do, but perhaps there will be space for *Aralia variegata*? Something about the silvered edges of *this* plant's splendid spread-fingered leaves seems to suggest more of a layered, disciplined shape after all. The royal fern, *Osmunda regalis* – so hard to establish in any remotely drained spot – is in its seventh heaven here, and ought to be kept in check. Grasses – the hard drinkers among them – love it too, but the Wisemans declare themselves beginning to tire of them. The gunneras are on the point of converting parts of the garden into Jurassic film sets – as usual. And that – sadly but truly – is also the impression one often gets now of the planting of tree ferns, even in Ireland where, unlike most of England, they actually flourish: the image all too often is of a tired, Hollywooden cliché. There are quite a number of dicksonias at Carraig Abhainn.

There is very much to enjoy for laymen here, the sort of people who, bit by bit, are beginning to take up gardening in Ireland for themselves. It is no surprise that the place is often locally chartered as a backdrop for wedding photographs. Long may it continue. But there is plenty for the plantsman too: rhododendron species, camellias exuding sophistication whether it be in the polish of their leaves or the poise of their flowers, those perfectly overlaid petals like the closed shutter of an old box camera. There are magnolias – a fine collection of the best, some of them only now becoming mature enough to flower. And allied with these is the rare and beautiful *Michelia chapensis*, its flowers goblet-shaped and the boss-like corona very much like a magnolia but the creamy-white petals edged with carmine. Here there are polished pittosporums blending well with camellias; maples blending well with the strawberry trees; *Piptanthus laburnifolius* with its wisteria-like leaves blending well with those of the several kinds of sorbus that populate this garden. Bottle-brushes abound, but you have to look twice at *Pseudopanax ferox* to see that it's not one of them dead and petrified. The same theme of airy, divided leaves is picked up again in the nandinas – the sacred bamboos – planted here and there. The Chilean *Desfontainia spinosa* blends mischievously with the European ilexes: which are the true hollies and which are not? There is a very interesting mimosa with bluish leaves, and that makes one look twice at the nearby *Eucalyptus parviflora*, the serendipitous kinship of narrow glaucous leaves making one smile. There is *Sinocalycanthus chinensis* (a wickedly tautologous name if ever there was one: how Chinese can you get?), a most beautiful shrub which needs time to bloom (and somewhere out of the wind), but when it does your patience is rewarded with quite large bowl-shaped flowers – like a single pæony – but the colours soft like watercolour pigments, cream or wine, according to variety – and very understated, very lovely, like the quietness of colour in a Gwen John.

Where do all these fine but unusual plants come from, you wonder. Once you are in the know, in Ireland, the answer is predictable enough. They come from fellow gardeners, that confraternity of inveterate plant-sharers. But the fellow gardeners, where did *they* get them from? From seed-shares perhaps. Or it may be that the plant

in question actually originated in this or that garden. And yet what about the more public, more conventionally commercial sources? Here at Carraig Abhainn and, I should think, in southern Ireland generally, more often than not the source will have been either Seamus O'Driscoll, whose Mill Road Nursery in Thurles, Co. Tipperary, is a marvel, or Bill and Rain Chase at Deelish Garden Centre, down the back lane to Baltimore from Skibbereen, in Co. Cork. Ardcarne at Boyle, Co. Roscommon has good plants, common and uncommon. So does Robert Miller's nursery at Altamont in Co. Carlow. For gardeners nearer to Dublin, there is Mount Venus Nursery, an extraordinary source of really fine plants. There are other good nurseries – one or two specialists of international renown among them, particularly in Ulster – and, in the nature of the trade, others will spring up too just as older ones may fade away. As far as generalist nurseries go, however, there is none currently to beat those listed above.

Carriag Abhainn is good, in season, for the person who craves incidents or, better still, *events* of colour, but it is probably even more satisfying for the slower, quieter enjoyment of leaf form. Everyone knows that paulownias stooled produce the best leaves, but paulownias grown in this kind, drip-fed soil make leaves as big as aprons. *Xanthorrhoea glauca* – the grass tree – is fun in the manner of a retro sixties haircut. *Saxegothea conspicua* – the Prince Albert yew – belies its name to be quite modest, but it's worth looking at carefully to enjoy the green cones, whatever the season. *Castanea variegata* is always interesting but, through no fault of its own, those variegated leaves remind one now too much of the edge-burnt, blistered and blighted leaves of its parent, the common horse chestnut, which we are having to get used to seeing in July and August these days. *Salix fargesii* shivers silver-green, of course, but the leaves contrive to be shaped a little oblong, like spatulas blunt from use. The Chinese persimmon, *Diospyros kaki*, is a character whose acquaintance you feel privileged to make.

It's the climate and the surrounding mountains which, in the first place, mark out this garden as Irish. And after that, it's the planting. You could achieve that effect – that Irish sense of place – in any number of ways, but two plants alone would do it here even if there were no vast supporting cast. Invariably good to see – though it's common enough in Ireland – is *Crinodendron hookerianum*, the lantern tree. White-flowered, vanilla-scented myrtles are common too – and you learn quickly to appreciate how their cinnamon-coloured trunks and branches soften the pitch of all the greens surrounding them – but *Myrtus ugni*, which you will find in Carraig Abhainn, with its softly pink flowers and sharply red fruits, is special, even by Irish standards.

Quite a number of pieces of wood and stone carving can be found in the garden and sometimes they articulate or punctuate the spirit of the place. There's a strange river god, for example, as well there might be, bearing in mind earlier ruminations about rivers, gods and Ireland. Perhaps there is also a witty cross-reference here to the famous masks of river gods carved onto the arches of O'Connell Bridge in the heart of Dublin. Other things – the frankly bizarre radial sun-god seat, which seems more suited to an Aztec Quetzalcoatl than to an Irish Cúchulainn – may be less successful. Still other things seem just bad ... but that's probably equally true of a lot of the sculpture at Chatsworth, Longleat or Powerscourt, so perhaps it – bad sculpture – is just a blemish of gardens so institutionalised everywhere that we either don't notice it any more or are inured to grin and bear it anyway.

Every now and then, however, there will be a little horticultural cameo that connoisseur and journeyman alike can enjoy: that favourite Irish rose Dublin Bay abseiling through the holly Golden King, for example. There are delightfully teasing moments such as when an impertinence of dahlias – be their colours ever so expensive (indeed episcopal, these days) and not gaudy at all – muscles in upon the perfect shapes and demure tones of classy cordylines, phormiums and the aristocratic *Beschorneria yuccoides*. And then, just possibly, there may be one of those epiphanous moments where a sense of place is framed by something special about the light, or an accident of sound spilt in from outside, or an extraordinary coincidence of recovered memory perfectly melding with something just seen. There was one such at Carraig Abhainn. From those oaks down on the shore came a rabble of rooks – a familiar sight of course: that shabby untidiness in flight, like flakes of singed paper ascending on the thermals of a bonfire, and one's heart going out to the one always being left behind. But this time it was different. These rooks were silent. No shouting. Nothing but the soft hiss of their wings as they passed overhead. Not so much a rabble as a rapture.

Even if something like that never happened at Carraig Abhainn, it would be a shame to miss the way in which the place somehow epitomises the spirit of a (good) garden in Ireland. When the penny drops about the place, you realise how perfectly it combines elements of those two characteristic *ur*-gardens: the groomed, public shrine to Mary (or Demeter, or Gaia, it may be, did we but realise it) and the wayward, secret holy well. That too would be a moment of epiphany, but of a different kind. It would be the moment when we realise that gardens, and what goes on in them – how they both reflect and find shapes to express avatars deep in the human mind – are far too important, far too interesting, to be left only to garden historians, connoisseurs of sharawadgi curves or the self-appointed arbiters of taste and fickle fashion in the weekend newspaper supplements. You realise that encrypted in the landscape at large and then artlessly articulated in gardens like this is the way an old, grown-up culture has moved beyond the historical adolescence of confrontation, beyond struggling with opposites and polar incompatibles, and instead has learnt to live with paradox, perhaps even actually to celebrate contradictions.

Go to Dublin, to the hub of this very old, mature culture and, for all its sophistication and surface coherence, you will find things culturally incoherent. Go to Airfield, once a grand Victorian house in the leafy southern suburb of Dundrum, probably quite successfully recovering both its soul and its cash liquidity as a local theme park, vintage car museum, rare breeds sanctuary, fashionable lunch venue, etc. There's an old walled garden there, but kept up and indeed rejuvenated at the very pitch of style. In it are modern sculptures of ravishing beauty and almost disarming erotic power. There is the most wonderful planting, wonderful for its flamboyance and panache, its palette of colour harmonies, the sheer lavishness and quality of the plants … and there are coke bottles wedged into the clefts of a cedar. There is a big space given over to an inspirational monthly gardening club for kids, and there are newly planted birch trees being bent and trounced by children, their parents looking on and doing nothing. There is a kind of signature planting of echiums – the big ones, *Echium pininana* and its kin – which recurs here and there throughout the place, and they are dense enough and their swaying spires near enough to the paths to induce a sort of Alice in Wonderland sense of dwarfed stature in the passing human beings, and it's a piece of sheer magic, but it's impossible not to look outwards as well, beyond the garden's perimeter, and there to see the huge visual litter of the Celtic Tiger's high-rise, upmarket apartment blocks, so flimsy in their architecture that they look like shanties from a South China Sea waterfront but so visually crass as completely to poleaxe the spell of the garden. It's an optical, cultural, even perhaps moral meltdown – equivalent to building a concrete wall ten feet behind a stained-glass window and blocking the light … a window by John Pyper if you're English, or by the incomparable Harry Clarke if you are Irish. Not contradiction but contempt, and if I lived in Dublin I'd be beginning to worry. The gods – whether they be the wodwos of liminal woodland or Our Lady of the Lilies – have given up on this landscape, that's for sure. They left so recently in fact – and so finally – that at certain times of the day you can still hear the resonance of the door slammed behind them.

Both of these gardens – Airfield and Carraig Abhainn – are distinctively Irish despite being quite different in style. The climate alone would achieve that, but there is something more too, something that recalls, possibly unconsciously but nonetheless powerfully, deep, deep cultural roots, roots in the way people connect with, understand and find meaning in their landscapes, the way they intuitively or intellectually decrypt the raw data of the places they find themselves in. It is as if there were local and regional chromosomes in the earth itself which will out no matter what we do. And the result is a visible continuity – a kind of subcutaneous harmony – between ancient landscapes, ancient patterns of thought, and the modern. The difference, however, is that in Carraig Abhainn those continuities are intuitively understood and respected, both by the gardeners and by the visitors, whereas at Airfield they are under siege.

Back in West Cork, when you are there, do look up the annually published *Garden Trail*, the descriptive list and a map. Copies can be had from any of the invariably helpful tourist offices. You couldn't visit them all in one day; nor, probably, would you want to. But they are all within the maritime region west of Cork city. Individually more or less distinct, they still share characteristics of the benign climate, though winds off the sea are a significant shaping, limiting factor too. There is one garden – Creagh, at Baltimore – that everyone looks for every year, so much has it been missed since it closed some years ago. (The *West Cork Garden Trail* leaflets are partly sponsored by the Harold-Barry Trust, and it was Peter and Gwendoline Harold-Barry who made the garden at Creagh after moving there in 1945.) Rumours of its rebirth circulate fairly regularly, but are annually disappointed. Kilravock, a mile westwards out of Durrus, on the road to Kilcrohane, should be visited for its beauti-' fully spaced, beautifully paced rooms and its collections of restios and dicksonias (though even in this benign climate they were damaged in the hard winter of 2011). Another of the gardens – the River House near Skibbereen – has an interesting English, rather than Irish, origin: it is the work of David Puttnam and his wife Patsy, who settled there some years ago. Also on the trail are Ilnacullin at Glengarriff, Bantry House, and then Lisselan near Clonakilty. These are old, established gardens with a long history of visitors. Drishane, in Castletownshend, is an interesting garden with the grandest of views over a tremendous coastline. There are several remarkable specimen trees there but just as interesting is the connection with Edith Somerville (she of the writing partnership of Somerville and Ross). Somerville lived, wrote, painted (rather well, in fact) and gardened here for most of her life. The other gardens are generally younger and smaller. They are, indeed, exemplars of that new generation of private garden that has begun to grow in Ireland. Several – Carraig Abhainn among them – are outstanding.

Mount Usher

COUNTY WICKLOW

County Wicklow – south of Dublin and facing east towards Wales over the Irish Sea – has the reputation of being the Garden of Ireland. Not quite like Kent for its orchards and hop fields, nor like the Cotswolds for the foreshortened scale (and, of course, the sheer prettiness) of its landscapes, nor even like the Vale of Evesham for its apple and plum blossom. Wicklow is the Garden of Ireland just because it has quite a lot of them – gardens, that is. When it isn't gardens, it's woods and steep streams, wild hills and mountains. The drive (or, indeed, walk) up and over the Sally Gap must rank as one of the world's great short journeys (going west is best, either morning or evening). Synge's favourite (very long) walk out of Dublin was to Glencree, and his first play, *In the Shadow of the Glen*, is set in Wicklow. Edward Lear said that it was the Wicklow Mountains that spurred him to be 'a painter of topographical land-scapes' (so what, incidentally, one wonders, was the spur that made him the unrivalled master of those short comic poems? And you can't answer 'Limerick'). The county has its celebrated beauty spots – the Sugar Loaf Mountain, Glendalough, the Vale of Avoca – the last of which is the setting for Tom Moore's 'The Meeting of the Waters', and really, he, and the song – making it famous – did for the place, but the others are well worth the visiting. There are indeed a good many gardens in Wicklow too, but they're mostly private and quite small. One, which is both large and open to the public, is not yet very much visited, but it is a remarkable place with some tremendous trees – tremendous in stature, some of them, and also in beauty – and it deserves more attention than it receives. That's Kilmacurragh, the country outpost of Glasnevin, the National Botanical Garden in Dublin. However, it is three other gardens that occupy most of the limelight: Powerscourt, Kilruddery and Mount Usher.

Powerscourt is an ugly, bullying brute of a house, burnt out by accident quite some years ago but, sadly, not burnt down (though the vast caverns of its basement have been restored anyway to afford vast opportunities for shopping, and cappuccino). Nevertheless, the bor-rowed view (of that Sugar Loaf Mountain) is stupendous. When you first see it, it fairly makes you involuntarily gasp; and later, when you look up and see the shifting drama of light and shadows on its slopes, it is pretty amazing too. But it is a *borrowed* view. Like quite a number of other features of the place, it doesn't quite slough off the impression of contrivance, of the surrogate, of the appropriated but not neces-sarily earned. For example, throughout the garden there are lapidary inscriptions here and there: grandiloquent Latin (but self-congratula-tory in any language) to the effect that such-and-such a toff brought this and that 'to perfection'. They – the Wingfields, latterly Viscounts Powerscourt – made their money out of booze (Powers Whiskey) and influence. (The serving of their own interests in the Upper House of Grattan's parliament at the end of the eighteenth century earned them and their cronies the collective nickname from the Dublin wags of

'The Beerage'. Though, oddly enough, the fourth Viscount refused in 1800 to vote for the Act of Union. He was one of only five Irish peers not to toe the line. It seems out of character for the man, and it is certainly out of character for *this* place. But it wasn't actually he who built the house; that was his grandfather and father. And it wasn't he who made the gardens – the most French, the least Irish garden in all Ireland; that was his son and grandson. So let him have the benefit of the doubt: on the morning of the day when this man is said to have thrown out the courier bearing the bribe of an earldom, Wingfield was behaving like a disinterested patriot. And bravo!) There is a pets' cemetery, said

to be the largest in any Irish private garden (and pets' graveyards are another minor, but recurrent, feature of Irish gardens as it happens), but this one is really just another pretext for the Wingfields to get their name into stone, with the names of the animals they purport to have been remembering merely incidentally attached: 'Teddy, pet of Mervyn Wingfield …' and much more of the same. Even so, there are some fine trees in the valley garden, and there is lavish and meticulous bedding in the parterres. The discontinuity between the formal style of the garden and the larger landscape beyond is negotiated very well: the change of register, the big shift of key, is an achievement, not a wrench or a stumbling block. The double herbaceous border in the walled garden is magnificent. The turf – everywhere – is superb. The waterfall a mile or two away is precipitous. And so on. But the abiding impression is of a Retail Experience – that, and the Corporate. This is a golf course in waiting. And the crowds are everywhere.

Kilruddery, not far away, just outside Bray, is an interesting place. It's the garden with the oldest pedigree in Ireland. The core of it is in the (French) style of the seventeenth century: formal water, *pattes d'oie*, a small, controlled repertoire of trees planted to make big impressions. A little dishevelled, and a little later in date than these original parts of the garden, is a lovely theatre of hedges. There's an almost natural, very steep rock garden at the end of a long walk, a long view. There's a charming period piece in the form of an octagonal model dairy. Then roses, a fountain, terraces, bedding. The early nineteenth-century house is in a style somewhere between Balmoral and William Beckford's Fonthill Abbey. Fonthill had the good grace to fall down of its own accord – an early example of jerry-building – but Kilruddery needed a little help. The family began to run out of money in the 1950s, so most of the neo-Elizabethan, baronial pile was demolished. These days, what remains is a popular venue for weddings and celebrity light music concerts, and – weather permitting – the garden comes into its own then as a very sociable place. Convincing in its own way (unlike Powerscourt), Kilruddery is not, however, an idiomatically *Irish* place.

Mount Usher is.

Mount Usher – the name – is misleading. There is Usher's Island in Dublin (where, in 1914, Joyce set the last of the *Dubliners* stories, 'The Dead', but now an area unimpeachably dull, built over by apartment blocks). There was James Ussher, first Professor of Divinity at Trinity College, Dublin, and later Archbishop of Armagh. It is his *Annales Veteris et Novi Testamenti* – calendars of ancient and biblical history (published 1650–54) – which are probably the source of the famous datings inserted into editions of the Authorised Version of the Bible after 1701. According to Ussher's calculations, God created the world on 22 October in 4004 BC (these dates are Old Style). The event took place at 6 p.m. Adam and Eve date from the 28th – six days later of course. But it is not so much by reason of these big time spans that Ussher's name lingers on, as his – sometimes miniscule – specificity. After all, the centuries-old carol had also kept Adam 'bounden for four thousand winter', awaiting the birth of Christ. But Ussher refined the date very precisely by four more years, and it was his dates which, in due course, became such a notoriously important focus for critical scrutiny and challenge from nineteenth-century geologists and palaeontologists. Perhaps it was one of these early U(s)shers who gave their name to the site of the garden in Wicklow. It would have been only a day's ride from Dublin. Or perhaps the name *Ashford* (the village where the garden is set) is another of those lazy anglicised words, in this case a version of a much older name, *Usher's Ford … Ushford*? It is possible. Like Mount Jerome (one of the most sought-after Dublin cemeteries, if you know what I mean: John Synge is there, for example; so is Jack Yeats), like Mount Stewart (the well-known garden in Co. Down), Mount Congreve (Co. Waterford) and, indeed, like Mount Isabel, the fictional demesne in Elizabeth Bowen's *The Last September*, the name Mount Usher is a sort of verbal fanfare rather than a literal topography. As often as not, there is no 'mount' to speak of, unless it be in the sense of a *socially* elevated spot. The second half of these names was originally proprietorial. It denoted the family of the people whose place stood there: a topographical fiction followed by a flag waved. In the case of Mount Usher, both geography and name are even more misleading than usual: the Ushers – whoever they were – have long gone (and anyway, the garden was made by successive generations of a family called Walpole, and not by Ushers at all). Or perhaps there *was* an earlier garden: Mary Delany mentions in a letter of 1752 a 'Mr Usher's Garden' and, later, that she was about to make an excursion there where 'there are groves of myrtle as common as nut trees', so was there a woodland garden of some kind? A house called 'Mount Usher' appeared on maps of 1760 and 1777, but it had gone by the time of the Ordnance Survey of 1839. And – amazing observer though she was (and fabulous recreator of flowers through her appliqué pictures) – Mrs Delany's focus on this occasion was not really on Mount Usher but on the house and garden on just the other side of the river, the place known then as Rosanna, now as Rossanagh. It was the home of William Tighe. He was something of a magnate in his time; his house was a favourite destination for Dublin's social elite and for visitors. Then Rosanna became – but two decades at least after Mrs Delaney's death in 1788, and at least a decade or two before what we now think of as Mount Usher Garden began to be made on the other side of the river – a much more famous place still as the home of one of the most widely read poets of the nineteenth century, Mary Tighe. She is almost forgotten now, and wrongly so. Her long poem *Psyche* (which anticipates Keats' poem on the same subject by fourteen years) went through successive editions after 1805 and enjoyed both critical and popular success – rightly so. Tighe died at the age of thirty-six in 1810. The commemorative sculpture by Flaxman in the family mausoleum in Inistioge, County Kilkenny – luminously white alabaster in the gloomy interior – is a fine thing. But I digress …

Mount Usher – the title – misleads not only by nominating the wrong garden-maker but also topographically. We expect an elevated site, not just socially but also geographically, but actually it is set in a valley bottom. There are hills all around, and steep, wooded cliffs along the Devil's Glen only a little further up the valley, but you don't see much of either from the garden. What you do notice – cannot possibly miss – is a lovely trout-lazy, sky-reflecting stream that, in flood, can be quite busy, but is generally pretty easygoing. It gurgles and murmurs its way down through the garden over a succession of seven low weirs on its way to the sea two miles away. Its name is the River Vartry.

Seamus Heaney has it that Irish place names and stream names articulate their own senses of mood, landscape and character. Of the place through which, as a child, he walked every day to go to school (somewhere whose name literally translates as 'place of clear water', but that's not the point at all) he says – his tongue relishing the naming word: '*Anahoris*, soft gradient / Of consonant, vowel-meadow …' In Book IV of *The Faerie Queene*, Edmund Spenser – living at Kilcoman Castle in County Cork during the 1590s – rhapsodised about the beauty of Irish rivers. Heaney goes further: his Irish rivers speak Irish. Of the river that flowed by and seasonally flooded his family's farm he says: 'The tawny guttural water / spells itself: Moyola'. And you can hear what he means, what the word – the river – sounds like. So far as I know, Heaney did not study the sound and sense of the Vartry (which is odd, in fact, because when he eventually settled in the Republic, having left the North, it was into a cottage at Glanmore, not much more than a stone's throw from Mount Usher, that he moved – hence his sequence of *Glanmore Sonnets*). It's too late now – Heaney died in the summer of 2013 – but if he had done so (he called the process 'bedding the locale in the utterance') I think he would have revelled in this river's two long, laidback vowels, its trochaic rhythm.

Mary Tighe is probably not quite in the same league as Seamus Heaney, but in her day and after her death she had a following for her very long, very Spenserian *Psyche; or The Legend of Love*. She led a peripatetic life in search of relief from an ill-judged marriage and (like Keats) tuberculosis, but again and again she returned to Rossana in County Wicklow, the house of her husband's family. The Vartry ran at the bottom of the garden. What is now Mount Usher is a short walk – or wade – away. Here she is fondly evoking the river – its silver tides and chestnut glooms – as she knew it in 1797:

Sweet are thy banks, O Vartree! where at morn
Their velvet verdure glistens with the dew;
When fragrant gales by softest zephyrs borne
Unfold the flowers, and ope their petals new.

How bright the lustre of thy silver tide,
Which winds, reluctant to forsake the vale!
How play the quivering branches on thy side,
And lucid catch the sun-beam in the gale!

And sweet thy shade at Noon's more fervid hours,
When faint we quit the upland gayer lawn
To seek the freshness of thy sheltering bowers,
Thy chestnut glooms, where day can scarcely dawn.

Mount Usher's garden now is a comfortable twenty acres laid out on both banks of this stream. Twenty acres sounds a lot, but the place feels accessible; there is nothing exhausting about it or daunting, and anyway, some of it is set apart as a private house and private buffer-zone lawn (on whose gate is a very peremptory KEEP OUT – which speaks volumes, I'm afraid, for the behaviour of some visitors and for a sore trial of patience on the part of the owner). Across the stream there are bridges from time to time, three of them – the best of them suspension bridges that buck and belch ever so slightly as you step across but offer almost no obstruction to the longer views up and down the water. That's why they're there: they are so insubstantial. As it happens, suspension bridges are another recurrent feature of quite a number of other Irish gardens, starting with the very early, very daring one built in 1810 across the narrow but deep gorge of the River Camcor at Birr in County Offaly. At Mount Usher, those twenty acres are subdivided into episodes of the circular walk you'll take if you are going to see the garden entire: a Maple Walk, a Woodland Garden, a croquet lawn – the only lawn to speak of really: the ratio of groomed grass to cultivation is very low indeed here – an Azalea Walk, a Eucalyptus Grove, a Fernery, a Palm Walk and, wittily, a Contra Riviera Walk. In reality, you can choose from almost any number of paths, but the choice is not bewildering so much as indulgent. The drift of the place is unstated but clear whichever paths you take: downstream with the river – go with it. The woodland is dense with mature trees and shrubs: eucryphias, magnolias, camellias and dicksonias – a signature plant of old Irish gardens and, here, probably several generations on from the originals – all underplanted with trilliums, erythroniums, willow gentians and other woodlanders. Lush growths of (herbaceous) ferns occur everywhere. It's the light and shade, the green and the generosity of it all that you take in, but there are several very special individual things too. There is *Lomatia ferruginea* – ferny foliage on a striking, beautifully formed tree thirty feet tall, and the new shoots are indeed ferrugineous: rusty brown and bearing eventually yellow/red/orange flowers. There is a very rare *Cinnamomum camphora* – a botanical name that speaks for itself if ever there was one. Most special of all is a pair of *Cunninghamia lanceolata* – very fresh, dazzlingly green, columnar firs of Chinese origin, and unrivalled in their size here. Apparently the most inquired-after tree in the whole garden is the *davidia*, though if they ask for it out of season the people must wonder what all the fuss is about, because it sports its handkerchiefs only in May.

The so-called coffin tree, *Juniperus recurva* var. *coxii*, grows and multiplies like a weed at Ilnacullin in the far west. I remember overhearing a pair of young gardeners there – who had clearly had their fill of this 'weed' – vilifying it in the most vernacularly disrespectful terms possible at the same time as they were correctly intoning its august Latin name. The extreme fusion of languages – from the sublime to the very basement of speech – was both bizarre and wickedly entertaining. When it is mature, as it is at Mount Usher, it looks as if it belongs in the cast of another surreal opera designed by Maurice Sendak – *Where the Wild Things Are* indeed – its doleful limbs sagging like the lower lids of a lachrymose bloodhound. It's a wonderful tree really. So are the *Nothofagus dombeyi* and *N. menziesii* – so-called southern beeches – and they're of incomparable size and presence here. The Eucalyptus Grove has its denizens spaced out informally but quite widely so that you can measure one species against another. You can savour the vaporous air too, but I think the gardeners must be forever raking up the leaf-fall: there is none of the smothering of the meadow grass (and of everything else) you'd get otherwise. The bark of *E. urnigera* – green, brown, buff and spiralling up and down the tree like a helter-skelter – is particularly interesting.

One of the most important elements of this garden is the care and thoroughness with which you can identify almost everything … if you want to. Labels are put in place at the time of planting and maintained thereafter. But it is discreetly done and, rather than a frenzy of force-fed botanical Latin, it is done with numbering. Numbers correspond to a comprehensive catalogue kept at the gate which you can consult if you need to (so you need pencil and paper to jot down the numbers of things you can't identify for yourself). Four different guidebooks are available there too – you can choose at what level you want to be informed. The simplest supplies a map and invites you to come in. The next singles out the fifty best trees and plants for the relative beginner or the person who doesn't want to be saturated. A third guide lists the best things by season and location. Yet another does the same, but with some more detail and information and with some fine photographs. All of them give a common name too, if there is one (but there's none of that striving to supply one against all the odds that you find in places where someone has been on a course for *Access* and *Approachability*). You would have to go a long way to find a comparably helpful, but

unpatronising, selection of guides in other gardens. They make it possible that, by naming something, you can fix an impression formed of it which would otherwise be fugitive. For example, because of its size and because of the distance afforded here, *Calocedrus decurrens* takes on a sort of submarine quality. It looks for all the world like a vast sea-anemone swaying, ebbing, flowing in the wind-water. But its common name as the incense cedar has never really convinced. Indeed, short of stamping up and down on a bit of it, I don't think you'd ever smell it. As a result, I gave up remembering its name years ago. But seen like this, I wanted to learn what it was and was glad to be able to do so. A *Rhododendron cinnabarinum* 'Roylei', with red bark peeling off every branch and bleeding onto the ground, was planted a century ago, but was still very much alive. Yet – with that discharging of its bark, its skin – it looked as if it had been flayed. Quite astonishing. The Marsyas of the genus. It demanded to be identified. Occasionally, this numbering and naming caused as much frustration as satisfaction: what was initially identified as *Bowkeria gerrardiana* (and you wanted to know what it was because of its interesting, perfectly unblemished, squeaky-clean bark) was reclassified by the master catalogue as *B. verticillata* – a name that for a long time after proved elusive. Only some years later did it begin to appear in any other book or catalogue, but it *was* botanically correct. *Euonymus bungeanus* was a name to relish for its sound alone, but there were ferns growing on the slopes of its drooping branches and doing so in such a way that you had to look twice or more to convince yourself that it was *two* plants – host and guest – and not *one*, which, without the number, you would never have had the chance of identifying.

Mount Usher, with more than five thousand different species of plants, is indeed a treasure house of the fine, the rare and the beautiful, of trees unusually great in stature, of plants almost impossible of cultivation except in the most benign of circumstances, but it isn't in any conventional sense a botanical garden. Conventionally – and correctly – it is classified as a Robinsonian garden, and that places it right in the mainstream of the best of Irish gardening since the publication of *The Wild Garden* in 1870. Mount Usher makes its deepest impressions not so much by its parts – its individual plantings – as by the *sum* of its parts, by its moods, its ambiences, its harmonies and occasional dissonances, by its old pensionable walls but the bright new buds and leaves cladding them, by the sight of water, the sound of water and the cleanness of everything rain- and water-washed. A Robinsonian garden is one where contrivance and artifice are altogether discounted, and so are formality and system, but not coherence, flow, sympathetic concurrences and cohesion. The great Robinsonian mantra is 'to pursue the natural'. But that poor word 'natural' is never more sorely abused than it is in gardening circles, garden writing, breast-beating gardeners' eco-credos. Robinson himself was quite often pretty inconsistent, I think, and, moreover, he was stronger on what he hated than on what he sought to espouse. And yet it is in Ireland that one finds some kind of fundamental endorsement of it after all, despite all the caveats that we really should not lose sight of. I mean, for example, in the way that the word 'natural' so often flows there (naturally) into its cognate 'naturalised' in a way that doesn't necessarily happen elsewhere. The reason probably lies in climate but, notwithstanding the causes, the results are distinctly interesting. Take that case of the dicksonias – tree ferns. They're everywhere in Britain: the trendy makeover garden, the municipal multiculturally tropical garden, the chic minimalist garden. And they look lost, ravaged, hopeless. They're gassed by barbecue fumes, roundabout fumes or just cant. They're a mute, heart-breaking indictment of the horticultural pillaging going on all round the globe despite all those internationally signed protocols to outlaw it. And they look terrible anyway. But not in Ireland. In Ireland, not only do they look right – *natural* – but they have actually become *naturalised*. The same is true of myrtles. And then there's the arbutus (and again it's the subject of a famous sentimental song, not by Tom Moore this time, but by his disciple Alfred Graves, son of the Protestant Bishop of Limerick and father, in due course, of Robert Graves … it is 'My Love's An Arbutus'). There are a few acres of the Dingle Peninsula – remote even by the standards of that place – in which *Agave* has really put down its feet – huge plants growing easily and smothering everything else.

Something similar looks as if it must be conceded for *Gunnera* around Bantry Bay. It is endemic there now, and it looks fine (though there are some who are trying to get up a campaign to eradicate it – puritanical, super-zealous, botanical cleansing – with industrial earthmovers. Or explosives, perhaps, as a last resort?). On the evidence of places such as Mount Usher, the genus *Eucalyptus* need no longer look bashfully exotic and out of place. It would seem to actually belong there.

I suppose it shouldn't be a source of wonder in a place where, after the shamrock, the iconic flower is the hedgerow fuchsia of the Atlantic coasts. It is impossible to imagine those far-western lanes without it. But in truth, it is not a native. It is *F. magellanica* (as in 'The Straits of Magellan', so it was originally from South America), and its introduction took place within the last two hundred years. Ireland's a strange place for plants. The potato is not a native, but it is etched more deeply into Ireland's culture and history than any other plant anywhere – more even than the endemic opiates of Asia and the Americas, in this sense probably the only possible rivals. The Burren – those limestone pavements on the Atlantic edge of County Clare – is world-renowned for its spring flora but, according to the logic of normally behaving continental endemics, none of it should be there. And yet it is – Mediterranean though it be, or belonging more properly still to the Azores, or classifiable only by that strange word *Lusitanian* – and you cannot fault it for looking unnatural there in any shape or form.

William Robinson singled out Mount Usher for particular notice in the 1897 edition of *The English Flower Garden*. He said it was quite unlike any other garden he had ever seen. He described it as 'a charming example of the gardens that might be made in river valleys, especially those among the mountains and hills. In such places there is often delightful shelter from violent winds, while the picturesque effect of the mountains and hills offers a charming prospect from the gardens'. (Perhaps in those days you could see over the walls and trees to the mountains, but it isn't easy now.) Warming to his theme, he continued with detailed approval of plantings: 'the eye wanders from the Torch Lilies [he meant what we now call kniphofias] and Gladioli to the blue Agapanthus, and thence to the Pine and Fir-clad hills' and he rhapsodised that 'to see it in the time of Lilies, Roses, Pæonies, Poppies, and Delphiniums is to see much lovely colour amongst the rich greenery of the rising woodlands' (and we notice in passing that 'natural' here means natural *colours* rather than the natural planting of natives that we conventionally associate with Mr Robinson, but never mind his inconsistencies).

Quite a long time ago I planted a yellow crocosmia in my own garden. That was long before crocosmias graduated from being mere montbretias, though I expect there were taxonomists even then who were on the case. Lucifer had yet to light his bonfire then: montbretias were orange, and that was that. As far as you could reasonably tell, there were no yellow or bronze, red or umbrous varieties. And if there were, they were probably dwarf day lilies. Unless, that is, you had some inkling of Irish gardens and of old Irish plants. Escallonias were Irish, of course. And so were one or two special (Irish) primulas and violas. (*P.* 'Guinevere', for example, and *V.* 'Irish Molly' – khaki, mustard and remarkable – and 'Molly Sanderson' who is jet black.) A few people quietly prized the very special blue libertias which were occasionally found in old Irish gardens, likewise the occasional sighting of unusual dieramas – all presumed to have originated in the old, lamented Slieve Donard Nursery. Most recondite of all – almost mythical, in fact – were the Irish snowdrops: 'Hill Poë', 'Irish Green', 'Ballynahinch', 'Straffan' (otherwise known to the cognoscenti as 'The O'Mahoney' or 'Cool Ballintaggart', to complicate and indeed obfuscate matters even further). The ladies were simpler: 'Mrs MacNamara' and the honey-scented 'Brenda Troyle'.

Our crocosmia, all those years ago, was pure yellow – no gold, no orange in it at all – and it did (still does) very well. I cannot remember now where we bought it. Perhaps it was the old, lamented Ramparts Nursery outside Colchester. But there was never any doubt about its name: *Crocosmia* 'Mount Usher'. And once the name (the place) had registered, you began to notice other plants with the same provenance – most notably *Eucryphia* x *nymansensis* 'Mount Usher'. You pricked up your ears too the next time you read Robinson and came across his unwonted rhapsody of the garden. You promised one day to go there and see it for yourself.

I have a private theory that the real test of a good garden is whether it touches children, and then how deeply it touches them. I found this in my diary for a day when I had been at Mount Usher ... once upon a time, and feeling a story coming on:

A little girl, along the path to the gate into the garden, pushed just a little past me, and her mother rebuked her, but gently. So I smiled at them both, the embarrassed mother and the child further on down the path now, her back turned to both of us.

I caught up with them at the ticket kiosk. Two grandparents, pleased to see that they got a discount, the mother and the girl in a lovely loose frock, the sort that only a mother could or would make. The little girl was a Down's Syndrome child, her face a little puffy, one eye sticky. And she wiped her eye with her cuff and the back of her hand.

Oh, how unfair, how cruelly unfair life can be.

I wished that one of the adults would hug her, would do something to make up for it somehow, but they were too sensible (too right) to treat this child differently – as if she were one of Nature's errors rather than their daughter, their granddaughter.

But how I wished they had hugged her, so that the love was lovely even if the face was less lovely than it might have been. To a stranger, anyway.

Then the child reached out for her mother, her hand on her thigh, her hip. And together they passed through the gate.

And out of sight. But an hour or two later I saw them again, and the little girl lovely because she was in love with the garden, so deep had been the delight she had felt. And her mother hugging her, while the child stuck the white petal of a dogwood on to her mother's cheek.

Once seen, Mount Usher can linger long in the memory. Very long indeed.

Wren's Wood

COUNTY WICKLOW

Perhaps the most engrossing new garden in Ireland is only a few miles away from Mount Usher, from Powerscourt, from the gardens of June and Jimi Blake. It is Wren's Wood, and you'd find it by following a quiet road with a long and beautifully wrought stone wall (it belongs to the Dunran demesne) on your right if you're coming from the east, on your left if you're travelling from the west … and there'll be a glimpse over it of Kiltiman Castle (a teasing pile – is what you see a late medieval tower house, but in very good condition, or is it the real thing heavily and imaginatively restored, or is it actually a brilliant folly?). Almost opposite, on the other side of the lane, is Wren's Wood.

This garden – more than almost any other I can think of – is at ease in its site, embraces it, goes with the flow of the land, of its natural flora, and does so on more than one level: there is diversity and integrity of space and place but also of a sense of time, time past, time present and the future. It is both effortlessly ancient and easily contemporary. The site of fifteen acres or so affords sheltered, enclosed glades but also huge views, over the land, over the sea not far off. A kindness of place allows feats of horticulture – brugmansia growing out of doors, for example – but forbids boastfulness about it. There is everywhere here a long span, a long scope, long life even, and then a short one too. A long, long spatial view – sometimes – but also a temporal one, a revision of time itself, most obviously in an Iron Age *rath*, deep in the woods now, which must once have scanned almost those same panoramic views we enjoy now from viewing places within

the garden. After all, according to the antiquarian Roderic O'Flaherty writing in 1793: 'the Irish date their history from the first aeras of the world … so that in comparison with them, the antiquity of all other countries is modern, and almost in its infancy' (*Ogygia, or a Chronological Account of Irish Events*, quoted in *Irish Dreamtime* by J.P. Mallory). A super-nationalist exaggeration, of course, the sort of thing that used to make younger nations – history's 'infants' – very self-conscious, but, if it were true, it would make us *all* blush. And – in a sense – it *is* true: Ireland hasn't any *more* history than anyone else, but what it has got seems to matter, to shape more the perception of landscape and identity and – yes – national narrative (but so much more than even that). It is indeed – sometimes – as if you must reckon with a fourth dimension in the landscape: time. And only then do you begin to understand.

And there is deep time – in this garden – in the ancient trees, of which there are many. The finest of them – unquestionably, I'd say – are the four oaks on the hillside to the east of the garden. Monarchies of light and half-light, of greens and greys, and the Gothic configurations of their limbs, the exotic cartography of the veins in their bark. Noble trees indeed.

But a shortness too. The venerable trees give way from time to time to new plantings, both woody and herbaceous. A handkerchief tree, for example, and magnolias, and dogwoods. There is a Judas tree, and a paulownia. There are young beeches, young oaks, young fruit trees in the orchard. And young platforms of newly laid dry stone – flat-topped cairns, levelled viewing stations – beautifully constructed and both satisfying to look at – to use, indeed – and thought-provoking to contemplate because they look so ancient at the same time as they are so modern. Already these are features of the almost-natural landscape. Sometimes they – and indeed the indigenous great stones too – have wittily modern names (the Grandstand, the Stone Heart), sometimes names locally topographical or aetiological (the Spring Rock), sometimes they function as elegies. The most evocative of these last is the Carnac Rock, a modern installation remembering a lost family member through invoking an ancient site in Brittany, quietly, mysteriously sacred. Sometimes they have a story. The Spring Rock, for example, remembers Marina, daughter of the family, and a moment in her life. She – aged eight then – had hatched a clutch of ducklings under a broody hen. They were about to take to the water and learn to paddle but a guinea fowl gave warning of an approaching fox. There was just time for the ducklings to be safely gathered in, and the fox was foiled. It was at this spot that it happened.

Go anti-clockwise round the garden. You pass first through some of the garden's box rooms close to the house. They are a loosely threaded series of intensely gardened, beautifully planted enclosures that follow the very local lie of the land: the lee of the wood, the rise and fall of the hillside, the heat-reflecting walls of the house, the shelter of hedges. There is something here for all seasons, beginning with spring bulbs and ending with puddles of winter-brave cyclamen, both hederifolium and then coum, only to start all over again in the new year. In late spring it is the dogwoods that effortlessly effect the transition from garden to woodland. Other fine small trees and shrubs gratify the rare-plantsman but simply intrigue and delight the ordinary visitor: *Neopanax laetus*, for example, a plant that lives up to its spirit-lifting name (*laetus* means 'happy') with the poise of its magnificent five-fingered leaves and then the pink-purple buds opening to white flowers and settling into orange-purple fruits (if the weather allows). This is a *prima donna assoluta* among plants. But if you miss that, there are the tiny light-reflecting leaves of *Azara microphylla* – odd to think it is of the willow family, until you remember the sparkle of the leaves – which counterpoints the darkness of the woods beyond. (This may well be the largest example of the species in Ireland. Size-spotters please note.) In August, the scent of *Myrtus luma* dizzies the insects and quickly makes them drunk. (But the taxonomists get full marks – on this occasion, at least – for changing its name to *Luma apiculata*, which means 'beloved of bees'.) In high summer there are abutilons, daturas (Brugmansias), and eucomis, the latter enjoying a more amenable common name – pineapple plant – than a literal translation of their Greek name strictly should allow (*eu* – 'well', and *komus* – 'hairy'). A stooled paulownia gently waves its impossibly large leaves in a breeze, leaves which follow on from its foxglove-like flowers in the spring.

Move on, through a gate, into the wood – beech, holly, ash and sycamore. Underfoot the path is springy with generations of leaf mould. There are mosses everywhere, the faint hazes of enchanter's nightshade, navelwort and dog's mercury – deep woodlanders, all of them – and patches of *Lamium maculatum*, the dead nettle, artfully planted here and there to afford varied patterns for the eye. Earlier in the year there have been foxgloves – rods of colour, pools of the rosettes of leaves visible in the light spilt through the canopy of the trees.

You reach Kiltimon Fosse, the *rath*. It is elliptical rather than round, an unusual thing, measuring about one hundred by one hundred and fifty feet. Such defensive enclosures are generally more or less circular, concentric, but always they'll have taken advantage of natural features anyway – a scarp here, and gully there – so shapes fit landscapes rather than the other way around. This one is classically formed of earth walls still as much as two metres high here and there, and a surrounding ditch (the fosse) which is quite steep and deep in some parts, while in others you have to use your imagination to reconstruct it. You follow its

shape with your steps as if running a finger round a bowl, to gauge, by feeling, its shape. The original entrance is on the south-east flank, close now to the garden's dry-stone boundary wall. In spring, before the trees are clad in all their leaves, the *rath* is at its best – bluebells below and the blossom of wild cherries above. Later on, when the woodlanders have come and gone, it is the occasional gleam of polished holly leaves or even the urgent scamper of the tutelary wren through the branches that catches your eye.

Down, down through the wood with the dry-stone wall on your right – the boundary – and you can hear but not see running water. Right at the bottom, there it is, running and muttering, through the wall, through a hole built for the purpose. It's a *lunkey*, a Yorkshire word apparently for precisely that expedient, an aperture in a rough stone wall to allow a stream to pass through. The simplicity and efficacy seem to demand an *applause of light*, at least, just as there's a sudden crescendo of water. Both the hole itself and the word for it surely deserve wider currency. Two streams converge here, so – with a facetious nod in the direction of another and much more populous haunt of tourists quite close by (and to the poet Tom Moore, whose song immemorialised it) – it is cheekily dubbed The Meeting of The Waters.

A butterfly-haunted grove leads suddenly into strong light and to more stoneworks. There is a pool here of almost still water. And the spirit of play that gently pervades this garden – wordplay, episodes of theatre, glimpses of a sort of psycho-geography that remind you of … Bunyan perhaps, or *The Wind in the Willows* – is evident again here. The pool is elliptical and it has a stone tail shaped like that of a fish, the same flat white stones marking the edge of the water as if they were the flaking scales of a great fish. This is landscape art employing the raw elements of stone and water and reflected sky. Pan, and perhaps Syrinx, are not far away. Another of these stone structures – the Spring Rock – like so much else here, connects past and present, hard eroding water with soft impermanent stone. Around it grow tall, damp-loving plants: the huge leaves of *Inula magnifica* and its comically small sunny flowers – mere smirks of yellow when you were expecting to be dazzled – and *Eupatorium purpureum*, both of them blending, in their energy and elan and the rough and tumble of their natures, with the indigenous hogweeds and mumbles and rosebay willowherbs. The place feels young, the stone fresh, but timeless with it. (The Cambrian rocks beneath your feet are generally grey/blue, but then there are occasional deposits of granite and quartz too.) There are young trees here which will bring an air of mature sophistication in due course when they get into their strides – a magnolia and a davidia – and others which will breathe the contrary, the primitive. I'm thinking of the dicksonias and the gunnera. It will be a magical spot. On a sunny day you will be looking at a picture by Douanier Rousseau.

That strong tug of timelessness pulls you towards a lovely piece of inscripted green slate: '*Cedant Curae Loco* / In This Place Cares Surrender Their Sway'. And so they do. But it takes time: here you must stand, must stare, absorb where you are, who you are, must spend time to lose time. The Latin words remember another garden where they also occur, that of the Villa Mattei built in the 1580s near Rome, a place of formal spaces and fountains, informal wildernesses and puzzle-mazes, orange groves and secret arbours. It is descendants of the same Mattei family who garden now at Wren's Wood, and perhaps there is a lineal trace visible in the occasional playful theatricality of the Irish garden.

Move on eventually … up the hill, either quite steeply by the thirty-nine steps – another literary trope, a quest mixing Buchanesque adventure with Bunyanesque labour – or by a longer, gentler slope, the zig-zag path. You are climbing Querquetulanus … which (who?) sounds as if it might be named after an ally of Boudicca, or else the site of the tumulus of a pre-Roman warrior … but actually it is another instance of the wordplay which flourishes here: the name (the word indeed) is invented … though the botanically informed will spot the word *Quercus*, Latin for the great trees which crown it. There are more long views and those magnificent oaks whose bark is the nursery of the silver-washed fritillary butterfly you might be fortunate enough to see. Enjoy the scribble of the twigs of these superb trees above you, giggles of occasional light on the grass below. There is an avenue of young hornbeams. There is a lovely inflection of the native rowan tree: the sorbus here have not red but yellow berries.

Rather forlornly a wooden chalet comes into view – forlorn and unused it is, but odd too. This is Troldhaugen (Hill of the Mountain Men) and there's a whiff of the Norwegian about it. You wonder what it's doing here, but there is a redeeming plan afoot. It may become the reward for your quest, a self-helping tearoom. Ah ... and let there be a piano ready to be played if mood and place make you feel like it. Grieg. The *Lyric Pieces* – they would do.

A winding old carriage drive leads through the woods again, a different part of the wood but a familiar spirit ... you cannot know where, because it won't run straight and let you see ahead, will not permit you to calculate upon a destination. You listen out for, look out for, the greater spotted woodpecker. It frequents this spot, but also favours the woods of the Dunran demesne across the lane. You may be lucky, or just teased by the skull-bashing *tock-tock-tock*ing you can hear but cannot see. Red squirrels favour the quieter trees and feast on the abundant acorns.

You cannot see where you are going but you do arrive. You come down into the spot where you began. Another applause of strong light. And another wonderful set of box rooms. Beautifully clipped hedges frame a tiered series of small gardens assembled like boxes in a Neapolitan theatre up a brief hillside. Cyclamen, eucomis, erigerons – small, abundant things which make you smile, like a table laid for tea in a doll's house, but also imposing clumps of crinum … and a blue room, with the pitch set in late summer by that astonishing intensity of colour you get with ceratostigma. You descend altogether and your feet are firmly on the level again – a fairly rare sensation in fact in this garden, though slopes and undulations are so cunningly punctuated by those stone platforms, standing stones, big views, special plantings, that you've hardly noticed and never minded anyway.

The dog Tilly greets you. She's a Dandie Dinmont, a terrier, and where did you first meet? In that painting by Gainsborough, was it? Or was it a memory of the curious connection with Sir Walter Scott (the dog got its name originally from a character – a proverbially dependable fellow – in Scott's *Guy Mannering*). Will the great man himself, leaning heavily on his stick as always, come round the corner and greet you? After all, he was indeed in Ireland in 1825. And his itinerary really did take him down the very same lane you took. He passed by Dunran – that we know for sure – may even have stopped … but whether he had a dog with him we do not know.

You enjoy a few more shrubs before you must go – late summer fuchsias flowering against the wall like bashful girls in their first party frocks. There's the bladder senna – *Colutea arborescens* – with its translucent pink pods (and its unthinkable medicinal properties!), a fig against the wall, the marvellous feijoa (*Acca sellowiana*) with flowers like a Disney princess' coronet. There's *Crinodendron hookerianum*, the lantern tree which has become almost a signature plant of Irishness in a garden (though actually it comes from Chile), and *Clerodendrum trichotumum* with its strange, lovely turquoise berries late in the year (which hails from Japan). There is the Japanese wine berry, one of the several different rubus species you will have met, here and there, in the course of the garden.

You'll leave. And want to come back, reminding yourself that it is only a small wonder that Wren's Wood has won regional and national awards. Like almost no other, this place plays so thoughtfully with time and space. Thoughtfully, memorably, beautifully.

I think of the pennywort growing in a wall, leaves like green coins, flowers like miniature foxgloves. A currency of memory. Spending time …

Ilnacullin

COUNTY CORK

Some time in the sixth century, St Brendan the Navigator left behind dry earth, safety, sanity (some would say), and set sail westwards over the uncharted ocean to find the Promised Land. We have his word for it: the little book, the *Navigatio Sancti Brendani Abbatis* – The Sea Journey of Saint Brendan, Abbot.

Promised Lands ... somewhere far away, over the sea. Hy Brasil is the usual, but not the only, name given for this place, first in Irish mythology and then infinitely repeated in British sea shanties. Sometimes the mind sites it not on, but under the sea: the Garden of Fand, again an invention of Irish fabulists but perhaps best known now in the beautiful tone poem of that name by Arnold Bax, a man English by birth but Irish by heart ... all these places imagined by idealists, millenarians, cranks, saints, escapists, psycho-geographers, call them what you will. In Ireland, as everywhere else, it is of course just wishful thinking, but in Ireland it is regularised, canonised even, into a common expression: Tír Tairnigiri, The Land of Promise, an island, a paradise, but elusive. It is always shrouded in mists, glimpsed only by sailors in their dreams and saints in their ecstasies.

Hy Brasil (possibly from the Irish *to embrace* – so, the place to hug, welcome, embrace; or the place to be hugged by – or, perhaps the same thing really, from the Irish *to bless*) was reckoned to be somewhere west of the Aran Islands, west of the west of Ireland, out there in the infinite ocean. Somewhere. So much and so widely was this fabulous zone spoken of that when Europeans did discover land more west (south-west really) than they had ever dreamed possible, they called it Brazil.

So much mentioned, discussed, retold was the story of St Brendan's voyage (there are versions extant in medieval Catalan, Norse, English, Occitan – a dialect of Languedoc – German, Dutch, Latin, Italian, but strangely not in Irish – they made do with the Latin) that the Vikings sailing to found their colonies in Iceland and Greenland seem to have used the *Navigatio* as their guide, inspiration first to imagine and then to locate new worlds. Sometimes these were found, and then lost again. But Paradise is like that, as John Milton knew well. The most documented of all new worlds was the one serendipitously bumped into by Columbus in 1492, but he mistook these islands off the east coast of a new continent for islands off the west of the old world – *West* Indies. Half found, then lost again in errors of oceanography. It took an Italian from landlocked Florence to understand where they were, what had been achieved. Amerigo Vespucci read the *Navigatio* as a child. He rectified Columbus' regressive old-world mindset (albeit that he, Columbus, was testing the *progressive* idea that the old world was round). Vespucci – schooled by idealists like St Brendan – understood that what had been discovered (rediscovered in 1499, seven years after Columbus' first landfall) signified not just a place on a map but also a place in the mind, a new, better, promised world. It – the idea – still promises, even when the real America sometimes disappoints.

The Irish, for one reason or another, have a near monopoly on imaginary places out there beyond the sunset, places almost – but not quite – beyond the mind of man to conceive. Early Irish saints had, in St Brendan, the trailblazer par excellence, and, because of him, during those early medieval centuries, they enjoyed an absolute monopoly before other seafaring, dream-making nations caught up. And not just a monopoly of religiously inspired navigators. *The Voyage of Bran* has its sailors pitch up for an ecstatic year on The Island of Women – the Tír na mBan – though only, and rather perversely, for them to get tired of their good luck, to begin to yearn to go home, and to overlook the fact that a year spent there was an aeon back in the ordinary world. The literary genre of the voyage tale is a stock of medieval writing, common, or fairly common, in quite a number of other European cultures. Ireland in the early Middle Ages did not have an exclusive monopoly of the form (though, in due course, in 1726, Jonathan Swift – with his *Travels into Several Remote Nations of the World* undertaken by one Lemuel Gulliver – would pretty well settle the custody question once and for all). But it certainly had the lion's share, and it had its own word for this sort of fable: *Immram*. One of them – *The Voyage of Mael Dúin* – enjoyed a British outing in the form of Tennyson's *Voyage of Maeldune*, written in 1880. The poet selected what he must have regarded as the insular plums from the Irish original: the Silent Isle, the Isle of Shouting, the Isle of Flowers, the Isle of Fruits, the Isles of Fire, of Witches, of Double Towers, and finally the 'Isle of a Saint who had sailed with St. Brendan of yore'. In fact, Tennyson had thirty-three in the original text to choose from. They included places specialising in Giant Ants, in Demonic Horses, in Birds that Spoke. The Fruits in the Irish original are narcotic, but Tennyson sanitised them rather primly into 'the poisonous pleasure of wine' (and this from an erstwhile Lotus Eater? Shame on him!). Once again, in the Irish original, the sixty warrior-mariners who completed the journey were in no doubt which was their favourite: the same Tír na mBan – the Island of Women – that we met earlier in the *Voyage of Bran* – but Tennyson missed it out altogether. Too racy for Victorian readers? Too likely to jeopardise his elevation to the peerage?

But also a reflection, perhaps, of another sort of culture gap: two nations united (after a fashion) by a common language, but separated by a sea of distinctively different attitudes.

Other cultures have named and located their Never-Never Lands in different ways, in different places. To the pre-Homeric Minoans and later the Greeks, it was Atlantis, an island perhaps, a drowned city perhaps. To travellers in the Hindu Kush it was Shangri-La. To intellectual Englishmen it was Utopia, the Never-Never Land invented by Sir Thomas More in his book of that name early in the sixteenth century; or, for Arthurian romantics later, it was Lyonesse, somewhere beyond Land's End. For the French it would have to be Ys, the drowned land off the coast of Brittany. In the first place some or all of these had a strong local currency, and sometimes, latterly, a wider following, but never anything as widespread as the Irish coining enjoyed. Though it was the Irish who had invented Hy Brasil, this place in the mind exuded an internationally compulsive appeal. It appeared again and again on Italian charts, on Spanish charts and on English charts, that is to say, in the currency of the three great late-medieval maritime nations. This place, that no one had ever seen, that no one ever *could* see except for one day every seven years – and then only if the mists parted and you were adept enough at the necessary magic to fix the vision with fire – remained on British Admiralty charts right up to 1873. Some Irish ascribe the English interest as simply commercial and mercenary (whereas the Irish view is dizzily mystical and pure, of course). Probably that was one element of it; several seaborne expeditions to find Hy Brasil were mounted, and those voyages were modelled on *The Bounty* rather than on the *Navigatio* of St Brendan, but nevertheless the view is essentially uncharitable. What you hear in all those British (not Irish) sea shanties in which Hy Brasil occurs is a yearning for an end to the sea at last, an end to the infinite endlessness of ocean, once and for all, almost a sort of death wish in fact. But also for a sort of Paradise. Hy Brasil was the first, the prototype, of an idealistic answer to an existentialist dead end. It's the Irish version of the albatross that appears out of nowhere to cancel that terrible sense of being directionless, pointless, meaningless, or just 'Alone, alone, all all alone, / Alone on the wide wide sea.'

Other cultures have configured their paradises in other ways. That in the Book of Genesis was an inland spot, well-watered, well-planted and walled: it was a garden. That prototype, that primary formulation of the single most haunting idea in the mind of mankind, probably originated in an ancient Persian word, *paradeisos*, which meant 'pleasure ground', or 'park'. But these very early Irish sailors and mystics, though they reconfigured Paradise still as essentially a garden, to them it was also an Island. That is probably the second most haunting idea in the collective mind of mankind. Islandness. An ideal of a better world ... a world apart.

St Brendan's voyage to locate – in the terrestrial world, and not just in the oneiric imagination – this Isle of the Blest turned out to be difficult, very long and wonderfully eventful – a succession of false paradises, promised lands which serially disappointed, a trial of the spirit and of physical endurance. Eventually he and his fellow monkish sailors got there, but the first port of call, the first red herring, was The Island of Sheep, the sheep 'so numerous that the ground could not be seen at all'. (Some scholars think it may have been the Faroes, but to be too geographically specific with the *Navigatio* is to risk losing its magic.) They sailed away and the next landfall was the Paradise of Birds. Here were 'groves of trees ... full of flowers' – it sounds quite tropical. Then there's an island upon which they draw up their boat. Sheep are grazing. They build a fire and begin to cook their meal. The island moves; it is a leviathan, a whale. Next is an island where a community of monks has lived already for eighty years (though it seems like no time at all to them, so absorbed and abstracted from time are they in their daily offices). On another island (but there are weeks, months, years between these landfalls; in fact, the *Navigatio* may really be a composite of several voyages, and St Brendan may be several sailors fused into one) they drink from a well and it induces a deep sleep lasting three days. They ply a passage through a strange sea whose water was 'coagulated' (the Sargasso Sea?) and beach upon another island where there are 'huge purple fruit that taste like honey'. They encountered in the flesh the mythical gryphon, they passed an island which seemed to them a 'crystal pillar' (an iceberg perhaps) and another which they called the Island of Smiths where the furnaces were fired by volcanoes (Iceland?). They passed Judas marooned for eternity upon a rock in the ocean and, taking some Christian pity upon him, they petitioned the demons who perpetually tormented him to give him respite, if only for a few hours. The demons, impressed by their piety, consented. On another island they met a lonely hermit who

hadn't eaten for sixty years, his soul feeding upon the still finer food of penitence. At last, they do indeed reach the Promised Land of the Saints. It is a land full of fruit-bearing trees, precious stones, sweet water and perfumes.

Islands. Islands to the west, always the promise of something, somewhere beyond the horizon. Curiously enough, there are almost no (real) islands on Ireland's east coast, but hundreds off its west coast. Off the coast of south-western County Cork there is Roaring Water Bay: biggish islands there like Sherkin, like Clear Island, and then smaller ones such as Hare Island, Horse Island, Goat Island; little archipelagos like The Catalogues, Skeam East and Skeam West, or Calf Islands Middle, East and West. If you have a mind to visit them all you'll have to find a boatman in Baltimore (the original Baltimore, parent of the American one) and set aside a few weeks to complete the odyssey: there are said to be more than a thousand islands in Roaring Water Bay, albeit most of them tiny. In Clew Bay, off County Mayo, there are a thousand more: great Achill Island where Paul Henry painted so often, Clare Island with Knockmore, the Great Hill, and then smaller ones like Inishbofin (the Island of the White Cow). Off the coast from County Clare you may see, on a good day, the Aran Islands – Inishmaan, Inishsheer, Inishmore (Middle Island, East Island, Great Island) where John Synge found the germ of *The Playboy of the Western World* that touched, at its first performances in 1907, a very sensitive nerve of another kind of Irishness, but perhaps an artificial one – the boast of impenetrably and impeccably chaste womanhood – provoking riots at the Abbey Theatre in Dublin, and at theatres in the States in due course. Robert Flaherty filmed his *Man of Aran* there, and fixed for a generation the definitive image of the Irish spirit faced with a life hard but real and honest. Ralph Vaughan Williams' chamber opera *Riders to the Sea* – probably the most compelling of all modern tragic operas – is set there.

Of all the fingers of land which point out into the Atlantic from Ireland's west coast, the farthest reaching is the Dingle Peninsula. Slea Head at its end is the furthermost westerly point of mainland

Europe: Ultima Thule, Finnisterre, World's End. But still there are islands beyond, the Blaskets, the holy ground of vernacular Irish writing, where *Twenty Years A-Growing*, *Peig*, and *The Islandman* – Irish classics all, *Fiche Blian ag Fás*, *Peig* and *An tOileánach* – were written. Next parish, America.

Westwards from the Iveragh Peninsula – the so-called Ring of Kerry – lies Valentia Island. The first Atlantic cable reached Europe here in 1858. On a good day, look out across the south-westerly ocean and you may see Skellig Michael, an Atlantic rock so remote, so inhospitable, that its sixth-century monastery must have represented both the darkest night of anyone's soul, but also perhaps the repaired soul's brightest dawn.

Further south, and off the end of the next peninsula down, is Dursey Island. You reach it – if you're lucky – by cable car, swinging and pitching over the strait of water and rocks far below. There is a new car now, safer perhaps but less characterful. The old one's floor was six inches deep in the dried dung of terrified cows, and there was a frieze of holes – hoof-shaped – all around the base through which you could watch the boiling sea below. On the door was the small item of instruction: 'To Carry Six People or One Cow'.

Islandness is written into the Irish psyche, an offshoreness that speaks, of course, of separation and even isolation sometimes, but also of a certain kind of purity, less contaminated by European preoccupations with war and empire and the material. The Blasket Islanders used to talk and write about 'going into the island': to their way of thinking, it was the mainland, and not their island, that was offshore. The tag 'Ireland, Land of Scholars and Saints' was always an exaggeration, but it was also essentially true in the sense that in the Dark Ages it was Ireland that kept bright the lamp of learning – Latin, Greek, patristic studies, the making and revering of books, beautiful books like *The Book of Durrow*, *The Book of Kells*, *The Book of Armagh*. That was twelve hundred years ago, but there are people who see even now an afterglow of those remarkable minds in the contemporary survival of (and indeed modern interest in) Celtic Christianity – something purer, more elemental, real.

If Ireland is Europe's own epitomous manifesto of islandness – Europe's own visionary place out there in the west, visited in the imagination if not in the flesh, a place of wild beauty, wild unfettered minds, beautiful wild people – then Jack Yeats speaks for Ireland's own perception of itself as the liminal place, the western shore, beyond which lie the last islands of all. Again and again, this idea haunts his pictures. Let one suffice. In *Many Ferries* (1948), once more the time of day is evening and the light in the west is setting, but lingering long enough for the figures – sometimes single, sometimes paired, always receding away from us – to form a skein of people complementing the chain of islands that also recedes out into the west, fading gradually out of sight. Islands ... leading, luring us ...

There's always an island at the centre of the stories that make up that literary genre of ideal worlds: *Utopia* at the posh end, *Cythera* for the classicists, *Swallows and Amazons* or the Darling children's Never-Never Land at the popular end. High-brow or low-brow, it's a sort of nirvana, a zone of adventures – physical adventures for the children, intellectual adventures for the adults, or at least the boffs among the adults – and always there is the literal or metaphysical picnic hamper to be gained at the end, even if this is not literally or metaphysically a *Treasure Island*. Even before Sigmund Freud invented the human mind and Carl Jung identified the archetypes of the Collective Unconscious, islands had always been the best places to be. That myth is powerful enough and universal enough to have underwritten the self-consciousness of Great Britain: it underpinned empire, it legitimated difference. The literature of that empire is vast but – like the idea of empire itself – neither trusted nor esteemed as much as it once was. Swift smelt the rat even as early as the eighteenth century. He sent the whole thing up by having his Laputa – after Lilliput, the venue for the next of his *Gulliver's Travels* – not just an island, not just a water-girdled kingdom, but an airborne island. It doesn't just float, it flies. Perhaps it would take an offshore man – an Irishman – first to have imagined that, and then to have written it.

In the middle of the lake at Larchill in County Meath is an island, and on it a diminutive stone castle, the walls only a few feet high.

It was built for children (and regressive adults too, I suppose). On the OS map of 1836, this toy fortress is clearly identified as 'Gibraltar'. Prospero's magical realm in *The Tempest* is, of course, an island. Hereward the Wake retires to the safety of Ely, his island fastness in the fens. Magna Carta was signed at Runnymede, an island – a symbolically neutral territory – in the middle of the Thames. Diana, Princess of Wales, queen of so many hearts, was laid to rest on an island in the grounds of Althorp Park, her childhood home. The most sought-after, most expensive of celebrity retreats are islands (not least that of Charles Haughey, former Irish Taoiseach, on the island of Inisvickillane in the Blasket group). Tax-free havens for the super-rich are sometimes behind 'hedges', but more often – and less inscrutably to the economically illiterate – they are simply offshore.

Islands cast a terrific spell over our minds, always have done. So have gardens, from Eden onwards. The two avatars – islands and gardens – are fused together at Tresco off the south-west coast of Cornwall, and again, in Italy, on Lake Maggiore. Isola Bella and Isola Madre are both islands *and* gardens, and quite a lot more than merely half of their enormous magic comes from that fusion. But it is in Ireland that islandness and gardens – and the fusion of the two – have reached their apogee. Gardens of the mind and islands of the mind … and then the translation of ideality into reality. Glanleam (Valentia Island), Rossdahan and its neighbouring island Garinish (off Parknasilla, County Kerry) are all classic Irish island gardens. But at Ilnacullin, offshore in Bantry Bay, we have the most perfectly sited of them all – perhaps the most perfectly sited of all gardens anywhere, not excepting those Borromean gardens in Tuscany. It is the one iconic Irish garden whose setting alone predicates magic, that most precious, most quintessential, most elusive of all the things we prize in a garden.

It is time for a summary timeline of this place's evolution:

In 1805, the British built and desultorily manned a Martello tower to defend Bantry Bay against Napoleonic invasion. The threat was real. Only bad weather had prevented Wolfe Tone from landing a French fleet there in 1796. This tower apart, the island – half a mile at its longest – was a waste of rock, bog and scrubby bushes, especially squat, windswept gorse and holly, hence the name Ilnacullin – the Island of Hollies.

In 1910, a Belfast businessman (and Scottish MP), John Annan Bryce, was holidaying at Glengarriff, a long-established Victorian village of charm and character at the top of Bantry Bay. He saw the island out in the bay and bought it from the War Office, intending to build a house, a garden and an island retreat.

In the same year, he invited Harold Peto, doyen of garden-designers in the Italian style, to visit the site. Bryce was something of an amateur botanist himself – particularly interested in plants of the southern hemisphere – and had envisaged a garden of tender plants taking advantage of what he correctly surmised to be the island's extraordinarily benign microclimate.

Between 1911 and 1914, over one hundred men were employed clearing the scrub, sometimes blasting rock, and building a new slipway (originally you came and went from a little pier off the Glengarriff–Castletownbere road, a mile out of Glengarriff). What little soil there was consisted of old red sandstone and shale, but heavy rainfall had leached out nutrients for centuries. Bryce and Peto brought in by small boats thousands of tons of soil from the mainland. They planted shelter belts of doughty evergreen trees. They levelled a central, sheltered area towards the north-west of the island, which became the only flat land. Beneath the thin soil here was a peat bog. Over the years, as it gradually dried out, the level of this lawn sank (by the equivalent of two steps to the loggia whose base had to be deepened to compensate).

Simultaneously with a garden, plans for a mansion, five storeys high, were commissioned from Peto: a fantastic (Italianate) confection of balconies, ambulatories, gables, stairways and loggias. In the plans it looks like an opera set for Verdi crossed with

John Ruskin's Brantwood. The house was never built. The Bryces ran out of money. Only a gardener's cottage was put up. In principle, Bryce liked the architecture of both the big house and garden, but thought he knew better than Peto about plants. He may have been right.

But the core idea – an Italian garden – *was* carried out: there are two buildings framing a sunken pool garden. The pavilion which looks outward north-west to the Caha Mountains – a stupendous view – is good (though the lines of the roof suggest something oriental rather than Italian and that is a little confusing unless you grasp that, in hardly any senses, is this garden a purist, doctrinaire conception, but a many-branched, impure hybrid). The larger casita (or loggia, as it is sometimes called) is a really lovely building. There are two collonaded wings, open except for ranks of pillars. Between them is a fairly modest room, intended originally to house Bryce's collection of antique sculpture and old-master drawings. (All the drawings and almost all of the sculpture were progressively sold off a long time ago, but a few lapidary inscriptions remain, and there were three Turner watercolours included in the bequest of the garden by Roland Bryce – Annan Bryce's son – to the Irish State.) The columns of the arcades are made of a variety of marbles, mostly Italian but some from Connemara. The casita itself is made of biscuit-coloured Bath stone. The pool is lined with blue tesserae, however, and that makes it look as if a swimming pool were originally intended. There are lilies in the water now, but the blue walls sit ill with them.

A temple was also built at the top of a flight of steps at the western end of the long valley walk. You cannot see this from the Italian Garden but it has the same antique flavour, and the approach to it is planted with narrow Italian cypresses (but, sadly, they are not growing well).

The large lawn (that gradually sank) on the other side of the casita was originally tennis courts. Now it is uneventful. Across the lawn is the entrance to the walled garden.

There are broadly three elements of the island garden as a whole – the Italian garden, the long valley walk, and the walled garden. Together they take up a little less than half of the island as a whole, which covers thirty-seven acres. The rest remains wild and rocky and heavily wooded. The walled garden has quite Italianate towers at its corners – one a gazebo and the other a taller, campanile-like clocktower – and there is a fine medicean gateway. Originally it was a kitchen garden. Some old, old apple trees remain. Now at least some of it is simply a mess, but a rather winning mess, it has to be said. The style and planting – such as they are – of this part of the garden are not Italianate at all, they probably never were, nor is that of the long valley, the Happy Valley. Though always marketed as an Italian garden, in fact only a small part of Ilnacullin matches that description – and then only approximately. Beyond the walled garden was (is?) a garden of roses and pergolas, but it is not accessible to visitors.

In 1928, a remarkable man named Murdo MacKenzie, a Scotsman, was appointed head gardener. He retired, but only slightly, in 1971.

On the death of Bryce's son, Roland, in 1953, the garden-island was bequeathed to the state, and it remains the jewel in the crown of Ireland's small, select portfolio of publicly owned gardens.

Ilnacullin – the Island of Hollies – can be reached only by boat. Do not be confused by the name Garinish (or Garnish). Ilnacullin and Garinish (which means 'The Near Island') are one and the same (though in fact there *is* another Garinish Island, on the north side of the Beara Peninsula). There are two little, locally owned ferries which ply between the island and the mainland: the *Blue Pool* to a jetty hard by the middle of the village, the *Island Queen* to a pier opposite the Eccles Hotel at the bottom of the village. Both boats make a point of lingering near the colonies of bored seals laid, on a hot day, like slabs of greying, mouldy butter on rocks in the bay. Notice the swallows – you saw them earlier in the village. Now they're out here over the water, scribbling invisible inks in the sky. The voyage takes about ten minutes, and it's wonderful. It sets the tone for a place set apart, it breaks with the everyday world, it is slow and it slows you down.

The slipway is visible only at the last moment. A wooded island comes into view, but no garden or hint of one either. Step off the boat.

Be reminded by the boatman which one it is (which one your return ticket was bought for) or you'll be delivered to the wrong part of the village when you go back. You'll go through a turnstile, having bought a second ticket which will allow access to the island. Still there is no evidence of any garden, but trees loom closely all around. There'll likely be two or three people keen to learn where the toilets are … because a journey over water makes you watery yourself. Get away from them as well as you can, and follow the sign to 'The Garden'. You'll climb a curving flight of uneven, foot-polished stairs. Because of the bend you cannot see where they lead.

The feeling of transition – even though the steps cover a short enough distance – is colossal. You enter another world.

In summer there will be fewer flowers than in the spring. Perhaps most obvious in summer will be the large knots of crinums. Out of flower they look scruffy, like the rude nests of swans – just heaps of this and that detritus. But once their strong stems grow up and over the dump, and the flowers open successively, they are very impressive. Only *C. powellii* is reliably hardy for most of us and only it is grown here, which is a shame. The more tender ones would flourish here, and they would be even more impressive. Nevertheless, such crinums as they do have – summer amaryllis is what they really are – look very good indeed. Behind them are abutilons – strangely insubstantial plants, unnoticed, unremarkable, until they flower, and then they are lovely – bells, bonnets, stamens poking out like bristles, a fusion of those elements, and one of those plants whose individual blooms immensely reward close attention. The rusty trunks and branches of myrtles are numerous. The colour catches your eye in summer and so, on a still day, does their scent but you may not, at first, realise the source. In these beds there used to be three distinct varieties of hoheria – one of the least appreciated, least blousy, most beautiful members of the mallow family – almost a signature plant in Irish gardens, in fact: *H. populnea, H. glabrata* and *H. sexstylosa.*

If you see one at all in England, it will almost certainly be a selected form of *H. glabrata* called 'Glory of Amlwch'. These other hoherias are rare, even in Ireland. To see (and smell) a hoheria in a garden is a real August event – blossom in abundance when almost every other summer garden is tired and dull. Only one hoheria remains here now, but it is still a fine thing.

In spring it's the magnolias and camellias that impress. This short path is like an haute couture catwalk of the best that horticulture has to offer in March, April and May. The volume and intensity of flowers is astonishing, but it is concentrated within a walk of only twenty or thirty yards, and then you come down a flight of steps – generous and even steps this time – and you are in the Italian Garden.

It is not all that large as Italian gardens go, but there is less architectural formality and there are far more plants than you find in the type, whether it be the real thing in Italy itself or in the countless derivatives elsewhere. In the centre here, and down another flight of steps, is the blue-lined pool, framed by the two buildings, behind you the casita and, in front, the temple. On either side are concentric formal beds and narrow paths, densely planted with tender fuchsias and leptospermums, callistemons and olearias, and these days – at the front – stuffed with bedding begonias too. There are taller plants towards the back – more camellias, pittosporums, Irish escallonias, azaleas and mahonias. Best of all are the rhododendrons, among them here Murdo MacKenzie's own favourite, *R.* 'Lady Alice Fitzwilliam'. The space is not so very large, and it is enclosed all about by plants, but it is not in any way cramped. And it is not quite entirely shut in either. To the west, behind and visible through the temple, is a stunning panorama of the Caha Mountains. It's a terrific *coup de théâtre*.

The mood and atmosphere of this garden are dependent upon the light. Of course, that's true to some extent of any garden, but never more so than here. On a hot balmy day, divisions between areas lit and areas in shade are sharper, clearer. Only strong colours survive strong light. On such a day the garden does indeed feel Italian. Mercury in the middle of the pool forfeits godliness in his small stature but retains his mercurial strangeness: what does his pointing finger mean? And is he really pointing, or does he beckon? What does he know that we don't? The stumps and capitals of antique (Italian) columns here and there become more than just stage properties, and you notice them more carefully: the light picks out the carving which is absorbed into a mere impression of lichen and shade on gloomier days. If it is really hot, you envy the water lilies and seek out a seat in the shade of the casita's loggia (they say it was in the casita that Bernard Shaw slept when he was here. They say he was writing *St Joan* at the time. And why not?). Originally there were the very clear pencil shapes of cypresses – signatures, of course, of the *ur*-Italian garden. The other tree (and much faster growing) which would have served to characterise the place in a distinctively Italian way would have been the

Lombardy poplar, *Populus nigra*, all of its forms tall and thin and looking as if they were painted into the landscape by a Florentine primitive or a latter-day Corot. But poplars will not tolerate the wind at Ilnacullin, so it had to be cypresses. And even those – the originals – are either gone now, or much less conspicuous. Others have been planted but they are rather feebly struggling. Nevertheless, you know that you are in the vaunted Italian garden of Ilnacullin.

At some point, however, an epiphanous moment may occur: this is *not* an Italian garden in the usual sense at all; it is a *Roman* garden, an evocation of the gardens at Pompeii that both Bryce and Peto knew well. Understood thus, it makes much better sense … the pool to flop in and out of, the sybaritic mood and, of course, all that antique sculpture. In reality, what we have here is not an Italian renaissance garden (in the manner of Boboli or d'Este or Gamberaia) but a pagan fantasy garden. Thus perceived, this garden, begun in 1910, fits perfectly into an era where neo-paganisms – everything from the Great God Pan in *The Wind in the Willows* (1908) to Debussy's *Prélude à l'Après-midi d'un Faune* (1894) to Isadora Duncan dressed like someone out of Pompeii – were very much in vogue.

Really strong though that antique-Pompeian flavour is, there is also something of the Orient here, a sort of heuristic, scattershot exoticism. Originally there was a collection of Japanese bonsai trees (but planted in Roman urns, troughs, etc.) One of them – a beautiful gnarled larch – is still there; it is said to be over three hundred years old. The stone lions at the bottom of the steps are two thousand years old but the lion was an animal so exotic to the Romans that when they sculpted it – as here – their anatomy was only approximate, conjectural or just fantastic. As a result, they look quite odd, quite oriental in fact. Another whiff of the Far East is caught again in the low lines of the roofs of the temple and the casita which we noticed earlier. Seen from the lawn, the casita is decked out in a big shawl of wisteria, and that completes the oriental trope.

Later in the day, when the light is longer but still strong, you notice more how reflective are the leaves of quite a number of the austral plants here (and indeed of the camellias too, though quite a lot of these are Italian-bred, rather than Chinese or Japanese). The crazed scaffold-like structure of the corokias becomes clearer, and the way their twigs and leaves interlock like answers on a crossword puzzle. The bottle brushes come out of the mind's kitchen and enter the swankier salon. The bruised leaf smell of the *Vestia lycioides* suggests Italian drainage, and you smile. The begonias just look cheap and nasty, but never mind.

Labels are woefully rare at Ilnacullin now, which – for the plants-man – is a serious deficiency. A lot of these plants are very special indeed, but out of flower, or late in the day, you might miss them. You'd also miss the special plants which belong here because they began here, either by accident or by deliberate breeding. Everyone knows (and some revile) *Griselinia littoralis*. The ordinary griselinia has long been recognised as a useful shelter plant and is famous for its salt-tolerance. It's a prolific weed here, so much so that it even grows epiphytically on other trees. The less common but variegated griselinia – not an Ilnacullin plant – is alright if you want a change, but *G. littoralis* 'Bantry Bay' is something else again: splashed green, light green, darker green, creamy green, it is a remarkable plant. MacKenzie found it in the garden in 1950. He was inveterately a modest man and he would not have it named after him, so it is just 'Bantry Bay'. It is a little tender, wind sensitive, and quite special.

Other Ilnacullin plants include a bottle-brush, *Callistemon* 'Murdo MacKenzie' (named posthumously) whose flowers are the usual red but with a purple undertone. There is an apple-blossom pink escal-lonia (*E. macrantha* 'Bantry Bay'), which would be planted everywhere if the Slieve Donard escallonias hadn't stolen the show. A very fine pieris – *P.* 'Murdo MacKenzie', and named long after his death – has the usual white flowers (but abundantly) in February, and bronze-tinted new leaves. There was a good leptospermum – *L. scoparium* 'Roland Bryce' – which had separate scarlet and pink flowers on the same bush, a curious but not unattractive plant, but the original is gone and now it is only spoken of, so far as I know. Finally – and a simply outstanding plant – is *Cestrum roseum* 'Ilnacullin'. The swags of flowers are really big. They begin a strong red and slowly fade to a lovely soft pink. It is slightly tender, of course, but only slightly so. Given a sheltered, sunny spot it thrives. It will be in flower for ten out of twelve months – long enough to depend upon it, short enough not to take it for granted. It is not commonly available but well worth seeking out. No one seems to know where in the garden the original plant is to be found, if indeed it is still there.

The name Murdo MacKenzie is cropping up again and again. He was Scottish (so were the Bryces, originally). At first his salary was to be £100 a year, plus ten per cent of the income from garden visitors – not a bad sum then, if it was indeed paid. But since 1938 his remuneration had been irregular, to say the least. By the time that the state took over the island, he (and the six under-gardeners) were essentially dependent upon the revenue from visitors. After William Robinson, MacKenzie ranks as the most influential, most respected of all Irish gardeners (gardeners in Ireland) so far. Bryce began to run out of money once the war (1914–19) got underway. Overdependence on investments in imperial Russia meant that after 1917 he was never much in funds again. MacKenzie arrived in 1928 when the shape of the garden was more or less settled, but its character – as conceived by Peto – was not. Peto had planned a rich man's playground. MacKenzie – as a Presbyterian, a bit of an ascetic himself – gave up on that (except insofar as it was a lure to the visitors who supplemented his salary) and consolidated the place as a plantsman's Elysium. He was, apparently, a stickler for weeds. As an old man he used a stick, but it had been designed by him to allow the screwing-out of weeds as well as supporting his old legs. He was a strict master, though held in enormous respect by his underlings. There was a lot of the gentleman about him – fairness, honesty, integrity, an educated eye. A lore is growing up around him now. My favourite bit so far is the story that, though he was tolerant of visitors' inanities with regard to what they said about the plants, the nuns – or some of them – provoked his patience. Apparently they would break off blooms, but then their courage or conviction or whatever it was would fail them and they would try to hide the stolen items inside their robes. The theft he could overlook, but the slyness he could not.

What MacKenzie made of the Happy Valley, the next area we move on to of the greater garden of Ilnacullin, we do not know. He might have approved of it – the name and the concept – in the sense that there are some extraordinarily happy (and rare) plants there. The classical undertones he would have respected: Arcadia of course, the Vale of Tempe perhaps – Apollo's favoured rural spot in the shadow of Mount Olympus – Pliny's out-of-town garden, etc. Centuries later, Thomas More's *Utopia* (1516) is bordered by 'Happiland', a place whose king is sworn to serve his subjects rather than himself, but the expression is (deliberately) babyish in the book, and that's a resonance unintended here in Ilnacullin's Happy Valley, though not, in fact, entirely unavoided. Johnson's 'Happy Valley' in his *Rasselas* of 1759 (which is where the expression was really first coined in this definitive form) is a little trickier, if it is indeed one of the models for Bryce's valley. Johnson has his Rasselas, son of the Emperor of Abyssinia, weary of the joys of the place because the inhabitants know only 'the soft vicissitudes of pleasure and repose'. Rasselas actually runs away from it, but Bryce was not a particularly bookish man, and perhaps he didn't know this. I wonder if there's an undertone of Samuel Palmer, the painter ... *The Golden Valley*; *The Valley Thick with Corn*, and so on. Bryce's contemporary, Yeats, certainly knew Palmer's work. Did Bryce perhaps own a Palmer? Or did he hanker after doing so? It would fit so well if he did. Certainly there were Turners in his collection, there were superb landscapes by Edward Lear. Whatever the case regarding Palmer, the broader connotations, the ones which would have been in the air when this garden was being made, were not of high-minded classical models at all but chiefly of colonial watering holes. MacKenzie would have been challenged there, I think.

At the western end of the Happy Valley is a flight of steps which lead to the last and least impressive of the Italian-flavoured buildings on Ilnacullin. It's a roofless tempietto. The building is only gestural but the view – again, towards the Caha Mountains – is stunningly good. The planting up here is all agapanthus and half-willing juvenile cypresses, some of which have failed already, and the rest will follow in due course it seems. But turning eastwards, and back down the steps, you begin the long valley walk. It feels like a valley because there are walls of trees, east to west, on either side of you, but the real valley runs with the stream, north to south. At the oozy bottom, when you get there, the mood is faintly oriental again. There are stepping stones for the nimble-footed, and skunk cabbages and sagittarius. Predictably, *Gunnera manicata* is there too. Gunnera is now virtually naturalised in West Cork. You see it in damp spots by the roadsides and in many a foggy bottom too. In Glengarriff, which seems to be the epicentre of the plant's invasion, they had a blitzkrieg against a colony of it in front of the police house recently. It seems now to be lying low, but I doubt if the battle was won. It would be interesting to know when, by whom and where it was first introduced. Probably not through Ilnacullin, which is not by any means the oldest serious garden in the district. Early in the century, the Daisy Hill Nursery in Newry, Co. Down, propagated and sold a golden (well, paler) version of *G. manicata* and three varieties of *G. tinctoria*. Those were innocent times before we knew better, and before deluvial rainfall – even in Ireland – became so conducive to these damp-lovers. It is sobering to learn that, eighty years ago, one of Murdo MacKenzie's big difficulties was watering in summer. Not enough water could be stored to carry the garden over dry times.

As you walk down and then up the other side of the Happy Valley, you are passing by fabulous plants everywhere you look. Most of them are rhododendrons – species and hybrids – so you need to be here in spring to see them in flower. Even out of flower, *R. sinogrande, R. maccabeanum* and their ilk are conspicuous by their huge leaves, by the silvery, dusty-red, downy-green indumenta of the undersides of their leaves, and sometimes by their peeling trunks. They all love the soil, the climate, the shelter and the rainfall here. So do certain magnolias, a number of choice Chinese and North American dog-woods, rare pines, thujas and cedars and swamp cypresses. There is a beetling southern beech, aromatic eucalyptus and always more rho-dodendrons. Competing occasionally with the flayed barks of certain rhododendrons is a similar thing occurring with arbutus. Usually it's the ordinary *A. unedo*, another Irish weed really, but here and there is *A. x arachnoides*, whose bark is really beautiful. It pays to keep on looking up as well as across and along. Some of the individual trees have superb profiles; seen collectively, these ever-changing ensembles are three-dimensional tapestries of leaf colour – infinities of green of course, but also blue and burnt reds, blacks and greys – colours and textures. Tree ferns have become a cliché of Irish gardens, so much so that one or two gardens now spurn them in favour of the more recondite, more reluctant restios. At Ilnacullin, tree ferns – both dicksonias and cyatheas – are not over-exposed, and they look just right here too, woodlanders and mist-lovers. Ubiquitous *Griselinia* seedlings, saplings, thuglets, grow around them, over them, sometimes even in their crowns. The other endemic Ilnacullin weed is *Juniperus recurva* var. *coxii*. Its insidious fecundity is not funny.

In 1989, a list was published of the more important plants to be found at Ilnacullin. It wasn't by any means comprehensive, but pretty extensive nonetheless: one hundred and fifty-four different plants, species or varieties, in the Jungle (where you cannot go now); one hundred and eighty one in the Happy Valley. A significant number of those plants are not there now, or they've been smothered by something else ... by the *Juniperus coxii* or the *Griselinia*! There have been new plantings, it is true, but a lot is now missing. No doubt some of them were plants which never would have thrived here (roses, for example ... hopeless!), some would have been short-lived anyway, some perhaps have changed their names. But given the scale of the garden, the loss is commensurately huge. It would be bad at any time of year, but in summer it is almost catastrophic: a few hydrangeas and desultory agapanthus apart, there is almost nothing in flower along the whole southern part of the garden. Where are the stuartias? Where is the bound-to-stun *Crinodendron hookerianum*? Even better, *C. patagua*? The embothrium? There are compensations, of course there are, but not enough to gratify a visitor led on by an expectation of an 'Italian garden', exceedingly hybridised and syncretist though that term has turned out to be at Ilnacullin.

One of the few plants to be labelled is one of those compensations, and it is a very great one too. *Dacrydium franklinii* is a New Zealander, precariously tender, very rare, and a great character. If Gollum had wanted to invent an appropriately lugubrious, definitively eccentric, Middle-Earth Christmas tree, it could have been this. Other trees stoop, wilt or stagger; some do it well enough to sidestep the cliché of the sentimentally lachrymose – *Picea breweriana*, Brewer's weeping spruce, among them – but only *Dacrydium franklinii* weeps, blubbers and un-mans even the most hard-boiled of clinical dendrologists. It is a most cherishable tree here.

Superb though it is, the quality of this tree is not exceptional; but the fact that it has a label is. There are very few other (visible, accessible, still-readable) labels. Given the extreme rarity and self-evident happiness of so many of the plants here, that is a great shame. A determined effort should have been made years ago to rectify this. And there have been some piecemeal attempts, but something comprehensive and systematic must be done before the island becomes merely a camera-clicker's day out. Many trees still bear an identifying number – that's good, that's serious and systematic – but it's meaningless to the visitor without a key to the numbers.

There used to be a good path away to the left and through the Jungle, where there were (are?) even more fabled, fabulously beautiful plants, where the freckles of the light on wet leaves compensated for the umbrellas and the damp feet. But it has been closed now. Access to some of the very best things on the island is no longer possible. It was always a slippery, yielding track, but that could have been mended enough to make it safe. It is time for the garden to be recovered for serious gardeners, serious tree lovers, grown-up walkers, as well as day-trippers (God bless 'em!).

You have no choice now but to climb the other side of the Happy Valley. The walk ends in three flights of steps. You deserve a seat at the top, but there is none. Views south over the vast expanse of Bantry Bay are good. Interesting too is the rough, rocky surface, the rough gorse and hollies, the birch trees which struggle to survive at all because of the wind. This is what the island was originally like. You can look over the Martello tower if you want to, but it's just a shell (and, unusually for Ireland-of-the-tall-stories, no one boasts that

James Joyce was ever here, but he *was* at the one at Sandycove on the shore of Dublin Bay if you're a student of Martello towers or the first chapter of *Ulysses*).

From the Martello tower you must descend quite steeply towards the walled garden. But before you do, from the viewing point up there, you can see this garden's context best. All around the island: water, mountains, starved rocky landscapes, Whiddy Island with its huge dug-in oil storage cylinders, so cunningly masked that you'd really never know; but Ilnacullin itself is densely vegetated. Yet almost none of it looks gardened, until you are right on top of it, right in it. You can see from here the Italianate clocktower of the walled garden, but you'd never know it belonged to a *garden*.

Down flights of gloomy, slippery steps – so much overgrowing all around you that you'd forgive even the growling, grinding,

tree-punishing sound of a chainsaw if it were to bring in light and air. Soon enough, however, you will be at the east gate of the walled garden, and before you, gently sloping down, is a path through a double herbaceous border. Plants spill over the path wherever they can ... which is nearly everywhere, because there are nowhere nearly enough (skilled) gardeners to keep it in order. Nevertheless, the disorder exerts a strong charm. There are no colour gradients, not much phasing of things coming into or going out of flower, only rough-and-ready arrangements of taller things approximately further back than the smaller things which are approximately at the front, and yet this is a wonderful piece of easeful gardening. No stress of worrying about abstracts like taste, style, tone. Not much worrying about material things like staking or dead-heading either. But an exuberant overgrowth of plants pleased to be here. A lot of them are simple plants – cottage garden favourites like erigeron, heliopsis, gaudy dahlias, silvery anaphalis, phloxes, penstemons and a lot of sedums. The disorder and the exuberance are exciting. Visually it's like a bus-load of kids who are normally regimented into uniform, mindless obedience and the sulky queues of habit and conformity, but today they have the school outing, they can wear what they like, and the bus spills them out into an anarchy of sunshine.

Occasionally there are out-of-the-ordinary plants: exotic daturas bedded out, the gorgeous *Hydrangea villosa*, one or two clematis flouncing about, smothering the voices of pittosporums or abutilons. But – exotic or common-or-garden – it's really the exuberance that impresses.

Once upon a time, this was the kitchen garden. There was a range of glasshouses along the (wonderfully wayward, crooked) south-facing wall. There were fruit trees. Here and there, the bones of these remain. There were annual crops of vegetables and perennial beds of rhubarb and asparagus. This is the best soil in the entire island. Now – except for that central walk between the long borders – it is mostly in ruin. The roses (there used to be lots) struggle or give up or, contrarily, they go berserk. Survivors have been pruned, but only to allow passage through them. They haven't been fed, and they don't flower much now. Most of the twenty-five clematis listed in 1989 have gone.

Rank weeds enjoy the fine earth, the shelter, the holidays from supervision and the stored warmth of the walls. But all is not lost. And even if it were, there is a special kind of enchantment in ruins, something of *Sleeping-Beauty*-ness, something atavistic ringing old bells about lost gardens, lost domains, secret gardens, childhood, mystery.

As it happens, one of Ilnacullen's special moments occurs here if you step out of the highway of the double border and relax and slow your eyes down and revert to simpler, black-and-white vision. Turn left the moment you enter the garden (by the eastern, Martello tower gate). It's a short walk up and into the corner where the walls meet in their right-angle. There's a stair to an upper room – a Gothic-Venetian window … Act Two, Scene Two of *Romeo and Juliet* about to begin as the dusk closes in … but underneath it is a grotto, a small cave, a large, gloomy, shallow alcove. Bryce and Peto were imagining a nymphaeum, I think, a watery, half-lit cave where spirits of the classical world – and latter-day skinny dippers? – could bathe. What remains of Bryce's collection of relief sculptures is stored (and approximately displayed) here. They're interesting, but it is the moment-glimpsed spirit of the place that catches at you. A moment of magic.

Emerge from the walled garden at its western end (inhale the scent of *Magnolia grandiflora* if you're there in July or August). You have almost completed the circuit of the garden. In front of you is the large, uneventful space of the casita lawn. But the brief, deep, south-facing border as you make your way back to the little harbour and the boat is often well-planted with new, adventurous things. It's an echo of what Ilnacullin must have been like in its salad days: exciting, risk-taking, young and a bit foolish.

Don't leave yet. Let there be one more piece of magic to remember the place by. Go back along the loggia (you can easily avert your eyes from the hysteria of begonias down there in the Italian Garden if you want to. It's okay.) Take the path – the only path – again to the Happy Valley. It's quite narrow, twisting, but not long. Just before you reach the broad walk, on your left there's a big, dome-shaped rock, bald and scalped except for a rose sprawled insouciantly over it. It might be *R. mulliganii*, it might not. It doesn't matter. It hardly flowers anyway.

The magic is in the louche, slouched abandon of it, the attitude. It looks like a half-hearted, slightly torn hairnet on an old woman's head. A very wise old lady, to be sure, even if she is nearly bald. It's terrific.

Just before you go, there's the tea room, the best thing to have happened at Ilnacullin in the last few years. Food and drink is excellent, it is shelter when it rains, and the company is good. And there's a very good class of dog, infinitely bored with the horticulture, infinitely patient for crumbs from the table. The last time I was there, the conversational company was a retired architect and his wife – Irish through and through, but it had been fifty years since they were at Ilnacullin – and now they could go home to Howth and tell their daughter that the tree which flowers at her garden gate and she never knew the name of is *Hoheria sexstylosa* ('and is that six leaves or petals or stamens? Oh, that man Linnaeus…!'). Then there are two sophisticated young women down from Dublin for a few days. Lace blouses. Fine tweed skirts. Deep in their conversation ('that rain last night, that was just un-*ray*sonable' which – by Irish standards – is saying something, so you know it must be true even though you slept right through it).

Keeping almost the best until last … climb again the few steps up from the tearoom as if you were going back into the garden, but don't turn right. Turn instead to your left, but only for a few yards. There you'll see the most fantastically shaped, the most lugubriously mournful, sagging but still going *Cryptomeria* of your life. You could be forgiven for thinking it was alive in a more than vegetable sense: a cryptic animal indeed, slinking through its own undergrowth. You mustn't miss it.

The best of Ilnacullin – the flagship, I suppose, of Ireland's great gardens – is its plants, the rare ones, the plain ones, the way they are so comfortable here. But the soul of the place is its islandness. For all that it's not what it used to be, not (perhaps) what it still should be, it's still a magical place, a special place and one that you'd come back to again and again, either in your memory and imagination or on that slow boat from Glengarriff. Of all island gardens, this one is the most magical. Isola Bella is theatre, but not good, grown-up theatre. Isola Bella is glad-ragged costume drama, a series of acts, a bit of horticultural music hall. Isola Madre is house-and-garden, rather than pure garden alone, and all those ridiculous peacocks are a joke. Ilnacullin – no house, no peacocks, no smell and ooze of money (really, at least not now), no balustrades or belvederes and no box or bougainvilleas – is the real thing, a garden for the sake of plants alone and for the glimpse of Eden recovered.

And this is not really an Italian garden anyway. It is just very, very Irish.

To leave Ilnacullin – to get back onto the boat, back into the swim of traffic, of life, of money to make, bills to pay: that world that Wordsworth thought was just too much with us (and that was two hundred years ago) – is to induce a sense of loss. I defy anyone to leave this place without thinking *Will I ever come back? Will I have* time *to come back?* It's the epitome of several themes in this book about Irish gardens: islandness, a sense of loss and exile, the strangeness of melancholy, that sadness we love to enjoy. Tom Moore, once more, puts his finger on it in this verse from *Sweet Innisfallen*. He is musing on a place – mythic or real, it hardly matters:

Where erring man might hope to rest –

Might hope to rest, and find in thee
A gloom like Eden's, on the day
He left its shade, when every tree,
Like thine, hung weeping o'er his way.

Weeping or smiling, lovely isle!
And all the lovelier for thy tears –

Strange. Not least because it is strangely – even embarrassingly – true to one's experience. Unmanned by a garden and what it can mean.

Of all gardens, Ilnacullin is the place where what it means is so much greater even than what it actually is.

Derreen

COUNTY KERRY

There's a certain school of thought – deeply unfashionable, mischievously attractive – which holds, contrary to all the best authorities from Doctor Spock right up to Oprah Winfrey, that not all the best things in life are well expended upon children; that some things are, in fact, *wasted* upon children. (I'll pause for a moment to let you catch your outraged breath.)

Clearly, children do need their iPods, their multi-channel televisions in their rooms, their ponies, their designer clothes changed at intervals of a month, and, by way of what used elegantly to be called 'finishing', their year out in the fleshpots of Thailand, the beaches of Sydney and the rest. There is no question about it. All is completely endorsed by the best thinking of the last thirty years in education, potty-training and retail sales-indexing. So what on earth can these flat-earthers be thinking of?

Well, take food for example. *Good* food is wasted on the young, isn't it? Of course, they need food, nutrition, per se, but put a plate of good, adult, interesting food in front of the average young person and you are wasting it. They will not eat it.

Or (but possibly more contentiously) travel. There are a lot of air miles expended these days in lugging minors round the globe, but I don't think I would be alone if I confessed to a growing suspicion that a lot of it is wasted, in the sense that the larger minds that used to flow from (much less) travel in the past do not seem so very much in evidence now. One must be careful, though. Perhaps travel itself, irrespective of the age of the person doing it, is becoming less fulfilling, a street in Sao Paulo being much the same now as a street in Kathmandu. Be that as it may, it's almost incontestably true that music, good music, tends to be wasted on the young these days, isn't it? Or perhaps one is simply becoming jealous (and crabby and grumpy). And yet ...

There may or may not be anything in it. But let us consider just one more example, one more piece of putative evidence in support of the thesis. Let us consider, for a moment, the case of gardens. Children, from the age at which they can walk independently up to (say) four, cannot get enough of gardens, but beyond that age any child, any adolescent, any young adult, who would actually go out of their way to engage with a garden – a grown-up space given over to trees, plants, earth, water, in short an outdoor space carefully reconfigured into a *considered place* – is an extreme rarity. He or she would have to be the exception to an otherwise infrangible rule: young people (and the age range in this matter easily extends way beyond the age of majority) find gardens unutterably boring; gardening itself 'sad' (as their own sadly reductive parlance has it), and gardeners themselves as generically geriatric.

Let it not be noised abroad too loudly, but actually this proposition – that gardens are wasted on the young – is true. And that fact, it has to be admitted – given that *we* number gardens among the seriously good things of life – may be rather depressing. Considered carefully, though, and used as a critical yardstick, it can reveal an awful lot about the meaning of gardens – why they matter; indeed why they matter more and more – which is otherwise almost universally overlooked.

Imagine, then, a real garden – a conventional place of trees and views, paths and fallen leaves, and not some sort of landscaped football pitch – in which children lose themselves for hours, in which they play, romp, explore, build fantastic kingdoms of the mind, and love every minute of it.

Almost beyond belief, and extremely rare though it is, there is such a place. It is called Derreen, and it's right on the edge of the Atlantic coast of south-west Ireland. I have visited Derreen on quite a number of occasions over quite a number of years and it has never failed to exert upon me a powerful impression: a complicated mixture, I suppose, of botanical awe, deep pleasure, in a sense-of-place beginning with the garden but then spilling out into the huge contiguous landscape of sea and mountain, lake and woodland, and, as well as the horizontal landscape, the kind of vertical sense – a sort of fourth dimension – you get as you gradually begin to apprehend a landscape with a past. Thus, a place with roots in an historical as well as dendrological sense, something which I believe the seasoned visitor to Ireland begins to find more and more important as the first flushes of familiarity give place to other ways of looking and enjoying, so that garden-visiting becomes a wider synthesis of perceptual skills – botanical and aesthetic of course, but also cultural, historical, perhaps spiritual too if it's not too ponderous and portentous a word.

Well, the last time I was at Derreen there were only two other vehicles in the car park – it was August and the rhododendrons were long over – and I sighed with the slightly guilty pleasure that goes with thinking that I should have the place, to all intents and purposes, to myself. But as I wandered off along the paths and through the trees, I could hear the voices of children. They were ahead of me, I think, and Derreen is a very large garden, but at any moment they might have turned round, or I might have caught up with them, but I never did. Always they were invisible, though often I could hear

them some distance away, always separated from me by trees, always on separate paths somewhere out of sight. There were shouts, cries of excitement, discovery, impersonation. 'It's my turn', or 'Look at me!', or 'I'm the king of the castle ...' All of it very good-natured and, of course, that made it a pleasure to hear anyway, but that's not my point: these children were absolutely engrossed in their games, and the games were absolutely integral with, and inseparable from, the place. *These* children loved *this* place.

I think they had been here before; they seemed familiar with its paths and with each new theatre for their imaginations that each succeeding grove supplied. Perhaps they lived here, or were on holiday in the big house, or lived nearby and came in often. Whatever the case, here was a garden which children understood (in the sense that it struck chords in the music of their own imaginations; that, in a kind of inverted Proustian sense perhaps, they recognised). And then, having subliminally understood it in possibly a very complicated though largely unconscious way, they set about simply but emphatically to enjoy it. This garden was not wasted on these children.

There's another school of thought – a fairly new branch of geography, I believe – which identifies the pleasure one gets out of landscape,
and the kind of personal and ethnographic affiliations and loyalties
that grow up as a result of that, with *recognition*: people dislocated
(from where they began) by pressures of social and economic mobil-
ity – or indeed displaced by warfare and by having had to flee for their
lives – sooner or later will gravitate (or want to gravitate) back towards
their places of origin, or at least to the *kind* of place they originated in:
psycho-geography. Like many of the best ideas, it is essentially very
simple, even obvious (at least in retrospect). By taking the easy word
home seriously for a change – stripping it of damage and accretions
bolted on by the building industry or corruptions inflicted upon it by
salesmen of every kind – and then simply by watching its magnetic
fields at work, you'd have stumbled upon it. Or by thinking carefully
about Aborigines in central Australia or Amerindians in Nevada, and
the tenacity with which they want to hang on to apparently empty,
hopelessly inhospitable places, would you not reach similar conclusions? Or just by reading Proust. On a big, geopolitical scale it might
explain how it is that a sense of personal freedom – in some minds,
some cultures, some situations – yearns to be underwritten by a landscape of big, open spaces. On a much smaller scale, it might explain
why people make gardens in the image of the (lost?) paradises of their
childhood, and why something as simple as a wall can come to beto-
ken something as colossally significant as safety, enclosure, indeed as
home. It's the kind of fascinating territory (of the mind) where playing
as a child – with all its connotations of care-freeness – can begin to
be seen to connect with something as ineffably serious as *playing*
Beethoven, or *playing* Hamlet.

Perceived as territory (in the mind as it were), I think it is one
of the most interesting avenues into Irish gardens, territories on the
ground – what they mean as well as where their particular styles and
character come from – not least because the Irish have an unusually
intense familiarity with emigration and all that that entails in terms of
the loss of a sense of *home* – perhaps even of exile. Writing about the
industrial town of Springfield in Massachusetts, a hundred miles west

of Boston, and the fact that it is where so many emigrants from the Great Blasket eventually settled over the span of the decades that saw the gradual depopulation of the island, Cole Moreton called his book *Hungry for Home*. Originating in the condition of exile, those words also suggest the metaphor which unlocks the forms and meanings of gardens in general (perhaps), and Irish gardens in particular ...

At any rate, that afternoon in Derreen it struck me with unusual force: something special was going on there, and that seemed to imply something special about the place. Upon reflection, I think that is indeed the case.

Derreen, the name, comes from the Irish *doire*, meaning 'oak-wood'. It's the diminutive, so '*little* oak-wood'. And it's cognate with *derry*, as in Londonderry, the place and the song. It's situated on one of those peninsular fingers of rocky land that reach far out into the Atlantic from the coast of south-west Ireland. The Fastnet Rock is farther out still, but it occupies the same sort of imaginative territory and engages the same sort of mindset: a wild, sometimes cruelly wild landscape which is also stirringly, unforgettably beautiful. Mizen Head is there too (for connoisseurs of weather reports). There are five of these peninsulas. The most southerly ends at Mizen Head. Dunmanus Bay (see the chapter about the garden at Carraig Abhain) separates it from the next, which ends (but after nearly twenty miles – these are *long* fingers of land) in Sheep's Head. Next comes Bantry Bay, at whose top lies Ilnacullin, or Garinish Island, the island-garden also celebrated elsewhere in this book. Then there's the Beara Peninsula, and that's separated from the Iveragh Peninsula – or the Ring of Kerry as it is also known – by a long, fairly narrow bay called (rather misleadingly) the Kenmare River. Finally there's Dingle Bay, and the Dingle Peninsula (off which – 'next parish, America', as they say – is that Great Blasket Island). Parts of these landscapes are so powerful the feeling amounts to shock: the shock of the astonishingly beautiful, the unsentimental, unforgivingly beautiful. Every prospect, every parish, is different, but never very far off they are all bony with mountain, rough with exposed rock, and sea-bruised, wind-brawned. Engaging as we are here with that atavistic, primary dialectic of earth and sea and sky, it's the intellectual territory of another great Irishman, Edmund Burke, who so perceptively differentiated the merely beautiful from the almost terrifying, almost awful: the Sublime. He might have been thinking of this very landscape.

Derreen belongs to this liminal territory on the very edge of Europe, almost at the end of the world. It is on the north shore of the Beara Peninsula – the whole area something of a well-kept secret, but those who know tend to rate it as perhaps the finest of all Ireland's wild regions. A rather oozy inlet, two miles deep or so – Kilmakilloge Harbour – marks most of the boundary of this big garden, itself a peninsula of about ninety acres. Like water itself, the garden basically flows from the conical hill at its centre, where stands the house – its highest point, but by no means a forbiddingly boastful edifice – down to the water. There's a fantastically barge-boarded, nearly invisible boathouse down there (and Ratty and Mole not far away, as it seems to me). There's a very handsome new belvedere right on the water's edge which lives up to the promise of its name in the prospects of water, and of mountains over water, that it affords. And like all the best places – real and imaginary, hinting at treasure somewhere – there really is a little island just off the shore.

The names of some of the paths are such as you might find on that mythically crumpled, long-lost map discovered among the papers of Long John Silver (or indeed, Kingdon-Ward): Shingle Strand, Goleen Walk, King's Oozy, Cappul Walk. Unlikely though it might seem, the prosaic explanations or translations of these wonderful expressions – 'Every name is a tune,' said the poet Marianne Moore in her 'Spenser's Ireland' – are almost as interesting as the magical worlds they evoke. A *strand* is simply a beach (thus the street in London, until the Embankment was built). *Goleen* (*góilín*) means inlet and, sure enough, the Goleen Path follows the edge of the inlet. King's Oozy was so called because Edward VII and Queen Alexandra planted a bamboo each on a visit in 1903, and oozy the place is, but it may also derive from a bit of now-lost Indian slang. The Cappul Walk has a view onto Cappul Bridge a mile away (Cappul probably from the Irish *capall*, horse) … and a huge backdrop of mountains. These mountains, and the borrowed views they afford, are one of the particular features of this garden – indeed, they represent why the garden was made here in the first place. Borrowed views, even as fine as these, are not such unusual things of course, but the skill with which they have been framed here – by people planting merely sapling trees as much as one hundred and fifty years ago, and by successive generations carefully cutting out excessive growths – is. The views from within the garden proper are carefully prepared by being sparingly offered. From the Broad Walk along the shore and from the Shingle Strand you can see for miles, but from only two places within the garden itself can you see such huge prospects. The impressions they make – not a little due to their prepared contexts – are like the finale at the ends of each of the two acts in a grand two-act opera, a drama moreover of distinctly heroic character. Having to climb a little up to these vantages, gently but nevertheless firmly, prepares you somewhat, but the rewards exceed expectations by large margins. From Froude's Seat (J.A. Froude, sometime tenant at Derreen, and opinionated Victorian historian whose lofty views of ethnic Anglo-Saxon superiority – in books first about Ireland, and then about the West Indies – caused exasperated readers eventually to coin the word *froudacity*) there is a tremendous prospect westward, over the great estuary and, on a good day, far off into the mountains, among them Macgillicuddy's Reeks, the highest mountains in Ireland. The second borrowed view is north across an inlet of the estuary to another mountain, but this time one very close. Knockatee rises to only one thousand feet or so, but at such a close range it looks mighty!

Given this, there is a sense in which a lot of the character and spirit of this garden falls into place. To judge by an early nineteenth-century painting, there had been a garden here, perhaps for a long time, but the demesne had been let out, and had never seriously attracted the attention of the owners – the Lansdowne family preferring on the whole to live at Bowood, their house in Wiltshire (where, incidentally, Tom Moore, their friend and protégé, had a cottage on the estate).

Neither the character nor the extent of this original garden is clear, though a vast encompassing wood of oaks seems very likely. Then, however, beginning in 1866, and by dint of much earth-moving, tree-clearing and massive planting programmes, the garden we see now was made by the fifth Marquess of Lansdowne. He had served terms as Governor General of Canada and Viceroy of India. This garden was a deliberate – and extraordinarily successful – evocation of a mountainous Himalayan landscape. The mountains needed only a framing of trees and, of course, a comprehensive planting of rhododendrons. That done, you have Derreen, or most of it. There are one or two other subtexts to this grand scheme, though: Australasian planting is an important element; indeed, Derreen is probably best known for its fabulously abundant tree ferns. And there are phormiums everywhere too. From Asia, bamboos. From the Americas there are a good many fine trees, and from Chile, impossible to miss here, redoubts of *Gunnera manicata*, green thugs in green groves.

I tried to estimate the girth of one of these old dicksonias. It must have been about seven feet round. Their soft, rusty, deep-piled trunks, their primitive 'leaves', but most of all their sheer size, make them seem like *ur*-plants, residual survivors from a Jurassic age. Perhaps that is why children (here) like them so much. In our gardens, exposed to lots of light, starved of lots of moisture, they look terribly out of place. But here, where dicksonias are completely naturalised, bathed in eighty inches of rain a year, and shaded everywhere by beetling trees and huge rocks (that even those other thugs, the bamboos, cannot shift), they emphatically belong. So do those rhododendrons. Originally a lot of hybrids were planted, but they grew too vigorously (and flowered too blowsily?). Now they are mostly species, mature or newly planted (the work goes on). Glorious in flower, they have to be seen in spring, but *R. sinogrande* – vast leaves; huge seed pods, like elongated figs – *R. falconeri* – touchable flock-covered under-leaves – *R. barbatum* – peeling, pink/silvery bark – and others of their ilk, are not to be missed at any time of year. At the other end of the scale, the small-leaved rhodos, protected from sika deer, remind you of the unlikely truth that they all belong to the *ericaceae*, the heather family.

Bark is one of the great things here. There's the dusty cinnamon of myrtle, the precise geometry of the vertically striated *Thuja plicata* (one of them here, with branches spiralling downwards – a helter-skelter for squirrels), the great sagging soft-brown limbs of *Cryptomeria japonica* 'Elegans', swagging down like tired flesh on old, old arms. Holly is one of the native colonisers that has to be kept back rigorously here, but the occasional gleam through the trees of its clean, silver bark – a vision for a moment, and then remembered for life, like Yeats' similarly silvery 'mackerel-crowded sea' – approaches the magical.

Sound is another thing: the wind in the treetops miles above your head; the breeze strumming the stems of bamboos, and they returning to the vertical and standing again like great choruses of organ pipes; the lovely hypnotic, melancholy drip of water, ticking as if from an erratic clock, its source invisible but likely to be somewhere in that scarcely credible all-blanketing sprawl of a single plant of *Vitis coignetiae*, embracing but not quite smothering at least five of the neighbouring trees; the fidget of ash keys somewhere; the satisfying crunch of leaf litter underfoot; the soft scratching of stem upon stem from the wild scabious, itself spangling the floor of a glade covered with bird's-foot trefoil; and now the far-off, ghostly barking of Larry (1946–52) and Conny (1989–2003), whose modest graves you'll have passed perhaps without noticing.

Derreen is best for flower in the spring. Seas of bluebells; reefs of buttercups. The sheer volume of blossom on the rhododendrons is simply thrilling, but there are very special individual things too: probably the finest stand of the tender, acid-yellow *R. burmanicum* anywhere; *R. auriculatum* in a remarkable sport probably peculiar to Derreen. High summer is not without its dramas too, however. There is *Embothrium coccineum*, the Chilean firetree; there is *Crinodendron hookerianum*, the lantern tree – difficult plants in mainland Britain, but flourishing easily here. There has been some recent planting of herbaceous things too, especially around the two ponds (tightly and imperviously lined with that blue clay that had to pass for soil elsewhere in the garden … where there was any soil at all, that is, and before soil and humus were arduously barrowed in

all those years ago). So you'll find water lilies, iris, hostas, the royal fern *Osmunda regalis*, lysichiton, crinums, as well as, of course, gunnera. Down there is a fairly new swamp cypress. In due course, it will take its place as one of the noble protagonists of this garden – which, given the majesty of so many of the older trees, is to expect much, but I'm confident that it will oblige. Hydrangeas are going to thrive too – deer permitting. Elsewhere there are new plantings of more trees and shrubs – particularly of mountain ash, maple and bottlebrushes – some of which, in this benign climate, may well become considerable trees.

The house at Derreen discreetly oversees the garden as far as a very far-flung lawn allows and before the trees begin. That's impressive too: the way the prose of grass gives way to the big poetry of trees, water, mountains. On this lawn, however, is a very large, low-domed rock, the almost-buried cranium of some huge, mythological creature, it could be. Or, for the time being, and ideally placed to be so, the first of the castles any child would leap to defend.

It is hard to go back into the mind of a child and start to understand what it is that makes them make friends so readily with Derreen. They would perhaps label the place and their games in it simply with the exclamation 'Magic!' and not bother about the ontological complications that word imposes upon us adults. As adults, we might wander the same paths and wonder at the magnificence of it all. We might register, perhaps, a pattern of exposed finger-like roots climbing down a rockface and remember – possibly even with a bit of a frisson – the spooky magical world of the Arthur Rackham illustrations in the books of our own childhood. We might see a single spot of red on the woodland floor and stop, in alarm as much as in curiosity – arrested by an epiphany of blood – but it turns out to be the single berry of an old, etiolated mountain ash, its stem silvery in the gloom. Or we might reflect upon the time-schemes invisibly embedded in a place like Derreen – these trees here long before, and going on long after, us – and learn again those lessons in being merely visitors, not only to this garden but also to the world at large: something invisible to the conscious minds of children, but intuited unconsciously perhaps for all that, and one of those profound reasons why gardens matter. Whether or not children do apprehend something of what adults construe of a place like Derreen, I don't know – certainly not the botany, that's for sure. But I'm fairly certain that Derreen, by a mysterious process of inversion, recovers just a little of the child in us adults, projecting – for all the difficulties of both words – just a little bit of magic, and just a bit of the wisdom that provokes a sigh of comprehending satisfaction: 'Ah, yes.'

When you leave, you must follow a different road out. Once more there are great trees on either side of you, and once again you get an impression of the sheer scale of the place. You come out on to the road through the village of Lauragh. Turn right and you'll begin a circuit of the Beara Peninsula. After five miles or so of fairly low-lying road, the scenery becomes steeper and wilder, the views over the sea tremendous. If you have time (or, better still, make the time available) take the turning offered to Dursey Island. It will be another five miles or so, but it is probably worth it just for the views (and there's a remote, lovely beach at Garnish) and then, eventually, the sight of the island itself. It will raise the temperature of your imagination: what would it be like to live on an island? Who lives on this one? Why? What does the balance sheet look like: you lose ready access to shops and to someone competent to mend the washing-machine, but you gain …?

People – a few – do live on Dursey. You could cross over yourself for a few hours (if the cable car were working, which it almost certainly won't be). You can transport yourself imaginatively there anyway. The name Dursey might come from the Old Norse *Thjorsey*, which might be a version of the Irish *Tarbhna*, but the Norse is cognate with *Thor*, the god, while the Irish means 'bull'. Some scholars think it comes from the Irish *dóirse*, meaning 'gate' – so the island marks the gate into the sound. Nobody knows for certain. On a good day you'll see whales and dolphins; if not, there is the herd of little islands – Bull, Calf, Cow Island – which lie out there in the ocean as if it were a field, and Dursey were its hub.

The Children of Lir came home to Ireland after their nine hundred years of exile (the tale is one of the canonic *Three Sorrows of Storytelling*), and their landfall was nearby. You can visit the Graves of the Children of Lir up a windswept lane just outside the village of Allihies. It – or the wind – will bring tears to your eyes. Arnold Bax wrote his gorgeous tone poem *The Garden of Fand* inspired by the sea beneath Mount Brandon on the Dingle Peninsula a few miles north, but it might have been here – a magic zone of enchantment where sea and land, mortals and gods, meet, connect. The union of Cuchulainn, the mythic, battle-frenzied but human warrior, and Fand, consort of the god of the sea, lasted as long as it took Mananann, the Sea God, to lose his patience, which is to say, centuries at least. But in the end, he shook his cloak between them and separated them forever, while conferring upon the mortal the saving grace of forgetfulness: he would never remember what it was that he had lost.

Dursey – because it is an island – is actually a pattern of garden-ness, of what gardens are and what they mean: somewhere connected but separate, somewhere that keeps out the wilderness and keeps in the secret, an oasis of calm, a recovery of Eden, a (gratuitous) act of grace but a compelling necessity too. There is, in fact, a tiny beautiful sheltered garden belonging to one of the cottages on Dursey, but the island as a whole is rough fields, low walls, tracks for droving. If you cannot get across, don't hanker too much: the mind has already made both the journey and the connection anyway ... and gardens are sometimes as much places in the mind as they are places on the ground – the best ones, anyway.

Go back along the lane. You are now travelling eastwards. You can turn left and go back directly to Lauragh (and thence to Kenmare, Killarney, etc.), or turn right and complete the Ring of Beara. Tennyson, Trollope, Thackeray, Virginia Woolf, the composer A.J. Moeran – they've all been here and had their minds stained by the experience. But there remains one more experience which they cannot have had, and which you must, if you can. When you left Derreen you could have turned left and taken the road directly to Kenmare. The mountain scenery is terrific, and it is a simple thing to see quickly how suggestively Himalayan it is and how this journey alone predicates the garden itself. But if you leave Derreen, then turn left (as if going to Kenmare), and then take the road signposted on your right to the Healy Pass, you will learn at first hand exactly what Edmund Burke was getting at when he identified awe and terror as elements of the sublime. The pass climbs one thousand feet over the Caha Mountains. It's stupendous (but it was only finished in 1931, which is why those earlier visitors would not have known it … though it *was* open when Woolf visited Glengarriff in 1934. There was an oversight in her itinerary or perhaps she suffered from vertigo and was warned off.) If, however, you did complete (anticlockwise) the Ring of Beara, you could still take the pass ten miles or so before you get back to Glengarriff. It is signposted at Adrigole. In any case, whatever your route, it is a wonderful journey … and not by any means unrelated to the experience of Derreen.

Mount Congreve

COUNTY WATERFORD

The Suir is arguably the loveliest river in a country oozing with lovely rivers. It hasn't got the epic east–west sweep of the Shannon. It hasn't got a bard of its own like all those other Irish streams celebrated in Book IV of Spenser's *The Faerie Queene*. There it is merely: 'the gentle Shure that, making way / By sweet Clonmell, adornes rich Waterford'.

It has not achieved the immortality conferred upon the Avoca by Tom Moore's *Melodies*, and it hasn't got the clout, the craic and the gravity of the Liffey, or the fabled loveliness of the lasses of the Lagan, or the piscatorial cachet of the Lee. But its admirers reckon it makes the loveliest journey of them all … and Spenser, who champions always his own Awbeg or the Aherlow River that comes down from the nearby Galtee Mountains, admits at least that 'the faire Shure' is where are bred a 'thousand Salmons'… so the fishing is good even if the goddesses and water sprites he awards to his favourites largely overlook it.

The Suir rises in the heart of Ireland in County Tipperary, dawdles through the Golden Vale, resists the temptation to flow south, and instead slips eastwards, through County Kilkenny, and into County Waterford. In spate it races, smothers and scours, but as a rule it

just bowls along, chattering when it's shallow, and muttering a bit when it's deep, occasionally raked by a weir, often delayed by a lazy bend. It flows quite unselfconsciously through classic, sometimes famous, Irish landscapes, or else quietly and self-effacingly through ordinary, simple Irish scenes. There's the Rock of Cashel – Cashel of the Kings – and the river snuggles into the meadow below, almost out of sight of this tremendous place. There's the lovely old bridge and timeless pastures, and then the church itself, at Holy Cross Abbey with its aisle not level at all but steep and you have almost to climb back to your seat. There's Grubb's Grave at Clogheen: it glowers out over the river from its bare hillside. It's a sort of *clochan* – one of those beehive-shaped buildings the sixth-century monks on Skellig Michael made, but inside this one – solidly built into the stone – is the body of the said Samuel Grubb of Castle Grace, thus interred, at his own wish, and upright (like Ben Jonson in Westminster Abbey, but that was because they were running out of floor space) in 1891. It's a very late date for what is really yet another Irish folly. There's Cahir, a turreted, barbicanned, crenellated castle such as boys can only dream of. There's Clonmel – Spenser's 'sweet Clonmell' – where *Tristram Shandy* and the world turned inside-out were first imagined. And then there's Carrick-on-Suir, a characterful small town of small shops and (these days) small purses – and probably not much the worse for it. Mind you, there are seven shoe shops, and there's Phelan the Victualler (in Ireland that means the butcher's, and Phelan's is 'Grade A guaranteed'). There's a Bombay takeaway (Mumbai has yet to reach Carrick), the Emperor's takeaway (Chinese), and Taaffe & Co (rare name, but Irish for all that – and it's the florist's). Only three streets to speak of. One of them gradually peters out past once handsome, now slightly decaying, Georgian front doors – but still with highly polished brass plates – until it brings you to Ormonde Castle, less a fortified building than an Elizabethan country house ('If locked, knock on the left-hand door of the entrance passage for caretaker, who has the key' – Harbison: *Guide to the National Monuments of Ireland*, the indispensable vade mecum for travellers.) Below, the Suir will be quietly slipping past; cacophonous, immemorial rooks will be taking

advantage of this unfrequented street's resonance to cough and quar-
rel and make a fine noise. Or, if there has been a bit of rain, rooks too
busy to throw their voices will be hammering the turf of the meadow in
front of the castle, and behind it the river will be harder put to maintain its characteristic insouciant slouch. There'll be flurries of foam
here and there, like the stuffing coming out of a pensionable sofa.

The Suir – pronounce it 'Sure' with the ghost of a second syllable on
the end – is conventionally said to mean 'sister' (which it does if you
spell it *siúr*, but you don't), and that makes sense – good geographical
if not lexicographical sense – with the way that it has two brothers (or
sisters, is it? Are rivers always female? Ol' Man River? Confusing!)
in the form of the rivers Nore and Barrow. Independently, these three
rivers drain a great deal of south-eastern Ireland; blended together in
their last moments, they form Waterford Harbour. Waterford – a rather
unlovely town, really – is on the Suir just before it meets its brethren.
Thus the riverine geography, but Suir (spelt just like that, as indeed
it is on the maps, the signs, the place names) doesn't mean 'sister',
but 'wooing' … which returns us to the proposition that it's one of the
loveliest rivers in a country already oozing with lovely rivers: the Suir
woos, it makes a pitch for your affections.

> How sweet 'tis to roam by the sunny Suir stream
> And hear the doves coo neath the morning's sunbeam,
> Where the thrush and the robin their sweet notes combine
> On the banks of the Suir that flows down by Mooncoin.
>
> Flow on, lovely river, flow gently along,
> By your waters so sweet sounds the lark's merry song.
> On your green banks I'll wander where first I did join
> With you, lovely Molly, the Rose of Mooncoin …

Not great poetry to be sure, but good enough to express the loyalty of
supporters for the often-victorious Kilkenny Cats, who are frequently
the winners of the All-Ireland Hurling Championships. Matches generally provoke the crowd to sing this song, penned originally by one

Watt Murphy in 1826, who was disappointed in his love for the Molly of the song when her father, the rector, disapproved and sent her away to England and safety. One way or another, you see, this river woos.

By the time it reaches Waterford and almost the sea, the river is tidal, muddy, a bit smelly in a salty, weedy way, and sad because whereas once there was a busy-ness about it, now there is not. Once upon a time, seagoing ships used to dock in Waterford, but now it's not deep enough for the newer, larger ships. And it's not posh enough for expensive yachts. In that respect, it's a lost cause, but there is still something to celebrate about this lowest reach of the river because four miles up from the city, where it's still tidal but less oozy, it rubs the banks of one of the great gardens of the twentieth century: Mount Congreve, a house, a garden, and an almost legendary proprietor, Ambrose Congreve, who died in 2011 at the age of one hundred and four. Give or take a year or two, the garden we see now is the work of fifty years, half a lifetime, and vast expenditures of cash and vision, vision and doggedness, doggedness fine-tuned to patience, the kind of patience that can plant and then wait for twenty, thirty years; the kind of patience that seeks out and prefers a garden which eschews for the most part the merely rowdily colourful, but doesn't court only the quietly contemplative either. It occupies instead a carefully edited middle ground.

The Congreves have been at this site since 1725. It is possible therefore – just possible – that the most famous Congreve of them all, William, the Restoration playwright, who was born in 1670 and died in 1729, could have visited. Certainly he grew up in nearby Youghal and went to school in Kilkenny. Certainly he studied at Trinity in Dublin. But whether he was ever here at Mount Congreve is not known. Nevertheless, associating him with this house is – at least in spirit – a viable proposition: the house is as elegant, as patrician, as mannered as can be, a piece of fine, understated Palladianism with a beautiful Irish inflection in the form of the tall, very wide but very shallow bow window, which leans out from the front like an intelligent bump on a bookish forehead. Congreve's work is like that: urbane, witty, worldly, polished and knowing. But his definitive location in a garden is not here. It is not even in Ireland. It is at Stowe in Buckinghamshire.

Stowe's political agenda is never out of sight, even to the most innocent visitor, but for most of us it is largely out of mind. Unless we are pretty fluent in Whiggery, in the ameliorist agenda of British eighteenth-century Enlightenment thinkers, and in the skills of bouncing the nuances of contemporary (that is to say, Georgian) political infighting off Roman and Saxon originals, we are left in the dark ... or actually in the simpler, clearer light of much bigger, timelessly archetypal ideas unedited by the local particularities of time and place. Put simply, this garden at Stowe is a pattern of Elysium, of arcadian bliss, of an ideal world. We can see and feel the literalness of the beauty of Stowe's Elysian Fields without necessarily grasping the metaphor, and that is one measure of the garden's achievement. Whether or not we understand, or are even aware of these precedents and principles, the place – its intimations of Elysium, of Paradise – works, at least on some level, even when you are blind to its original agenda and narratives. But even the most innocent visitor is likely to want to know who is who in the Temple of British Worthies, who is on top of the Grenville Column, and, in the end, what sort of people they were – these Lords Cobham of Stowe – who could so blithely sprinkle their territory so immodestly frequently with their own family name, Temple. There are, after all, distributed throughout the garden, thirteen fanes – indeed, temples – albeit that they are ostensibly dedicated variously to Virtue, Janus, Liberty, etc., and not to the Cobham dynasty at all.

Several of these temples contain portrait sculptures – most notably that Temple of British Worthies, the Temple of Ancient Worthies (Homer, Socrates, Epaminondas and Lycurgus) and most wittily the Temple of Modern Virtue ... which is a ruin, and the sculpted figure has no head, no features, no credibility (Robert Walpole, decoded for our times!). But it has to be said that, as sculpture, as works of art, none is all that distinguished even though they were reckoned top-of-the-range in their day. Scheemakers's *King Alfred* is at best an essay in generic kingship, but has no real character; Rysbrack's *William III* looks like a parody of a noble Roman trying not to notice that someone has broken wind.

There is, however, at least one piece of reasonably good sculpture at Stowe: the monument to William Congreve. Not so much monument as affectionate remembrance, it is a cryptic, witty, quite modest pyramid upon the top of which perches a monkey. Like Congreve in his plays, this monkey holds up a mirror to the world (though, being made of stone rather than glass, this mirror looks more like a medallion; and it doesn't make sense if you haven't grasped that a mirror is intended, so an explanation is indispensable). The diminutive pyramid is of undressed stone and the monkey himself is quite gruff and ready, as indeed befits a buffoon who is nonetheless licensed to act as critic of the follies of the world in which he dwells. In very high relief on one of the four faces of the pyramid is an urn: Congreve is dead. But his spirit lives on in each of the three grinning, frowning masks and their accompanying emblems on the other three faces: Eros' arrows, Mars' sword, and Pan's panic-inducing or soul-soothing pipes.

It's a charming, capricious piece of work (William Kent, probably), a bit of frozen miniature theatre in a place of otherwise big stone

events, all with designs upon your mind. In the context of all of Stowe's high-mindedness, it is refreshing to encounter the shade of a cheeky, wise, puncturing poet. In one of his very last poems – 'Of Improving the Present Time' (1728) – Congreve picks up on the great theme of Lord Cobham, Stowe's creator – the moral and political improvement of the age – and gently mocks it. Cobham and Congreve were friends; the grandee would have taken it in good part. Congreve imagines his patron exhausted and finally frustrated in his life's work to whiggify the world (and keep his own preferred place-men in all the seats of power too, of course). He retires from the world, disappointed, to take up garden-making at Stowe. The tone and sentiments of the verse are suitably august and elevating until you begin to notice the less-than-dignified mixture of perfect and (deliberately) imperfect rhymes, whereupon it becomes deliciously mischievous and charming:

> ... dost thou give the winds afar to blow
> Each vexing thought, and heart-devouring woe,
> And fix thy mind alone on rural scenes,
> To turn the level'd lawns to liquid plains;
> To raise the creeping rill from humble beds,
> And force the latent springs to lift their heads;
> On wat'ry columns, capitols to rear,
> That mix their flowing curls with upper air?

Stowe in England and Mount Congreve in Ireland share a certain grandeur in their respective houses, a certain patrician effortlessness in their sheer scales, and also the spirit, at least, of an ancestor in the poet and dramatist William Congreve. Beyond that, they could hardly be more different. There are probably more stone flowers than real ones at Stowe. Even the daisies in the grass – those 'level'd lawns' – must dive for cover should a gardener approach. Mount Congreve's colours, on the other hand, are probably visible by satellite, even in winter. The water at Stowe, the lake – Congreve's 'liquid plains' – is an instrument of geometry, its flatness and reflective surface not just scenery, but stage scenery. It is there to point up – indeed, to elevate

– by contrast with its horizontality, the aspiring verticality of trees, columns, temples and, of course, noble thoughts. It's there to give occasion to the fiction of needing a bridge – a Palladian bridge, and very beautiful too – but really only another bit of theatre. It's there to say something about man's (rightful, as they saw it) mastery over nature, man's prerogative to shape and reshape the natural world, be it water, earth or woodland.

Bridgeman built the ground-breaking ha-ha at Stowe, Gibbs did the Palladian bridge. Vanbrugh made the rotunda and some of the temples, Kent was responsible for other bridges, temples and the Elysian Fields – and, indeed, for that monument to Congreve – but Capability Brown did the Grecian Valley. It is, of course, at least partly man-made, man-excavated, though there was a bit of a valley there already. Nevertheless, it is Brown's cunning plantings that make it seem both steeper and longer than it really is. The estate accounts record sums paid for 'earth-moving'. Exactly how many thousands of tons of earth were, indeed, moved, dug, barrowed and relocated – dragged by men, dragged by horses – we can only begin to guess. Likewise the sum of the labour and the volume of the spoil from the Eleven Acre Lake. Of course, Brown himself didn't literally do any of it. It was Irish labourers – *navvies*, men otherwise employed digging Britain's canals, the *navigations*, the arteries of Britain's Industrial Revolution – who did that. It was Irish labourers who made the great English landscape gardens: another link between these two Congrevian spaces.

But the Waterford garden of Ambrose Congreve – the parts where earth was moved – are not Augustan but relatively recent, and whatever earth-moving there was (done by machine?), it was modest compared with Stowe. Moreover, Stowe is conceived as part of the countryside around it – that countryside epitomised and clarified, the distilled epicentre of an ideal world, an England perfected: context is built into concept and both are meant to be very visible. That is why Bridgeman's ha-ha was so important and so enabling. Mount Congreve is conceived not as a part of a larger world but as something apart *from* it. For all that there are occasional glimpses of that River Suir, it is largely inward-looking, it is walled away, hidden, reclusive. The walled garden alone covers about four acres. The woodland garden entire is more like seventy. To walk its paths – all of them – would take all of a long summer's day. Even a simple circuit is a matter of two miles at least.

Originally modelled on Exbury, Mount Congreve shares a similar wooded, riverbank site, and both places are rightly famous for their rhododendrons, magnolias and camellias. Though at first (in 1955 or so, when garden-making began in earnest) Mount Congreve was a rather gawky upstart, the two gardens must be rated equals now, fifty years on: their respective national and international reputations are similar, the imprimatur of their names on important plants bred in each place is similarly respected and bankable.

Ambrose Congreve has gone down already as one of the twentieth century's great garden-makers but, in some respects, he was quite a forbidding man. He was dogmatic about some things, opinionated about others. The establishment was considerable – a staff of thirty-five in the garden in the 1980s – and head gardeners enjoyed his respect, but those lower down might not have loved him much. On one occasion there was, indeed, a strike of under-gardeners over what was reckoned to have been a particularly high-handed fiat of Congreve's. The garden was only ever open once a week, and that conferred a sense of occasion and privilege upon visitors, but also carried a faint undertone of admittance on sufferance. Dogs were never allowed. Children were forbidden. And he didn't mince his words: visitors were required to respect the integrity of the place, and pilfering of cuttings, seeds and seedlings would trigger criminal proceedings as a matter of course.

Other things were excoriated too. Eucalyptus, for example. They were under ban. But it never seemed a forbidding place. On the contrary, the welcome by one of the garden staff was invariably individual, warm and beautifully modulated somewhere between the formal and the unbuttoned – an epitomously Irish etiquette, as it happens. And anyway, how much more grown-up it seemed bluntly to forbid something than blushingly to dub it 'inappropriate' or some comparable drivel peddled on a course run somewhere by the Human

Resources industry, probably. Moreover, the brief but firm list of things anathematised seemed to encompass – unspoken but essentially undisguised – all those other pestilences of our times: mobile phone use, the fumes of burgers and barbecues, the horrors of the latest must-have celebrity plant – that sort of thing.

After the sheer scale of the garden itself has been grasped, probably the next of its bold elements to impress itself on your consciousness will be the sheer scale of the planting, and this remains true though Ambrose Congreve himself is no more. If you or I can afford it (both the cash and the space) we want to plant in groups of three or perhaps five. Not so at Mount Congreve. Fifty is the general rule – not just of lily bulbs, or astilbes in a bog, or echinaceas in the walled garden, but fifty of any one tree, any magnolia, any rhododendron.

In flower, the effect is colossal. It is impressive both as a plausibly *natural* visual experience (because huge drifts of any one plant which has naturally colonised a hillside, in the Himalayas, in the China of Augustine Henry one hundred years ago, are indeed a natural phenomenon), and as exotic – regal, plutocratic, Vanderbiltean – because only the enormously wealthy could indulge their gardens with either that level of expense or that single-mindedness. In flower, the effect is tremendous … as of a long, long gallery of successively vast canvases. But rhododendrons and azaleas, magnolias and camellias, *out* of season, what happens then? In a sense, that's where the very best of the *genius loci* at Mount Congreve lies. It is when someone has spotted, and then exploited, talents for association latent within discrete plants, when someone has seen that to associate this plant with that one – however superficially unalike – will work because they are, as it were, visual anagrams of each other (indeed like the words *latent* and *talent*): *Sorbus aria lutescens*, for example, with *Magnolia grandifolia* (the leaves and their spatulate shape, their ribbing, the openness of both trees, their poise). Or placing a stewartia next to a *Magnolia wilsonii* where the respective flowers are very similar indeed but the magnolia faces downwards and the stewartia upwards, and they don't flower at the same time. Contrary to what you might expect – the enormous risk run of tedious vistas of never-ending foliage once the star plants have finished flowering – it works. Without ever compromising the essence of the place as a woodland garden, there is just enough variety of form, of tilt and pitch of paths and slant of borders, of the occasional anarchy of some unruly climber, of rhododendrons giving place for a while to groves of pittosporums, or of mahonias, or of pieris, and then – sometimes writ large, sometimes small – the gradual unravelling of the ever-changing middle-distance view – tall trees, thin tall trees, big-leaved tall trees, those glimpses every now and then of the Suir, and then the surprise of just one stand of late-flowering magnolias – to keep the visitor engaged. It is very artfully done, and it works.

Analogies? Certainly with landscape painting. After all, the people who conceived of places such as Stourhead, or Rousham or Stowe did so through their experience of looking at a Poussin or a Salvator Rosa. They wanted the pictures on their walls to be duplicated by what you saw when you looked out of the window. But analogues with music are sometimes revealing too. Christopher Lloyd – he of *The Well-Tempered Garden* (and thus of its Bachian title) – knew a thing or two in this respect. Everyone talks and writes now of colour *harmonies*, of seasonal *crescendi* in their long borders, or of *choruses* of pelargoniums (or whatever) – clichés all of them by now – but there is life still in the fundamental impulse to draw an analogy here, a comparison there. The impression you absorb of Mount Congreve is not, as it were, like listening to – let's say – Bach. There is no layered texturing of colours and forms and narratives, no polyphony, no maths infinitely humanised. It is simpler, bolder: slabs of colour like the lumps of sound in a Bruckner symphony lumpishly conducted as they so often are. Or in painterly, landscape terms it is not (say) John Nash – apparently simple but still somehow mysterious, mostly because there is never a figure in evidence. Even so, a Nash landscape is never forbidding, but always subtly domesticated. Mount Congreve is not quite like that – domesticated it isn't. No, it is Ivon Hitchens – big-brushed, bold and very strong, but not necessarily comfortable because the invariable absence of human beings in *his* pictures amounts to a prohibition on us, an eviction. Not necessarily any the worse for it either: the grandeur and gravity of simplicity – whether we're talking about gardens or music or paintings – can be a very impressive thing indeed. At Mount Congreve it is essentially the single-mindedness of the woodland spirit and perhaps (as with a Hitchens) even of that sense of being here conditionally which defines the place and its strong, bold character, but it is further underwritten by the all-pervading naturalism – a lack of (visible) artifice – and that, of course, has a particularly Irish dimension through the example of that same natural style's originator, William Robinson, the most influential and international of all Irish garden-makers and garden-thinkers.

The garden – the woodland garden – is much longer than it is wide. The paths along its length run roughly parallel with the estuarial Suir, but at two levels, one virtually along the shore and thronged with hydrangeas loving the damp, and the other higher and with longer views. Without realising it (probably), the visitor will be making a circular journey, first outwards, down through dells and up slopes, only occasionally being able to see very far ahead or far behind because the path twists so, but sometimes with lateral views, views across garden, valley and river. You can digress – indeed, you should – but probably not visiting all the paths on any one day. After all, if all the paths were unravelled and their collective lengths totalled, their sum would be sixteen miles. There are signs to guide you, and one at least – 'Quo vadis'… where on earth am I going? – to amuse. There are framed garden occasions, the Rose Lawn, the Beech Lawn, Monty's Lawn, the Bell Gate Lawn, each very different in character and very aptly identified by their names. Each comes up with a different answer to the question of what is the ideal ratio of grass to planted areas. The differences depend upon how an area is lit, how it is planted and how various leaf textures and tree profiles act up to the flatness of a lawn.

From time to time you get a larger view out over the valley of the river, and sometimes there is a little train that chuffs along the river's bank and makes a noise like a comfortable knitting machine with a cog loose somewhere. There are set pieces of dazzling horticulture: ranks of wisteria grown, trained and woven in as columns; a grove of mature tulip trees, their laterals pruned so that they too are almost columnar; old clematis whose stems – liana-like – are so stout you won't get your hand around them; a group of young magnolias pollarded (and you wonder what will be the result when they are mature and flowering: a great table-high plaza of them?). There is a copse of red maples blended with cut-leaf elders, a cunning and curious mix, like a tweed with subtle and random variations of colour density and thickness of thread.

All the time there is the sound of birds, near or farther off if you find yourself in one of the intense, gothic-gloomy spaces, like a medieval church, created where lower branches have been cleared but the leaf canopy above kept dense. Woodland birds and estuary birds. Occasionally there's the sound of water because you must pass a pretty spectacular one-hundred-foot waterfall, or because your feet are squelching in a boggy patch of path. There are scents too, of course, heady and fascinating like a woman back from Paris in the hedonistic sixties, and all the more fascinating because often you cannot at first identify the source of the wicked seduction. But then, if you are in the garden on hedge-clipping days, you get the smell of cut box near the house – acrid and vast like the stink of old armpits from the rugby club changing rooms.

You are passing by several thousands of distinct and very fine plants (three thousand, five hundred rhododendron species and hybrids alone – the largest collection in Europe) but even so some rise above the others. There is *Rhododendron* 'Lady Alice Fitzwilliam', for example, possibly the most scented of all its kind. The trusses are large and bold but because the individual flowers are quite tightly funnelled it has a grace and poise about it despite the promiscuous volume of blooms. It is white, pink-flushed. It was the outright favourite of Murdo MacKenzie, a man not easily pleased. Head gardener at Ilnacullin for more than forty years, and a humble man, he is nevertheless one of the great figures of Irish gardening. 'Lady Alice' is a fabulous rhododendron in both senses of the word: wonderful to behold and smell (though famously difficult to place so that it will thrive), and indeed in the sense that it has become legendary.

Towards the end of March and two or three weeks into April, there is a meadow framed by thousands upon thousands of snakehead fritillaries. They dance and chime in the wind; on a still day, they stand – and so may you, awestruck. Then there's that cascade – one hundred feet down the perpendicular sides of an old quarry – and that's quite stunning too. Primrose, skunk cabbages and royal ferns enjoy the edges of the pools at the bottom. It's all man-made, but you'd never know it. On the other hand – and very self-consciously artificial too – is the tall narrow Chinese pagoda that you come upon in due course. You have to look down on it from above. The colour is so artificially red it is shocking. So, perhaps, is the theatricality and exoticism, but some people love it. The two chestnuts which preside over the Rose Lawn must be the most noble, most effectively placed trees you could hope to see anywhere west of the Theatre Lawn at Hidcote. The image is so powerful mostly because it is so simple, but how much sophistication does it take to achieve that level of simplicity, one wonders?

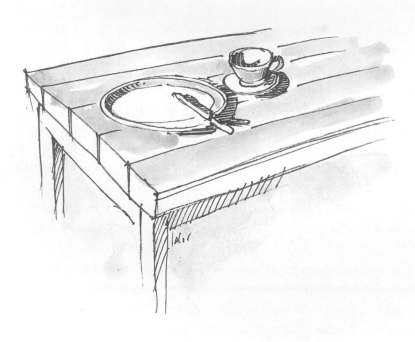

And then there are the walled gardens. Or discrete areas within the fine old walls, walls that you can only occasionally see, so densely clothed are they in climbers – honeysuckles, wisteria, passion flowers, clematis, star jasmine, climbing hydrangea … and then the rarer things, astonishing in the apparent effortlessness of their voluminous growth: *Lapageria rosea, Mutisia ilicifolia, Pileostegia viburnoides* (not a particularly difficult plant but unaccountably rare, and so good!).

The first of these walled enclosures grows vegetables and fruit, and does so in an industrious, no-nonsense way which – it must be said – is not necessarily what you came to see, but the long, straight path through all this region of brassica and onion is. You are flanked on both sides by battalions of three infinitely repeated plants: nepeta in front, herbaceous pæonies in the middle ranks and, behind them, delphiniums, all of them framed by enormous swags of climbing roses right along the back. Simple, bold and very strong in its effect but not ostentatious or boastful (and there is mare's tail in profusion, a *felix culpa* if ever there were one! A collective noun for this sin in a context like this? A *heresy* of mare's tail, I think).

Through another gate and a great sloping lawn spreads out on either side. Once again, abundantly clothed walls surround you but there are deep borders too and, facing you, a grand old eighteenth-century glasshouse. Inside, in masses of fine clay pots, are lilies, streptocarpus, pelargoniums, gerberas, orchids, everything that would have seasonally graced a great house years ago (and now corporations and government departments pay millions to Dutch contractors to deliver and then to take away, as the very same plants come in and go out of season). Something about the diminutive size of the panes of this great glasshouse, and something about the predominance of horizontal, rather than vertical glazing bars, is serendipitously evocative of the De la Warr pavilion at Bexhill … that and its whiteness, of course. Outside and all around the very large, long lawn are those deep borders. The planting is lavish – every sort of copper-bottomed herbaceous plant (and not a few blended shrubs too, sometimes rare but always beautiful: *Crinodendron patagua*, *Correa lawrenceana*, *Hydrangea sargentiana*), arranged according to season, then colour, then habit and foliage, and then stature – you see them first as massed washes of colour, but the closer you get, of course, the more they become individuals: words, sentences, then paragraphs of plants. Successively each has its climactic days (or weeks), only to give way to the next plant which will complement it or contrast with it. Collectively the effect is stunning, magisterial, most uncommonly beautiful: that classic, consummative skill of Western gardening, and probably the most demanding too, the herbaceous border ... but the bounty of it here! And brought to such a peak of textbook horticultural perfection.

There are individual episodes within this vast chapter of the garden – too many to enumerate comprehensively, but let there be recorded just a few of them to serve as examples. There is a venerable *Ginkgo biloba*. The tree, when it grows true to type, is quite tall and eventually tapering, but this one is crumpled and dome-shaped, and very characterful indeed. Beneath it is a circus of cobbles and then, around the trunk itself, there are bluebells, both white and blue. The cobbles must be hellish to weed and to keep clear of falling leaves, but the job is nevertheless accomplished somehow. Once again, success draws largely upon simplicity, but here the effect is not so much magisterially simple as simply charming.

Mount Congreve has been the source of some very fine new plants, such as *Magnolia multipetal*, an important new tree spotted in the garden by Peter Smithers in the eighties. As time goes by, and as they mature and begin to flower, it is a safe bet that further new magnolias will occur (though let us hope they are graced with better names than 'multipetal', for goodness' sake!). A race of fine pieris was bred here: 'Mount Congreve Scarlet', 'Carmine', 'Coral' and 'Mahogany'. There is *Rhododendron mucronatum* 'Marjorie Congreve', and there is a characterful watsonia (*W*. 'Mount Congreve'), the colour of weathered Tudor brick. All these are plants that revel in the Irish climate but can be difficult to place elsewhere. And nowhere is this more true than in the case of what is possibly the most attractive of all the plants originating here, *Pseudowintera colorata* 'Marjorie Congreve'. The foliage begins a lovely shrimp pink and dusty green. Later there is a glow in it of old gold. It sounds implausibly exotic, even vulgar, but in truth it is a really beautiful thing – not gaudy at all but quite shy. It is a very covetable plant, but susceptible to even a rumour of frost or wind or drought.

The nursery at Mount Congreve propagates not only its own named plants but a great many others besides. It is a major source – sometimes the only source – of many distinguished species and varieties, supplying an international market.

Ambrose Congreve set his sights upon a kind of immortality. Now, after his death, his chattels have been auctioned off in London – the vintage cars, the rare books, the furniture, etc. – but years ago he willed his garden, the place which bears his name, to the state to hold in perpetuity after his death. It would join a small band of other gardens held by the state: Glasnevin, the National Botanical Garden in Dublin, and its country cousin Kilmaccuragh down in County Wicklow, Altamont in County Carlow, and then Ilnacullin, the fabled island garden in Bantry Bay. Most recently, Annes Grove has joined the list. Currently, all of these are starved of cash to a degree only just short of the liquidation and meltdown suffered by the Irish economy at large.

Mount Congreve is a world-class garden. There is no question about it. And, of its kind, it is unequalled in Ireland. It has become a dependable cynosure within gardening circles, a magnet of the better kind of tourism offered to visitors. It has set and sustained benchmark standards for tidiness, husbandry and velvet-fisted control. Admired, respected, more and more emulated, even revered; it is all of these, but ... does it provoke affection, is it a place you feel protective towards? Photographers love it, but do gardeners? For an Irish garden, it is a latecomer. On the ground it is very well established indeed. You might think it were an old garden. But it isn't. And though it appeared in George and Bowe's *The Gardens of Ireland* published in 1986 – the earliest of the current generation of serious surveys – it is not there in Connolly and Dillon's *In an Irish Garden* published in the same year. And it is absent from both Whaley's *The Gardens of Ireland* (1990) and Olda Fitzgerald's *Irish Gardens* (1999), the standard books on the subject for years and years, and doesn't really reappear until Georgina Campbell's *Guide* of 2006 and now Shirley Lanigan's *The 100 Best Gardens in Ireland* of 2011, in both of which it is – rightly – very highly rated, even though both books tend anyway towards breathlessness and impossible photographs. Jimi Blake reckons Mount Congreve is now the pre-eminent woodland garden of Europe, which doesn't settle the matter definitively, of course, but it does make you think.

If Mount Congreve (so far) does not exactly prompt affection, does that really matter? Probably it ought not to, but in practice it probably does, it probably will. Negotiations ground on between the trustees and Dúchas – the Office of Public Works. No doubt, both parties' minds were particularly exercised by costs. It began to look as if the nursery were being wound up, but it had been through the nursery that the garden paid for itself (if it ever did so at all), so what was the rationale there? There is the house and an estate, but could they be made to support the garden? Did the garden have to be that big, that labour-intensive? At what point would 'commercial viability' effectively destroy the place anyway? And so on, and so on.

The Irish state hasn't got either a large remit or a large budget ... for mortgage relief in cases of negative equity, for completing half-built capital building projects – roads, schools, hospitals – for combating the *Chalara fraxinea* fungus identified in its ash trees a few months ago ... so it certainly hasn't got a popular mandate to take on any more posh demesnes. And yet there's a far-sighted sense in which Ireland – the Emerald Isle indeed – is moving gradually towards a perception of itself, at least in part, as the world's garden (and larder too, perhaps), if only because – if you turn a blind eye to the periodical blots on the landscape such as unregulated out-of-town development (every town, everywhere, it's almost all uniformly awful), such as hideous new identikit housing estates, such as monstrous ranch-style bungalows slapped on to beautiful open hillsides – the country, so much of it, still looks *so* good. In which case, in the medium and long terms, and with the looming likelihood that Ireland's most successful, post-tiger, money-earner is going to be, once again, tourism – to have missed the chance of a place such as Mount Congreve would have been a grievous mistake. Nevertheless, in the short term, where was the money to come from?

But eventually an agreement *was* reached, a settlement both financial and conscientious. The garden is now safely in the hands of the state.

Gardens often do not survive their makers. Their ephemerality, like the constantly changing characters of their plants, like the sum of their visual impression, is actually – somewhere deep, deep down – part of their meaning. But perhaps in the case of Mount Congreve it was right that an exception should have been made and the ephemeral allowed to last after all.

Perhaps it is fitting too that a small gesture of continuity between past and future, between the Congreves at Stowe three hundred years ago and the Congreves at Waterford yesterday, should have been put into place. There is now, here too, a temple: six graceful ionic columns supporting a light copper dome, and from it a lovely sylvan, riverine prospect ... 'In memory of the late Mr and Mrs Ambrose Congreve'. Cousin indeed of Vanbrugh's rotunda at Stowe.

Altamont

COUNTY CARLOW

It is one thing to give your name to a plant – thus *Forsythia* (Wm. Forsyth, superintendent of the Royal Gardens at Kensington in the late eighteenth century and then author and purveyor of a famously quack remedy for weeping saw-wounds), *Davidia* (Père David, missionary and botanist), *Buddleia* (the Rev. Adam Buddle, friend and English correspondent of Père David who discovered the buddleia in China, and named it after him). These are the names of genera, of course, but some varietal names have also become part of the botanical canon: mention *Mrs Sinkins* and you hardly need the specific *dianthus*, ditto *Bowles' Mauve* (erysimum), *Mrs Hegarty* (schizostylis they were; now renamed hesperantha) – and, turning over the coin of eponyms, it is not, even now, unusual or eccentric to name your daughter after a sweet-smelling, bonny-looking *Daisy* or *Rose*, *Rosemary* or *Lily* (or *Susan*, if you prefer *lily* in Hebrew). But calling your offspring after a tree is a bit more exotic (unless perhaps you were a footballer and not quite sure how to spell 'beach' but wishing to memorialise a romantic liaison at (say) Copacabana, in which case perhaps: 'Come 'ere Beech, and eat up your Frosties,' would be alright). Even so, *Willow* is still possible. *Linden* used to be quite common, and I once knew a Mrs Smith – Hilda for most of her life, but in her latter years she was always affectionately known as *Apple.* To name your daughter *Rhoda* probably suggests an intention to imbue her with a bit of Welsh flavour, and it would only be a pedant who pointed out that, in principle at least, you would be harking back not so much to Cymru and Wales as to roses (again), though this time in Greek. However you look at it, it is probably best not to put too much store by what's in a name. But it's still fun. And why not go the whole hog and call her *Rhododendron*? After all, there's *Laura* from Laurel; there's *Daphne*; there's *Veronica*, so why not *Tree of Roses*? That would be its literal translation, and it's not such a bad moniker perhaps.

One of Ireland's most single-minded rhodo collectors was a man by the name of Fielding Lecky-Watson (and who needs botanical nuance with a name like that!). His collection ran into thousands but,

even among so many, he had a favourite, 'Corona'. It's a medium-sized hybrid with gorgeous coral-pink flowers, pitched somewhere between the boudoir and the ballroom, whose parentage has been lost (or mislaid, perhaps, in Left Luggage at Waterloo Station? It is of that prurient Edwardian vintage) but which is still worth taking the social risk to plant. It flowers in May.

Lecky-Watson named his daughter after this rhododendron, and she, under her married name, Corona North (and helped or hindered by her name as the case may have been), became a legend in her own lifetime. She had interests in all sorts of local affairs in and around Carlow, but her greatest passion was for the garden she inherited from her father at Altamont, a few miles away, which, 'to save it from the digger and the chain-saw', she gave to the nation when she died in 1999.

Altamont – the name – has the flavour of something Spanish, I think. Something conventual. You'd expect an abbey ruin at least, and perhaps a flight of penitentially high steps up to the 'mount'. But although there is a Nun's Walk in this garden and – they say – a misty origin in some far-off religious order, the presiding spirits of the place now are pretty paganly chthonic, I think. The gods here now are those of earth, stone, water, sun, sky. But if we cannot directly or even indirectly attribute the origins of the place to nuns, *monks* are marginally more possible – Cistercian monks, in particular – as attested by so many tellingly situated monastic sites both in Britain and Ireland. They had an uncannily sharp eye for where to build: somewhere remote and set apart from the world, but also intensely *of* the world too, at least in another sense – the physical world of (God's) beauty embodied in nature wherever you looked, be it out of your refectory window, or on your meditative walk between the offices of *none* and *vespers*, or from the vantage of your work in the monastery fields. There's an interesting and appropriate transcultural test case for this: Tintern Abbey, famously and beautifully sited in the Wye Valley of Monmouthshire, and its sister house – also Tintern Abbey – in a remote and similarly beautiful riverine spot in County Wexford. One day, the County Wexford site will find its own poet to memorialise the place as definitively as do Wordsworth's 'Lines written a few miles above Tintern Abbey' in the case of the Wye Valley site. And then the comparability – largely through the sheer beauty of both spots – will become unmistakably apparent.

Altamont is rather like that too. Notwithstanding the puffs of the tourist brochures, it is *not* well signposted. It is, in fact, quite challenging to locate and reach, though the rolling countryside of County Carlow is a pleasure in itself, even if you haven't a clue where you are. And having got there, one of several indelible impressions is going to be of the panorama – a drama indeed – of the surrounding hills: the Blackstairs Mountains to the south, Wicklow Mountains to the northwest and, far away to the south-west, great Galtee Mor. A typically Cistercian site, in fact, because it is both beautiful and remote.

There was a Lord Altamont in the 1790s whose pile was at Westport, but that's miles away in County Mayo, yet however that may be – those arcane and finer points of the Irish peerage – the house at Altamont in County Carlow is a happy incident in the visual itinerary of the garden, rather than its focus. It tries to be eighteenth-century, grey stone and stucco, but mostly it's ivy and ill-disciplined clematis. The principal feature – in fact, a regular component of Irish vernacular generally – is a great, two-storeyed bay window with a conical slate-smooth roof like a squashed pepperpot. One day the house will be talent-spotted as an idiomatic, faintly decayed, relaxed film set for a William Trevor script. The Office of Public Works has the place in hand, but I hope they are not too diligent in their ministrations, particularly in the matter of the wonderful blue *Rhododendron augustinii* which is holding up the east end of the place. (The *augustinii* is not another ecclesiastical residue but points to Augustus Henry – Irish customs official in China and plant collector – he also of *Parthenocissus henryana, Lilium henryi, Begonia augustinei*, etc.)

In front of the house, like an apron spread, is a long sloping soft-turfed lawn. Down its centre a path leads feet and eyes to the lake, but not in a rush. There are yews to enjoy, placed formally like buttons on a frock coat, and clipped into plump egg shapes. And there are big splashes of roses between them.

To the left, under fine old trees, is a very deep, very long mixed border sumptuously and skilfully planted for colour and character, for seasonal interest, and for neighbourliness with adjacent plants, so that elements such as the grey in the leaves of *Romneya coulteri* chime with the smoky mauves of *Cotinus coggygria*, but the papery-white crêpe flowers counterpoint – and can easily be mistaken for – single roses, the rugosas especially, and the flowers of the many single clematis. The latter are everywhere in this garden and, for a place that does not boast all that many walls, the bounty, frequency and variety of them is both surprising and head-raising. Another combination working well here is chalky-blue agapanthus blended

with smudges of Pritchard's blue campanula – but the similarity of colours is belied by the difference of shape. China and Prussian blue delphiniums complicate and enrich the colour schemes further, but it's not an essay in blues alone. There are plates of achillea, blades of crocosmia (and bifurcated ferns too if you want forks laid also). Asters, penstemons, dahlias, thalictrums, heleniums, lilies, eremurus and, in low spots, geraniums. *Kitaibela vitifolia* – another plant that blends and extends the palette – is planted here: it has flowers like a hibiscus, or are they more mallow-like? The leaves are white-dusty like a vine in a dry, high summer. The base of the petals is cut away to reveal a green calyx, so they appear to be bi-coloured – both classy and curious.

There are grand old trees almost everywhere whose slow greenness and stature are a marvellous foil to the high-summer, short-lived excitement of the herbaceous and shrubby things at their feet. They are carefully labelled three times over: Linnaean system's Latin, comfortable English, and then fascinating Irish. So hawthorn (cultivars) begin as *Crataegus monogyna*, of course, but then blossom into *Sceach Gheal* (which sounds something like *she-ark gull*), and that gently opens the door not only to a vernacular which rightfully belongs here, but also to a great undertow of folklore about trees. To take just the hawthorn: in England and Ireland it's also the whitethorn, the flower of fertility and the May, and it is the grail-thorn of Joseph of Arimathea at Glastonbury. In Scotland and Wales, it's the switch of choice if you're stealing cattle or even just warding them. In Ireland, it's especially associated with holy wells, those hidden, numinous places where water and rock are saying something about life and its sources. As often as not, it will be on the hawthorn that those votive ribbons will be hung which puzzle strangers who stumble upon them in out-of-the-way places in Ireland. They're called 'clooties'. They strike me as northern versions of the supplicant and prophylactic prayer flags you might see in Tibet, but blended often with the wishful thinking or the sympathetic magic entailed in washing a wound with a bit of cloth, then tying the rag on to a tree which, in turn, takes on, assumes, the wound, suffers for us, and releases the person originally bleeding. The blood-red haws attest in due course to the efficacy of this process and to the tree's vicarious suffering on behalf of the suppliant. Oak, ash, yew and hazel were sacred to the Celts – and most famously of all plants, mistletoe too, of course. But it is the whitethorn, the hawthorn, the May, which, according to a survey reported in Mary Low's excellent book *Celtic Christianity and Nature* (1996), turns out to be the most frequently encountered tree at sacred sites – something just over fifty per cent of all trees recorded were whitethorns. Whether this reflects Celtic origins or Christian preferences we shall never know for certain, but it seems likely that the tree's aura transcended any crude pagan/Christian dichotomy and was passed seamlessly from one religion into the other. Actually, this potency in the hawthorn is not only a locally Irish lore, but elsewhere it is inflected a little differently. In England, you admire the May out of doors but never, never cut it and bring it into the house. You'd *never* decorate a church with it, no matter how tempting that might be with Easter very late. To crown a maypole with sprigs of it, however, would be a good move towards the propitiation of the earth spirits. Yet, in Ireland, to cut down a whole tree would be dangerously to tempt fate, which accounts for why, even now, so many country roads take a bend around a May tree before reverting to their course. If a tree should blow down, however, then you'd be at liberty to use the wood, and a loaf baked in an oven fired with hawthorn knows no equal.

The first systematic book of the wild plants of Ireland – a book that uses scientific but pre-Linnaean taxonomy – was the *Synopsis Stirpium Hibernicarum*, written by Caleb Threlkeld, doctor of both divinity and medicine, and published in Dublin in 1726. The first of its kind, it was also almost the last for a long time to give names in Latin, English *and* Irish. Here is Threlkeld on the plant we have been discussing, *Crataegus monogyna*, the hawthorn: 'Oxycanthus, sive Mespilus Apii folio Sylvestris Spinosa, *The White-thorn*, or *Hawthorn*, Irish *Sceach*. The *Haws* are accounted Diuretick, good for the stone, Gravel, and Pleurisy.'

As it happens, on 28 October, the day after the publication of this pioneering book – and in London, not Dublin – there was published another book which, in its way, also distils so much of Irishness between its boards. It was *Travels into Several Remote Nations of the World* by one Lemuel Gulliver. Unlike Threlkeld, Swift did not publicly own his book straightaway. Both were enormous commercial successes.

Most of the old trees at Altamont are bigger and rarer than the haw, if (pharmaceutically and magically) less potent. There is a very fine tulip tree, for example, and a davidia too. There's an important collection of sorbus species. There's a *Fraxinus excelsior* whose close-grained bark is silvery from the passage of many snails. There's a fern-leafed beech (*Fagus sylvatica* 'Asplenifolia') which, to judge by its size, may well be almost as old as the introduction of the cultivar itself (the tree was first recorded in 1804). In common with the best of its kind, it has a misty miasma to it and, in a breeze, it moves like vapour from a pot of steaming green tea. This particular example is a paradigm of the species: I can think of no rival to its special presence and beauty here unless it be the one (planted possibly by Wordsworth, no less!) at Rydal Mount, near Ambleside. A similar and complementary airiness belongs to the deodar cedar, perhaps the grand old man of the entire treescape here, though collectively, and indeed individually, those august beeches in the Nun's Walk by the walled garden would take some beating. Together, these and all the others form a second and third dimension – the horizontal and the perpendicular – around the great flat lake, whose one-dimensional surface lies at the heart of the garden. It was dug by hand, not, as so many earthworks were, as a local Famine Relief Work in the 1840s, but during the 1920s, though in a similar spirit really: a responsible landlord trying to help people hit hard by the Depression. Elsewhere, that same charitable impulse to provide employment and thus a source of income to the otherwise destitute, has left Ireland with probably the greatest concentration of follies in the world – most, but not all, of them in gardens – but there is none at Altamont. (As so often, it is this haunting by history that constitutes really a fourth, and special, dimension of Irish gardens: the enclosing of the demesne by those beautiful walls – mile upon mile of them – the lakes, all those follies, all kinds of earth-moving, and then, though ghostly now, the colossal human distress that they bear witness to even as they signal real attempts to alleviate it. Perhaps, too, they are memorials – muted now but not quite silent – to uneasy consciences which linger on even after the acts of charity have been committed.) Follies are not uncommon in England, but they are endemic in Ireland; they surely reflect – and not only in the history of Famine Works – something in the collective psyche, a spirit of fun, a cherishing of the absurd. Folly building was at its peak in the nineteenth century, but it's good to report that the spirit (of folly, of calculated, serious foolishness) is still alive now. At Oakfield Park (near Rathoe, County Donegal) there was built in the garden, during the 1990s, a new 'castle' on the lakeside. The spirit has been kept alive too by timely restorations. A number of these were made possible through grants from the Gardens of Ireland Restoration Programme. Money – essentially EU money – was given between 1994 and 1999 for the restoration of twenty-six Irish gardens. In some cases, it was quite a lavish funding, but probably none of it was wasted. Even so, it wasn't enough to save several of them. There were at least two great successes, however: at Birr and at Kilruddery. Kilruddery, being essentially a seventeenth-century garden, has no follies as such, but at Birr there are several. And not just as incidental eye-catchers: even where there are no buildings as such, the whole place is still shot through with this spirit of grave folly.

At Altamont, but not as a Famine Works, the labourers excavated a shallow bowl of two and a half acres in extent, and then flooded it. There are three islands, but so thickly planted that they'd resist now any attempt at a landing. On the flat table of the water's surface there are picnics – banquets indeed – of lilies, and of the still water reflecting the inverted images of trees and the castles of clouds in the sky above. There are excited sounds of a gabble of swallows. A number of balustrades lend a theatrical air to the place here and there, in the manner of Rex Whistler (to English eyes, perhaps) or Oliver Messel (to Irish eyes). Messel had connections with Birr, in County Offaly, and I wonder if he, or his spirit, visited Altamont. I suspect so: Lord Rosse (of Birr, and Messel's brother-in-law) certainly was here. The *Clerodendrum trichotomum fargesii* by the door to the house was a gift of his.

The planting around the lake is very rich indeed, lazy pinks and purples rather than the stricter, stronger colours closer to the house. An excellent dusky-red crocosmia, for example – 'Mrs Geoffrey Howard', the helpful label says. Meadow rue, foxgloves, lots of lilies, grasses, flax lily – their feet in the lake – maples, dogwoods and hydrangeas, hostas everywhere. It's relaxed, abundant and skilfully set off by perpendiculars – above all, two perfectly symmetrical swamp cypresses, *Taxodium distichum* – against the horizontal, level surface of the water. Somewhere between the horizontal and the vertical come the clematis which clothe and re-clothe so many of the trees. One, a particularly remarkable plant, has only small flowers but it flounces them above and about in such profligate abandon, such dense, creamy clusters, as to resemble washing put out on the bushes to dry in days gone by. And the lower stems of this particular climber are truly tree-thick.

It is down here by the lake that most of the rhododendrons stand – 'Corona' among them – but blended with plenty of other fine trees too: embothriums with their impossibly exotic tomato-red blooms, eucryphias – those signature plants of so many Irish gardens – an august *Nothofagus obliqua*, an uncommon (southern) beech, but looking quite like an oak – a *Podocarpus totara* looking, as *they* always do, like a yew out on probation, but cocky about it anyway.

Following the path clockwise around the margin of the water takes you tunnelling through lugubrious undergrowths of rhododendrons. There are fantastic contortions of tree trunks and of gnarled, peeling branches. You find yourself stepping softly past a badger sett. And – surprised – you are enjoying the confusion of feelings brought about by the strong smell of things decaying – leaves and spent petals – and the sight of things vernal, primroses especially – 'things dying … things new born', as Shakespeare has it in *The Winter's Tale*: a confluence and congruity where you had expected a contradiction. They – and you – are making the most of an amnesty between the just-about plausibly aesthetic and that musky smell of the rotten and the rotting. The writ of Health and Safety runs only loosely here. There are luxuries like puddles and the fantastic wefts of roots reaching up through the earth. You walk carefully over and through them, but the pleasure easily overwhelms the caution. If Messel or Whistler were the tutelary spirits of the garden up to this point, what lies beyond strongly evokes the fantastic, the gothic edginess of an Arthur Rackham or a Mervyn Peake. The rhododendrons continue, but the path becomes less and less orderly, and it is not plants so much as rocks which engage the eye and exercise the feet. The further you go down into this wildwood, the more elemental it becomes: rocks and moss, lichens and fern-dripping cliffs, a soft but precipitous stream, pools of sharp light alternating with pools of bright water, peaty and delicious to the taste. In a garden which has almost no sculpture to speak of, it is these living, raw rocks which engross the eye – boulders and amazingly sculpted tree trunks, tree limbs – nature's own artefacts so much like works of human art, simultaneously they might be both primitives and moderns. Some sort of order emerges as you digress into a glade deliberately made over to bog plants but it's not necessarily a comfortable one – gunnera brandishing their clubs, insects staggering about in nectar-induced orgies of intoxication, the bruised stink of skunk-cabbages. Children of the right mettle ought to love it down here. For adults, it is a deeper lesson in culture and anarchy. Down and down you go, between walls of rock fitted together like Aztec masonry. There is a ladder of waterfalls. Down. Down.

But before long – and consistent with the abrupt, unmodulated changes of mood which characterise this garden – the trees and the rocks, the streams and the ancient gloom, all of them come to an abrupt end. You find yourself suddenly out in the open on the banks of a river. It is the Slaney, a long, easy-going stream which eventually debouches at Wexford sixty miles away. An oak, nearly full-grown but by no means ageing, has slipped and tumbled into the river, and puzzled birds are flying through its ruins. A single weir sculpts the water like wet, green clay, then shatters and spills it into prisms of light and sound. A dragonfly settles on to a spire of loosestrife and the swallows are here too, their chatter competing with the sounds of the water – muffled chuckles, murmurs, rumours of the sea.

A climb of a century of steps (so they say) takes you back up through the wood – awash with bluebells in the spring, the colour, the scent – and out onto a wide hillside. At the top, a Temple of the Four Winds. (This name for a garden building has a particular Irish, progenitive tendency: the parent of them all is at Mount Stewart, County Down.) You can see for miles and miles – those huge panoramas – and the air is sweet and cool after your climb. The wire of the fence is wadded with scraps of wool, though it is not sheep you see but, on your right, on the sloping meadow between the hilltop and the woodland garden quite far below, a herd of Friesian cows. In the dewy grass of the path, here at the top, there are ecstasies of tiny slugs and smears of silver everywhere, but you can't chide these gastropods – however numerous and slithey – if they have the decency to prefer the view up here to the hostas down below.

Soon, you are back in among the trees, and turning into that beech-lined walk. The stature of these trees is astonishing – both humbling and heart-lifting. At their feet are cyclamen, but also – woven through ferns, *Liriope muscari*, arisaemas, epimediums and hellebores – there is a collection of snowdrops. I counted some twenty different ones, but there are said to be a lot more. Galanthophiles would have a

field day here, but in summer you are left with their names alone to give you pleasure, not all of them Irish by any means, and not all of them of the quite legendary status some of the rarest snowdrops have achieved, but easily enough to satisfy: Blewberry [sic] Tart, Mrs Backhouse No 12, Tilebarn Jamie, Barbara's Double, Coolballin Taggent, Straffan, Anglesey Abbey, Little John, etc.

The last chapter of a visit to Altamont may very well be the best. In any case, it is certainly a kind of summation. Turning left out of the cathedral of beeches you find yourself looking down a double border, nearly but not quite exclusively herbaceous, pretty deep, and carefully graded for colour along its length and, for height, across its depth. It was planted in memory of Corona North herself. The original design, execution and subsequent maintenance are the work of Robert Miller, a close friend of Mrs North. Glasnevin's famous double herbaceous border is longer (but the box edging, when I saw it last, was terminally scruffy), the borders at Annes Grove are arguably even better planted (but much shorter), and the borders at Powerscourt are more lavishly planted and perhaps better groomed (though too deep for not having walls behind them to close the view, and gaudy with far too much yellow in high summer). Altamont's borders seem, somehow, to be lacking in nothing at all (if one is indulgently blind to the presence of a few strappingly rude weeds and if one takes a relaxed view of dead-heading). There is an old medlar and there are some pensionable roses but most of the plants are young, and kept young by division. Together they constitute a sort of anthology of Irish gardening because they were given in memory of Mrs North by her friends – proprietors, many of them, of the greatest gardens scattered all over the land: Birr, Glasnevin, Airfield, Beechpark, Mount Congreve, the Dillon Garden. Robert Miller's achievement is to have melded what was probably an almost impossibly heterogeneous group of plants into two stunningly good borders, good because they are so convincingly coherent.

Distinct from this border, and back now through the gate, there are four people employed in the garden at large which is now the property of Dúchas, the Office of Public Works, but there is no sign whatsoever of the throttling, homogenising, dead hand of institutional oversight we would probably have to expect if this were the National Trust or the RHS – bloated now, as they are, with too much cash and corporativeness, and surely losing their way did they but know it. If theirs had been the sway here, those paths through the woods below – narrow sometimes, uneven with roots and rocks, challenging with puddles, pungent sometimes with sap and with that furtive, strong stink of fox, but always free from an imposed doctrinaire aesthetic and (olfactory) hygiene, from social and architectural detergents masquerading as safety regulations – they would have been widened and flattened, so that gardeners (who *used* to wear boots and push wheelbarrows and have dirty hands, do you remember them?) might now get through in their buggy-trucks, the air smudged with their fumes, the birdsong wiped out by their engine noise and the chatter of their mobile phones. As a result, the place, the spirit of the place, would have been deeply confused. But it hasn't happened here yet, and long may it be resisted.

Robert Miller's status at Altamont must, I take it, have been separately provisioned under the terms of Corona North's will. A certain tension between the two incumbencies would seem to be evident. Such signs as there are to Altamont tend to be duplicated on the spot by another sign to *Altamont Plant Sales*. That's Miller's superb nursery in the walled garden behind the commemorative borders – well worth a visit to find excellent plants for your own garden, and to enjoy the two Hidcote-like pavilions which oversee it. Garden and nursery occupy essentially the same site but do not share the same proprietorship, and perhaps not quite the same spirit, but nothing of that necessarily impinges upon the visitor who comes away with an impression of Altamont as an Irish garden of much more than just Irish significance.

Kilmokea

COUNTY WEXFORD

One way to catch and pin down the spirit of a place, indeed of a garden – assuming that it is a good garden, and that it has a spirit – is to ask yourself who might live there, which characters, what plays, which novels might be set there? Interrogate your impression of the place, but start with some relatively easy questions: could you, for example, stage *A Midsummer Night's Dream* here? Would Puck be at home? Or, if you settled the first act of Shaw's *Mrs Warren's Profession* here, would it approximate sufficiently to 'a cottage garden on the eastern slope of a hill a little south of Haslemere in Surrey'? (Why didn't he actually give a map reference and be done with it?) Or would something more sylvan – 'a wood, dark and mysterious; in the background the faint glimmer of a lake' – be more fitting, as prescribed in the stage directions for *The Immortal Hour*? It is not necessarily an entirely whimsical pursuit, this scene-setting: suppose not Chatsworth but some hitherto obscure house had been identified by literary scholars as Austen's model for Mr Darcy's Pemberley. What then? A very lucrative boost indeed, in terms of visitor numbers, bookings for television dramas, etc., I should think.

Whimsical perhaps, though anyone with any pretensions to the understanding and appreciation of eighteenth-century gardens would not so much rush in to mock as seek diligently to learn the trick of how to do it as soon as possible because, of course, those gardens and their sculptures were deliberately conceived, each succeeding glade, as a series of invitations to precisely that sort of perception … this spot as belonging to Pan, that as where zephyrs do blow, and this a pool where Diana might discreetly bathe and Actæon not stumble upon her. Tutelary spirits all, but only some of them – Pomona, Ceres, Vertumnus – specific to horticulture. Others more to do with mood and aspiration, the whole place populated with their likenesses in the

form of stone or lead statues: the entire many-layered trope inviting us to see the garden – if only we make the leap of imagination – as a place peopled by gods: a special, magical, even hallowed zone where dull, all-too-human cares might be sloughed off for a while, and at least a glimpse of the immortals achieved.

If a match cannot be made between your favourite book (or play, or poem, or pantheon of Greek gods) and a garden newly visited, that is not necessarily the fault of the garden. Rather, it serves, by a process of elimination, towards an understanding of precisely what sort of garden you are engaging with. And some gardens won't work with it at all, so it is not an infallible tool anyway, though once you get into the habit of it, it is hard to break, and quite often you come across something that is quite revealing: a connection, an analogy, an association, which precisely frames what you feel about the place. (Try Levens Hall and *Alice in Wonderland*. Try Lady Bracknell with anything municipal, but rose-thorny and strewn with notices saying *Get Off The Grass. Know your Place*. Try Miss Marple with hollyhocks and a bicycle propped against a wall … Or any number of heritage walled vegetable gardens with an invisible but all too chillingly sensed sign which would say – if indeed you saw it – *Mr MacGregor Works and Holds Sway Here*.) The possibilities are endless, so it is fun, and so are the windows of recognition each placing in a garden opens upon the mood, manners and even the morals of the place.

Sometimes you can sense not one but two people in and behind the spirit of a place. That's literally true of a garden by Lutyens and Jekyll of course, and there are other people, other places, whose spirit is binary: both Burlington *and* Kent (at Rousham), Sackville-West *and* Harold Nicholson (at Sissinghurst). And it works – it *can* work – with literary characters sensed in real gardens too. Pan and Psyche is an obvious, well-rehearsed one (very usefully, very schematically binary: the sylvan as against the riverine, the rough and shaggy with the groomed and smooth, in sum, the male and the female). I wish someone might try Don Quixote (but, please, not Phlox of Sheep) and Sancho Panza (a scarecrow, off-duty, eating a raw carrot and ruminating, scratching first head, then vast backside). Of course, it depends upon what your reading is, but sometimes the connection approaches the definitively iconic willy-nilly. I defy anybody to visit parts of Kensington Gardens and not encounter at least the ghost of *Peter Pan*, for example.

Many gardens have more than one zone, one mood, one style, but for all that variety they generally strive for continuity between the parts as well as contiguity, for kinship as well as contrast. There might well be a gate to mark the transition from one zone to another, but it would be low and you could see through it – a dog-deterrent but not a frontier for people; or it would be high but, made of wrought iron, no barrier to vision at all – on the contrary, an invitation to peer through, then pass through, at least in your imagination. You wouldn't expect a heavy wooden gate, thick with hinges and handles, impenetrable to vision either through, over or around it, a long iron bolt sliding, but not all that easily, through entrails of oak and rough stone piers. Unless it were a gothic film set. Or Kilmokea.

Actually, there are only four gates in this garden – and they are not really gothic at all – but gates of such character and positioned at such critical junctures that they linger in the mind long after you have left. They take up permanent places in the conscious and subconscious mind. They assume the status of (newly discovered but incontrovertibly authentic) drafts of a Robert Frost poem about fences, neighbours and gates; they remind you of the map on the endpapers of the copy of Bunyan's *Pilgrim's Progress* you won when you were nine – all journeys, gates, wickets, obstacles and then, far off, a destination, but only if you were very focused, very good. They – these gates at Kilmokea – definitely suggest to you some Alice-like kinship with yourself as you pass through. With gates like these, you gradually lose sense of where you began, where you are going to, and does it really matter anyway?

These are not the kind of gates that stand on ceremony at grand entrances to announce wealth, power and property to the forelock-tugging world outside. These are essentially internal thresholds, forceful in their differentiation of spaces and places but modest in their materials and their bossiness. Yet they lack not a jot of character.

One of them opens onto a lane – a public road, in fact, though the traffic is notional by any standards. It is a real surprise. You think you must have mistaken your way and stumbled out of the back gate – a boundary marker declaring that there's no more garden beyond – a terminus rather than a threshold or rite of passage. But a yard or two in front of you, and facing you across the lane, is its brother: heavy, wooden, taller than you are, emphatically stock-proof and almost certainly recently negotiated by none other than the Mad Hatter. Or the spirit of David Price.

David Price (1907–94) moved into Kilmokea with his family in 1947. It consisted then of a handsome but crumbling eighteenth-century house, with a kitchen garden long ago lost, and the rest of the demesne given over to copse and fields (though – a first, teasing hint of possibilities – a local dowser promised to find a long-lost but useful-sounding well, and indeed did so). Sixty years and seven acres later, we have a garden with such a sense of place that it knocks spots off many a more famous, more visited destination. To confine the scope to Ireland only, you could argue that places such as Powerscourt or Mount Stewart, Lismore or Kilruddery, can very well flaunt a sense of *occasion*. Indeed, they can and do. Large gardens tend to be good at that. But a sense of *place* is a more elusive and almost infinitely more interesting thing. Kilmokea claims a space in the imagination of the visitor almost straight away as you pull in at the gate (negligible, this one): self-sown *Echium pininana* strut about the edges of the yard as you park your car in it. Clearly, they'll take over soon, shove concrete and hard-standing aside, and claim the space for their own. You think you have come to a sort of Irish Tresco … except that the freedom these plants are enjoying is such a glorious snook cocked to conventional order, moderation, discipline, taste: these plants are taking liberties. This is (as *The Devil's Dictionary* has it, if I remember rightly) a case of that disobedience which is 'the silver lining to the dismal cloud of servility'. And it's terrific.

You enter the garden proper through a low-arched carriageway and door, and you help yourself to a map (though you take note of the invitation to put it back when you've finished, if you like. Or to keep it, if you like. But the unspoken hint is to not just throw it away. Already you know you're in a sensible, liveable place.) You pass through a passage, frescoed and echoing, and you come out into a sheltered, old-walled courtyard. A sleeping cat ignores you. Already something about this place has taught you to interpret this not as rudeness but as a compliment. A rickety table of plants, home-grown and for sale, easily tempts you to risk getting earth spilt onto the back seat or the carpet of your car. There is no one demanding an entrance fee. A trowel and a bucket relax on a low wall, meaning business of course, but not just yet. An Edwardian conservatory will supply you with tea when you're done (and indeed claim an entrance fee when you're ready), but in the meantime cat and proffered cream are in a state either of amnesty or of suspended animation: neither and no one stirs.

It is a deeply satisfying little cameo within the larger sense of place that Kilmokea exudes – August, somewhere half a mile away a tractor

humming, a wasp rendered harmless through intoxication … and that sublimely careless cat. But then you see the flowering tree by the gate (aperture, threshold, page-turn into Act One, Scene Two – these little rites of passage so characteristic of this remarkable garden) and it's extraordinarily beautiful. A crinodendron, is it? Something about its leaves? Yes, though you know that that's a guess, and it isn't *C. hookerianum*, the lantern tree you see quite often in Ireland but almost never in England. In fact, it's *C. patagua* – bell-shaped, creamy, clematis-like flowers. Small, tough leaves. Wonderful. I know of only one other and, curiously, that too is placed just inside a gate: look to your left as you enter through the Swan Walk gate of the Chelsea Physic Garden.

You expect rarities there, but Kilmokea is full of rare plants too. That's one of several good reasons why it should be visited. Other gardens have them too, and sometimes they swank about them, but not at Kilmokea (or, let it be said, in the Chelsea Physic Garden either). Here, in this quiet garden in a quiet south-eastern corner of Ireland, rare plants have had to be interesting (as well as rare) to have gained admittance.

Once past this beautiful thing, you find yourself in a brief, intense, formal rose garden. Then there's a bed given over to *Vestia lycioides*, cheerful in the spring with its yellow tubular flowers, interesting later for its acorn-like fruits, and arresting no matter what the season for the smell of mentholated beef gravy its leaves give off when gently rubbed. After which (developing the theme of food, perhaps?) you come to a kitchen garden. Most of the vegetables served with the (rather famous) meals in the house – which takes in guests and spoils them rotten – are grown here or in the vegetable garden proper behind the wall. This is probably the only chance you will have to get the measure of the soil at Kilmokea because, unusually for the garden as a whole, here some of it is bare where something has been removed for the kitchen and the table. The mould is deep, old and quite light, the result of years and years of husbandry, I should think – a lifetime's achievement in itself. The quality of the husbandry in the garden is outstanding: unobtrusive, thorough, and conscientiously going with, rather than against, the grain of the place.

Beyond this, and through another space-defining aperture, you come upon a lawn rolled out in front of the house. Everything about this building is just right: symmetry, dignity, modesty, presence – golden sections everywhere, restful ratios of three to four (panes across to panes down); three storeys up, four bays across; three bass reliefs but four windows; and the roof: two right-angled triangles meeting and cut off to take a long, low chimney of eight pots (two by four). No curves, no Hogarth, except in the subtle falls of the curtains glimpsed through the windows, and in the lazy sighing of the connecting walls at either side of the house itself. Curves – Hogarthian, or just witty – there are in the garden, however. Topiary abounds. That old evergreen joke about peacocks-in-yew competing for poise and couture with the real peacocks strutting their stuff in front of them. It makes you smile, no matter how often you see it, and always it rekindles a debate with yourself about which is really the more artificial. The crisp edges of topiary and hedges are smart, of course, but they are more than that, more than just a manifesto of standards of housekeeping, or style, or attitude. The sharp lines, the definition, are precisely the right visual rhyme for the geometry of the house. And there is wit too: earlier you passed a bay tree clipped into the shape of a bulging, tall-standing thistle.

On the right of this, the only lawn in the garden, there used to be a large bed of lupins, but lupins are quite hard work (renewed every two or three years?) and not, these days, to everyone's taste anyway. For whatever reason, they're no longer here and the grass has been reinstated, though lupins – something of an Irish habit, actually – survive here and there elsewhere.

On the left there has long been a fine herbaceous border. In David Price's day, this was the work of his wife. And you'd have needed something quite tall, quite substantial, here because, without some sort of masking screen, you'd have seen and sensed – not from the house, necessarily, but certainly from the garden – the presence of a very old graveyard, just behind the wall. In its own right it is a beautiful, wild place, but melancholic and not something you'd necessarily want to integrate into your garden. Thus the herbaceous border, which masks both wall and mortality, and keeps its secrets to itself. In fact, it is not unusual in Irish gardens for some accident of place – something accidentally unearthed, a view outwards onto an historically charged landscape, the hint of an association with Maeve, with Morrigan, with someone of mythic stature – to set up a layering of the way it is perceived: diachronic, synchronous, according to how much you know (or, indeed, want to know) of these resonances. That opportunity – probably and understandably because graveyards may induce some gloom – has been eschewed at Kilmokea. (Though mausolea – garden houses at the end of the world, as it were – are, in fact, a rather Irish speciality ... in a minor key, in a quiet way. See Maurice and Michael Craig's classic, *Mausolea Hibernica*.)

Originally the border was blues and yellows. Now it is more catholic and polychrome, but no less impressive: hollyhocks and crocosmias (reds); Japanese anemones and phlox (pinks); achillea and helianthus, lysimachia and solidago, then the ligularias, both Othello and Desdemona (yellows and golds); echiums, asters, cardoons and echinops (blues); acanthus and foxgloves (creams, browns and mauve). And enormously tall, virtually arborescent, clumps of *Melianthus major* majestically lording it over everything and flowering profusely. In-fillers might be geraniums, might be fraxinellas. The picture overall is stunningly good – carefully graduated in size, modulated in colour and texture, paced to flower successively over the whole season.

There is a pool garden, a few paces round a corner and further on. Very formal, with a shallow-pedimented Doric temple closing it off at one end. (It is these same columns which are echoed in the front of the house where, I have to say, their whiteness and manifestly fibreglass weightlessness – ditto the flat roof above, which manages also to slice across the eighteenth-century fanlight – make them look faintly silly.) The pool is a shallow rectangular tank busy with dragonflies and patrolled by those vain, mincing peacocks. This is a suntrap rejoicing in roses, cistuses and dieramas. Earlier in the year there are the flasks of magnolias toasting the waxing spring. There's topiary here too, parodying, mocking those catwalking peacocks, did they but know it. Stone and branch alike bloom with lichens silver, grey, golden and pewter – testament to the clean air hereabouts (though even here things aren't what they used to be: the river was once crowded with salmon and trout, the fields and woods with partridge and pheasant. No longer, though.) Self-sown valerian and alchemilla blur the edges of formality. A walnut tree promises fruit (and stained fingers) in due course, should the nut-thieving crows – another Irish habit – allow. Doves croon, as well they might, because close by is the loveliest-looking columbarium you will ever set eyes on – a steep-roofed, stone-rough house with forty-two apertures for very fat birds, set in a wall beneath lines of shingles that curve just a little upwards and inwards towards the centre of the roof like a quizzically raised eyebrow. It's a gem. The paving is a pleasure too: old, worn, leather-beaten stone. Perhaps some of it may have come from nearby New Ross and the Rebellion of 1798. Tradition has it that the Irish tore up the flagstones there, then used them to repulse the rebellion-snuffing British.

Kilmokea has a great many seats scattered over its acres. Having places to sit is sometimes part of what marks out a good garden from the merely pedestrian, or distinguishes the garden that has not lost sight of what it is really for from the place which has: the place for sitting, pausing, idling even (as well, of course, as working) from the sort of garden which is really just a species of compensatory therapy, a machine-for-needing-me-to-look-after-it ... obsessively. But if you have seats too many and too formal then the place becomes municipal or baronial, just as, if there are too few, it will convey an impression of tacitly urging you on, on and out, if you please, like the message your backside gets after five minutes of penitential seating in a McDonald's. Placing is important too: some seats need to be sited so as to arrest a particularly good view – like a frame frozen, a still, in an otherwise moving picture. But others need to reward the climbing of a slope, or to be almost hidden – somewhere two people could hold hands in if they wish and not feel self-conscious. Kilmokea has all of those, and bothies, and arbours, and *sitooteries* to boot. All in discreet abundance. The sitting and pausing makes you notice things ...

seen from lower down, the light coming *through* those banana leaves
– so much more interesting than light bouncing off them, like so much
ocular latex when seen, as normally, from above; that juvenile tree –
not a plane or a maple after all, when you take time to look closely, but
a tulip tree. That stone marker-post … it was once an old lawn roller
now stood up to attention, and the like of which you haven't seen since
that end-sculpted one by Eric Gill in an exhibition in London years
ago. That pennywort in the wall, it would be lost growing anywhere
else, but just there it is a jewel. Seats – but they must be well-placed
– really do make a garden.

The best of this place is still to come, though. In the late 1960s,
David Price resolved to see what could be done with a field of bog
and four acres on the other side of the lane behind the garden so
far. The resulting transition from formal garden to what became the
woodland garden is what occasioned the best pair of gates you will
encounter in any garden anywhere. They pull faces at each other
across the lane. They have massive stone piers the shape and size of
pillar boxes, but a bit taller and quite a lot rougher, one for salt, one
for pepper. They look as if they have been borrowed, grumpy and
very likely dyspeptic too, from a frame in a graphic children's story
by Maurice Sendak. Fantastic.

Close one gate behind you, cross the lane, and open the other. Is
there any other garden so emphatically bisected by a public road?
Yes, there is. Giverny. But there the road is to be ignored, only just
about tolerated, or it is actively resented. There's nothing of that at
Kilmokea. Here, it is what encourages the mind to expect change.
Once through the gates, once across the lane, you are in a very different kind of garden altogether, but the path gives very little away.
It is quite narrow. It weaves and ducks so that you cannot see where
it is going. You must trust it or give up and turn back. Here and there
on either side are impenetrable thickets of bamboos, nervous in the
breeze. Tunnels of leaves, then swags, flourishes, buntings of blossom,
absorb and draw you further and further in – rhododendrons, magnolias, myrtles, camellias, all carefully, closely planted, to support each
other through life and the weather's trials, to take it in turns to take

the limelight and, effectively, to prevent you – the visitor – from ever quite knowing where you are.

You come upon quite a large lake in what you take to be something like the middle of the wood. Lazy trout and a lazy boat moored in a charming little boathouse hunkered down among the reeds. Hydrangeas flouncing about here and there, but not taking themselves all that seriously somehow: something improvised and informal about them, like children having raided a dressing-up box from the attic. The lake was formed by damming a stream, but you'd never know it now, the concrete dam being almost invisible. They found bits of a medieval water mill – a wooden flume, a curiously horizontal bit of gearing and a millstone. The rest of the bog, downstream, was trenched, drained and introduced to the habit of trees – originally larch, spruce, firs and hemlock – shelter belts which enjoyed the acidity and served to drain it a bit more. It was a far-seeing, long-spanned project to reform soil and context. The result, fifty years on, is a dark mould, springy, damp, but not wringing wet, and singularly hospitable to the sort of plants Price had in mind: those rhododendrons and magnolias and camellias – eucryphias too – which throng the place now. There are a lot of special trees and shrubs here but, on the whole, they tend to be modest in stature. Though, having said that, there are big scarlet oaks (*Quercus coccinea*), their trunks beginning now to show those characteristic fissures which come with age and maturity through which you see the bright red new bark beneath. There is a terrific *Podocarpus totara* (and its relatively diminutive cousin *Podocarpus andinus*, which doubles exactly as a yew till you look closely at the fruit which are oval rather than round, yellow rather than bright red). And there is *Eucalyptus viminalis*, an unexpected lesson in compatibility: eucalypts so often looking a little uncomfortably exotic among native broad-leaf trees, but blended with myrtles here (which flourish so well in Ireland as virtually to have become naturalised) they seem to adopt vicariously the almost-native airs of what are, in fact, their allies, both belonging to the same genus, the myrtaceae. Those myrtles, and the eucalypts too, mix well with pittosporums which grow to considerable sizes here; and the pittosporums – being southern hemisphere plants, perhaps –

prepare us for that other staple of Irish gardens, so integrated now as to have become almost part of the vernacular: the tree ferns. They are thriving in this damp, mild, sheltered spot, so much so that it is all too easy to take them for granted. That would be a mistake: even here they must be fairly close to their limit of tolerance of frost, however rare those frosts might be. Similarly not to be missed if possible is the really rare and no less really beautiful *Eucryphia moorei*. The white single-rose-like flowers are smaller than those of the eucryphias more usually encountered, but possibly even more numerous. It too is nervous of frosts, even in this benign climate. (And the *moorei* in its name does not on this unusual occasion signify David Moore, but his much less celebrated brother, Charles.) In contrast with these plants, whose size affords them considerable presence, most of the rhododendrons here are smaller species and cultivars; some are even dwarf. They are planted pretty closely, and they work well. You get an impression not of congestion but of associative cohesion. The underplanting, which tends effortlessly to a rude health and stature even the most optimistic of nurseryman's catalogues would blush to claim, supports this impression because there is nothing merely gestural or timid about it.

There are lakes and pools of *Omphalodes cappadocica* where puddles would be the norm; *Blechnum tabulare* – large clumps of it – and individual fronds so tall you could ladder the backs of your chairs by them; and a *Melianthus major* (again), in the outfall to the trout lake, which is virtually a small tree.

Everywhere there are big rugs of primula – tall candelabra ones, *P. pulverulenta* and *bulleyana* – drifts of that aristocrat *P. japonica*, so stunningly modest in its eye-soothing classiness, and (I think I spotted) *P. edgeworthii* and *P. griffithii* 'Guinevere', fine Irish cultivars both of them, harbingers (and gene banks) in their way of an impressive new generation being bred by Joe Kennedy and beginning to attract a good deal of attention. Mostly these primulas are dark-leaved, like the old 'Guinevere'. Their names read like an atlas of Ireland: 'Avoca', 'Drumcliffe', 'Tara', 'Glengarriff, 'Carrigdale' and 'Claddagh'.

Clearly a significant proportion of the planting in this woodland garden postdates David Price. The garden (and guest house) are owned now by Mark and Emma Hewlett. One or both of them must be committed and skilful gardeners. But there is no straining either after a religious adherence to Price's style and attitudes, or else after its opposite, an iconoclastic bonfire of his favourite plants. Gardens – the best ones – go on changing, and Kilmokea is no exception. The process here, however, is seamless, and all the better for it.

There's no telling accurately, for example, how long crinums have been here (though it's tempting to measure the girth of really mature bulbs, because they do indeed grow to such a prodigiously impressive size). Crinums have only fairly recently become staples of English gardens, but in Ireland they have had their feet under the table (their roots under the tree-cover, or beneath a south-facing wall, or against an old conservatory) for years. And not just the rather soho-pink of *C. x powellii* (which is a cross between the species *C. moorei* and *C. bulbispermum*). *Crinum x powellii* 'Album' is a classically simple, pure white, hardy amaryllis-like, summer-flowering beauty – all the more stately even than a lily for having no leaves on its stems. It is quite hard to come by, though *Crinum moorei* is harder still. The colour here is white but with the faintest rumour of pink … or is it lilac? Originally from Natal, it is something very special, possibly the most beautiful thing you'd see anywhere in late summer. It was named by Joseph Hooker after its discoverer, David Moore (yes, the much more famous of the two brothers this time), director of Dublin's Botanical Gardens at Glasnevin from 1838 until his death in 1879, and the man who strove so hard to identify the famine-dealing fungus *Phytophthora infestans*. In my experience, this plant is very hard indeed to find, and certainly not to be missed when you do.

Tree ferns – dicksonias – and the very large echiums both love it at Kilmokea, though it remains a little surprising that they should enjoy virtually the same conditions with only a little bit of inflection in the way of more shade here or more sun over there. The conventional wisdom is that echiums like it dry and sunny whereas the tree ferns like it damp and shady. But both loathe frost, and neither likes wind, and perhaps that accounts for their cohabiting so easily here.

Such is the density and intensity of tree-planting here that it's not necessarily easy to see any particular specimen entire. Plantsmen and purists might grumble, but for the rest of us the mood of companionable closeness easily compensates and, since you can rarely see the tops of trees, you have to settle instead for their foliage and flowers at head height, or the patterns of their roots, the gothic shapes of the boles, the texture of bark on the trunks. Complementing those trunks will be the perpendicularity of the bamboos, or the singularity of rare and engaging climbers and clumpers. There is *Muehlenbeckia complexa* for example (black twigs, not as many leaves as you'd expect for that quantity of twigs, and an insect-like swarming habit, upwards and outwards. It's the sort of almost other-worldly elemental plant you'd expect to find in a painting by Graham Sutherland.) There are the ghostly white upright stems of *Rubus cockburnianus* supporting their crowns of thorns. Details everywhere engross: the seed capsules of *Magnolia wilsonii* dripping orange pips; the ubiquitous black pods of the almost embarrassingly (and certainly unusually) fertile camellias here; the cinnamon dust on top of the leaves of *Rhododendron pachysanthum*, the silver patina beneath. Or you can enjoy spotting who's currently in and who's out of the Literary Corner; or the amusingly self-conscious (im)posture of an obelisk – three-sided and somehow unconvincing as either serious or durable (and actually it isn't either: it was salvaged and carried off from a theatrical stage set).

So, in the end, who does live here? Well, a certain Tristram Shandy (gent) would be my nomination, and he shoving Uncle Toby along the paths in a rickety old bath chair, the pair of them happily losing themselves and the cares of the world in the fastnesses of the wood – people with an eighteenth-century dignity, of course, but with a twenty-first-century need to laugh and laugh again despite everything. And as it happens, Laurence Sterne (gent), their creator and the author of *The Life and Opinions of Tristram Shandy* (1761), was born and brought up only a few miles down the road in Clonmel, when the paint was still wet on the house at Kilmokea.

Or we could just settle for the plants themselves – the rudely flourishing, astonishingly various plants – as the rightful and proper occupants. The plants … and the swallows fretting the summer air, the dragonflies revising the laws of gravity and of what should be aeronautically possible, and the flocks of humble hedge sparrows, all too rare now elsewhere, but chattering volubly and successfully to set the world to rights. At Kilmokea.

Postscript (2015): the *Crinodendron patagua* has gone, replaced by a glass and plastic tearoom. Let's hope that – in contrition – they will plant another somewhere else in the garden.

Mount Stewart

COUNTY DOWN

Cyprus, Eritrea, Palestine, Catalonia, Cashmere, the Basque Country – all famously and sometimes bloodily contested territories. So is Ulster (or Northern Ireland, or the North of Ireland, or the Occupied Territories of the Six Counties, or …). Sometimes, and until fairly recently, the heat of passions and burning buildings, the rattle of gunfire and rhetoric, is such that you'd seek out the safety and quietness of a garden to get away from it.

There are several fine gardens in the Six Counties. Soil, climate and material prosperity have served well both plants and gardens, and then the maintenance of them. History, however – the visible surface tensions and invisible fault lines beneath that surface – is more ambivalent.

Mount Stewart, fifteen miles south of Belfast, lies quite snugly on the eastern shore of Strangford Lough. There are a good many people who rank it as one of the finest gardens in the British Isles (British in the political sense, and then in the larger geographical sense which includes, willy-nilly, the whole island of Ireland as well as mainland Britain). Some claim it as the finest of them all. For my part, I wouldn't go that far. Contested territory.

Curiously enough, it is more or less contemporary with Sissinghurst, the place that most people would say epitomises, along with Hidcote, the English garden. Edith, Lady Londonderry, embarked on her garden in 1921. The Nicholsons, Harold and Vita, after a trial run at garden-making in their first home, Long Barn, got to work at Sissinghurst in 1930. All three gardens – Mount Stewart, Sissinghurst and Hidcote – owe their origins and characters to the contested territories of peace of mind within the lives and experience of their makers. In the case of Mount Stewart, it is only occasionally that the character of the garden betrays very much about its maker and her life until, that is, her death: the garden, and her gift of it to the nation, were – in the end – a gesture of contrition, perhaps even of expiation.

Mount Stewart covers about eighty acres, some intensively cultivated, quite a lot lightly gardened as a sort of woodland Arcadia. Most of the garden faces south, none of the garden is more than (say) a quarter of a mile away from the Lough. Strangford Lough is itself a fine view. The Lough and the panorama behind it looking south to the Mourne Mountains is very fine indeed, but nowhere at all is any of that visible from Edith Londonderry's garden. Even given that shelter beds of trees were and still are necessary, it is an extraordinary omission – some might say oversight, some might even say fault – but there it is. The small, enclosed *hortus conclusus* of the monastic or college garden is one thing, but if ever there were a big, world-in-miniature-sized garden from which the world outside is actually excluded, it is this. Exclusivity is an age-old badge of the aristocracy, but they usually like hoi polloi to catch a glimpse or two of what they are excluded from. Not here. It's as if there were something to hide. This is not just a place that turns its back on, offers respite from, perhaps even hides from a hostile world outside – specifically in this instance, the contested territorial struggles of Ireland's northern tribal factions. Lots of gardens do that, though not usually upon such a violent world-outside as Northern Ireland turned out to be in the seventies and eighties. Not just a place turning its back on topography, locality, history, context, etc., but a place which represents a contested territory of its own – not on the ground, but in the mind.

First to be made at Mount Stewart was the very large, very formal sunken garden. Jekyll had a hand in it. Originally it was themed blue. Now it has orange-flaming azaleas in spring, but still in summer it is more or less blue – delphinium blue, aconitum blue, echinops, solanum, ceanothus blue. There are whites and yellow, oranges and

creams too: white phlox, yellow and cream day lilies, all revolving around blue as if it were the tonic of a piece of music whither they will eventually return – lavender, campanulas, that charming rare plant *Jovellana violacea* – rare and difficult for most of us but effortless at Mount Stewart.

This sunken garden is terraced around its perimeter on three sides with a pergola walk. The very fine stonework of the pillars suggests the influence of Lutyens, a garden of golden Edwardian afternoons with the day of reckoning indefinitely postponed. You inhale nostalgia everywhere. In this instance it is rather like sequences of Strauss waltzes at a ball in Vienna on the eve (but you'd never know it) of the First World War. At a simple, not too serious level, nostalgia is not necessarily a bad thing. But at the deepest, most atavistic level – the recovery of private and collective Edens – it is probably at the very heart of what a garden – this garden, any garden – really means.

There were no lazy longueurs, however, about the building and planting here, in the earliest of Mount Stewart's new gardens. It was up and running by 1923, a rapid evolution over only two years or so. That was thanks, first, to a team of labourers and gardeners. Originally there were twenty or so of them, then forty, then sixty. Edith Londonderry didn't stint; she didn't have to. Her husband's vast wealth, deriving from coal mines and influence, saw to that. The family had four other houses besides, all in mainland Britain, the grandest of them, Londonderry House no less, in London's Park Lane. Their style there was proverbially lavish and the establishment of servants generally in the region of forty to fifty indoors (and never mind the gardeners, chauffeurs, etc., outside). England was strapped for cash after the First World War, still more so was Northern Ireland, but the Londonderrys generally retained at Mount Stewart something like thirty-five servants.

The tree and shrub planting in the Lily Wood, along the drive, and on the slopes around the lake, did not begin in earnest until the late 1920s. Oddly enough, the rationale of employment in the garden rather reflected the patterns of one hundred years earlier in Ireland as a whole. In the 1830s and 1840s, humane landlords tried to mitigate the hardships of the struggling poor by creating employment with Famine Works. In the 1920s and 1930s the beneficiaries were, first, demobbed soldiers from the Great War and then, later, those who had lost their livelihoods in the Depression. And – not entirely coincidentally – one of the earlier Londonderrys, the 3rd Marquess, had been particularly active in his efforts to relieve local hardship almost one hundred years earlier.

The sunken garden itself, the terraces and the pergolas, are framed by a hedge of Leyland cypress clipped smoothly – a local plant, bred across the lough at Castlewellan – and used to excellent effect here because it is controlled. If every Leyland hedge were grown like this one the plant would never have gained its evil reputation ... but to achieve that perfect control you need twenty, forty, sixty gardeners!

All the formal gardens were begun and essentially completed in the two decades, 1920–40. Some of the men responsible for this were immensely skilled. The mason, elderly Joe Girvan, for example, and the concrete master, Thomas Beattie – he cast all the balustrades and almost all the statuary. The head gardener then was a man called Thomas Bolas. He served here for thirty years. Often he must have been asked to do the impossible, to situate reputedly tender plants outside – lapageria, banksian roses, acacias, rhododendron arboretum species – and often he proved that it could be done, at least in the benign context of Mount Stewart's microclimate.

There are five formal, set-piece gardens within the greater garden. The sunken garden is the earliest, arguably the most impressive, but not the largest. That distinction goes to the Italian Garden. The Londonderrys themselves, and all their visitors too – royalty sometimes, plenty of the powerful and rich, sometimes the interesting, if Edith had her way – reached the house by way of grand gates and a drive. That took them to the main (front) door, the north front, but visitors now arrive via the car park and the ticket booth to the east of the house and garden. Particularly after her husband's death in 1949 and during the ten remaining years of her life, Edith Londonderry occasionally opened the gardens to the public. In a sense, that simple-seeming fact is the key to understanding not the origins of the gardens, but the significance of them in 1955 when she willed them to the National Trust – the significance then and, indeed, their abiding meaning now. But that is to anticipate. As it happens, entering the estate as you must now, through the back door, does afford a glimpse of a little Gothic gatehouse, a minor gem of Irish dolls-houserie, which grander visitors would never have seen. That is good, but coming in this way also skews perception of the place in general and of the garden(s) in particular, which are laid out along the south and the west of the house: you are delivered straight into them; you lose the intended preface and prepared approach – along the drive, through the house, out on to the terrace. You lose the intended and conventional hierarchy of house and garden.

Be that as it may, the first of the five gardens you will encounter now is the most recent. It is called the Mairi Garden because, so the story goes, Edith (no, not Edith, but Edith's maid!) would put out the pram of her youngest daughter, Mary (Mairi), there so that she could doze in the sun and benefit from the fresh air. The colours here are simple – mainly white and blue, nursery colours really – and plants are bedded into a very large pattern which follows the shape of a 'Tudor Rose', possibly a tellingly English thing to do. It doesn't work though (because unless you are a bird you cannot see it), but it hardly matters. Scent makes up for absent pattern and absent concept – roses in summer, the rhododendrons in spring, and eucalyptus all the year round pretty well drench the place, especially because the scent is trapped by enclosing hedges and trees. If this were indeed a children's garden, they would feel safe here. But it is piece of adult whimsy really – the 'silver bells' of the nursery rhyme are agapanthus, campanulas and galtonias, and, if you still haven't cottoned on, there are 'seashells' embedded into the paths. A bit of adult whimsy, and it only just gets away with it.

There have been several false starts in this, the youngest garden. The blue and white nursery theme seems to have been the original idea but latterly others have been laid on top of it, like Graham Stuart Thomas' attempt to make roses an important element of Mount Stewart. Mercifully there are no (remotely likeable) blue roses, here or anywhere else, but the white ones have crept in alright, though culturally (in both senses of the word) it has been a struggle. There was a new wave of planting (in 2012), slightly suggestive of the Orient and strongly echoing the (then) current Irish vogue for plants which belong to the araliaceae – not the best plants for a nursery garden as it happens, given their tendency to throw out thorns, but there we are. *Schefflera fantsipanensis* (what a wonderful name! It's more or less a contraction of its place of origin almost on the Chinese border of North Vietnam: Fan Si Pan Mountain) is one of these new plants and another of the many rare and exotic things here and elsewhere through the entire garden which impress specialists, tickle the curiosity of the ordinary visitor and delight anyway because they are usually beautiful as well as curious. These aralia-relatives apart, there is also a promising new magnolia of Vietnamese provenance. Probably the best tree is that old stalwart of Irish gardens, a hoheria, flouncing white like a summer frock, scented, airy, its leaves slender and slightly glossy.

Your direction now will be westwards into the adjacent Italian Garden, but don't hurry. Beneath the balustrade marking out the boundary with the Spanish Garden is a quiet row of memorials to pets – there is *Mouse: border terrier. d.1967*; then *Tuppy: miniature dachshund. 1956–1973* and *Macky: cockatoo. May 31st 1996*; then *Edward: macao. d. Nov. 5 1987*. Pet cemeteries are not uncommon in Irish gardens, but this seems less a burial ground than a roll of honour and, unlike some, it is discreet, and rather touching.

Look back and towards the house. On your right is another terrace there, and it is well worth the looking. Walk along it and you will come face to face with some of the strangest, most amusing, most intriguing bits of sculpture or garden furnishings anywhere in Ireland, and that in an island already quite generously endowed with such things. This is the Dodo Terrace. Its centrepiece is a stone ark, a really characterful little *Titanic* with a tubby, carvel-built hull and a hopelessly unwieldy house above – a cross between a tall-doored giraffe house and a round-towered medieval chapel. Water lurks beneath the ark's pedestal, spewed out of the carious gob of a goggle-eyed frog. It's grotesque and funny and really very interesting, and it sets the tone for the group of sculptures around it. They are animals, or grotesques of animals, always the eyes too large and watchful, and their distended mouths on the brink of laughter. They have names, or rather they are caricatures of the names given to various members of an invitation-only club that Lady Londonderry founded and fostered. Under her auspices, high-society people and politicos mixed with the intelligentsia. They all had club names, generally silly animal versions of their real names – Beatrix Potter meets Tenniel's *Alice*. Chamberlain was 'Neville the Devil', Baldwin was 'Bruin the Bear', Hazel Lavery (the most recognisable woman in the Republic because she was the Erin on the new banknotes there) is 'Hazel the Hen'. Churchill was 'Winston the Warlock'. Edith Londonderry herself was 'Circe the Sorceress', and it was indeed through her powers of enchantment that she assembled and presided over this motley crew. Apparently they 'all scratched, pinched or bit each other jocularly or argued fiercely together', but all answered to their Ark Club names when called.

John Buchan's wife thought it was 'silly and vulgar', but that is probably to miss the point (or perhaps it was just that she hadn't been invited to join). Edith Londonderry was in pursuit of pleasure – that was the role she was born for, the lifestyle she had married into, and something she could very easily afford – but something else was going on, over and above that, too. The membership was exclusive but very clearly not tribal. She never disguised or masked what her caste was, what tribe she belonged to – titled, Tory, tax-exempt and effortlessly patrician – but the group of people she gathered around her were Liberals as well as Tories, there were intellectuals, actors, writers, painters. They were not drawn by any means exclusively from the ranks of the moneyed, the influential or the blue-blooded – the cream of society who were on the whole, as Samuel Beckett so memorably and unfairly put it – like cream indeed – just 'rich and thick'. Nor were they all Anglo-Irish or British, even when they met in London. In the air at these meetings were probably most of the prevailing smells of that time and of those elevated classes: money, anti-Semitism, the demonising of Bolsheviks, the possibility of war in far-off places such as the Balkans, and so on – but Bernard Shaw was quite a frequent attender and he was no reactionary, still less so was Sean O'Casey, the playwright. He was publically Marxist, conscientiously under-dressed and much given to plain speaking, but Lady Londonderry didn't cut him. On the contrary, in 1935 she underwrote his American Tour. In 1928, he had given her a copy of *The Silver Tassie* – the play which was famously too strong even for Yeats at the Abbey Theatre and the cause of their bitter falling-out – and inscribed it 'With warm regards and sincere wishes'.

Most interesting of all about the inmates of this zoo was the way in which, far from endorsing class and tribe, they transcended them, and above all they rose above the tribalisms of deeply entrenched Irish loyalties. Her father-in-law, the sixth Marquess, had fought, lobbied and machinated tooth and nail to obstruct any form of Irish Home Rule. Indeed, Churchill recorded in his diary that, in his opinion, the methods of the Ulster Unionist Council (of which this Londonderry was the Chairman) amounted to 'treasonable conspiracy'. History largely confirms that opinion. Edith's husband, Charlie, the seventh Marquess, while having eventually to accept the partition of Ireland and the secession of the Republic, broadly shared his father's views – the views and prejudices, indeed, of his class and caste: 'The Southern Irish can be very charming but they certainly are an inconsequent race – in fact, very like children and when given too much latitude, they get out of hand.' And yet his wife was entertaining Irish nationalists and international socialists.

Silly and vulgar the Ark Club may have been, but this Dodo Terrace, with its sculptural representations of some of the members, is not. The spirit of Bomarzo's strange figures hangs over it but none of Bomarzo's menace. It is more than possible that one of the models for the terrace was indeed the *Sacro Bosco* at Bomarzo: Edith Londonderry was given to quite promiscuous borrowings from other gardens, other traditions (and sometimes they don't really come off. For example, the white stag up behind the lake: startling the first time you see it, but then – like a piece of twice-visited conceptual sculpture – obvious and spent. And anyway, it was lifted from Wordsworth's *The White Doe of Rylstone*.)

But here, on the Dodo Terrace, the flavour convinces. Borrowed or not, mere epigones or not – and as a group, the figures are remarkably stylistically consistent – the impression is of lightly modernist gargoyles, grotesques, Swiftian inversions (Horses, and Madmen and Midgets – Houyhnhnms, Laputians, Lilliputians, call them what you will – Rule Okay!), and of whackiness – a certain distillation of a certain kind of Irishness in fact, not least because several of these elongated, etiolated, bloated, grimacing forms are uncannily reminiscent of figures and animals – similarly stretched, compressed, toothy or prehensile – in the margins and on the great carpet pages of *The Book of Kells*. As pure forms – and never mind their facial features – several are really beautiful: minimalist, proto-modern – particularly the spoon-billed waddling dinosaur-like creature with its know-all, penetrating eyes.

Who designed these things? I wish someone would tell us, but in the absence of evidence to the contrary we can only suppose that designer and maker were one and the same, Thomas Beattie. It was he who cast them (they aren't sculpted but cast in very convincing stone-like reinforced concrete). Was he another of that race of inspired but strange Irish geniuses? Harry Clarke in glass, Myles na Gopaleen (and Swift too) in words, Jack Yeats in paint, and now Thomas Beattie?

It's appropriate that this terrace is on the brink of botanical anarchy as well. But in the thick of the riot there are some very fine (very rare) rhododendrons, a *Magnolia* x *watsonii* and an outrageously arborescent *Melianthus major* which wants to take it over. Quite right too.

The Dodo Terrace overlooks the Italian Garden, but it isn't vantage enough to see the fountain and these two large parterres at anything like their best. From the south terrace proper in front of the house you would see more (but visitors are not allowed on to it). Probably only from the upper windows of the house could you see it to real advantage – and the need for that elevated viewing point is to be expected with any parterre, which is why Elizabethan gardens had mounts or belvederes. As it is, at Mount Stewart you see this garden level on the ground, and it doesn't really work. Even when you have primed yourself by studying the aerial views in all the guidebooks, you cannot really thread it together on the ground. What you see – that is to say, the defining character of the garden as it is perceived – is flat and uneventful, the shapes of the beds only to be guessed at. They are edged with clipped purple-leaved berberis. Box was *herba-non-grata* apparently. Some clarity and shape and formality are lost; some variety is won.

There are camellias, callistemons, abutilons and other marginally hardy plants in abundance, and they are clearly happy. A little less so are the roses. They are mostly locally bred, McGredy's or Dicksons: the over-egged custard colour of 'Whiskey Mac' (but at least it is spelt right, in the Irish way), the cheerfully plebeian 'Bright Smiles', then 'Baby Bio' whose flower is only marginally less horrid than its name, and the over-exposed 'Iceberg' (but it's local, you see … Harland and Wolff, icebergs, the *Titanic*). One – 'Lady Edith Helen' – is covertly more than usually at home; its name is a version of Edith, Marchioness of Londonderry. Herbaceous planting is lavish but rather pedestrian – clots of phloxes everywhere, *Crocosmia* 'Lucifer' chiming against them like the primary colours in a child's first paintbox. This planting is not really effective, but not altogether through a fault of its own. It is just that seen horizontally, as the visitor must see it, the geometry, the stitching, of the parterres is largely invisible, and that's a serious shortcoming. A carpet with bits of the pile coming loose is what you see, as if you were a very lowly dog with no overview of his world available because he is so short. Less serious, but still disappointing, is the evidence of undigested, unassimilated borrowing and second-hand designing. The herms are straight out of the Villa Farnese, the paired columns from the Boboli Gardens, the profiles of the balustrades from those at the Villa Gamberaia, etc. To call this eclectic is to let it off lightly. A comparison with the other Italian garden in Ireland – at Ilnacullin, in Bantry Bay – would not be, in any respect, to Mount Stewart's advantage. And then there are the fountains: even by modest English or Irish standards the *jeux d'eau* are feeble; by Italian standards they are pathetic. There is, however, one small – perhaps serendipitous – element of this

Italian garden which almost redeems the other shortcomings. Down the steps from the house terrace are spills of self-sown erigerons. They look unflinchingly, almost challengingly, unofficial. The cognoscenti will know that precisely this effect (in precisely such a situation) was a classic signature of many a Lutyens/Jekyll garden. It's as if while Miss Willmott famously scattered her eryngium seeds when no one was looking in the gardens she visited and which she deemed in need of improvement, the ghost of Miss Jekyll has been doing something of the same here. A charming effect.

Down another fight of steps and you are in the Spanish Garden. This too is somewhat gestural as far as its theme goes – some majolica tiles here, oil jars there – but the place certainly has a presence. It is enclosed by very tall, slim (Leyland) cypress hedges trained and cut into continuous arcades of tall, narrow arches, with only a narrow continuous string of growth along the top. Like a cloister? Very much like those distinctive arcaded, neoclassical facades that Mussolini's architects affected – clean, quite severe, visually so rhythmic, like human-scaled columbaria really. It's a shame about the politics, but some of those buildings were really rather beautiful, and so is this. Helen Dillon took Mount Stewart's arched hedges as the model for a much-shortened arcade in her own, Dublin (Ranelagh) garden. They work (worked) very well in both places.

There are several informal gardens at Mount Stewart. The Lily Wood (cardiocrinums and lily of the valley are the eponymous lilies here) is lovely. The area is not great but the density of small trees with tremendous beauty and character is remarkable – rhododendrons especially, but sympathetically blended with various pieris, eucryphia, a lovely old stooped *Myrtus luma* swaddled in a rampageous *Actinidia chinensis*. There are meconopsis, blue and yellow, and adventitious foxgloves everywhere – those fifth columnists of the natural and the Robinsonian – then clematis, given their heads and allowed to romp. Here, perhaps more than anywhere else in the entire garden, either the absence of plant labels or labels so faded that they are hard to read is really exasperating, but the plants themselves are wonderful and so is the atmosphere of this Lily Wood.

The gate, out of the Italian Garden and into the Lily Wood, the Vine Gate, is very beautiful indeed – great petals of gold leaf shining out of the wriggling grilles of black wrought iron.

The Lily Wood blurs into the Memorial Garden (but you wouldn't really know that, so blurred is the character of the latter anyway), and then, if you drift first to your right and then veer as if going back to the house, you will find yourself in the last of Mount Stewart's formal gardens, the Shamrock Garden. The hedges, yew this time, enclose a three-lobed space, a shamrock leaf – or it *would* be if you were above and looking down. And there are further emblems of Ireland. High up in the centre is a topiary harp (but the 'strings' are more or less broken and it looks a bit shabby) and, set out in begonias (or something else red-leaved when begonias are out of season) is a large hand, rather like the old Ind Coope logo but with the fingers more splayed. It is the Red Hand of Ulster.

Ulster is a minefield for the unwary or the uninitiated. Everywhere there are innocent-seeming words and symbols which actually have loaded meanings and coded tribal affiliations attached to them, but the Red Hand, an ancient badge – originally of the O'Neill clan from whom the Londonderrys claimed descent – has managed to evade a lot of the stain of sectarianism. Event at the height of the Troubles in Ulster, it was never a target for discontent. In a Northern Ireland context it is uncontaminated, but not necessarily so in Ireland at large. In fact, it is not so value-free as it seems (or, given the super-sensitive antennae of Northern Irelanders, as perhaps it *should* be). If it symbolises simply the province of Ulster – one of the four great 'fields' of ancient Ireland itself – then it would be natural to look for corresponding symbols, occasionally at least, when you are in Munster, or Leinster, or Connaught. But you won't find them. Only Ulster brandishes its badge ... because only Ulster feels that it needs to make a point? Only in Ulster is there a felt need to wave a sort of territorial flag – albeit non-sectarian, something to mark out its territory, to stake its claim. *The Red Hand of Ulster*, interestingly enough, is the title of quite an important novel. It was written in 1912 – not yet at the height of the resistance in Ulster to Home Rule, but astonishingly prescient of what was going to happen – by George Birmingham (real name, Canon James Owen Hannay). In it, Edith Londonderry is easily recognisable as Lady Moyne, and her hopeless husband is, of course Lord Moyne – a curious locution suggestive of *Boyne* (the battle of that name, fought on 1 July 1690, that settled protestant hegemony in Ireland for the next two hundred and thirty-one years) but also an anagram of *money*. Ah ...!

When Northern Ireland is peaceful, no one notices these things – verbal badges, quiescent symbols and tokens – still less their encrypted tribal meanings, but when tension in the streets begins to fester and riot squads are again a presence in the towns, the smell of burning in the air, the thin skin of mutual tolerance broken again (as indeed it was at the time of writing and, ironically, precisely because of a symbol: the Union flag, by decree of the fragile government, allowed henceforth to fly on public buildings only occasionally) then you have to wonder if a garden is an appropriate place for a quasi-political symbol.

Even with these large formal gardens, most of Mount Stewart is lake and woodland, and very beautiful it is too. The lake, dug between 1846 and 1848 as a Famine Work, looks wonderfully natural. Swans, ducks and wading birds think so too. Around the shores are slopes planted with fabulous things – once again rhododendrons above all, but lovely deciduous beeches and birches, and then magnolias, clethras, a *Sophora tetraptera*, quite a lot of different sorbus (a favourite tree of Irish woodlands), tree ferns, groves of eucalyptus (sieving the wind symphonically, and really thrilling in a gale!), maples by the score, an old, arching-over cork oak whose sunny side is host to small ferns and lichens. Close to the water are royal ferns up to six feet high, thickets of bamboo, cathedrals of gunnera, and in the leafy vaults beneath them the shadows of strange gods.

Looking across the lake from the south side can be seen one of the world's masterpieces of garden theatre. Almost but not quite hidden in the trees, halfway up the slope, is the cone of a pointed tower, then another, and then a taller gatehouse, square and windowed. A sleeping beauty of a pocket-sized castle? It certainly looks magical and it casts a terrific spell. Even more so when you learn its name, and the meaning of its name: Tír na nÓg, the Land of the Ever Young.

In Irish mythology, Tír na nÓg is whither the souls of the dead are borne away, a place of carefree afterlife, a sort of secular heaven, open to all. There Oisín – the Irish Orpheus, I suppose: poet, musician, almost-god – presides over a world of forgetful joys. Jack Yeats, in his 1936 picture *In Tír na nÓg*, painted later than this place in Mount Stewart but completely synchronous in terms of spirit, has a golden-haired boy drowsily sprawled on a green-golden turf. He has an open book in his hands. It is an illustrated book but, having stimulated his imagination, it doesn't hold it. He gazes back over his shoulder towards ethereal figures standing on the shore of the world behind him. A boat approaches … warm light bathes the painting but there is a pool of shade to his left. It is cast by such a tree as never grew on ordinary soil. This tree's branches hang almost over the boy like a willow or a silvery, weeping pear, except that the leaves are red like a poinsettia, gold like ripe plums, ruby like arterial blood.

Latterly, Tír na nÓg became also the name of a chain of shops all over Ireland that specialise in children's clothes – a clever appropriation of a gentle, lovely word and its seductive meaning.

This walled, turreted enclosure at Mount Stewart is actually the Londonderry burial ground. It was built in 1926–27. Close up (you can't get in, but you can peep through a bit) it's a little gem – Art Deco stained glass in the windows, superb Arts and Crafts ironwork hinges on the door – and not gloomy at all. The planting in the woodland around it is once again bountiful. But best of all is that view of the embowered towers from across the lake. Arthur's last journey across his lake to Avalon – even when Tennyson tells the story – pales beside this. There is nothing like it.

Or is there? Bits of Scottish castles? Bits of Ludwig II's Gothic fantasies in Bavaria? The great gatehouse to St Nicholas' Church in not-far-away Carrickfergus has similar features, a similar profile.

Actually, there *is* another place very much more like it still – the turrets, the way they are half-hidden by trees, the fairy-tale ambience. It's at Castell Coch in the Taff Valley, Glamorgan, and the similarity is striking (though the Welsh building has chimneys). Castell Coch was built first. It was completed to a commission by John, third Marquess of Bute, in 1879. The architect was William Burges, a man not by any means unknown in Ireland, having designed and built St Fin Barre's Cathedral in Cork (1865), one of the most visible, most prestigious building projects in mid-century Ireland. Burges built nothing in Northern Ireland, and only St Fin Barre's in the south, but he was well known in mainland Britain, not least for Castell Coch and, I imagine, it would have been eastwards to Wales and England rather than south into the Republic that the Londonderrys would have looked for inspiration. In any case – whether it was Cork or Castell Coch that first caught their eye – it seems very likely indeed, on grounds of imitative style, that Burges (posthumously and without being credited) provided the model for the Mount Stewart mausoleum. Whether or not Mount Stewart's Tír na nÓg was built with Castell Coch in mind I don't know for certain, but the idea – the notion of a Land of the Blest, an Irish (sylvan) Elysian Fields – is all its own and it's marvellous. There is room enough in the world for two such beautiful places, but only for one Tír na nÓg: it's there, in the head, really.

Mount Stewart is famous for its rich tree plantings, for its scale, for its tidiness and staking and pruning and tying up, and for the generosity of the bedding out, for design elements such as the arcades in the Spanish Garden, the control of the formal and the looseness of the informal, the risks successfully taken with marginally hardy plants – all in all, the classiness of the place. Nevertheless, it is probably not a garden of the first rank. It is not homogeneous – not so much a unitary garden as a skein of separate gardens, none of which relates all that much to the others, individually all of them too large to be constituent 'rooms' (parts) of a whole. Having said that, however, if Tír na nÓg is something out of a fairy tale or a vision of bliss, even more perfect still is the building a mile away at the other end of the garden, The Temple of the Four Winds. It does not relate to, has really nothing to do with, the rest of the garden, but – given that the whole place is characterised by a cultural eclecticism, a cultural syncretism, and not by a perceptible, unifying coherence – that is neither here nor there.

This octagonal belvedere cum stand-alone dining room – probably the most precious and perfect element of the garden – was here long before Lady Londonderry made the rest of the garden as we know it now. Architecturally, it is in a different league altogether from the (pretty dull) house, which is later anyway and, in terms of the garden, the temple plays no real part. It is not really an eye-catcher, not a component of an arcadian vision, not a host to climbing roses (or, as some members of the family wanted it, a mausoleum for deceased grandees). It was commissioned by Robert Stewart, the son of the original Alexander Stewart who bought the estate in 1744 Mount Pleasant it was called then – and he renamed it Mount Stewart – but the original Irish name had been Templecrone. How potent, in terms of dominion, is the naming of a place. To name is to claim. To rename is doubly so.

The architect of the Temple of the Four Winds was the Scotsman, James Stuart – 'Athenian' Stuart, he was called, because in 1762 he published a hugely influential survey, the first comprehensively accurate one, of all the buildings remaining from Greek antiquity. Lavishly illustrated, it was very widely admired. Stuart, apparently a famously relaxed man, designed only a small number of buildings, but they are all of outstanding quality, and this is the only one in Ireland.

Built in the 1780s, it is closely but not slavishly modelled on the Tower of Andronicus Cyrrhestes, a clocktower (water clock) and sundial, presiding over the (then) new Caesarian Agora in Athens – a late classical building, and a beauty. Beautiful proportions, beautifully blent elements of dignity and modesty, something of grace and something of gratuitous generosity.

The Irish edition of this ancient building has windows in walls that in the original were blind, a kitchen in its fundament and a panoramic view over Strangford Lough. The workmanship is second to none – floors in marquetry, gorgeous plaster ceilings, perfect masonry. Oxford's Radcliffe Camera is another, but less distilled, version of the same original. And there's a temple by Stuart's co-traveller in Greece, Nicholas Revett, at High Wycombe, but it barely approaches this.

Ireland has one of the richest collections of garden buildings and follies in the world. They range from the well-nigh sublime Mussenden Temple overlooking the sea at Downhill, County Derry, to the dotty, such as the beehive pyramid at Clogheen, County Tipperary, which is called and indeed *is* Grubb's Grave (one Samuel Grubb is buried inside, upright on his own instructions). Or there's the ziggurat-cum-helter-skelter pigeon houses – consorts of the very worthily named Wonderful Barn – near Leixlip in County Kildare. Together and separately they reflect aspects of the Irish Mind: a love of the craic, a nostalgia for lost enchantments, the knack of self-deprecation and the giving-in to the temptation to self-aggrandisement, all blended with a natural kinship towards the absurd, and a tendency to perfection. The Temple of the Four Winds reflects all of these, and a bit more still when something of its latter history comes into focus. It was built originally as a pleasure house (for social occasions such as small banquets), but in 1822 there was a strong swell of opinion in favour of using it as a mausoleum in which would lie the mortal remains of Robert Stewart, second Marquess of Londonderry, better known to posterity as Lord Castlereagh. The idea to rededicate the temple not to pleasure but to obsequies was resisted, thank goodness, by his brother, the third Marquess, of whom more in due course.

But the ghost of Castlereagh hovers over Mount Stewart even though his bones are elsewhere. In Ireland, only Oliver Cromwell is more execrated than he. As Chief Secretary for Ireland, Castlereagh oversaw the passing of the Act of Union between Great Britain and Ireland in 1800, the dissolution of the Irish Parliament, the final, definitive moment of England's conquest of Ireland. Never mind that he also resigned in due course because George III would not countenance Catholic Emancipation in any shape or form whatsoever (even though it was the carrot that was dangled to sweeten for Catholics the pill of the loss of sovereignty), in Ireland Castlereagh was perceived as a villain of the first order, perfidious Albion personified, but worse even than that because he was, himself, Irish not English. In fact a complex, introverted man, troubled and driven by demons of his own, he never stayed for long at Mount Stewart. He had never really warmed to the place but, even if he had, he would have been too busy. He had been overseer of Britain's continental wars. He was architect of post-Napoleonic Europe through his role as puppetmaster of the Congress of Vienna. He should have been hailed as a statesman in England even if he were vilified in Ireland, but he wasn't. He was seen as author and mastermind of the years of repression that characterised Britain (and Ireland) in the second decade of the nineteenth century with their sometimes draconian restraints upon civil liberties enforced by a narrow-minded king and the government of the Prime Minister, Lord Liverpool, of which Castlereaagh was simply one – albeit very senior – member. These were years of censorship, surveillance, of the suspension of habeas corpus, imprisonment of pressmen and of free thinkers, the Peterloo Massacre, the Gagging Acts, years in which fear of the bogey of Republicanism bred its own kind of reign of terror in the very country that had waged war partly to expunge that very thing in France. Castlereagh certainly did have a hand in it – he was not called the Irish Robespierre for nothing – but he probably didn't entirely deserve Shelley's famous 1819 damnation of him in his angry young-man's poem *The Masque of Anarchy*, written in response to the Peterloo Massacre:

I met murder on the way –
He had a mask like Castlereagh –
Very smooth he looked, yet grim;
Seven blood-hounds followed him:

All were fat; and well they might
Be in admirable plight,
For one by one, and two by two,
He tossed them human hearts to chew
Which from his wide cloak he drew.

Nonetheless, that was how most people saw him. At his death, his funeral cortege was cheered, his coffin hissed – and that was in England.

His father had systematically clambered up the stairs of social and political preferment leading eventually to ennoblement: first, in 1786, he became a Privy Councillor in Ireland; then, in 1789, Baron Londonderry; in 1795 he became Viscount Castlereagh; in 1796 Earl of Londonderry; and, finally, Marquess of Londonderry in 1816. Though this last – the apogee of his social ascent – was conferred on Robert Stewart (*père*), it was earned really by his son, the Londonderry whom we call simply Castlereagh, won by dint of his public offices first in Ireland then in England. He inherited the title for himself on the death of his father in 1821. In 1822, he committed suicide. He used a pen-knife to cut his own throat. He was fifty-three. In Irish eyes, Castlereagh had sold his soul and his country for a mess of foreign pottage: eventually, a British peerage. In Irish eyes, Mount Stewart was tainted ground.

Nevertheless, his successor, the third Marquess, was, and was seen to be, a good fellow. Largely he kept out of politics but plunged instead into deeds. He was Wellington's aide de camp at Waterloo (and you wonder if, later or earlier, they discussed their common Irish origins). In the years of the Great Famine, this Londonderry did his bit, did it more than most: famine relief schemes, Famine Works (indeed the digging of the lake at Mount Stewart), leniency with rents, charity even. And perhaps in part – great or small, we don't know – it was the presiding dark ghost and reputation of his brother that drove him. Lawrence's portrait of him has this soldier raising a second-rate painter to almost first-rate stature ... and you wonder, you ponder: Why? Whatever the case, when this Londonderry died, his 'grateful tenants' built Scrabo Tower out of the same soft-coloured, hard-textured stone that the Temple of the Four Winds is built. Scrabo Tower (which unfortunately is ever-so similar in profile to the sinister towers drawn by David Hockney to illustrate his edition of the Grimms' fairy tale, *Rapunzel* – but that is coincidence only ... I think) can be seen clearly, punctuating the horizon, across the water from Mount Stewart's pleasure house/would-be mausoleum because, ironically, that is the only part of the garden (and no part at all of

Edith Londonderry's garden, because it is much older) from which you can see the world outside.

Looking back over the history of her Londonderry forebears, Edith, the seventh Marchioness, would have had to recognise a family's image that was tarnished, to say the least. The Irish are famous for their collective memory, its span and its depth, and in terms of history going back further than the first Robert Stewart – and bearing in mind that though he paid good money (£42,000) for the estates in 1744, they were originally 'planted', that is to say they were lands 'confiscated' – the euphemism current then for 'stolen' – the (Catholic) landlords or tenants or yeoman farmers dispossessed, and 'planters' (usually, in Ulster, Scottish Presbyterians, but elsewhere often just English bootleggers and adventurers) given the freehold. The family of the man Alexander Stewart bought the estates from would, almost certainly, originally have been 'planters'. Mount Stewart was tainted earth. In crude terms of virtue and head-counting, the family in the first three generations had racked up one (the first Marquess) who was described by the Reverend Steel Dickson, a neighbouring Presbyterian radical (a man who should have been after his own heart) as 'weakened by a toadish coldness, and haughty distance of deportment'; one (Castlereagh) who was seen as irredeemably vile; and only one (the third Marquess) who was perceived as a decent man. The fourth and fifth Marquesses kept their heads down, probably wisely. The sixth, Edith Londonderry's father-in-law, had hoped for the post of Viceroy of India but had to settle instead for the job of Lord Lieutenant of Ireland. His vice-regal court in Dublin, right from the outset, was not a success. The Lord Mayor and the entire corporation of the city refused to give him the customary, formal, official welcome. The Catholic population at large loathed him and expressed their feelings in public mockery. He was not trusted: his immense private wealth, deriving as it did from coal mining in County Durham, was seen as an indication of where his heart, as well as his business interests, really lay: not in Ireland at all, but over the sea in England.

Edward Carson was the charismatic, lawyerly brains behind the Ulster Unionist resistance to Home Rule but, in the London courts, he was also the (successful) barrister, defending the Marquess of Queensbury, by means of the vicious ad hominem attacks he made upon Oscar Wilde which so much characterised that trial and which the popular press so much enjoyed; then, through the murky, clandestine international weapons market, he was also one of the men who organised in April 1914 the gun-running into Larne from Germany of weapons to arm the resisters; and it was he who was lurking behind the Curragh Mutiny, the plot whereby British officers would pledge themselves to refuse to enforce the law should the Home Rule Bill be passed and implemented. A busy man, then, he was even credited with particular powers of meteorology: the expression 'Carson weather' – the rain that tended to dampen the UVF parades – entered alike the speech of damp militiamen and the over-heated journalists of the *Belfast News Letter*, the morning paper of choice for the Protestant minority. But from the outset, it was the sixth Marquess of Londonderry and James

Craig, later Lord Craigavon, who were the highest-profile figureheads in the Unionist fight to keep Ireland British or, failing that, to keep the six counties of Ulster British. Carson was initially the *éminence grise* behind the formation of the Ulster Volunteer Force, from 1913 the Protestant militia raised to resist Home Rule, but a lot of the money and even more of the networking came from this sixth Marquess. Latterly Carson shared with him the limelight of public leadership. The marquess, and his son, Edith's husband, both held high (para)military offices throughout the six counties (at the same time as the son held a commission in the Royal Horse Guards and the parliamentary seat at Westminster for the constituency of Maidstone in Kent). More locally, they assembled companies comprised of their tenants and estate workers and had them drilled in military manoeuvres at Mount Stewart. At its height, and measured throughout the province, this citizens' army numbered something like one hundred thousand men – abysmally led but quite well armed – and probably sufficient to have resisted the will of Westminster if that Home Rule Bill (which passed into law in 1914) were ever to be implemented. In the event, the Great War intervened. The Act was suspended for the duration. Britain needed compliant soldiers, not disaffected agitators. Conscription in Ireland to the British Army was very seriously considered and only narrowly thought better of. These men – the rank and file of the Ulster Volunteer Force – were essentially the same men who, by 1916, comprised the 36th (Ulster) Division of the British Army, fighting on the Ancre Salient in the Battle of the Somme – the same men who would suffer more than five thousand fatalities in the first two days of the battle: a blood sacrifice indeed to demonstrate to the Mother Country how unwavering was their loyalty to the Crown … and to require, if necessary, a reciprocation of the same once the war was over and the Home Rule Bill would be resurrected. These dead men were five thousand out of the total of something like fifty thousand Irishmen killed in the war, at least half of whom, we know, were Catholic (and therefore presumably Nationalist). There was no such intended, conscientious agenda of sacrifice for them. It was not these, but the sixteen men whom the British executed in the yard of Kilmainham Gaol in retaliation for the Easter Rising in the same year as the Somme who became indissolubly associated with a sacrifice of their blood for Ireland – in their case, an Ireland freed from British rule. The symmetry between the two – the men of the Ulster Division who died on the Somme and the men who declared Ireland's independence in O'Connell Street and then faced a firing squad – is appalling in its deadly precision. Even custody of the forms and imagery of loyalty – the semiotics of Irishness – became a contested territory.

Through Irish eyes, the Londonderrys were seen as partisan, un-Irish and self-interested. By the Ulster Unionists they were seen as pillars of support for a threatened noble cause, British Rule in Ireland. Contested territories; contested hearts and minds. This was the seedbed of the next chapter of Northern Irish history, slow to mature but deadly when it did, fifty years later: the bullets and bombs, assassinations and self-immolations of the Troubles. A complex of time and place where, as Edna O'Brien puts it, 'courage and criminality overlap', where, in the minds of the participants, those bigamist marriages of principle and bigotry, passion and deeply manured tribal loyalties, take place. A deadly place sooner or later and one in which it would never, easily, be possible to reconcile heart and mind, emotion and reason, what you deeply, irresistibly feel with what you know to be wise and right, because while murder is compelling it is not reasonable. Contested territory; contested heads and hearts.

Then, on the death of the sixth Marquess in 1915, came his son Charlie, husband of Edith, she who made the garden at Mount Stewart. This latest Lord Castlereagh – as he styled himself in his minority before his elevation finally to marquess – was neither wise nor clever, but imbued with that trait familiar in his caste: a sense of himself as having a natural right to govern. As it happened – and perhaps also in conformity to his patrician upbringing – he also took a relaxed attitude towards his own marriage vows. He was serially unfaithful to them and to his wife, which irked Edith no end. Qualified neither by talent nor experience, he was variously Northern Ireland Secretary for Education, Air Minister in the British Cabinet and Lord Privy Seal, until he was relieved of public office in 1935, found out and thrown out by his own mediocrity, because with the rise of Hitler, government was no longer the playground for those indulging in a hobby that it had used to be.

Then came the worst damage of all to the family's image. As a private man he had achieved little, but done little harm either. As a collegiate member of a cabinet he had enjoyed only a limited scope for getting things wrong but, having been dropped by Chamberlain, he embarked upon a very ill-judged mission of his own: to wine and dine, at his houses in England, Joachim von Ribbentrop, failed champagne sales-man, Nazi enthusiast and – at this juncture – German Ambassador to London (vividly caught by the novelist Kazuo Ishiguro in his novel *The Remains of the Day* – and also where his Lord Darlington is a thinly disguised portrait of this, the seventh Lord Londonderry). Simultaneously with this, Londonderry set about to write and pub-lish in 1938 a feeble, foolish book called *Ourselves and Germany*. Probably he saw himself as would-be saviour of his benighted, mis-guided country. Perhaps. And in the meantime, he sought to ingratiate himself with the Führer. He believed – sincerely perhaps – that this was the best way to prevent a second world war. Edith subscribed to the illusion too. When she met Hitler, she described him as 'a man with wonderful, far-seeing eyes. I felt I was in the presence of one truly great. He is simple, dignified, humble. He is a leader of men.' In the tradition of Edith's Ark (and remembering 'Danny Boy' too, of course), those critics of the Londonderrys who were in the know mischievously dubbed Ribbentrop the 'Londonderry Herr'.

First the original Robert Stewart, then Castlereagh, then the sixth Marquess (and Carson), and then this! In 1955, when Edith, since 1949 a widow, willed the garden and some of the house to the National Trust, it was of course a tax wheeze. The family had lost almost all its money (the nationalisation of the mines saw to that) but lost almost all of its credibility as well, its right to respect or even self-respect. To live with straitened circumstances is one thing; to live with shame is another. On the whole, she, a highly intelligent woman married to a fool, was 'guilty' by association only, but the sense of contamination must have been unavoidable. The only thing left – conceivably – was to try to go down in history as a great gardener ... and to hope, perhaps, that by redeeming her own image she might also mitigate that of her family at large? But before that could happen, she had to find a way to make amends. In the event – by giving the garden to the nation – she achieved at least something of both.

In some senses, on some level, Mount Stewart is an act of contrition. This beautiful place, originally conceived and then developed as a private toy, became in the end a gesture of atonement.

The Dillon Garden

DUBLIN

Dublin's Phoenix Park is the largest public space of any European city. So much space is there that though you might occasionally witness a crowd (as in 'a crowd of us went out to dinner') – for a race meeting, a hurling or a football match, for wedding photographs (it's a popular venue) or for the zoo – you'll never find it crowded. It isn't a garden as such, or very little of it is. It is a lightly wooded succession of open spaces – the Fifteen Acres, the White Field – and groves – the Wilderness, Fury Glen, Oldtown Wood – linked by roads, footpaths and rides, with the occasional bit of shrubbery and cultivated beds. The name seems straightforward enough (though the fire-fuelled phoenix is not necessarily a bird you'd associate straight away with cool, watery Ireland) but actually it isn't.

It probably comes from – is a bastardised English version of – the Irish *Fionn Uisge*, the Fair Water. But the spirit, if not the real name, of its far-off origins – a deer park, an outside larder – lingers on in the warily grazing herds of deer.

There are something like thirty other parks and public gardens within a three-mile radius of O'Connell Bridge. They range from the very large space of St Stephen's Green – but still much smaller than the Phoenix Park, it's an eighteenth-century Georgian square really (as is Merrion Square, close by), but larger, I should say, than any in London – to the almost tiny but charming Millennium Garden in Dame Street. And then, of course, there's the Glasnevin Botanical Garden, but that's of a different order altogether, both of magnitude and of character. As with any other city, no matter how good the planning, the planting, the horticulture (and the bedding-out in St Stephen's Green is annually stupendous: imaginative, lavish, immaculately maintained), the best of the municipal almost anywhere is just as likely to have been an accident as it is to have been planned. So it is with Dublin, or so it seems to me: the cathedral of gloom and green thoughtfulness formed by the plane trees in summer in Lower Baggot Street; the accident of light and water, shadow and swan on the Grand Canal by Huband Bridge; the sightlines on to the flower market in Grafton Street opening and closing, contracting and widening, as the crowds ebb and flow, the available colours ever shifting as if somewhere a vast kaleidoscope were being cranked by some invisible, insomniac functionary of Dublin Corporation.

If there are thirty public gardens in or close to the heart of Dublin, there is probably no greater number of significant private ones – that is, gardens worthy of the name. That might seem an impossibly mean estimate, but the same could be said, and equally accurately, of London or Paris, Berlin or New York. As a rule, you don't either expect or find good gardens in the heart of a city.

There was, however, really only one private garden in Dublin that you would have been foolish to have missed if you were there in late spring, summer or early autumn when it was open. There may have been one or two others of comparable quality (though I doubt it, and they were not open to the public anyway) but only this one had earned for itself the stature of a kind of landmark in Dublin and – even more interestingly – a kind of benchmark, here or anywhere, for what it is possible to mean by that curiously self-cancelling term 'a city garden'.

It is a contradiction in terms really, isn't it? City *and* garden? Conventionally, from Pliny onwards, the time-honoured locus of a garden is in the country. But, of course, it is not really that simple. The heart of the country garden lies in the way it mediates between itself and the larger landscape around it. It is a transitional zone between the more or less natural and the more or less artificially cultured and cultivated. And it derives a good deal of its *raison d'être* from a dialectic, a sort of visual conversation or debate or even argument with the larger landscape around it, literally and most conventionally in the form of borrowed views, but also suggestively and more subtly in the way, for example, its (artificial) straight lines may give way to (natural, unregulated) curves here and there, topiary and clipped hedges may modulate into (unclipped, shaggy) shrubbery, the scale of one specimen tree (set in a lawn, say) may prefigure the scale of the undisciplined, free-spirited trees out there in the larger landscape, or a mown sward in the garden may hint at a scaled-down version of the sheep-cropped pasture visible on a hillside a mile away. At its best, it is a rich succession of visual rhymes, as it were – some of them calculated, some of them accidental – between the cultivated garden and the free landscape.

But it follows – it surely must follow – that if this is true of the garden in the country, it cannot be true of the garden in the city. The city garden does not borrow the view; on the contrary, it generally strives to shut it out. The city garden is not a cultivated, mediated version of the natural world around it. It is the obverse of that world: a deliberate, conscientious rejection of it, a place whose *raison d'être* is not the presence but the absence of a surrounding context of the gratefully rural (or the ungratefully urban).

But then, on the other hand, there's the argument from necessity: gardens rightfully belong most where they are needed most. And that enormously favours the town garden over the country one, a privileging that would be true of city gardens in any country (and certainly not least in Ireland because – except for old, central Dublin and the smaller, old country towns – urban, industrial and suburban growth nationally has been pretty poor from the visual point of view. As a general rule, Irish towns – the bigger ones – are pretty bad places for the eye.) It is the rationale behind the whole ethos of the Garden City. But there is a special circumstance in the case of Ireland that makes it even more persuasive: so much of the countryside is so pleasant to behold, so suggestive of a garden, even in its raw state, that the need to garden there is slighter than ever. David Thomson, in his beautiful, elegiac book *Woodbrook*, chronicling life in 1930s rural Sligo, has this to say about the neighbourhood:

> many gardens were hedged by fuchsia bushes, beautifully red in flower, but no small flowers were to be seen, and between Carrick and Sligo I cannot remember even one house with roses, nasturtiums, marigolds, wallflowers or Michaelmas daisies about it.

(And you have to remember that those fuchsias – spectacular though they are – are not cultivated but wild.) His explanation is most interesting, but strange too, and not flattering to those inclined to imperial nostalgia: 'I have read that these paucities originated in the old colonial system. I think that is true of vegetables.'

The Irish famously had their 'potato gardens' of course and, fatefully, little else when it came to facing the Great Famine. (And did you know that until very recently the most popular potato to be grown in Ireland was a variety called British Queen? Some irony intended there, perhaps!) Thomson continues:

> But even the internationally educated Irish people ... had a gap in the visual sense peculiar to their country; it seemed as though their choice of pictures, distemper or wallpaper happened quite by chance. Perhaps the dearth of flowers in the gardens of poorer people was caused by a similar blindness. Most of the simpler seeds and seedlings could be bought in Carrick or Boyle, but were bought only by the Anglo-Irish and their gardeners.

I believe he is right. That certainly is one of the reasons: a legacy of British rule and the residue of an aesthetic originating in division between masters and servants; and, ninety years after the writing of that book (almost one hundred years after the British were finally expelled and Ireland achieved its independence), it is fascinating – perhaps depressing too – to find Helen Dillon remarking in one of her columns for the *Irish Sunday Tribune* that 'the backbone of Irish horticulture consists of Protestants alone' – that is to say, the residual Anglo-Irish. I hasten to say that the context was light-hearted and the tone exaggerated, calculated and not serious, but the germ of a truth remains (even when that adamant 'alone' can be incontestably disqualified in a not insignificant number of cases). In any case, there is certainly at least one other and more cheerful reason, and that is that the need (for a garden, for a place of heightened beauty) was then, and remains now, very considerably less compelling if you live in the context of such a lot of naturally beautiful landscapes – boreens sweet with cowslips and mulleins, foxgloves and fuchsias, meadowsweet, tangled ribbons everywhere of bright crocosmias, hedgerows a riot of hawthorn, sorbus, honeysuckle and the rest. And yet ... even when the full weight of this argument is duly absorbed, the degree of artifice – the extent to which a town garden has to pretend to be natural – strains to breaking point the simple, fundamental idea of a garden as nature (but mediated): hence the internal contradiction in the term 'city garden', I suppose.

In many respects, Dublin is almost the same as any other city – densely built-over; hectically busy, noisy and anonymous; hard under foot, visually cluttered, relentlessly mobile – except for at least one cardinal fact: the heart of it remains even now, both in fact and in spirit, an eighteenth-century Georgian city – indeed, arguably the most beautiful and characterful in the world, notwithstanding Bath even – which means, among other things, that there may be window boxes or tubbed and clipped box on the steps up to the fanlit front doors, but there won't be any front gardens as such – not until you get out to the nineteenth-century residential suburbs (and, now, of course, those of the twentieth and twenty-first centuries too ... though you have been warned about them!). In a sense, this is simply to say that even without gardens (though, of course, there are exceptions to the rule, and there are those two beautifully gardened squares, St Stephen's Green and Merrion Square), Dublin tends to be a feast for the eye: the patterned regularity of the streetscapes (but subtly differentiated by small, telling changes of roof height, brick colour, the patterns of the fanlights, and so on) is a very pleasant thing indeed. The very new Pevsner/Casey *Guide to Dublin* is fatter on this diet of extraordinarily fine buildings than any one of the familiar single guides for a whole English county – as well it might be. But, of course, Georgian houses did have gardens, not at the front but at the back – long and narrow back-*yard*ens, whose principal function was not horticultural at all but to allow the offices – the privy, and its accompanying malodours – to be situated as far away as possible from the house. Thus the typical long, thin rectangular shape of the town garden is with us still, though bereft of its original rationale.

You may wonder where all this is leading. The answer is to that one garden in Dublin that no one should have missed, to 45 Sandford Road, Dublin 6 – or, as it was much better known, throughout Ireland and beyond, the Dillon Garden.

Dublin 6 is Ranelagh, an old, well-heeled southern part of the city. From the crest of a road or the top of a bus you can see the Wicklow Mountains quite clearly. Walking along the wide pavements you can smell the paint on the latest mews conversion. You'll discreetly notice the superior class of stuff in the charity shop window. And the deli is well stocked and well patronised. No. 45 was a dignified Georgian house, a perfect exemplar of the old virtues of town planning, claiming its own visual space but disclaiming any vulgar superiority over the street as a whole.

True to the originating form of the town garden, the space was rectangular, though it came over as neither long nor thin. It seemed, instead, justly proportionate to the size, age and style of the house: neither too great nor too small, though actually it wasn't possible to judge confidently either the size or the shape of the garden as a whole, so invisible were most of the boundaries.

The overall scope and scale may have been cunningly masked and blurred, but as you and your eye moved from perimeter to centre, the design became progressively more visible, more clearly deliberate and stronger, and more geometrically regular. The principal feature – a long canal down the centre – had a classical simplicity about it, and a classical dignity too, but without any assumption of gravitas – nothing pompous, nothing declamatory. Once there had been grass here, but this garden was famous for changing, for refreshing itself over and over again during the thirty years or so of its celebrated life. That was especially true of the detail of planting but also, from time to time, of the larger pictures. The building of a canal had been just such a protean event. Out with the lawn and the grass, in with the limestone pavement, darker granite edge and a thirty-foot-long stretch of water. Straight away this looked very fine indeed – the materials, the proportions, the way flat surfaces of stone and water down the centre of the garden formed a still, calm, almost uneventful hiatus in the middle of graduated banks of plants on either side. But in fact, it achieved more: at a stroke, this town garden was furnished with the means after all to borrow the view, the only available *beautiful* view: the sky reflected in the water. And it worked for the ear as well as for the eye: there was the murmur and the ghost of a gurgle as the water slipped down over a succession of low steps. Patrick Taylor, in the new *Oxford Companion to the Garden*, spoke of this garden as 'dominated by a central canal of Islamic character'. But the effect of the canal, I humbly submit, was not really Islamic, nor was it one of domination. I'd have likened it more to orchestration: it was the almost still, almost flat, almost colourless, almost uneventful heart of this place, otherwise thrumming with colour, shape, texture, incident all around. Or, to take the musical analogy further, this was an episode of *recitative* – leaner, quieter, closer, denser – in the midst of a big, essentially symphonic essay.

The garden measured something in the region of three quarters of an acre, and that included the house – but in no sense at all did it appear small or cramped or, and this was crucial, capable of being taken in all at once. Always honest, and on occasion a savagely self-critical gardener, Helen Dillon once wrote that she thought the place had been 'over-gardened'. The risk was real enough, in this or in any other defined space – to avoid at all costs an impression of the *defined* equating with the *confined* – but she was too hard on herself. It was neither over-planted nor over-gardened, and that alone was a measure of the skill (in planting, staking, pruning, placing and replacing) engaged here – engaged, but not even remotely visible. Irrespective of season, the place invisibly trod that fine line between (grateful) abundance and (choking, cluttered) superabundance, and got away with it. The abundance was felt in the impression to be gained of a really generous profusion of individual plants, which were clearly flourishing and closely planted, but not so close or rampageous as to induce a sense of competition degenerating into thuggery, or over-population threatening an impression of teeming ghettos. Individually some of the plants were actually potential mobsters (macleayas, romneyas, for example), but here they had been invisibly disciplined and schooled into good behaviour.

Helen Dillon was (still is) a plantswoman through and through. That is not to say that she sought out novelties and rarities and scorned the common-or-garden, nor that she collected plants as others might have collected postage stamps. It meant just that she was deeply scepti-cal of the idea that out-of-the-way plants necessarily deserved their obscurity. It meant that she was critically alert to the sort of soil and situation that would enable a plant to thrive, and took serious steps towards providing precisely those hospitable conditions. It meant always that her vision was bifocal: some – perhaps most – plants blended, and looked their best when blended; but some simply had to be savoured alone. Somehow her garden achieved both these modes, and that was no mean thing. There were rarities here whose iden-tification would have defeated most of us: *Senecio petasites* – large, tactile, green-silver downy leaves, lined and radiating like maps of river deltas, big trusses of brassy yellow flowers like ragwort, soften-ing to a smoked haddock colour later; *Justicia carnea*, with tubular red flowers in club-shaped bunches and leaves shaped, coloured and puckered like a loquat, but more comfortably upholstered, and a rich mauve-bronze underneath … I could go on and on. But their rarity was not their reason for being here. It was because they were beautiful. The genus of the plants you were looking at – canna, for example, or dahlias – might have been ordinary enough, but the varieties found here might well have been unidentifiable … thus far. Look in any trendy magazine or shop in two years' time, however, and there they would have been: the latest must-haves.

There were interesting (that is, rare and beautiful) trees and shrubs here too. *Polylepis australis* baffled me entirely, but its flaking bark was not to be missed; nor was the way it anticipated the much more familiar bark of *Acer griseum* a little further on. I was a stranger also to *Tetradium daniellii*. Looking it up later, I learnt that it is of the rue ilk, but I wouldn't have guessed that from its arborescent habit.

There were familiar plants treated in unfamiliar ways. *Desmodium elegans*, for example, still with its lovely lime-green leaves and pea-like flowers but stooled – like the paulownia nearby – and much denser as a result. Or strobilanthes, but as tall here as aconitums and somehow (a secret of cultivation?) with the same smokey, dense-smouldering blue, rather than the thinner, emulsive watercolour of the type.

Helen Dillon would possibly have resisted the idea of signature plants, but two in particular approached that status in her garden writing, and in the gardens of other people who had consulted her. One was *Hydrangea arborescens* 'Annabelle' – creamy-white with the ghost of green in it, flowering almost all summer, and very fine. The other was the genus *Celmisia*, silver-leafed Australasian daisies that are a bit of a challenge to grow, a challenge much more commonly taken up in Ireland than anywhere else so far. In the first place, David Shackleton, at Beech Park outside Dublin, was a great apostle for them. One of the best hybrids bears his name. They are quite common now in Irish nurseries, but less common flourishing in Irish gardens. Bought and planted on a high tide of excitement, sooner or later they would fall victim to their own fussiness. They revelled at No. 45, however. Helen Dillon declared a love of pæonies and hellebores also, perhaps not only for their intrinsic beauties but also because they too presented challenges to the gardener: they are quite difficult to place. What do you share their space with for the rest of the year when they are out of flower? Selection, she said somewhere, is at the heart of successful gardening, but it was not only that. Whom you invited to dinner mattered, of course, but just as important was the choice of the person you sat them with at table. She would have been good at that too.

The Dillon Garden lay on either side of its canal like two pages of an open book. On the left was a deep border of mixed planting with a spectrum, broadly speaking, of reds and mauves: roses, dahlias, tender big lobelias, *Knautia macedonica*, *Eupatorium purpureum*, black elder, gorgeous cannas, asters, mauve all of them. But the red ebbed into pinks (more roses, and the flowers of those elders), or into orange occasionally (hedychiums, heleniums and more cannas), and they were all set off subtly by secondary pools of blue: asters again, and delphiniums. Foliage and stems were significant too: the tea-colours of the new growth on roses (stems and juvenile leaves), aristocratic darkness in dahlias (whole benches of various 'bishops', of course). Sometimes there was a plant whose intensity of colour made a point about quality (of colour), where quantity – the tyranny of mass plantings – would have missed the point entirely. I'm thinking especially of *Tibouchina urvilleana*, the richness of whose blue/mauve flowers, bunches of buds the colour of cheerful pink-cold faces in winter, and recurved silvery leaves, defied even the most immodest description. What got planted in this garden – and where – was governed by carefully considered principles of proportional representation rather than the crude psephological simplifications of first-past-the-post. Those colours, and the smooth sophisticated jazz of the rhythms with which the border as a whole was comprised, belonged to our times, indeed, to a city garden of our times, and (I'm guessing) to someone who had enjoyed looking out over it in the company of (say) Duke Ellington and a bottle of good wine. It came as no surprise to discover in Helen Dillon's own writings utopias of summer evenings on the terrace with Gentleman's Relish sandwiches.

Roses must have presented a particular problem when it came to questions of inclusion in a town garden, partly because there were so many that justly claimed attention, and not least because it may well have been that it was in a town garden, being enclosed, that roses as purveyors of scent would be far more successful than they often were out in the country, but also because it took a rose on a wall or a rose bed on the ground to have created a certain sort of ambience – classic, summer-lazy, romantic perhaps – if that was what you wanted. But roses are the most *un*placeable of plants, unless you have acres of space and an impermeably municipal caste of mind. The answer was, of course, to mix them, to underplant them, to blend the ramblers and climbers with other climbers, and to prune like mad: but it is easier said than done. Two roses here, on south-facing walls, worked very well indeed by means of that critical combination of the right choice in the first place with the best situation and thorough cultivation. 'Florence May Morse', a venerable Irish Rose, was a charming old lady on an old wall where her red flowers showed to advantage. 'Rhapsody in Blue' was nothing of the sort, thank goodness. This was (still is) a rose of shy, dusky, damson-mauve flowers. Both bloomed profusely here. But both magnificently ran counter to the generally prevailing Irish slowness to plant roses at all, let alone as exuberantly as here. Was there something endemically Anglo-Saxon about that classic, summer-lazy ambience that roses at their best induced?

On the other side of the canal was the celebrated border which probably did deserve the title 'Rhapsody in Blue' given to it by a journalist in the then new (and rather excitable) garden magazine in Ireland, *Garden Heaven*. This border was never the same from one year to the next, and on Helen Dillon's own admission it had been the work of years to have got it to this condition anyway. But she, or her husband Val, was quite likely to sidestep the applause and, instead, to have regaled you with accounts of failure, promise unfulfilled: the mildew on the little annual centaureas, for example. And they were right, of course. You should never believe what you read, never should succumb to other people's hyperbole … until the next beguiling seed catalogue arrives in the next damp, cheerless November, and your critical faculties are lowered somewhat by the mellow firelight and Mozart or 'Mood Indigo' massaging the torpid mind.

Helen Dillon was mightily exercised by matters of succession, filling in the gaps after the tulips had finished, the delphiniums had been cut down, the agapanthus and larkspur had gone over, and so on and on through the long, demanding season from April to October. Like almost no one else, she would have known that if you played your cards right you *could* have had aconitums in flower from May (*A. napellus* subsp. *napellus* Anglicum Group) to October (*A. carmichaelii* 'Arendsii'). She would have known not just that the mauve-white *Galega* x *hartlandii* 'Lady Wilson' was almost indispensible from late June and blended incomparably with certain of the salvias just coming into their own, but also that there was another goat's rue, *G. orientalis*, much less well-known, which started six weeks or more earlier and, being a measurably darker blue, complemented the best of the Dutch iris in that earlier phase of summer. She would have known that autumn-sown nigella was a better bet in a mixed border because, being stronger plants, they could hold their own in a competitive field. But possibly only she would have had the reckless, self-undeceiving, utterly winning candour to describe a plant (*Campanula lactiflora*) as 'seriously easy to grow'. Above and beyond all this (and her own seriously impressive aconitum seedling which grew to nine feet at the back of the border), the plants here were the ones you would have expected to find – at least, in a border that did not flinch from defying puritan orthodoxy by blending blues with mauves, white and (occasionally) even pink and red. So you would have found eryngiums, clematis ('Perle d'Azur', of course, but also the herbaceous *durandii*), white foxgloves, blue lupins, *Knautia arvensis*, lots of geraniums, big cornflowers (*Centaurea cyanus*), at least seven different groups of delphiniums, *Baptisia australis* with its rich rugby-bruise-blue peas, *Verbena bonariensis*, *Salvia uliginosa*, perovskia and campanulas. There was nepeta too at the front, and airy tall dieramas at the back, picking up and fidgeting with whatever there was of breeze. Aster 'Little Carlow', blue *Malva sylvestris* and anchusas joined the cast also. But then there were the plants you wouldn't necessarily have expected, the silver-leafed plants that served so well to show up the blues: various willows (clipped hard),

Melianthus major, black-flowered *Salvia discolor* with its sticky silver leaves and, of course, those signature celmisias. The impulse to have filled in with dahlias (which would have been foolish to resist if there had been any blue ones, but there weren't) was expressed with a new plant whose source had been Nutty Lim's garden in Cornwall, and Helen Dillon, who cultivated good writing as well as fine planting (for years she was columnist for the *Sunday Tribune* and has several good books of her own), had dubbed this plant 'Negligée Mauve' because of its 'extraordinary luminous colour only found in 1950s nightdresses'. Cunningly placed – which was to say sparsely placed so that they made their mark by surprise – were occasional poppies, scarlet *Papaver rhoeas*, the field poppy, and one or two *P. orientale* ('Patty's Plum' – imagine the colour), and they fitted extraordinarily well.

Blues need light to grow and flower at their best, but they need half-light to cast the best of their spell and be enjoyed at their most

bewitching. The south-facing border in the Dillon Garden in the twilight was just such a place, magically, suggestively half-lit like a deliberately under-developed photograph. It recovered precisely that resonant blueness in the expression 'blue remembered hills'. Indeed, it was hard not to think that the whole place had been conceived with at least half an eye on what it would have been like in moonlight.

Everyone who came here went away with images impressed on the retina of memory. Some would recall the ivy- and rose-clad allée, and the way it continued the visual rhythms set up by the canal. Others would remember the affection and respect afforded the two venerable apple and pear trees. Some would have chuckled at the way the rose 'Paul's Himalayan Musk' masked the wall and the boundary (but, when you looked closely, actually it lived next door). And speaking of next door (on the other side), those inclined to appreciate continuities would have enjoyed learning that Augustine Henry (he of *Lilium henryi*, *Parthenocissus henryana*, *Davidia involucrata* var. *vilmoriniana*, etc.) once lived there one hundred or so years ago, and perhaps his spirit lived on a little even then. An abiding impression which everyone would carry away, however, was of the sheer quality, not only of the plants but also of the gardening. Helen Dillon revealed not a few tips during the course of her writing. For example, *Osteospermum* 'Whirligig' would lose its 'spoons' if it weren't settled in direct sunlight – lots of it. Or, 'Rolls-Royce quality compost heaps are all very well, but the only difference between a compost heap and an (organic) rubbish heap is the time it takes to make one'. Or, 'much of the excitement [of gardening] is imagining how the replanted area is going to look, not tending a dated area of planting, constantly wiping its bottom'. On garden furniture she had this to say: 'My opinion is that you can get away with white close to the house, such as on a patio, but elsewhere in the garden white is too prominent.' And she had the knack often of fixing her wisdom in unforgettable terms – as when she complained of 'constipated old soil', or described the flowers of *Helleborus orientalis* as gradually dissolving from 'dim to beautiful understated hues, old rose and mauvey greens, reminding me of faded dowagers'. She could be hilariously tart: 'A serious frost might also solve the cabbage problem. The ornamental cabbage, I mean, a frilly monstrosity, the leaves a shocking combination of white, green, pink and purple. The proper place for a cabbage is on a plate of corned beef and not in the front garden.' Or 'Man in the garden likes to advertise his presence. The more noise he makes, the better he feels. My theory is that his passion for motorbikes metamorphoses overnight (around thirty-something) into an obsession with mowing machines. They serve equally well as rattlers of tranquillity to the neighbourhood.'

Reading these words, you might reasonably begin to wonder, first, what were Helen Dillon's own favourite gardening books? (Answer: Christopher Lloyd's *The Well-Tempered Garden*; Graham Stuart Thomas's *Perennial Garden Plants*; Vita Sackville-West's *Garden Book* – you guessed, I expect.) Secondly, why is it that a good writer and a good gardener are so often one and the same person? Does the one feed into and fertilise the other (and vice versa) or is it merely coincidence? Helen Dillon did a good line in ribbing her 'co-gardener' husband Val. She said that they had rows about missing secateurs daily, and rows about thorny bits in the compost weekly. On the occasion from which the following quotation is drawn, it was again the contents of the compost bins that generated the division of opinion:

> The dead heads of the bulbinella (an early flowering herbaceous plant, somewhat like a kniphofia) were destined [she said] for the compost heap. In this garden, the compost heap reigns supreme. Like a monster animal, in its wooden-slatted cage in the yard, its great mouth lies open, ever ready for a snack. My co-gardener, unreasonably fussy about its diet, was uncertain about the suitability of bulbinella heads. (If he had his way, it would be fed on a souflé of grass cuttings and freshly minced weeds – I would simply chuck in everything regardless.)

And there was quite a lot in the same vein elsewhere, though it was abundantly plain that Val himself knew a thing or two about gardens and gardening. There was no grass any more at the Dillon Garden. The lawns – the 'bullies' of gardens, Helen had been known to call them – having gone, she could not berate him any longer about the noise of a mower. So far as I know, he had no motorbike, so there was no bone of contention there either. But there was, in the potting shed (the old Coach House in the mews, whose yard accommodated the all-consuming compost bins – three of them, to be used in strict succession), a pile – indeed a palette – of cans of Czech lager, and Val swore by the efficacy of this otherwise pretty small beer to see off any number or character of snails and slugs – organically and anaesthetically. On the evidence of the garden itself and the lack of damage to plants, I think he might have been right as well as a good, open-bordered European. And then there was the visitors' loo. The plumbing was standard but the décor was amazing: every surface was encrusted with brightly coloured shells. Reached by going down a short flight of stairs, it was a perfect and surely deliberate evocation of Pope's own Twickenham grotto. The joke was both recherché and spot-on.

So, in what senses – if, indeed, in any at all – was this an Irish garden? Self-consciously, deliberately, it was Irish hardly at all. It went with the flow and tempo of the Irish climate, of course, but, given that by most standards that climate is so very kind and comfortable anyway, it would have been foolish to have done otherwise. No: it was not a calculated, induced Irishness which struck one about this place, still less something deliberately, clumsily chauvinistic (and surely it was all the better for that?). And by the same token, it was a deeply refreshing relief that there was no brandishing of 'style' about the place (beyond a consummate skill in husbandry). Like yesterday's stylish clothes – even in fashionable places such as Dublin 6 – the charity shops of the mind are full of yesterday's styles and yesterday's designers, and that's as true of the trendily designed garden as it is of the contemporary, labelled, designer outfit. Nor did this garden subscribe all that much to that spirit (spirit, rather than style) which most sympathetically reflects the character of Irish weather, the Robinsonian. It is hard, perhaps even daft, to be Robinsonian in a city. There were plenty of Irish plants here, though: those Henryi lilies, *Rosa* 'Souvenir de St Anne's' (an Irish sport of 'Souvenir de la Malmaison', and a long-flowering old thing at its full-hearted best in the half-hearted heat of an Irish summer and autumn), *Hedera colchica* 'Paddy's Pride' (often denuded of its Irishness elsewhere and sold as *H.* 'Sulphur Heart'), *Osteospermum* 'Irish Lavender', *Primula* 'Guinevere', *Bergenia* 'Ballawley' (which originated in Ballawley Park Nursery, Dundrum in the 1940s), Agapanthus 'Lady Moore' (the name commemorating Phyllis, wife of Frederick Moore, Keeper of the Garden at Glasnevin. She lived and gardened at Willbrook House, Rathfarnham, Co. Dublin.) But the incidence of Irish plants in this garden fell far short of a crusade. Once, in her writing, Dillon gently pointed out that that pillar of the English gardening establishment, Penelope Hobhouse, was actually Irish, and that sort of thing was a slight but important correction to one's natural but skewed inclination to suppose that the centre of gravity in world gardening was Wisley, or Kew, or at any rate British. But it was not a big issue: she and her garden were not on an Irish mission. My feeling is that in the first place the Dillon Garden was important and influential and bench-marking as a garden *in* Ireland, rather than a particularly Irish garden. And that in the second place, what it represented as an example of what could be achieved in a town garden anywhere far transcended any local or particularly national agenda.

That said, and even though (if you listened carefully) you might have caught the sound of an Irish breeze strumming the catkins of a garrya or playing the stiff, nervous stems of certain grasses growing tall on a regime of Irish rainfall, there remained something about this garden which, though not exclusively Irish, nevertheless came close to being a national treasure: silence, or pockets of silence, even here, close to the heart of a great city, or pockets of silence framed (she was writing about the garden at Mount Usher) by the 'mild chattering of rooks high in the trees and the buzz of a tired wasp', or indeed the rhythmical hum of a tractor in fields half a mile away somewhere out there in the Irish countryside. That was very Irish – that silence or near-silence – and treasurable.

And something else too: looking out through the long Georgian drawing-room windows at the garden spread out below, over the still canal, over the borders with their colours softening into the twilight, conjured a very Irish moment – fine, soft weather, the scent of some far-off, fragrant plant, and blue-remembered silver-ghostly planting. Yeats had a line about really satisfying achievements, things deserving and demanding to be remembered, celebrated and passed on, all compressed into one resonant image: 'We the great gazebo built'.

In the much-loved poem from which this line comes ('In Memory of Eva Gore-Booth and Con Markiewicz') it is a parallel and comparable scene that he is evoking: a balmy summer's evening, an eighteenth-century Irish house, a garden richly planted. It rhymes well with one's remembered experience of the Dillon Garden:

> The light of evening, Lissadell,
> Great windows open to the south …
> Blossom from the summer's wreath …
> … that old Georgian mansion …

Postscript: The Dillon Garden – house and garden, the entire property – was sold on, with effect from October 2016. And the Dillons themselves moved to somewhere else. Helen Dillon – now getting on in years – said she wanted to be 'a creator, not a curator'. And indeed, within a space of only two years, we hear that there is a new Dillon Garden! It's in Monkstown, Co. Dublin. And it can be visited (see the Dillon website for times and directions).

I'm eager to see it. Aren't we all? But, notwithstanding whatever it is that we find there, the influence, the achievement and the memory of the old Dillon Garden in Sandford Road will remain. Like it or not – and surely we should – its presence, and now its history, will last, and last.

Four More
Dublin Gardens

The Hugh Lane Gallery

The Hugh Lane Gallery on Parnell Square has been through several
incarnations. It began, in 1736, as Charlemont House, the town-
house of the lord of that name. Only the façade, the entrance hall
and the stair hall survive, but they are superb examples – even in
the pretty crowded field of eighteenth-century Dublin – of elegant
architecture and the finest skills of the carpenter and plasterer. The
door (to your left as you go in), which perfectly follows the curvature of
the wall, would, on its own, stand as a masterpiece of craftsmanship,
style and elegance. Between 1931 and 1933, the house (or rather

the space behind it) was remodelled into what we now call the Hugh Lane Gallery, but was then the Dublin Municipal Gallery of Irish and Modern European Art. Six years later, it became the subject of Yeats' magnificent poem about paintings and friendship, one of the finest in another crowded field, the collection *Last Poems*. It's called simply enough 'The Municipal Gallery Revisited'. After reviewing the portraits of Irish luminaries – to some of whom time has been unkind, but most of whom we'd still recognise: Roger Casement, Kevin O'Higgins, Arthur Griffith, Hazel Lavery, and then of his friends Augusta Gregory, her son Roger Gregory and the playwright John Synge – Yeats makes the sort of hugely revisionist, humbling, ennobling claim that only someone old and very wise would dare to articulate. Evoked by his sense of 'this hallowed place / Where my friends' portraits hang', there follow three commanding imperatives – in that tone of voice such as only someone absolutely sure of his ground and very short of time to live could get away with – to close the poem: we must *trace*, must then *think*, and finally *say*, must speak out: 'Ireland's history in their lineaments trace; / Think where man's glory most begins and ends, / And say my glory was I had such friends.'

Hugh Lane's imprecise will occasioned the British government's purloining of the best of his thirty-nine paintings – French impressionists, mostly – and keeping them in London for however many years and predictably protracted lawsuits it took to get it sorted out (1961). Lane died when the *Lusitania* was torpedoed off the Old Head of Kinsale in 1915, but there had already been a commission to design a building fit to house the paintings in Dublin. Lutyens had won it with a design for a gallery built across the Liffey itself. The philistines on the Dublin Corporation – as Lane and Yeats and Lady Gregory, Lane's aunt, saw them: the self-appointed arbiters of taste in this 'blind and ignorant town' – wouldn't fund it. In one of those moments when, retrospectively, the tides of history beach people far out of our reach, out of our sympathy, they refused not only on financial grounds (and now we might consent to their fiscal prudence!) but also on 'moral' grounds. (After all, these pictures – some of them – were *French!*) So Lane moved all the paintings to London. Then changed his mind, but the late codicil to his will was unsigned. Too late by far to satisfy the ghost of Lane, who'd been dead by then for nearly twenty years, the Municipal Gallery of Modern Art (previously Charlemont House) was envisaged in 1929 and finally opened in 1933. It contains *some* of Lane's French paintings, modern sculpture (by Irish men and women and Europeans such as Auguste Rodin,

Michael Ayrton, etc.), Harry Clarke's finest work in stained glass – *The Eve of St Agnes* – and several rooms of great Irish paintings (by Jack Yeats, William Leech, William Orpen, and so on).

Then – in 1998 – the heir of the Irishman Francis Bacon (who himself had died in 1992) left not only a number of paintings but Bacon's entire, unreconstructed London studio to Dublin. It was photographed, catalogued, three-dimensionally itemised, packed up and finally removed to the Municipal Gallery of Modern Art, where it was reassembled in a room of exactly the same proportions as Bacon's anarchically confused studio in London. Some sort of revenge was visited upon Britain (if you like Francis Bacon, that is, and some people don't) but it necessitated a radical rebuilding at the back and side of the old gallery. The architects were Gilroy McMahon, and what they came up with was good: something fresh but in no way contesting or divorcing the original eighteenth-century building.

Go, if you will, to the Hugh Lane Gallery – Dublin's Municipal Gallery of Modern Art – for the paintings and the sculpture, for the chance to read Yeats' poem *in situ* as you walk around the rooms, even for the paint-spattered walls (floor, ceiling, tables, chairs, door, dead fly, fossilised coffee in a dirty mug) of Bacon's studio, but don't leave without taking a look at the courtyard garden which was created when this latest round of construction took place. It's very small – perhaps twenty-five square metres in all – and situated at the bottom of a deep well of circumambient buildings. The light is capricious; but the gloaming is of the essence. Water, ferns and bamboo. There's a steeply leaning wall dripping with leaves – *Rubus tricolor* mostly – and two dicksonias staring up at the sky a long way overhead. Look up with them and your vision is sieved through an urban forest of fire escapes and steep slate roofs. Then there's a long, lazy weir spilling into a clear pool at the bottom where another dicksonia and a grove of arching black bamboo hold court. It's small and almost perfect (though there are six silly hanging baskets, unloved, unwatered and mostly unliving – somebody's afterthought of what a garden should have, I suppose: flowers). But the rest is a really convincing fusion of art and artifice, with the artifice there for all to see … and applaud, probably.

It takes the form of a plain, perpendicular wall painted cream behind the leaf-dripping scarp, but the really big wall at right angles to it is hung with a green gauze screen. And the whole thing is doubled up, as it were, by a wall-sized mirror at the back of the room (the tearoom actually) from which you view the garden. Superb!

You can see it on the level of the cafe, and again from a window on the next floor above from which vantage you are level with that cliff of leaves. There's a bit of decking and – capricious weather permitting – you can sit out, but it seems better somehow (for a gallery garden) to be framed and penetrable only to the eye and the imagination. Whoever designed this – Des McMahon himself? Someone else commissioned by the architects? – was a genius. Whoever maintains it – so carefully, invisibly – deserves elevation to the Irish peerage.

The whole thing must be very vulnerable to neglect, and perhaps to litter blowing in, but none of this is the least bit in evidence. It is vulnerable also, however, to vagaries of the light, but even those have been built into the idea of the place by the mirror (which must double the light as well as the apparent size). Perhaps it can be lit at night. In which case, it would be purely magical. I have never seen such a perfect courtyard garden, nor – really – can I imagine a better. Do go and see it.

St Audoen's

Come out of the gallery, cross the road, pass the Memorial Garden (there's a powerful sculpture of *The Children of Lir* by Oisín Kelly, but the paving, the walls and the pool may disappoint), pass the Gate Theatre on your right and you'll be at the top of Dublin's principal thoroughfare, O'Connell Street. At one end the Parnell obelisk, at the other O'Connell himself, and in between, the Dublin Spire. It's eye-beggaring, mind-boggling. It was intended to impress – Dublin's biggest Millennium project – and it does. It stands on the site of Nelson's Column. This was erected in 1808–9 (Thomas Kirk was the designer) and blown up in 1966, and it too was intended to impress, but not in a way necessarily appropriate to Ireland. For the Dublin Millennium (in 1988, one thousand years since the foundation of the city by the Vikings) a sculpture in bronze – gilded bronze, some of it; bronze and granite – was set up there. It was called *Anna Livia Plurabelle* (after the anglicisation of the Irish *Abhainn na Life* – the River Liffey, and, of course, her personification in Joyce's *Finnegans Wake*): a voluptuous goddess lying back with water streaming over her golden shoulders and down her golden hair. She was witty and admired, both as *Spéirbhean* (literally 'Sky Woman', goddess) and as simply woman. There was a ledge almost all the way round the fountain basin and always people would sit there – gratefully or just lazily. For some years there was a woman who would dance there – rhapsodically, ecstatically, completely absorbed. Something atavistic was going on, something devotional far deeper than conventional religion. Strangers would gawp. Kids (sometimes) barracked her. Dubliners, on the whole, accepted her, however eccentric. Her name I learnt years later: it was Mary Dunne.

With that special Irish blend of badinage and affection, the sculpture (it is by Eamonn O'Doherty) attracted Dublin nicknames. She was *The Floozie in the Jacuzzi*. Or sometimes *Bidet Mulligan*. (Say 'Biddy'). But her fountain basin was always a trap for leaves falling from the plane trees and, sadly, litter. She was allowed to become a mess and, predictably, the mess and litter attracted more mess and more litter. Clowns put dye in her water (and sometimes she looked rather good, actually). Less amusing were the bubble baths. Not amusing at all was the accumulated litter that some people shoved in and no one was taking out. She was renamed *The Hoor in the Sewer* (you have to say it with a Dublin voice to get the rhyme). And finally, she was taken away.

Then came the (other) Millennium, and it was decided to revamp the whole of O'Connell Street. All the dozens of mature plane trees were cut down and dragged out – chainsaws screaming for weeks – and people nodded their approval: *Dirty things, them aul trees. And the leaves skidd'n everywhere.* Somebody came up with something very chic, very expensive, and reckoned to be complementary to the spirit of the new Dublin epitomised by the Spire (by Ian Ritchie). It was pleached sorbus trees in rows along the edges of what is the very wide *rambla*-like space down the middle of the street, the traffic running along both sides. As a result – intended or not, it is hard to say – there was every conceivable deterrent to anyone lingering to enjoy that space as they used to: no shade in summer, no shelter in winter, nowhere to sit, to chat, to smoke, to watch the world go by. The poor sorbuses are beginning to try hard (after several years now) but it is almost hopeless: the diminutive scale of their leaves, of the sum of their presence in such a big space, puts them at serious risk of looking silly – lilliputian in fact, though I doubt if the Irish irony was intended. Plane trees are legendarily tolerant of traffic fumes, sorbuses not … and why was there nobody telling the Dublin Planning Department this? Or, if they were, why was nobody listening? In any case, all of these poor sorbuses are aesthetically unequal to the challenge; some of them have been able to stand it no longer: three out of twelve (in two of the bays I counted in 2014) had died, and their trunks had been sawn off level with the concrete. The cost of the maintenance of these trees far exceeds the cost of sweeping up the leaves from the old planes. There's the ongoing pleaching of the trees; there's the scrubbing of the Spire to keep it sparkling. The *New Pevsner* describes the latter simply as 'nasty', which is probably too hard, but it was supposed to be self-cleaning, and it isn't. However you look at it, though, the whole thing was a grave mistake. A noble street, the equal of any in Europe, had been rendered a bit daft – just like those little trees brought into Westminster Abbey for a royal wedding: silly gestures of designer-chic. It's worse in Dublin because removing the original mature plane trees had the unexpected consequence of exposing the architecture of the street for what it is: pretty poor. Except for the General Post Office and the Gresham Hotel, there isn't really a fine building the whole length of it. No fine buildings, but quite a number of really bad ones. Poor old Dublin.

Blackly ironic too. Here is a piece of doggerel I haven't been able to date (though I found it in a book of 1878). It sounds and feels like one of William Gilbert's *Bab Ballads* (1869) but, in fact, it's referring to the fashionable buildings and thoroughfares of Dublin in the first decade of the nineteenth century when the plan was originally mooted to plant trees the length of Sackville Street (latterly O'Connell Street), a noble space to be sure, but bare. (A 'cit' must be an abbreviated 'citizen'; and 'clown' is an old word for 'yokel'):

> How justly alarmed is each Dublin cit,
> That he'll soon be transformed to a clown, sir!
> By a magical move of that conjuror, Pitt,
> The country is coming to town, sir!
> Thro' Capel Street soon, as you rurally range,
> You'll scarce recognize it the same street;
> Choice turnips shall grow in your Royal Exchange,
> Fine cabbages down along Dame Street.
> Wild oats in the College won't want to be tilled,
> And hemp in the Four Courts may thrive, sir;
> Your markets again shall with muttons be filled –
> By St Patrick, they'll graze there alive, sir!

Dublin used to be grand (sometimes), and – at least in some parts – shabbily characterful when it wasn't. In the case of individual buildings and of whole streets and squares (mostly) to the south of the river, the grandeur and style remain, and – despite the depredations of property developers – a good deal of the genteel shabbiness too. On the whole, it is not to be derided. In another twenty years what remains of it will be cherished. You can follow the trajectory of what has happened to the city (without being beguiled into calling it 'progress'), if you turn left just before the post office and walk west along Henry Street. Huge, faceless chain stores in glass and stainless steel. A young Italian contemptuously flinging away the security tag from the pair of boots that his girlfriend has just thieved from H&M's. The competitive crescendo of sound: people using their phones begin to shout because other people in the street are making so much noise in order to be heard, because the person next to them is shouting … There are street sweepers everywhere but still a scurf of plastic bags whips around your feet. It is *very* bad indeed, but it is what has happened to the centres of almost every city, the world over. Total retail immersion. A few old *shawlies* will still sell you plums and pears from dilapidated prams, people still hawk balloons (if you're lucky) and fake designer watches (if you're not). But continue along the street and gradually the scale reverts to the human, the shopfronts become less regular, the crowds more genial. There are people lingering over a drink or a meal inside or out of the converted St Mary's Church, the first neoclassical church to be built in Dublin (begun in 1700). Almost at the end (Henry Street, the name, having morphed progressively first into Mary Street, then into Mary Street Little, and finally into Mary Lane) you find Mr Middleton's Garden Shop. It smells of bulbs, as well it might because, in season, there are hundreds and hundreds and hundreds of different crocuses, daffodils, tulips, eremurus, scillas, anemones, lilies in small boxes waiting for you to pick them out and put them in brown paper bags. Seed packets rattle when someone opens the door. A cat yawns. The foxy scent of ... what is it? Ah yes, crown imperial bulbs! The place is irresistible.

Back down St Mary's Street and turn right towards the river down Liffey Street. Shabby shops full of dubious bargains. Almost at the junction with Ormond Quay there's a sculpture (by Jakki McKenna) called *Meeting Place*: two women sitting on a granite bench, passing the time of day and taking off their legs the weight of their shopping bags. Go over the Halfpenny Bridge, and through the arch into Temple Bar. Enjoy the small streets, cafes, the Claddagh Record Shop, the Irish Print Studio, the boutiques. Sooner or later, you'll probably come out upon the wide thoroughfare of Dame Street. If you turn left you'll come to Trinity College and Grafton Street, but if you turn right and keep going, you'll pass first Dublin Castle – less a castle than a bit of a palace really, or it would like to think so – then you'll come to Christchurch, one of Dublin's two medieval cathedrals. Do go inside if you have time (or make time later) but walk a little further anyway (Dame Street will have blended into Lord Edward Street and now into the anonymously named High Street). You will think Dublin, the characterful city, has ended and only dirty or dull or coarse buildings remain – the so-called Liberties – and there's a fierce amount of traffic at the junction, but just before you give up and go back into the city (by way, perhaps, of Fishamble Street, to see the site of the first performance of *Messiah* in 1742) look to your right and you'll see, first, a very impressive, classically severe church – so stern that you might take it for a secular building – a law court, perhaps, rather than a place of worship. This is St Audoen's, or it is the Roman Catholic Church of St Audoen. The Church of Ireland St Audoen's is almost adjacent and very much more modest. (So – in a cameo – you have Catholic triumphalism bent on eclipsing the 'alien' reformed faith … old, old battles, lost or won, but part of the historical fabric of Ireland anyway.) The classical, Catholic St Audoen's is massively impressive on the outside but much less interesting within (and it's nearly always locked anyway), whereas the humbler Gothic church very nearby is interesting on both accounts, inside and out. It is the only remaining medieval parish church in Dublin. The sympathetic design and materials of the new entrance porch are entirely plausible, thoroughly laudable. The large, square-mullioned perpendicular window that faces you is really beautiful: if only light were always edited thus! Do go in. But before you do, stop to take in one of the loveliest pieces of gardening in all of Dublin. On either side of the steep steps down into the church, wild flowers have been sown. It's what you'd wish to wake up to after you've died. The sheer liberty of it all.

> Now it is open country again;
> Delicate birches hold raindrops along the roadside,
> 　　　　… Audoen's tower
> Standing like a corner of a crumbling wedding cake
> When the bubbles have died and the talk is elsewhere …

I really enjoy constructing in my mind that image of the tower as a piece of Havisham-like confectionery (these are lines of a poem called 'Walls: John's Lane 1978' by Pádraig J. Daly). It must have been true then: the birches and countryside notional, the decay of the building real. Thirty years later and the tower is secure, the garden real.

Call it *rus in urbe* – the country in the city. Or Elysian Fields … which, these days, seem to occur – or at least be striven for, if not quite achieved – more often in cities than in the countryside. In spring it's Orphic. You'd be half-hearing Gluck – a rehearsal for *Orpheo ed Euridice*, the *Dance of the Blessed Spirits* – heard impressionistically from half a mile away. Or is it that the stone walls of the church are distancing the sound of an orchestra playing within? Or is the music simply inside your own head? Whatever the case – remembered sound, perceived wild meadow – it is very, very beautiful. It will strongly remind Londoners of what happened naturally in their city, in the years after the Blitz, but not in the sense that you'd be looking at a bombsite, a mess, a derelict oversight in an otherwise built-up environment, albeit in the process of reclamation by nature. Rather, in the sense of a small miracle of survival – those demonic juggernauts and pantechnicons thundering past a few feet away –

of survival against the odds in a place, a city, whose dynamic is for more concrete, more noise, less permanence, more speed. A more topical parallel with London leaps to mind with the memory of the best of the 2012 Olympics: the flower meadow leading to the stadium.

There are two paths into and through this wonderful space in Dublin: straight down the steps, or windingly, slopingly down a path which curls more or less around the edges.

As a doctrinaire wild garden it would not pass muster, it would fail the test of the puritans. There are *cultivated* plants, or cultivars of wild plants here. The birches on your right are not quite the vernacular *Betula pendula*. They are varieties of the Himalayan birches – *jacquemontii*, or 'Jermyns', or 'Grayswood Ghost', whose bark is more metallically silver, indeed more ghostly, especially at night. There is an enormous fatsia (that Irish infatuation with the *Araliaceae* again. In years to come it is what will date this place.) This, the biggest fatsia you'll ever see, is the great beast, the vegetable Shere Khan, the Lord indeed of a jungle to whom all the other plants defer; it's monarchical, pontifical. In orbits around it are silvery celmisias (nothing wild about them, but they fit, they really do). There are the spires of yellow verbascums poking up, like Wren churches in orbit around St Paul's. There's ragwort, the jazz of its yellow rhyming with the yellow verbascums, but best when it goes over, and then its brown buttons stud the scene like dusty old waistcoats in a costume museum. There are oatey tall grasses, fountains of their silvery seeds, and the stems are twanged by the turbulences in the air generated by the rushing traffic a foot away. Towards summer's end – when a cultivated Irish garden has nothing to offer but tired hydrangreas, hypericums and montbretias (eucryphias, but only if you're lucky) – this wild-tending garden is fantastic. Bindweed – each flower an oculus staring at you and blinking in disbelief when the wind shakes it – scrambling purple vetch, ox-eye daisies, buddleias colonising impossible cracks, mountain ashes splashing about so much red that you can feel a myth or two coming on (... and the blood of Oisín hung like dew on the branches, hung there, beads gripping, and refusing to fall ...), red valerian, that other great colonist of stony no man's lands, and feral Japanese anemones requisitioning spaces any cultivated plant would despise: not just a garden but a spirit … of anarchic vitality, vegetable joy. At full volume, in May, in June, it's Mozart transcribed for brass band. By September it's even better still: it's a one-man band – cymbals, drums, castanets, saxophone, harmonica – a huge variety of colours compressed into a single, infinitely ingenious space. And lording it over the flight of steps, over the rather comically outclassed hardy geraniums here and there and a bizarrely incongruous leycesteria (what? why?), lording it over everything really, are seas and the white surf of the ripe seedheads of rosebay willowherb. It is simply stunning.

This garden is several years old now. Was it made simultaneously with the new porch to the new museum in the converted church? I don't know. But whatever the case, it must have been designed, thought-out, conceived by someone very skilful in the first place. I've been told it was Dominic Murphy, but no one in the Office of Public Works, the custodians, really seems to know. I think I can imagine whoever it was drawing up a plan, supervising – indeed, performing themselves, I hope – the initial sowing and planting, and then keeping their fingers crossed. For a year – two years, three? – they would have to resist the impulse to intervene; they would have to let the spirit of the place find its own levels, let the plants fight it out between themselves. That has happened, and it's a triumph of the most conscientious inertia it's possible to imagine. Since then someone must have come in and done a bit of this and a bit of that – cleared up in the autumn perhaps, dead-headed nine out of every ten ragworts, perhaps shaken verbascum seeds about a bit. Perhaps someone else – a garden puritan of the old school – had smuggled in that heretical leycesteria. (Or perhaps not: leycesterias do escape from gardens, they do seed themselves, but it does look incongruous here, it really does.) Someone else again probably needs to keep an eye on the lemon verbena (there's a *lot* already), the dandelions, the thistles and most emphatically on the Japanese knotweed by the fence. Someone must be clearing up the inevitable windblown litter because a site like this, lower than the surrounding streets and in the very centre of a city –

even with the best will in the world – would otherwise long-since have become a natural sump for it. One beer can only was what I saw the last time I was there. Someone – the Office of Public Works? A *public* body? Could it really be? – is taking care of this place, and long, long may it last. It is one of the glories of Dublin's Fair City.

Fernhill

The third, but not quite the last, of these largely unconsidered Dublin gardens had the air of having been doomed, or at least almost abandoned, when I first visited (perhaps ten years ago). That is to say, it hadn't opened to the public or advertised itself for several years. And it was a shame. Fernhill, along with Airfield, used to be a premier league Dublin garden. In a more literal sense it overlooked Dublin because its situation afforded really big views north over the whole of Dublin Bay. The garden was spread over forty acres or more, and birds, squirrels, even deer seemed to have known it as a haven, though always there'd be the white noise of traffic from the city. There were tremendous old trees and huge clumps of rhododendrons. There was a small herd of cows and a dog called Helga who knew only Finnish, and would ignore instructions in English. The flavour of the place was faded but charming – strongest, but still only vaguely Edwardian, especially near the house (faintly Tyrolean-crossed-with-Home-Counties?) and in the bountiful kitchen garden.

But it was prime real estate. Through the trees you could see the roofs and aerials of new and nasty blocks of gimcrack apartments. The Celtic Tiger was at the gates, licking its lips in anticipation of the meal. When I was last there, the house and garden had just been bought 'by some rich businessman', the three remaining gardeners said quietly and apprehensively (and Helga understood not a word of the threat to her charmed life). After that I heard nothing, saw nothing, for years. Perhaps it might have survived, I thought, but rather hopelessly. *Sic transit gloria hortorum*. It is in the nature of gardens to be transitory. I hoped someone had the presence of mind to propagate

Rhododendron arboreum 'Fernhill Silver' (pink, campanulate trusses, silver indumentum beneath the leaves) before it was too late. We could probably spare *Crocosmia masonorum* 'Fernhill' (orange, with pale yellow throat), but nothing has been heard for some years of the fabled Fernhill rheum that certainly grew here up to the mid-1980s. Apparently, it was edible, indeed it was described as 'apple-flavoured'. The Tiger – whose tastes were emphatically carnivorous – might have overlooked it, and maybe it survives still in some forgotten corner? I hope so.

But in 2013, surely enough, the 'rich businessman' did indeed parcel it all up and flog it off to developers. And then he went bust himself. The garden seemed doomed to concrete. But, actually, it survived! Now publicly owned, a new 'park' opened in late 2017. Whatever its new shape, hurrah!

Baggot Street's L'Écrivain

To end more cheerfully, here is one more – almost certainly also ephemeral – Dublin garden, ephemeral but very special while it lasts. For several years now, this garden has delighted passers-by as they trudge along Baggot Street Lower on their way to work, to school, or to the restaurant L'Écrivain, which is the occasion of this blessed spot. (The name alluding, presumably, to Baggot Street's dusty, dubious, ink-stained past as *Baggotonia*, home – give or take a street or two – to so many writers: Brendan Behan, Maeve Binchy, Flann O'Brien, etc., and, of course, Kavanagh's famous *poste-restante* in Parson's Bookshop, during the mid-twentieth century.)

The garden in question measures about two feet by four feet and, in summer, it's sumptuously over-stuffed with plants blue and red: lobelia, pelargoniums, clematis and a vine climbing up a trellis jammed into the corner of the mews which affords this little space its living. The centrepiece is usually a dianella. It makes the impression of a miniature flax or blade-waving libertia. Towards the end of summer those characteristic seedpods appear, shaped like miniature peppers but coloured the unmistakable blue of Thomas the Tank Engine (with a hint of having had a black eye ... that darkening mauve bloom!). And as it happens, these berries chime almost exactly with the blue of the seeds of the *Tropaeolum speciosum* – the climbing, perennial nasturtium – which now you see threading its way through the spent clematis, though you hadn't spotted it before. Together they trap the eye from far away and you have to stop and look and enjoy and smile, and start your day all over again.

Butterstream

COUNTY MEATH

Immemorial images of Ireland? The shamrock, of course. A pint
of Guinness? James Joyce's mischievous, shaggy face, with the
weasly, wire-rimmed glasses? The Halfpenny Bridge across the
Liffey? The title *The Emerald Isle*? Anything green. Rain.

Irish has different words for *rain*, *pelting rain*, *light rain*, *golden
rain* and (ominously) *the rains*. There is a noun for a day (or a stormy
day) which we would have to translate as 'a soaker'. The language
has verbs and idioms for *raining*, *raining fast*, *raining cats and
dogs*, *raining presents*, and *raining the great water*. Rain is the great
national treasure. The Irish love to moan about it, curse it, boast about
it. There has even been talk of trying to sell it. If water covers seventy
per cent of the Earth's surface, it must underwrite, in the form of rain,

the openings of at least seventy-five per cent of Irish conversations. And it is the greatest of all the several patrons of Ireland's fabulously kind horticultural climate. It's strange, under the circumstances, how little attention garden writers have given to the subject. It has been left to poets and novelists, diarists and historians to do it justice, and then only occasionally.

Take Heinrich Böll, the Nobel Prize winner, for example. In the 1950s, he recorded in his *Irish Journal* a railway journey he shared with a fractious little girl, her nervous mother and a young priest. The mother has come over from California, sent by her (Irish) husband to meet her parents-in-law for the first time. She is afraid that she, or the train itself, will miss the stop, such a tiny, rural station as it seemed to her from the directions she had been given. The priest speaks soothingly, but her mood resists him. Even if they do get out at the right place, she still has:

> another twenty miles [to go], by bus, then on foot, across the bog – I'm afraid of the water. Rain and lakes, rivers and streams and more lakes – you know, Father, Ireland seems to me to be full of holes. The washing on these hedges will never dry, the hay will float away – aren't you afraid too, Father?

'It's just the rain', intones the priest, but the woman goes on fretting. The countryside, she is sure now, is depopulated compared with how she remembers it before her own emigration. Patiently, philosophically, laconically, the priest gives it as his opinion that: 'It's the rain.'

And she 'can't get used to pounds [punts, as they were] shillings and pence any more,' she says, 'and you know, Father, Ireland has got sadder.' The priest gives up resisting, but he stands by his original explanation: 'It's the rain,' and the rain and the train roll on through an ever more diluvial landscape where:

> wet dogs barked … the farmers rowed around in boats on their fields and fished up the grass in nets … A barber was standing in his doorway, snipping with his scissors as if he wanted to cut off threads of rain

... hills round about were covered with faded ferns like the wet hair of an aging red-haired woman.

It's the rain, you see.

I think I can imagine native Irish readers revelling in this picture. They'd relish indignantly taking up the posture of defending Ireland's reputation, bristling with injury, and wanting to know what right had this Böll, a mere foreigner, to visit such prodigious precipitation upon Ireland? And then they'd secretly beam with pride at this independent corroboration of the myth of their country as *Ireland of the Umbrellas*.

Thirty years on, the weather forecasts in the 1980s would still invariably close with some inscrutably calculated estimate of how likely you were to get the washing dry on that particular day, or whether hay could be safely gathered in. Twenty years further on still, I heard a young vet from the County Clare clinch an argument (about dog-racing, I think) with the unanswerable formula that: 'There's no question about it. After all, it's been raining steadily here for five years now.'

Any visitor to Ireland will confirm, firstly, that the Ireland of fact (as opposed to the Emerald Isle of popular myth) is not an impossibly drenching place and, secondly, that pleasure in your visit will increase fold upon fold the more sensitive you are to what's said around you and sometimes written too: the sly hyperboles, the ironies insinuating themselves through the perennially permeable damp-courses of adherence to facts, the rich allusiveness in metaphor and simile, as artlessly slipped into conversations as a tip to the waitress; and not infrequently the quotation from or allusion to books and authors you thought only crossword compilers had ever heard of. At least, that's how it might appear to the visitor.

Take that canonical expression 'It's a soft day', for example. You consider the words carefully and then compare them with the self-evident facts of the matter: it *is* raining. Of course it is, but only so much as to mist your glasses or rinse your breath when you suck in to register your confusion. It *is* raining, but if it weren't you'd have to forfeit that epiphany of light on the hillside a mile away where a shaft of sunlight streams down through a gap in the clouds, and it looks so magical, so theatrically stage-lit, and yet so natural, that it takes your breath away. It *is* raining, but the backpackers' smiles when you pull up to give them a lift redeem the flicker, a moment earlier, of small-minded misgivings about drips on your car's carpets. You've earned a bit of a foothold in heaven one day.

Soft means so many things, but the bottom line is that it denotes weather to be grateful for, because – even in Ireland where there's no malice in the meteorology – it might have been a great deal worse. But however you gloss the word, it's clear that its meaning is a moveable, liquid thing and, like scent in a pelargonium leaf, something to enjoy even as you fail precisely to identify it.

Take the word *Buttersteam* now, a proper noun. What are its resonances? A Land Flowing with Milk and Honey, a Promised Land? Do you have a vision of cows heavy with buttermilk, swaying their homeward way through meadows golden with the evening sun and knee-high in buttercups? Or do you perhaps hear a mellow chiming of *Butterstream* with Buttevant, site of the picturesque ruins of a Franciscan friary near Mallow? Perhaps there's something nostalgically childish about it, Beatrix-Potterish even? To those of a literary bent, is there a remembrance of The Isle of Butterflies, one of that legendary archipelago the Fortunate Islands, somewhere west of the Pillars of Hercules? There, goats grew old with ears finer than velvet and large enough to be sewn into coats – after which amputation, the ancient goats turned into lovely women. Nearby, from a mountain of butter (prototype for the EU, I suppose) rose a river of milk, and the trees bore cheeses, knives to cut them, and finally gold coins (silver if they were attacked by worms; there were no pesticides there, you see). If we were to confine our lexical field to plants alone – and never mind goats, curds and doubloons – we would still reap a rich hay of butterwort, butterchurn, buttered eggs, butter pumps, butterchops, butter daisies and, of course, buttercups.

At any rate, however in the end you construe the word, I think you'll agree that it resonates as somewhere essentially idyllic. But given this fecundity in the word itself, you might wonder whether any place actually named Butterstream could possibly live up to its lineage in lore and literature. And yet there really was such a place and, by and large, it did.

Butterstream was the name of the garden begun single-handedly in the 1970s by Jim Reynolds. But bit by bit, he appropriated more and more of a field of his father's farm at the edge of the small town of Trim (Baile Átha Troim – 'The Place of the Ford of the Elder Tree'. Words again!) in the lush Boyne Valley, north-west of Dublin in County Meath. The name of the new garden must have been his own invention, though there is a stream running through it and, to make the garden, grazing cows must have been displaced – and old hedges, and old farm buildings and sundry undistinguished trees too no doubt, though enough of them survived to affect a good blending of the garden into the landscape as a whole.

In those days, Reynolds, an archaeologist by profession, was a man on a mission: he wanted to demonstrate to himself first, and then to Ireland at large, that you could have a garden independently of a big (probably Anglo-Irish) house, that a garden could, or even *should*, be free-standing, and not just an appendix to a building. That was to strike out in a very new direction in Ireland then, but it was an idea whose time was long, long overdue. In a sense – fifty years after the establishment of the Republic – Reynolds was making the first independently, truly Irish garden. With the wisdom of hindsight, it is simple enough both to applaud and to spot the fundamental flaw in the conception, something which in due course would ruin the undertaking, but at the time, and indeed for several years following, Reynolds and his garden were the talk of the town, of the Dublin cognoscenti and beau monde and of the gardening gurus and nabobs. Reynolds published what amounted to a manifesto – the leaflet that was given to garden visitors – and in it he declared his ambition, he spiked the guns of sniffy critics by candidly acknowledging influences, and he nailed his colours to the mast of innovation. Not that this was going to be a modernist garden, not that at all, but that it would cut loose from the all too familiar associations of gardens with money and class and tribal fealties, which up till then had characterised all (?) the great gardens in Ireland. His garden grew incrementally – year by year, enclosure by new enclosure – and thereby, probably, lay some of the seeds of its downfall. The compartmentalised garden was then – and still is now – epitomised by Hidcote and Sissinghurst. Reynolds openly owned up to these places as his models. But it's hard – impossible, probably – to imagine any garden growing incrementally and not resonating at least a bit with Hidcote and Sissinghurst, even when its style and planting and spirit deviated wildly from those of the putative parents.

The trouble – for Reynolds, and for his garden – was the very culture of resonances that he was trying to break: Sissinghurst and Hidcote were English. The whole enterprise resonated with what an Irish nose, so disposed, could recognise at a hundred yards: West-Britain-ness. Embedded in the very pattern of the garden's layout was the contamination of the Irish ideal.

That wasn't what Reynolds meant at all, but that was how it was construed … by some, by enough to spoil it in due course. It's astonishing, I think, that Reynolds was blind to what he was letting himself in for. Should he not have known better? It's easy to say so now, but no one had ever explicitly fingered the Irish garden as a contested territory in cultural, or even political terms, in that fundamental way before. And, in any case, it wasn't just the garden that grew piecemeal, it was also Reynolds' guiding principles. Beginning – he said – with Sissinghurst, he soon moved on further with the idea of contiguous but not necessarily continuous small gardens, only loosely linked, which didn't necessarily have to amount to One Garden Writ Large.

For my part, I don't think that was a very good idea – the elevation of incoherence to the status of a design maxim – but I can imagine how it grew in his mind, because it precisely paralleled what was going on in the evolution of the garden on the ground. Whether the idea led the work or the work followed the idea, there is no telling now. I suspect a bit of both. Hidcote is less homogenous than Sissinghurst (because it lacks the unifying focus of the tower, the leitmotiv of the Tudor red-brick walls, the collegiate shaping of the courts). Perhaps that was where the Irish drift of the (English) model was going anyway.

Reynolds himself used the analogy of a menu for an episodically extended meal. I can follow that, and its internal logic, except that the unifying factor of a meal is rarely what is being eaten so much as the people who are doing it, the eaters. Dishes change, diners don't. I want to think that a better analogy might have been with a mixed Summer Show at the Royal Academy – a dog's dinner when it's least coherent, but exciting nonetheless because of the variety and the occasional serendipitous juxtapositions. Better still might be an analogy with a baroque suite, a musical sequence (of dances, perhaps, so you'd have a minuet followed by an allemande, a courante, a gigue, and so on). Or to blend the aural with the visual, there might be an analogy with Mussorgsky's *Pictures at an Exhibition*. There we'd have a group of 'pictures' (garden rooms) loosely homogenous in style (because they came from the pen of one man) but very different in subject and content, but linked anyway by a recurring brief promenade theme as the listener moved from one picture to the next. Reynolds himself pointed to a third garden model: Crathes Castle, Aberdeenshire, famous for its hedges and topiary. From this he would have learned the seminal principle that the frame (to move from a musical to a painterly analogy) – in this case the formality of the hedges, the sharp right angles, the critical punctuations imposed by end-stopped vistas – the frame can sell the picture. Moreover, the tensions and contrasts between the strict geometry of the hedges and the capriciousness of the topiary sculptures are fundamental: by themselves each of those two elements could have been either individually dull or collectively confusing, or both. Ironically, the small-scale topiaries of Butterstream, especially those be-tubbed balls and spirals, would look, today, absolutely à la mode, but they were reckoned eccentric back then in the 1970s and not yet fashionable when Crathes gripped Reynolds' imagination. Were the garden still there now, it would be hailed as the cutting edge of the contemporary, but even that wouldn't be true: Butterstream did not merely represent the contemporary, it was actually prophetic of the future. It led. It showed – by the use of old-fashioned topiary, albeit slightly inflected in a modern way – how much of the future lies in the recovery of the past. Of course, that has probably always been true – true of music, of clothing styles, of architecture even – but as a design mantra (the *Shock of the Old?*) it was never going to catch most people's imaginations. Reynolds was certainly ploughing an adventurous furrow.

Butterstream began as an English and Scottish garden translated to Ireland, but only structurally. It was indeed a succession of rooms, fifteen of them in the end. One of them was (too predictably, probably) the White Garden. There was also a laburnum tunnel, almost a cliché now but interesting then because it both looked back to a classic (the laburnum tunnel at Barnsley House, Gloucestershire) and cocked a snook at the *démodé* people who sneered at laburnums as *so suburban*. And the spirit of Geoffrey Jellicoe clearly haunted the pool garden, even though the Doric temple reconstructed there was incontestably Irish ... and the garden plan called it the Italian Garden anyway! There was a Gothic bridge, as charming and as gimcrack as Strawberry Hill itself. The Kitchen Garden was probably the largest room (the Lawn and Summer House Garden apart) but it was always going to be the most vulnerable to neglect – and that tended to show. The earliest – the Hot Coloured Garden, the Blue Garden and the White Garden – probably seemed in proportion and right when the box hedges were young, but as the hedges grew (wider, not taller) the rooms became more and more cramped, sometimes feeling like broom cupboards or like riotously cluttered children's rooms. The planting was tremendous but the idea (the ideology, was it? Reynolds was nothing if not polemic, combative) was distorting the horticulture and the spirit too, I think. Be that as it may, in summer you noticed lots and lots of roses – far more than you would have found in any other Irish garden – and that, however unintentionally, carried with it a sort of ideological subtext: the flavour in that respect was that of a west-British garden.

Having said that, though, Butterstream was Irish in its soul if not in some of its more superficially visible anatomy. This showed itself in a number of ways. First, and probably most obviously, it was almost evangelically Irish in its planting: old Irish primulas, old Slieve Donard eryngiums, old Irish crocosmias; even a lot of the roses had

Irish provenances. Secondly, there was something essentially Irish about the relaxed spirit: no standing upon ceremony, no straining after grandeur, a natural lushness replacing what would have been a groomed plushness if it had been a garden kept by the English National Trust. The box, hornbeam, beech and yew hedges were shapely but not barbered. The roses sprawled, scrambled or loitered. There was a blissful absence of signs and notices, directions and instructions. Even the absence of plant labels – as a rule, a circumstance likely at least to frustrate at first and then to irritate no end – here seemed like a gesture of freedom … and anyway it was usually possible to find someone who could tell you the name of a plant you'd admired but not recognised – particularly of the small, beautiful but strange trees which were a marked feature of the place.

There was a discreetly Irish flavour of wit here. Presiding over the White Garden was a white tower, the climbing of which was impossible to resist of course, and the larger views from the first floor were rewarding. It looked to my eye like something out of Alphonse Daudet: a windmill minus *l'Arlésienne*. Inevitable was the cheeky local sobriquet *Reynolds' Rapunzel*! And throughout the garden there was an echo of a very characteristic feature of the Irish countryside as a whole, where every other field has a pair of serious stone gate piers but – as likely as not – no gate to speak of. There were quite a number of these self-mocking gates at Butterstream. Like the hedges, they articulated the structure. They were the punctuation marks. The Obelisk Garden – whose severity and simplicity were masterly in fact – had two ranks of clipped box pyramids, seven in each file. One signified the Virtues, the other the Deadly Sins, but – given their identical appearance – you had to wonder which was which and, indeed, which side *you* were on.

A fourth sense in which this garden broke with English models and, indeed, departed from the pattern of the classic old Irish garden, especially those on the west coast, was the very marked absence 'of rhododendrons supplemented with conifers and heather for added boredom' – thus the rebarbative Reynolds; and thus Russell Page whom he enthusiastically quoted in an earlier prospectus for

Butterstream: 'Most rhododendron collections are as artistically interesting as a wallpaper catalogue'. Is this Reynolds taking advice from Oscar Wilde to choose 'his enemies with care'? Certainly it must have raised a lot of eyebrows and hackles in Ireland in the seventies. But – and provocation apart – he was also serving notice of a radical revision of the prevailing spirit of Irish gardening then (and still now): unlike Ilnacullin or Annes Grove, the lower garden at Kilmokea or the meadows at Birr, Butterstream would be a labour-*intensive* garden. And anyway, wasn't Reynolds being a trifle disingenuous? Even if he had wanted to grow rhodos, the limey Meath soil would have baffled him. Did he not know this or understand this? It is things like this – either an economy with the facts or else a rank error – that sometimes made one wonder if Reynolds understood as much as publicly he seemed to know, variously sometime author of the gardening column of the *Irish Times*, lecturer, talking head on television, chairman of the Great Gardens of Ireland Restoration Programme, etc.

The last of Jim Reynolds' garden rooms was an essay in the formal: two mirrored pavilions (and very much like the Hidcote pavilions they were indeed), peering down onto two sky-reflecting canals end-stopped with stone obelisks, and the whole standing to attention with files of limes. I didn't warm to it much, I have to say, but not on stylistic or ideological grounds, but rather contextually: it didn't fit. This and other inconsistencies in Reynolds' principles – on the one hand deriding the patrician, and on the other espousing it – were confusing and undermined his claims to be taken seriously – not so much as a garden-maker, but as a garden-thinker. The lurking suspicion that one already had (and didn't necessarily mind, in fact) that there was indeed a stylistic incoherence at large in the garden itself was enormously compounded when this last garden was unveiled. Roy Strong – whose garden, The Lasketh, in Herefordshire, bears a marked similarity to what Butterstream was – would probably have loved this latest room more than any other. Olda FitzGerald, in her *Irish Gardens*, reports Reynolds as admitting to the pavilions as his 'acts of folly'. I'm not sure which sense of *folly* was intended, though.

Physically, and perhaps emotionally too, the heart of Butterstream was the Herbaceous Garden. Whereas the classic Irish herbaceous garden tends inevitably to be summer-seasonal, this garden had an active life of unusual length. Beginning with tulips and closing with asters, it ran from April to October. It follows that it was also quite extraordinarily greedy for the gardener's time and attention. The beds, none of them straight-edged, were deep – in fact, as much as twenty-five feet deep in some places – but the gradients of plants from back to front were still quite steep: macleayas, crambes and aruncus at the back, down through kniphofias, all sorts of phloxes, bergamots, salvias and the taller geraniums, with violas, low campanulas and erigerons at the very front. The planting ran – and ran deeply – all round the perimeters of this garden room and then through a vast island bed in the middle. I reckoned it then as probably the most sustained essay in non-woody plants in Ireland. It was certainly one of the very best.

It rained here, of course, and with it came that characteristic of Irish lushness, but the exuberance was not confined only to the hydrangeas, the astilbes and the hostas, the plants which traditionally serve as reliable indices of dampness in a garden. At Butterstream there was also an abundance of meconopsis – a delightful surprise, for in those days these poppies were rare, indeed almost mythical. There was an attractive playfulness – cheekiness perhaps – in the place given to plants which conventionally would not have been reckoned as well enough bred for 'proper' gardens. I'm thinking especially of the wild foxglove (not the posh species like *Digitalis ferruginea* or *lanata*, or *lutea* – beautiful things to be sure, but expensive to come by). These were good old *Digitalis purpurea*, foxgloves, blobs, clothes pegs, sheegie thimbles (or in Irish, the dismally reductive *Lus Mór* the 'Big Plant'). And there was white rosebay willowherb too, and meadowsweet and toadflax and field poppies. Here they weren't patronisingly let in as 'part of our endangered heritage' (to a ghetto more often than not, but we'd have preferred the designation 'Wild Flower Meadow'). Here they were the equals and coevals of delphiniums and heleniums, eremurus and agapanthus, fine pæonies and regal lilies. True blending like that would be radical were it done even now; but back then it was nothing less than rudely jacobinical. In the same spirit, ferns – abundant in the open countryside but at best only tolerated in most Irish gardens (and then probably only because, should you try to get rid of them, you'd never succeed anyway) – were very welcome in Butterstream too.

Butterstream, those years ago, marked a special place in my appreciation of plant associations. Only a few days earlier, over in the deep south-west, the air rinsed by Atlantic rains, I had been seeing for the first time the brilliant extrovert red of *Crinodendron hookerianum* and then of *Embothrium coccineum* flounced up there in the branches of those big trees. Here at Butterstream, I saw for the first time what seemed then an apotheosis of The Hedge: it was *Tropaeolum speciosum* running through and over an eight-foot wall of green, and then festooning it with swags of its vivid scarlet flowers. As the swags got heavier, they were oozing off the hedge like icing off a bun, and by August the characteristic blue fruits were visible too. As the season advanced, you could have had all three phases overlapping, as they were then at Butterstream. A revelation, I thought at the time, and I still think it's marvellous now. It might be taken for shamelessly brazen washing put out on the hedge – and this time to dry in earnest. Years, and many attempts later, *Tropaeolum speciosum* performs pretty well through a hedge of my own. Sober yew mine is, and that seems the best because the slowness of growth reduces the temptation to clip the hedge while it's host to all this intoxication of flower. Mine lacks something of the sheer elan of Butterstream (it's the rain, you know), but it's not at all bad, and first-timers now – as I was then – can hardly believe their eyes when they see it.

The Irish never really took Butterstream to their hearts. The last time I was there, there were only four other visitors. The lady taking our money reported sadly that the tearoom had closed. There were no plants for sale, where there used to be lots, and good ones too. When Diarmuid Gavin took a busman's holiday for his honeymoon, his guide was a book called *The Hidden Gardens of Ireland* where Butterstream was identified as 'a glorious place of endless inspiration', (and most of the other standard superlatives too) but, as it happened – and probably significantly, I think – Butterstream was not on the lovers' itinerary.

Only an hour away from Dublin, you would have expected people to have been queuing up to get in, as at Sissinghurst. But not so. The Irish have taken to garden centres, especially the sort which offer virtually a day out – cafe, spa, endless retail experience – but gardens themselves (as places to visit, to think about, to begin seriously to value) have yet really to catch on. Perhaps there is something in the national psyche which makes attitudes to gardens as complicated as attitudes to rain – sometimes, but only sometimes, proudly proprietorial, and then sometimes with a sense of soul and body mortally injured. William Bulfin, even though writing a long time ago, might be speaking to this curious mixture of affection and long-sufferance:

> Irish rain of the summer and autumn is a kind of damp poem. It is humid fragrance, and it has a way of stealing into your life which disarms anger. It is a soft, apologetic, modest kind of rain, as a rule; and even in its wildest moods, it gives you the impression that it is treating you as well as it can under the circumstances.

Grand, and rather orotund (under the circumstances, indeed) though old Bulfin is, I prefer this from Winifred Letts – a beautifully simple, gorgeously damp poem:

> White elder-flower and thyme,
> And the soaking grass smells sweet,
> Crushed by my two bare feet,
> While the rain drips,
> Drips, drips, drips from the eaves.

Especially I enjoy the complexity of the mixture of feelings there, but above all – and never mind the rain or the poetry – I'm here to praise Butterstream as it was and to offer it not just another litany of horticultural plaudits, but an expression of affection. Of all the great Irish gardens, this, for all its faults, was truly the darling of the pack. Perhaps I say that because I am an Englishman responding to a place that bore marked, if unintended, characteristics of an English garden.

That may be the case somewhat, but not entirely so by any means. For all its faults, I'm sorry it is now no more.

It is in the nature of gardens not to last. It might actually be that the lesson entailed in that is one of the things that make gardens – the understanding of them – important. Even those that do – apparently – last (because they are preserved in the photographic faithfulness of how they were in their prime) pose problems. If a garden itself is an artifice, there is a sense that a garden indefinitely preserved strikes us sometimes as an artifice-too-far. And the tedious, technical squabbles about plants' historical authenticities bring out the worst in some of us. There is at least one other once-great Irish garden which has gone within the last few years: Creagh, near Baltimore in West Cork. As a matter of fact, it was at Creagh that I first saw the Chilean lantern tree in flower, *Embothrium coccineum*. Dublin's Fernhill, on the other hand, seemed doomed too. But actually not quite so (see p. 278). Nevertheless, eclipse is sometimes what happens. Conceivably that's what *should* happen to gardens? I wonder.

In the long run, Butterstream – its spirit – is not lost. That pioneering idea of a garden as something ordinary but passionate people, and not just toffs, can do – perhaps *should* do – is gaining ground. So is labour-intensity in a garden (as in June Blake's Wicklow garden). So is the structural principle of a garden of rooms. The latter idea was never original to Butterstream of course, but Butterstream was the first Irish garden to show it off. Other Irish gardens have taken it up – most notably The Bay Garden near Enniscorthy in County Wexford. Like Butterstream, the problems of scale and proportion there remain perhaps to be resolved: rooms too small, too many, too fussy, the whole garden not having enough overall coherence. But the die is cast, and – critically perhaps – the principle no longer seems alien, English, un-Irish. There is nothing toffee-nosed *or* un-Irish about the garden of Carraig Abhain in Durrus, but there's emphatically nothing slovenly or pinched about it either. These things and these gardens – or gardens like them – would have happened anyway, but they happened earlier rather than later because of the example of Butterstream. The Garden is dead; long live the Garden.

Rowallane

COUNTY DOWN

Rowallane, the house, has been the regional office of the National Trust in Northern Ireland since 1977. Rowallane, the garden, has been the Trust's property since 1955, but its origins lie much earlier with two men of the name of Moore. It has been a curiously recurrent name in Irish gardening, and a digression into the people of this name – quite an extended one in fact – seems to be in order.

Least well known is the Rev. H. Kingsmill Moore, one of that small but very intense body of people – pteridomaniacs, fern-fanciers – who flourished in middle and late Victorian Britain and Ireland. This Moore was a respected authority on ferns – bifurcated, crested, great-crested, polypods, lady ferns, male ferns, shield ferns, sensitive ferns, royal ferns, tabulate ferns, etc., etc. – and, by the standards of the clan, a relatively sane one: he actually argued for restraint before you claimed a new varietal feature on the basis of whether a plant's aura misted up your glasses or whether there were bells on the fingers as well as bells on the toes (and how many toes were there anyway?), but he couldn't resist discovering at least one himself, *Phyllitis scolopendrium* 'Concavo-capitatum'. Despite its name (which conforms punctiliously to the convention of ferns having nearly impossible monikers) it's actually a hart's tongue with tasselled endings to the leaves, and sometimes these are creased back on themselves, 'like a sheet of notepaper' he helpfully says (but really it sounds ghastly!).

Then there was a Captain Moore. His address – Eglantine in Co. Down – sounds like the period piece it probably was. He spotted one branch of an ash in his garden in 1830 that had single (heterophyllic) leaves which were variegated white and yellow. He took it off, successfully grafted it, and passed it on to Ogle's Grove Nursery who cultivated the plant commercially. A genetic accident, it sounds rather attractive but seems now to have been lost.

A whole family and dynasty of Moores spawned first David (of whom more in a moment), then his brother Charles, then David's son Frederick, and – a plantswoman in her own right – Frederick's wife, Lady Phyllis Moore. Charles worked not at Glasnevin, like his brother and nephew, but at the old botanical garden in Ballsbridge belonging to Trinity College. He spotted an interesting new eucryphia when he was in New South Wales. Its leaves are ash-like and get wider towards the tip. The flowers are small but abundant and, since eucryphias love Ireland, it's good to hear of yet another, however obscure, having an Irish origin. It isn't all that hardy, and its name – *Eucryphia moorei* – is usually read to mean either David or Frederick, but actually it's Charles.

David Moore was appointed curator of the relatively new National Botanical Garden at Glasnevin, Dublin. In due course he became its first director. Named after (or by) this Moore are some important plants: *Aubrieta mooreana*, the most floriferous of them all, a good rose-tinted hellebore *H. orientalis* 'Dr Moore', various narcissus, some of them raised through a very productive association with the celebrated Canon Ellacombe, probably the most beautiful of all Irish orchids, *O. latifolia* var. *bartonii* as well as *O. latifolia* 'Praecox Major'. There's a curious prostrate willow that he found near the summit of Muckish Mountain in County Donegal (and no one has been able to find again since). *Salix* × *grahamii* nothovar. *moorei*. It's still quite widely grown. But best of all the David Moore plants is the crinum that bears his name, *Crinum moorei*; it is white, flushed lilac, beautifully scented. The flower stalks rise up from the side of the huge bulbs, not from the centre. It has to be the most beautiful of all summer-flowering bulbs.

Looking back, we can see that David Moore put Glasnevin on the international map, where it remains to this day. A great botanist, he was also a great humanitarian. He worked long and hard to try to identify the cause of the failure of successive potato crops in the 1840s.

Against the tide of received opinion, he recognised it as fungal (because he alone noticed it in other members of the solanaceae), not a consequence of atmospheric conditions. Like a scientist working in something as unfashionable, unremunerative, as geriatric medicine now, Moore was the only person then in Britain or Ireland seriously studying the disease, and the spectre of famine knocking ever louder at the door of the poor and landless. Histories of the Great Famine invariably quote Moore's postscript (in a letter of late August 1846 to the amateur botanist Miles Berkeley, an honorary member of the Dublin Natural History Society and the only other man who seemed to care very much): 'Our potato crop *is lost* without exception I believe throughout Ireland' – words as chilling and laconic as they were correct. He failed to find a solution in time to prevent the single worst man-made disaster of the nineteenth century, but not for lack of trying.

David Moore's son, Frederick, succeeded him as director in 1879. He has numerically far more plants to his credit than his father, but they tend to be of the more recondite ilk (coelogyne, epidendrum, masdevallia, saccolabium, etc.) But there is a fine agapanthus, *A. campanulatus* 'Mooreanus' which is still widely grown, likewise a primula, *P. capitata* subs. *mooreana*. His name is found on two very good nerines, 'F.D. Moore' and *moorei*, the first a strong crimson and the latter a deep, bright scarlet. Interestingly – in view of the plethora of Moores in this most extended of digressions – this bulb's name is wrong. It should, of course, be F.*W*. Moore (there was an F.D., but he was this Moore's son and a soldier not a gardener). Who can blame the taxonomists, though, given that there were so many Moores to contend with. F.W. – it is most certainly he – also has two hedychiums which bear his name.

His wife, Lady Phyllis Moore, had a celebrated garden at Rathfarnham, in the south Dublin suburbs. Her one-time neighbour was W.B. Yeats. She has an acanthus, a handsome plant, which bears both her name and leaves which are cream edged while young. A lovely *Papaver or.* 'Lady Frederick Moore' is salmon with a black blotch at its heart, very much like *P.* 'Cedric Morris' in fact but with considerably larger flowers, and there's a gorgeous pæony,

'Phyllis Moore', which Graham Thomas describes as a plant 'most fetching – small flowers dark yellow with large mass of crimson stamens'. It must have had some of the same blood as that other fabulous Irish plant *P.* 'Anne Rosse'. She also has two candelabra primulas, not to be confused with a hose-in-hose viola which she introduced in 1925. The latter seems to be lost now, which is probably a shame. Like her husband, she has a nerine named after her, 'Mrs F.W. Moore', and she is also a rose.

All that said, the Moores who most concern us in the context of Rowallane are the Rev. John and his nephew and heir Hugh Armytage Moore. They were not related to any other of the Moores, so far as I know. John Moore fits precisely into that classic mould of the clergyman amateur gardener – like Canon Henry Ellacombe indeed, and so many other nineteenth-century gentlemen. He bought the farm, as it was then, in 1858. He built the walled garden (but used it for vegetables), the stables and much of the house, modest though it is. He certainly planted a number of the great trees that enormously enrich the garden now, particularly the noble pines. In all, he is reckoned to have planted upwards of seven thousand trees, but quite a number – having served their purpose as shelter, and then outgrown their space – have been felled. The weird stone pyramids (of which, more later) are his too. In 1903, the estate passed to Hugh Armytage Moore. It is he who was responsible for the great majority of the planting, though not perhaps entirely for that defining character of the place which marks it out as one of the world's most enjoyable gardens – that easiness about it, that lawnlessness, that gratuitous generosity of planting and spirit. These two Moores did not give their names to any of the plants that originated here. Instead, they simply and modestly bear the name 'Rowallane'.

Into the garden itself. John Moore had bought a farm – small fields marked out by low walls, probably quite a bit of mixed old timber here and there, some parts well drained, some boggy. There was a very modest farmhouse, and you reached it (I would guess) by a more or less straight track connecting with the public road. That journey now, from road to house, quite short though it is (a quarter of a mile?), represents one of the most interesting overtures to any garden anywhere. It is overhung by trees, sometimes densely, sometimes thinly, but the impression is of a forest, the floor fern-strewn, boulder-difficult, moss-slippery. The light theatrically varied, nowadays we'd say *gothic*, generally dark but locally spot-lit by shafts of intense brightness. It certainly wasn't like this in 1858; both planting and atmosphere are man-made (though, of course, both seem perfectly natural now).

There are very big, tree-sized rhododendrons, very large deciduous trees, and the record-breakingly high *Chamaecyparis lawsoniana* 'Kilmacurragh' – an Irish tree for an epitomously Irish garden, tall, slender, very handsome indeed. But these are not the only things which attract attention. The private road, which was almost certainly originally straight, meanders now, deferring arrival while increasing anticipation, and along the way are not only the moody splendour and agenda-setting of these trees but also some undeniably strange artefacts: rough stone seats, rough walled shelters and two cairns. Cairns they're usually called, so they'd be piles of stones to mark a boundary, a summit, a prayer-station, or a grave, but these are cairns the like of which you will never have seen before. They are six or seven feet tall, steeply pyramidal. Almost perfectly geometrical and comprised of sea-worn, round boulders, too big to be cannonballs, too smooth to be accidents, too numerous (seventy or so in each pyramid) to ignore. What did the reverend gentleman mean by them? Why did he build them (they are most certainly 'built' – the stones are not local but presumably from a seashore, and they are each mortared into position), one on each side, but informally staggered, along his drive? Nobody really knows, but the question persists. Insofar as the drive was contrived as an introduction – a mood-setting, palette-sensitising hors-d'oeuvre – to the garden proper, what are we to make of it, and what sort of garden does it prepare us for?

Vaguely, the cairns resemble those iconic stone huts (so-called beehive huts) and oratories you get in the far west of Ireland. Even if he had never seen them for himself, Moore would have been familiar with the images – marvellously atmospheric images – in books such as Coyne and Bartlett's *Scenery and Antiquities of Ireland* of 1842. Once seen, a modern photograph of the monks' cells clinging on to the sea-crashing rocks of Skellig Michael far out in the ocean is never forgotten, even now in our image-saturated times. And then there was locally the Giant's Causeway, and these cairns are suggestively vertical variations on that theme. So the cairns are *ur*-Irish, icons of ancient Ireland? Taken together, the seats, shelters and pyramids are (but so vaguely) suggestive also of the raths and stone circles and cliff-hanging Bronze Age fortresses that are not uncommon in the larger Irish landscape (the awesome Dun Aengus on Inishmore off Galway, for example), and there is, in fact, a vestigial rath on this very County Down estate, way beyond the present garden and out in the woods and fields ... but perhaps Moore had always had his eye on it, to make the garden grow around it, to make a definitively *Irish* garden around it. However you look at these 'cairns', once you begin to spot the visual rhymes it becomes harder not to infer something about what he intended his garden to be, to mean – something mysterious, timeless, anciently Irish. And yet the pyramids are also grotesques – only mildly, but nevertheless inescapably so. That would put them quite a long way not only into the great tradition of Irish folly-making, but also into a wider, pan-European tradition of grotesquery. Conventionally the masks of river gods are often grotesques, so are gargoyles of course, but these things can also be less physiognomic, less specifically just faces. The *locus classicus* as far as gardens are concerned is Bomarzo: the whole place is full of sculptural flights of fancy – sometimes funny, sometimes nightmarish, sometimes perhaps allegorical. It's not hard to see here the twin roots of the tradition in, on the one hand, fun (albeit of a grotesque tendency) and, on the other, in those chilling memento mori in medieval and sometimes Renaissance tombs: a sculpted skeleton visible within, the skulls and bones conventionally carved in relief and framing the name, etc. At Bomarzo the weird figures loom, leer and lurch out of the natural rocks of the landscape and then, just as mysteriously, merge back into it. Placed in a sort of Jurassic forest-like ambience, as here at

Rowallane and indeed at Altamont, the subliminal message – *Here be monsters* – can be funny or it can be a bit chilling, take it as you will. Georgina Campbell, in her *Ireland for Garden Lovers*, uses her Irish eye to capture the Irish humour – albeit anachronistically – in what she sees as piles of giant-sized Ferrero Rocher chocolates. That – the spirit of laughter and fantasy – is certainly there, but so too is an echo of something resembling a many-papped fertility totem. An Artemis of the Irish woods?

What *are* they for? What sort of garden do they presage? What, indeed, would such a garden be for? If all that sounds somewhat excessively theoretical, philosophical, so it probably is. Once you are in the garden, the strangeness – eccentricity, wackiness, edginess, whatever it is – recurs only a little and only in very much less obtrusive registers. It's incontestably benign too; there is nothing disturbing about it at all (I'm thinking particularly of the gates and the turrets in the Walled Garden). But the memory of those cairns does gently linger on. What – as conceived by its originator – was this garden for? Manifestly for plants, for a sense of nature's astonishing bounty and variety, and, by extension from that, for a sheltered, privileged glimpse of a sort of earthly paradise (and not forgetting, in the first place, for growing food). Unusually for a big garden, Moore seems to have had no sense whatsoever of making a social statement – a statement about his social standing – by his garden. Unusually for a big private garden, it is – with the exception of the Walled Garden – not in the least bit labour-intensive: it is not a machine for keeping himself (or other people) busy. Quite unusually for a private garden belonging to someone historically in the thick of the culture of plant hunting, there is no evidence at all of a mania to collect, to assemble 'albums' of plants. I say this only because the Rev. John Moore's garden, while not exactly giving away what he *did* have in mind, is not – even as it stands, visibly and not in any sort of coded way – quite as simple, quite as conventional, as it ought to be.

Some major renovations have been going on at Rowallane of late. The provision of retail experiences seems likely, and quite probably visitors will find their footsteps and itineraries being subtly marshalled in the direction of sales both before and after a garden visit, once the master plan is unleashed. On the whole, you'd view the prospects with some apprehension but, as a matter of fact, some improvements would be welcome. The car park is shabby and muddy (though it is invisible once you've left it, and that is a blessing not to be sniffed at). There are no decent guidebooks or plant lists or history, but only a leaflet or two and a map. The second-hand bookshop may be open, or it may not. Ditto the tearoom. But to organise the place and drill the visitors too much – or even to encourage more people to come – could seriously damage it. It's a familiar dilemma, and there is probably no ideal solution, no matter how hard we try to find one: to avoid destroying the very things we come to admire and enjoy. There is space at Rowallane, but the spirit of the place is not even remotely compatible with crowds. What we have there is precious and vulnerable.

As things stand now, you are given your map and a bit of a tree trail. Better than nothing, but only just, though actually it is in the nature of the garden not to have an obvious beginning, a logical itinerary thereafter, and a definitive end. For 'end', read 'gift shop and restaurant' in due course I suppose, but for the time being it does not matter where you begin, where you go from there, or what you save till last as long as you give yourself time to take in as much as you can of what the garden has to offer. This could be a long circuitous walk – two or three hours at least – which would afford something of everything. Or, exchanging quantity for quality and intensity, you could spend two hours or more in the Walled Garden alone and not waste a minute of your time.

Season matters interestingly little here. Of course, there are hotspots and high seasons for azaleas and rhododendrons, but they are planted thickly or thinly almost everywhere. Spring bulbs in the Spring Ground are an obvious (and very lovely) seasonal magnet, but later in the year the same space is full of wild meadow flowers, the sort of things that people would have been able to take for granted on field margins before agribusiness did away with them, and along the roadsides too before the control manias and tidiness regimes of local authorities killed them off there also.

I tend to think that visitors to Rowallane will, more often than not, begin in the Walled Garden and, like the garden itself, will radiate outwards from there, but it would not surprise me if not a few of them have to go back to that garden to look again, to convince themselves that they really did see such a wonderful place, before they leave.

The Walled Garden then. It is large – almost two acres – but intimate. You cannot really see across it, or even through it for very far. You certainly cannot take it all in at once. There is no emphatically central axis, though some paths are broader and straighter than others. It is perhaps approximately concentric, with the open space of a small lawn – the only lawn as such in the entire place – in the middle, and progressively taller and denser plantings as you move outwards towards the walls. Perhaps.

One of the walls is not straight. The garden is not square, nor is it on a geometrical grid. No serious attempt has been made to coerce it or beguile it into very much of regularity either. And yet it doesn't look or feel in any way like an *awkward* square.

There are some large plants here – *Magnolia watsonii, Hoheria sexstylosa* among them. Not so large, but very fine indeed is *Viburnum plicatum* var. *tomentosum* 'Rowallane'. The flowers in May easily outnumber the leaves. Individually white and pink and small, in the mass they are stunning. Rather than the work of the parish bees hybridising new generations of older plants with the garden, as is probably the case with the other named Rowallane plants, this was likely to have been a chance seedling from one of the many seed shares Armytage Moore was entitled to as a subscriber to expeditions by the likes of Frank Kingdon-Ward, George Forrest and Ernest Wilson. The formative years of this garden coincided with the last golden age of plant hunting. They also coincide with the twenty-four years that William Watson, devoted head gardener, served here. But there was another historically important factor also at play in the making of Rowallane, in the shaping of its character, its quality, its variety. Probably the two most celebrated Irish nurseries of all time just happened to be close by, the Donard Nursery (Slieve Donard) at Newcastle and Daisy Hill at Newry, both – like Rowallane itself – in County Down. Both businesses are now sadly defunct, though so many of their plants live on. When Armytage Moore was making Rowallane in the first decades of the twentieth century, both were at their apogee. Leslie Slinger, proprietor of Slieve Donard, became a good friend of Moore and a frequent visitor to Rowallane. It was he, apparently, who spotted the adventitious natural cross between the two tender hypericums, *H. leschenaultia* and *H. hookeranum* 'Rogersii', which we know now as H. 'Rowallane', easily the finest of all its tribe. Those two seminal sources would have been more than sufficient for a score of major gardens but, in fact, there was more. Between a group of three County Down gardens – three gardens but four gardeners – a wonderfully fertile confraternity grew up. Armytage Moore's sister, Priscilla Cecilia, had married into the Annesley family, who were much engaged in making the garden at Castlewellan, the source, of course, of the golden leylandii, the almost infamous *X Cupressocyparis* 'Castlewellan Gold', but let that not be held against it because there were also first-class (and manageable!) varieties of pieris, of eucryphia, juniper, pittosporum, and a beautifully sad, low-growing, pendulous larch, *Pseudolarix kaempferi* 'Annesleyana'. Castlewellan, twenty miles away from Rowallane, belonged originally to one of the core Irish gardening families, the Annesleys. It was also where Hugh Armytage Moore was working, as land agent, when he learnt of his inheritance of Rowallane. It is now the National Arboretum. At another of these gardens – Rostrevor, as in the eucryphia and the embothrium and the olearias that bear its name – lived Sir John and Lady Ross-of-Bladensburg. They too were sharp-eyed in spotting new plants and generous in passing the good ones on. Rostrevor, like those two great nurseries, has gone now, but its name will surely live on … on the strength of that lovely eucryphia alone, I should have thought. In combination with Rowallane itself, these three gardens and their four gardeners both literally and metaphorically cross-fertilised each other.

First there were these two superb general nurseries feeding into (and being fed by) the birth of three great gardens, and then – as if that were not enough – there were nearby two families of world-class rose breeders. The Dicksons: there was Hugh at Belmont in Belfast, Sandy on another site in the same town and Alexander at Newtownards ... and there were *three* generations of Alexander Dicksons! And then the Sam McGredys (not three but four generations of them) at Portadown.

The matter of symbiosis and reciprocity, whereby good nurseries generate good gardens, and vice versa, is an important but largely overlooked component of garden history in the past and garden-making in the here and now. As it happens, it is possibly nowhere more in evidence than in Ulster, and at precisely that time when Armytage Moore (and the Annesleys, and the Rosses-of-Bladenburg, and, a little later, Edith, Lady Londonderry at Mount Stewart, once more in County Down) were making their gardens. The subject would make an engrossing book, but suffice it to say – and for the moment speaking only of Rowallane – that the frequency of (say) dieramas here is no accident either of taste or of style: they were all bred during precisely these years at Slieve Donard. So were the meconopsis that are still such a fine feature of the Walled Garden. In addition, it is no mere caprice of nostalgia and so-called heritage gardening that *all* the roses are scented: they are exactly the roses bred originally by the Dicksons and the McGredys.

So it has come about – quite unselfconsciously – that Rowallane (and the Walled Garden in particular) can be read as a sort of library of classic Irish plants: those roses (Rambling Rector, Mrs Sam McGredy, Dickson's Gold, and so on), the (Slieve Donard) escallonias, the dieramas and meconopsis, the throngs of (Daisy Hill) heathers, the eucryphias (*E. x intermedia* 'Rostrevor', *E. glutinosa* 'Daisy Hill', *E. x nymansensis* 'Castlewellan', etc.) A host of famous single plants with an Irish origin, plants such as the herbaceous *Clematis recta* 'Purpurea' (bred at Daisy Hill), the pampas grass *Cortaderia selloana*, the ubiquitous purple-flowered *Solanum crispum* 'Glasnevin', and so on. A comprehensive list would fill pages (ninety-four from Daisy Hill alone in the monograph by E. Charles Nelson and Alan Grills) and so very many of the names would be still familiar. Strangely enough, the garden really is a 'library' – a national collection – of penstemons, about fifty of them, but ironically only two of *them* were actually bred in Ireland. One, 'Evelyn', is an old Slieve Donard plant; the other, 'Beech Park', came much more recently from David Shackleton's garden at Clonsilla, Co. Dublin.

Within the two acres of the Walled Garden the sheer bounty of the planting is astonishing: the little (but exquisite) *Echium russicum*, orchid-like with a jewel of deepest blue at the heart of each rust-orange flower, and then its beetling cousin *E. pininana*; tree peaonies, herbaceous pæonies, dozens of them; misty thalictrums and crambes; intervals of the foliage of bergenias, pulmonarias, stachys, hostas and rodgersias; strong thickets of the tall yellow scabious, *Cephalaria gigantea*, and then its rival for rich yellow flower heads, the king of the knapweeds, *Centaurea macrocephala*; episodes of summer bulbs – cardiocrinums, galtonias, lilies, crinums and their cousins *Amaryllis belladonna*. Earlier there were the flowers of magnificent small trees – the magnolias and *Rhododendron cinnabarinum* var. 'Blandford', and the early species roses, *R. moyesii* and *R. glauca*; later, the flowers of the hoherias, the belief-defying celery pine by the gate, *Phyllocladus alpinus*, and of Rowallane's own famous hypericum.

At one point the prevailing informality is brought into the sharply contrasting focus of a geometric herb and salad garden, presided over by an unusually well shaped, indeed almost geometricised, *Magnolia stellata*. Correspondingly, it is quite difficult to see, now that the plant is mature, but the famed viburnum is actually planted in the matrix of a Celtic cross – another instance of the geometric. The box-hedged salad beds are mulched with that old staple (and presumably waste product of Belfast's cloth industries) shoddy, which seems – unlike modern prophylactics both chemical and organic – actually to work in deterring the slugs.

A little further on is a double-sided walk of *Allium moly*. The stink is – shall we say? – raucous; the joke (is it?) quite good too.

The walls are quite good also. The hopelessly indefensible miniature turrets beg for, but probably do not quite live up to, games of chivalric derring-do, the rescue of damsels in distress (from the smell of onions?), and the reinvention of gunpowder and siege machinery. But they are too narrow and too stumpy. The walls, however, are a different matter. They are never less than eight feet high, sometimes as much as twelve – certainly high enough to afford masses of vertical space for climbing plants. In themselves – and never mind the plants – they are interesting to look at, being striated. You get six feet or so of a grey stone set, jigsaw-like, in a much lighter mortar, and then two or more narrow strata of red brick. If the colours were not so fresh, you might be looking at the slim courses of Roman masonry. Each layer is only two courses high but very visible because of the differentiated colours. Then there's more stone, topped off with a coping. These walls look like blueprints for the modern brickwork – faintly Victorianly themed, of course – in countless contemporary Barratt Homes all over Britain. More interesting still, the courses of brick are evident only when you look at the walls from the inside; from outside the Walled Garden, the walls are entirely of stone. Stranger still, and even more enjoyable, are the gates, three of them. They fit perfectly into that noble tradition of the Irish folly that you find so often all over the island, where a sense of humour has not been smothered by ghastly good taste (though there is bit of that too, here and there; Powerscourt, for example). In a normal garden – let's posit such a thing as a *normal garden*, for the sake of argument – gates conventionally serve as scaffolding for armorial boastings, or as forbidding bits of security, or – sometimes – as eye-teasers: you can *look* through the gate but cannot *pass* through it. At Rowallane they were probably built in such a way as to be impossible ever to close, even if you wanted to, which – contrary though it is to the very nature of gate-ness, and given that even these really *are* gates – is an eventuality probably no one ever imagined happening. Nevertheless, the architectural extravagances of these gates at Rowallane – rebuttments, and urns and finials and flourishes – are such gentle parodies of pomposity, or of Palladio for that matter, that the ghost of laughter is never very far away.

All walled gardens ought to promise something of a secret garden, but usually they disappoint. Once inside, usually everything and everyone is comprehensively visible. The only remotely mysterious zone will be the dark steps down into the furnace for the stove house, and they're out of bounds. But whoever was responsible for Rowallane's Walled Garden – John Moore built the walls but Armytage Moore did the planting – they must have read their Frances Hodgson Burnett. Once again, there is a perfect synchronicity of events: *The Secret Garden* was published in 1911, eight years into Armytage Moore's tenure of Rowallane. The spirits of both book and place are extraordinarily complementary, both essentially using the idea (and indeed fact) of a garden as a metaphor for a paradise lost, and a paradise recovered. In Burnett's case, exile – from happiness and from home – was all too real, all too painfully in need of a metaphor to make sense of it. Her childhood was blighted by the death of her father when she was four, the decline of the family fortune and the consequent impoverished removal to Tennessee. Her marriages were miserable. Her son died in 1890 at the age of fifteen. Armytage Moore's life has still to be written, but his garden itself can be read well enough. Nothing as crudely, reductively Freudian as 'an arrested emotional development', or 'the fantasy of a refugee from a hostile world', etc., etc., I trust. Something much more three-dimensional than that would answer better, because the yearning for something beautiful is not actually a psychosis but something common to us all.

Whatever the case, in Rowallane's Walled Garden, children could play hide-and-seek for days and no one – no adult – need ever know. The metaphor of secrecy works on the level of plants and planting too. So apparently light is the hand of the gardener over most of the space – a clump of meconopsis here, of primula there, or of galtonia somewhere else, of goat's rue tickling the air and your skin as you brush past – that it *seems* artless, invisibly gardened, almost gratuitous, and you feel privileged to have seen something that is invisible to everybody else. Of course it isn't, but the spell and illusion of secrecy is very strong.

By way of contrast, the controlling hand of the designer – tricks of managed perspective, gradients of colour, pattern-books of fashionable plants – is utterly absent, and absented with a rigour that cuts both ways. There isn't even a whisper of the voguishly 'heritage' about this place (though it is manifestly a period piece), but nor is there even a consolatory corner where, as a sop, a modern designer has been given their head to practise for Chelsea at someone else's expense. No designs on the ground, no designs on our perceptions, and absolutely no designer chic. Just a simple structure determined by the lie of the land, by how and where people are likely to want to walk, by its orientation to the sun and to shadows.

Leave the Walled Garden by the western gate and walk to your right. You'll be in the Outer Walled Garden: more walls, a pond; it's L-shaped. It was once a nursery, probably because it is sheltered and accessible. The original plant of *Chaenomeles x superba* 'Rowallane Seedling' is still here; it's an intense dark red, and the leaves are glossy and camellia-like. (And this might be the right moment to clarify how you say Rowallane, as you must if you're seeking the garden itself or one of its plants in another nursery. It's not *Row-a-lain*. It is *Row-allen*, which would rhyme with – say – *No-talon*.) Much more recent than the garden's own chaenomeles is a collection of lace-cap hydrangeas settling in. They enjoy the damp soil and the shelter, and they were a favourite of Armytage Moore anyway. By adoption and adaption, they have become stalwarts of Irish gardening in general over the last few years, despite labouring under the handicap of some of the worst new names for plants for quite a long while: *H.* Annabelle morphing into Invincibelle, into Hanniball, into Incrediball, etc.

In 1921, Moore paid eight shillings (40p) for a juvenile plant of *Magnolia dawsoniana*. Today it is one of the rarest trees in the garden and one of the most beautiful in flower – pale pink, smaller flowers than the show-buster magnolias, very classy! Almost as uncommon and, like the magnolia, unnoticed except when it flowers, is *Cladrastis sinensis*, a stunning little tree: leaves like a refined laburnum, wisteria-like clusters of soft white flowers. In July, when it flowers, the ambient scent is like a debutante's dressing room and, withal, the tree has character, poise, and an ideal airiness and deportment. It is uncommon, and it is sensitive to draughts, but it should be planted much, much more than it is. There are several other fine things here, but the same could be said of every zone of the garden at large.

Retrace your footsteps and you will be in the Haggard. For Shakespeare, a *haggard* was a species of hawk as yet untamed. Then it became not a noun at all but a gloomy adjective, as in Keats' 'O what can ail thee, knight-at-arms, / So haggard and so woe-begone?'

But until not so long ago it was still a noun all over Ireland, and pretty common too, signifying variously a stacking yard or a kitchen garden. Now it is rare, except in Ulster. Seamus Heaney has his 'Servant Boy' in hard times – indeed 'wintering out' as both poem and the title of his third book attest – following a 'trail / broken from haggard to stable', carefully carrying a clutch of warm eggs. *Haggard* here means simply 'farmyard'. And that's the case also at Rowallane, though this yard is now planted up with good trees. The one you notice in late summer is *Populus maximowiczii* because it's shedding its white down everywhere, as if an old mattress had burst just round the corner. Those of a tidy inclination hate it and want to sweep it all up today, tomorrow, and the next day, and then to cut down the offending tree. The rest of us – and children – love it.

Out of the Haggard, and in front of you lie the Spring Ground, the New Ground, the famous Rowallane Rock Garden, the Hospital (for sick cows originally, not plants) and the Stream Ground (more fun for children here: the stink of the skunk cabbages!). Sometimes the transition from one area to another is clear, sometimes it isn't, but everywhere there are grand trees, masses of rhododendrons in groves, on banks, and in the valley of the stream, sometimes half-lit, sometimes bright with sunlight. There are champion trees here for the trainspotters, old favourites like the handkerchief tree, trees very rare indeed (like the *Carrierea calycina* on your right before you enter the Paddock – it took ninety years to flower), and at least one of stupendous majesty, the Macedonian pine – *Pinus peuce* – in the Paddock itself.

The Rock Garden is special. No matter how much we appreciate the rationales of rock gardening (for steep drainage, for successions of tiny microclimates to isolate and harbour small, often exquisitely flowered plants, and the resulting clarity with which you can spot them) a rock garden always looks contrived, doesn't it? Even when it's well done – as at the University's Botanical Garden in Cambridge, a classic of the genre, or indeed at Glasnevin – it still looks false, and always disfigured by far too many labels, like rashes of botanical acne. Correspondingly, when it is *not* well done, it just looks silly, hopelessly incongruous – as at the RHS garden at Hyde Hall in Essex, a region of the British Isles where there is no *natural* stone, there never has been and never will be, until such time as concrete is reclassified. At Rowallane it looks right. Because it is right. True, County Down is not the Alps or the Himalayas, but none of these rocks was imported, they all belonged here originally, and it looks like it. All the Moores did was scrape off, where necessary, the shallow layer of soil which clothed them. Smaller rhododendrons, azaleas, ferns, saxifrages, primulas (including the tall, confident 'Rowallane Rose'), heathers and, if you look carefully, that charming little plant of Irish hillsides, the sheep's bit scabious, a drumstick primula in miniature, and primula-like too in the pastel softness of its colour except that it is an impossibly soft, lovely blue. There is virtually no bare soil at all and it is this above all which distinguishes Rowallane from almost all other rock gardens. This is the very model of how to do it … but actually the lesson is that if you haven't got a natural one, it's best, perhaps, not to try at all. Ah, but there's Sizergh Castle (in Cumbria) I hear you say, and indeed the rock garden there is very good – which is to say, it convinces, it looks natural, believable (and the old, wriggled maples there, the pillowing, mothering moss, the brief but intense chaos of rock, they all look so good). But step out onto the fell a mile away and that – albeit *sans* maples and *sans* the sheltered intensity – is essentially what you'll see anyway: Sizergh simply clarifies, epitomises, intensifies its natural context.

All told, you will now have completed roughly one half of a figure of eight. Roughly speaking, the Walled Garden is at the middle of where the two lobes of the eight meet. What remains to be seen – the other lobe – is the Pleasure Ground. Probably this is the oldest part of the garden. It is a parish of small hills, dells, slopes, exposed rocks here and there, marshy bottoms – the very distillation of the landscape at large of rural County Down. Those drumlins, those wallowing and clambering meadows populated by dairy cows and rooks – there's nothing quite like it except perhaps the countryside of Jutland, the rural heart of Denmark. The essence is its scale – everything in proportion but subtly reduced: scaled-down hills especially. At Rowallane the density of woodland is not great, so the effect is of a landscape of companionable trees sharing interlocking spaces in such a way that none has room to boast of itself only, but none will languish unnoticed either. There is indeed space enough for each to reveal its own character. There's a lovely old lachrymose *Tilia tomentosa petiolaris*. There is the fantastic geometry of the bole of an ancient chestnut. Rhododendrons are everywhere at Rowallane but not usually as gloriously expansive as this one vast plant of *R. fortunei max*. There's a monkey puzzle that the lower branches long ago and the smothering ivy recently have both been removed from. The growth rings revealed in the bark look like coils of rope on a capstan, and the long-mended wounds, where branches once grew out from the trunk, stare out at you appealingly like goggle-eyed ETs. Around the feet of lots of the trees are skirts of buttercups.

Planting still goes on, carefully, sparingly. There's a small specimen of *Fraxinus mandschurica* (a name I could not trace in any other source until later, but that's certainly what the label said). The new leaves glitter like iced sugar. It hasn't the schematic horizontality of *Cornus controversa variegata* – which is what I thought it was from a distance – but the airy white lightness of it is the nearest you'll ever get to a tree in song (and, please! Let it be immune to ash die-back).

The Bandstand (originally from the Prom at Newcastle) is incongruous in this landscape, though the Edwardian flavour matches something about the house and perhaps about the Walled Garden too. Bandstands belong at the seaside with lots of municipal bedding, or in summer spaces in old parks. There's one such iconically placed in the heart of St Stephen's Green in Dublin (the finest public garden in the world? Maybe …) and in July and August it is indeed manned by bands that stomp old jazz or smooch film classics. But at Rowallane the thing neither looks nor feels quite right, and it doesn't seem to sound at all. But were there a band there you wouldn't sit to listen to it anyway, unless you didn't mind a damp rump. The word is that there was an 'existing stone dais' here already, and the orphaned bandstand merely took up a rightful place there. Moreover, so they say, there always was a band-stand here and 'the Revd John Moore would preach from it to his flock'. By flock, I infer sheep. But, while enjoying that image of ovine piety, in general I am not convinced. Nevertheless, better a vintage bandstand saved than a pile of iron and dust in the landfill.

On your way back, you should look out for some more gates to enjoy – small, undemonstrative rites of passage between one space and another. None of them is grand, none of them prohibiting and, probably, none of them ever closed … except the one on the space where at last you can let your dog off its lead. The ironwork of these gates would have been from a local smithy serving local farms, at least a century or more ago. One of the gate pillars deserves attention too. It's a bit of Irish Toy Fort, I suppose, but the crenellations erupt out of the top with such a fierceness! And with such unmilitary abandon. They bristle, they poke up and out like a cavalry-busting *chemin-de-frise*, but more than that they look like the rather crumpled prongs of a party hat.

In fact, if you know what to look for, you can tell roughly where you are in Ireland by the style, size, character of the gate pillars – slim, doughty, round, square, tall, squat, domed, flat. Someone should write a book about them (there are already lavishly illustrated but essentially serious books about Irish doors, Irish walls, Irish shop-fronts). Someone should also write a book about Rowallane. And what *is* a garden for? We are surrounded by them, but we hardly know the answer, important though the question is, and indeed growing almost daily in importance (addressed at last in a book just published by Rory Stuart. It is called simply *What is a garden for?*). But if ever there were a pattern for whatever it is that tends towards perfection, satisfaction, Eden-ness, in a garden, you could do worse than mention Rowallane – something utterly gratuitous, very deeply affecting.

The Gardens of
June and Jimi Blake

Drive south from Dublin and you choose between two roads. One follows the coast – Bray, Greystones, Arklow, the sea on your left, the Wicklow Mountains on your right – and eventually down to Wexford. The other – the N81 – runs beneath the western slopes of the other side of the Wicklow Mountains and leads also eventually to Wexford, but the journey and the country-side will be quite different. The fields are large, the woods tall and the villages boasting a prosperity reflected in some of their names: Barrymore Eustace, Roundwood, Blessington, Hollywood (this is

the original, not the Californian scion). You pass a great water and it is so eye-catching that you wonder if natural 'capabilities' have not been 'improved' – and you would be right, partly: it's a Victorian reservoir serving Dublin – superb pump houses and dams in the very best of that slightly comical Irish style affectionately known as Toy Fort. Seen from the road it's idyllic, the flat surfaces of water a foil to the memory of the mountains and rushing streams of the Sally Gap behind you (if you came that way, through the mountains). Seen from Russborough House – a beautifully poised Palladian palace a mile away – you'd think a certain Mr Brown had been employed – and no expense spared – simply to gratify your eye, so strong is the impression of Arcadia, of Wilderness Redeemed.

Count on one hand the number of water supply systems which make an appearance in world-class books: it's not easy, but this will certainly be one of them. Talking to himself – as usual – Leopold Bloom, in *Ulysses*, interrogates the tap from which he has just filled a kettle:

> Did it flow? Yes. From Roundwood reservoir in county Wicklow of a cubic capacity of 2400 million gallons, percolating through a subterranean aqueduct of filter mains of single and double pipage constructed at an initial plant cost of £5 per linear yard by way of the Dargle, Rathdown, Glen of the Downs and Callowhill to the 26 acre reservoir at Stillorgan.

And it leaves us dumbfounded as to why, precisely or just generally, we needed to know any, let alone all, of that. But exactly the same could be said of most of the millions of pages emanating from governments, defence procurers, local planning departments, estate agents, technical specification dossiers, *et alia* … which is possibly Joyce's point after all!

Turn off the N81 to the right at Tinode. You can do this twice, the turnings half a mile apart, one a public lane up Lamb's Hill, the other a private but welcoming track. Both will lead to landmark Irish gardens. In style they are as distinct as Virgil from William Blake, the pastoral idyll from the combatively eccentric, the consummately structured and polished from the innocently anarchic. In spirit, however, and when you look closely at plant repertoire, they are subtly complementary. They are in fact the works of a very remarkable pair of siblings. Up the metalled lane is Jimi Blake's Hunting Brook Garden. Half a mile away, or less to the bee or the butterfly, is the garden of June Blake. Separately they are cornerstones of contemporary gardening, first in Ireland itself and then further afield. Two gardens, two closely related gardeners: it would be easy to conjure up a matrix of binaries – similarities and polarities, convergence and divergence, affinities and disparities. It is superficially tempting, so great are the apparent differences, but even more interesting than these are the subtle, formative continuities – different but compatible inflexions of modernism, different but companionable inflexions of Irishness.

June Blake's garden you approach up a wide green-dark avenue of beeches. They were planted (one hundred and fifty years ago?) to consolidate the three-foot-high dry-stone walls they stand on. And, of course, to make a formal statement of measured approach, stage-managed arrival. Perhaps there was a big house up there once. Perhaps there still is, but it's invisible now, obscured by the theatre of trees built to frame it. These trees now have aerial roots reaching like tentacles over and down the walls before they delve into the earth. The tap root will be plunged down through the earthen core of the wall itself, but all the others take first a deep breath of air, and clamber down the *out*sides of the walls before disappearing into the earth. And the Gothic rib-effect is reproduced in the interlocked branches above, shutting out the light and then enclosing the space in a vast vault of tracery and green-stained fenestration. Arthur Rackham would have loved it.

To reach June Blake's garden you must take a sharp right out of the beech avenue, and the green spell will be broken, though not perhaps the possibility of another taking its place. On your right is a field: old trees and grazing donkeys, the trees' branches all chewed off at cow height or horse height – or at the height of goats standing on their back legs, as they do to reach the last digestible twig – so now these oaks are poised like ladies hitching up their skirts to tread through the mud. On your left is the billowing edge of the garden.

The site is clearly old: the trees and walls and a certain formal, arched, vernacular dignity to the range of farm buildings tell you that. You make your way to the garden past two warily curious cats, the honesty-box, and an argosy of seriously good plants for sale. Trees in handsome rusting tubs mark the transition into the garden.

The reputation of this celebrated place is that the planting takes priority over design, and I suppose that is broadly true because the design(s), though bold, are simple and not necessarily clamouring for attention, but there *are* elements of design here – a curious spiral stair-case up the hillside, a very stark geometrical tank, and a tutelary tree, sculptural, perplexing in its pale deadness, and beached in a cairn of sea-worn stones. These elements claim eye-space and mind-space: they have to be thought about, they ask for an investment of imagination.

The pool is perhaps problematic. It is austerely formed, formally perfect, almost perfectly abstract. Clouds and tall grasses are reflected in it, but not – or not yet – the soul of the place. The residue of thought, in this case, is of a space that doesn't yet make sense in this context.

The staircase, the spiral of old railway sleepers up the hillside behind the garden and the house, is another matter altogether. This too is not just a feature of the garden; it is an event in the mind, indeed, something that goes on and on gently fomenting in your memory long after you leave. In material terms it is simple enough: a broad, rising, spiralling path – planted generously with spring bulbs, fritillaries especially, but later on in the year just greensward – which leads to a flat platform. You can see the whole garden from here … and away to those Wicklow Hills in the distance. You can appreciate, in the geometrical abstract below, the grid upon which the garden lies. You can see in really broad brushes of colour and texture what are only provisional impressions on the ground: you lose the local and the particular, and you gain a very big, very impressive picture. And you *feel* the elevation too. Even if the formality of the garden's grid did not necessarily remind you of earlier, geometrical styles of garden design, the structure of the ascent and its clear goal hint at and allude to the idea of a formal garden mount overlooking a formal Elizabethan parterre. But the permeation of allusion does not stop there. The path up is regularly punctuated by these weathered beams laid flush with the earth for most of their length but actually with a bit of a cant too, so that first the right-hand and then the left-hand tip slopes up above the ground. They are ribs … of a beached whale, of an excavated Viking longship, of a Mesolithic toboggan run, of a ghostly railway line whose rails have vanished (well, you saw them earlier on your way in, but probably the significance – their place in a magnetic field of allusion – escaped you) – all pieces of a complex but fractured, cubist imagery whose whole you have yet to grasp. Up on the hillside, the 'rails' have gone, but the bleached, weathered sleepers remain … which is why they foment in the memory.

The third arresting design element – functionally an old-fashioned eye-catcher, but poetically so different – is the torso of an elm. It is dead, inverted, flayed of its bark but lumpy with burrs, and it is astonishing. It catches the eye because it stands at the edge of the garden, at the head of the geometrical tank, and because its stony, bleached surfaces duplicate the carefully graded gravels and sea-washed boulders that you walk over and through everywhere else. The tree itself is grounded in a cairn of just such boulders. It catches the eye effortlessly; it captures the imagination in much less systematic, predictable or, indeed, comfortable ways.

Beholders must make of it what they will, but the visual allusions are manifold: a sea henge; something of a petrified forest; a lot of that oft-said, little-considered fact that there is as much of a tree below ground as there is above (that inversion, you see); and perhaps two particularly Irish inflexions – first, as a piece of immemorial bog oak petrified into whiteness, and secondly as a mischievous remembrance of the *Sidhe*, those displaced, disaffected spirits that live beneath the ground we blithely walk upon. Whatever June Blake's tree puts you in mind of, it won't last forever. See it while you can!

Quite frequently sited around the garden are pieces of modern (man-made) sculpture. There's a delightfully wacky bronze bench which you'd possibly be reckless to trust your weight to but, as a magic carpet to platonic benchness somewhere in the ether of the artist's imagination, it's superb. There are several steel, welded sculptures whose rigid shapes make interesting counterpoints to the never-ending flux of swaying stems, wind-jingled leaves, in the garden which surrounds them.

And finally there is the garden itself, the plants and planting.

No doubt there's something to see and enjoy in every season of the year here: in winter, the tango of wind in the stems of the many clumps of grass, in spring those fritillaries and the early foliage of the maples almost everywhere, in early summer there will be flowering dogwoods – there's quite a collection here of varieties of *Cornus kousa* – a fine Judas tree, and much more besides. In high summer, lilies, lovely drifts of bog-loving primulas, masses of monardas, Kremlins of the spires of alliums, lupins, echinacea, agastache, persicaria, geraniums low down – especially that classy, smoky, mauve Anne Thompson –

and verbenas and cosmos high up. That said – and if you can't visit in each and every one of those seasons – best of all must be late summer: the overall impression of abundance – sheer lavish abundance – of colour, of the most generous planting, of subtle associations on the one hand and big gestures of colour-scheming on the other, of textural variety. It's stunningly good. This must be the most thoughtful, the most lavish, successfully modern inflexion of that classic icon of gardening, the herbaceous border, that you are ever likely to see.

It isn't, of course, one long colour-graded border at all, but it is largely herbaceous, and supported by well-placed clumps of annuals, and shrubby plants too. But it is contemporary in a number of subtle ways, probably the most important of which is that most of the beds in the garden-grid are raised. Sometimes it is only a matter of eight inches, often it is more. The result – whatever the degree of elevation – is that you are almost never looking down on, but almost always *through* the plants. The difference is critical in forming the character and spirit of the garden: you become significantly more aware of textures, of leaves, and where they are in relation to the flowers whose

colours you are being prepared for by tones in the stems – the pink veining in eupatorium stems leading up to the effusion of pink in the flowers, for example – preparatory tones in the leaves, in the undersides of the leaves (the silver of kirengeshoma, for example), leaves whose dissections (those acers, lots of cut-leaved elders, etc.) are so much more visible because you see them against light, not just against each other or against other unsympathetic leaves, or even against bare earth. Remarkable new aspects of plant association become apparent at every turn. Bishoprics of dark-leaved dahlias seen through thickets of dark-leaved elders, for example, and again and again it is the leaves and not just the flowers that make the impressions.

Not having to stoop, the impulse to touch is compelling: the tickle of red hairiness on ricinus, the spitefulness of aralia thorns, the dustiness of *Primula pulverulenta*, the felt of *Senecio petasites* (a good plant you'd see quite often in Ireland but rarely anywhere else).

There are not many labels in this garden, but from time to time, if you know them already, you spot and admire one of June Blake's own plants: the particularly good foliage of *Pulmonaria* 'Blake's Silver', the sweet modesty of *Primula* 'June Blake' whose yellow is ever so slightly sharper than that of the species *Primula veris* but whose stature is shy and the rosette of leaves tighter and smaller. *Antirrhinum majus* 'June Blake' will sound curious rather than collectable (its foliage begins tinged red with cream variegation; flowers are red and pink) but it's better than it sounds.

The marked gravitational tendency in late summer towards purples, plums, ebonies, the ripeness of oaty grasses, the tawny crispness of papaver heads, and so on, has the sort of cachet of a gallery of old masters that have been spared the attentions of varnish removers: the colours are rich rather than fresh. But there are brash modern moments too of colour outrage, and occasional episodes of something in-between: the brisk whiteness of the bottle-brush flowers of some baneberries, for example, but growing on classily purple-stemmed, purple-leaved plants.

There are episodes and moments in this garden of unusual thoughtfulness too – unusual for gardens (and paintings, and musical compositions) in our emotionally stuttering times. Modern gardens are good at wit (try Bryan's Ground), good at concept (try anything by Charles Jenks), good even at irony, at politics, at taking up positions (try Little Sparta) – and good, of course, at nostalgia, but that's another, much more ambivalent and contentious matter! – but they're not very frequently good at poetry, at sense-making conjunctions, at epiphanies of sheer beauty. June Blake's garden, however, is not under a ban of expression, not subject to some kind of sensory starvation posing as cutting-edge minimalism. The clearest such moment is that inverted dead tree. But there are others. There's a large moss-covered stone … something altar-like about it, something very Irish when you recall all those stony Neolithic sites on remote hillsides, on mountaintops, and then those hidden-away Mass Rocks where forbidden rites were conducted secretly in very, very bad times. And sure enough – closeness and physical association inducing metaphysical connection – close by there's another stone raised up: a bench, if you're tired, or a Stone Age cromlech if you're an habitué of Peter Harbison's *Guide to the National Monuments of Ireland*. Then there is, indeed, a poem, a prayer:

> May I have courage today
> To live the life I would love,
> To postpone my dream no longer
> But do at last what I came here for
> And waste my heart on fear no more.

That's by John O'Donohue, but it speaks for, and speaks to, a bit of us all, and it's so much better than either the oozy kitsch of 'You're closer to God in a garden …' or the coy postmodern itchiness of (say) the Diana Memorial Garden. Some of the poetry is serendipitous: a stupor of nectar-drunk insects, twenty or thirty or more of them, on the flat heads of wild carrot (wild but not banished from this garden), and the same again on the nearby mauve, flat heads of *Angelica gigas*. Some of it is possibly just the caprice of the visitor. Arched over by a gaunt minimalist world-weary larch, stooping penitentially – the oldest plant in the garden, surely – is a sort of brief but very formal avenue of approach: a deep border of soft velvet pinks on your left, the house ahead of you up the slight slope, and under your feet different sizes of gravel, marked out by slim iron beams laid flush to the surface, rusty of course, and suggestive of a very wide-gauged private railway line for the few yards it takes to reach the house and, indeed, the entrance to the garden. An Adlestrop moment, you might think. And then you take in the modest but striking house – better, 'a cottage' – an 'estate manager's lodge, nineteenth century', I've read, but I don't see that at all. It's quietly but emphatically un-Irish. It is – bizarrely, I suppose – in the distinctive style of French railway buildings, or so it seems to me. Strange, but there you are. Or perhaps not. The fact of the matter – for what facts are worth – is that this cottage turns out to have been designed by one George Ashlin, and he was the sometime partner of Edward Pugin, and *he* was second son of Augustus Welby Pugin … whose finest work in Ireland has to be the cathedral at Killarney – very Gothic; not French. No railway connotations there either. And yet, Pugin (the son) and his partner George Ashlin built not only estate managers' cottages in Wicklow but also churches, Gothic churches, French Gothic churches. Their masterpiece has to be the Cathedral of St Colman at Cobh, overlooking the sea-roads into Cork Harbour. It – its elevated position above the vast water, its soaring spire, its authority (I suppose) – is terrific, and in style it is probably the nearest thing you'll get to La Sainte Chapelle of Paris itself. So perhaps there is more going on than immediately meets the eye. And perhaps there *is* something of the *chemin de fer* too: turn the corner and you're in the garden proper; you see that staggering, cherishable, ancient larch from the other side … and a cloud-clipped myrtle. But are they 'clouds', or are they puffs of smoke?

The last time I was in June Blake's garden coincided with a Wagnerian downpour of rain. Nowhere remotely was there shelter from that volume of water, but one of those cats – custodial and generally hostile – had been keeping a wary eye on me all round the garden, and now it showed the way. It ran, jumped, scrambled, skidded in the direction of a small canvas gazebo at the other end of the plant sales area (which, under normal meteorological circumstances, is absolutely not to be missed). I ran for it too. That cat was furious. It scowled, hissed, stared me out – Out! The rain pelted down, the roof drummed like hammers in a pewter workshop, but the cat had to share this little, dry space for the duration. The moment the percussion of rain stopped – as abruptly as if the conductor's baton had summarily arrested an orchestra – the cat dashed out and was seen no more, but my eyes were lured towards what had happened to the big rust-ironed tubs, each planted with a tree, at the other end of this terrace. The wet iron was now the colour of damsons, and on the surface of one tub – diameter three feet, a big area – was a veritable garden in miniature: dollops here and there of mossy uplands and between them tiny jewel-like sempervivums spilt over the surface like coins emptied from a pocket. And now glittering with beads of trapped water. In a garden of big symphonic gestures, here was a little bagatelle of exquisite beauty.

Jimi Blake's garden – so geographically close, so stylistically remote from his sister's – is a sustained modern essay in one of the fundamental issues of our times. How do we, how can we, how should we configure a sustainable relationship between nature in the raw – ungroomed, unregulated – and nature as it is edited in horticulture (and, indeed, in agriculture) – edited, disciplined, regulated? How much can cultivation be shaped by culture before it becomes self-defeating, self-destructive? The issue is central to agriculture, to the matter of feeding the world's seven billion stomachs, but between the organic allotment and the chemically-fuelled arable prairie the scope for fudge, for emotive overstatement, for distortion by commercial interest, is dauntingly vast. In the concentrated miniature that horticulture allows – in the garden, in fact – it's possible to see better what the parameters of the sustainable really are, or really should be. Gardens are very literally trial-grounds – laboratories, even – for the Good Life, for Edens-recovered, places to exercise what Robert Pogue Harrison reckons is what, in the end, makes us human – a 'vocation of care' (in his marvellous book *Gardens*). But without excluding that most unquantifiable of components – how something looks – to which generally only lip service is paid in the larger economic/ecological debates. Curiously, there is an especially Irish dimension to this very thing. Traditionally, historically, the Irish have starved – not always, only off and on, but sometimes very seriously – and yet they live (the further west you go, or here in the Wicklow Hills) in a heart-stoppingly beautiful part of the world. You can't eat beauty. No, you can't. But – and here's the controversial rub – it does actually help a bit, doesn't it? Does *how something looks* matter, matter so profoundly that we haven't a clue even to begin how to measure it? And is that because if it matters at all, it is to the soul, and we don't really know what we mean by that word either though we're pretty certain that, in some sense, it's there, if not in us, then at least in gardens? And does it matter, does it have this effect, even when your stomach is aching for food?

Only Geoffrey Dutton's marginal garden in the Scottish Highlands seems comparable in scale, ambition and single-mindedness to this of Jimi Blake. Even though the climates are very different indeed between them, the weather of the mind is close, very close.

You reach Jimi Blake's garden up a lane. It looks east over the valley and towards the Wicklow Hills. In a quiet, undemonstrative, but beautiful way, the view matters. To an ordinary – or eighteenth-century – gardener, there would have been a lot of scope for borrowed landscape, but this is not a garden of big views … though there are big gestures of planting within it. On the whole, you must foreshorten and sharpen the focus of how you look at things here, and see plants as characters and individuals first, and as constituent components in larger pictures only in a secondary, perhaps even an accidental sense. This is, in other words, a plantsman's garden. But it is not without its own *spiritus loci*, its own sense of place. Much of it is woodland – steep paths through strong old trees, water sometimes steep, sometimes easy-going – the Hunting Brook of the garden's name (and originally the name of the Blake family farm on this site). The ambience is a gift to ferns and fern-growing, and the gift has not been spurned. True to its type, plunging into this woodland makes you revise, bit by bit, your expectations of what constitutes a garden. Moss and lawn cease to be hostile contraries. Decaying logs are features not blemishes. Pools of light are occasional events, not the norm you take for granted. The colour spectrum contracts into infinities of browns and greens only. Something edgy – primitive, dangerous even – insinuates itself into your field of perceptions when fungi appear, both alluring and repelling, promising and cheating. Rocks and stones and leaf mould displace soil as the prevailing medium, the blank canvas of gardening, and the impulse to active intervention gives way to passive letting-be. Cultivation yields ground to contemplation.

And yet the natural here is really as artificial as it is in the conventional garden. Turn a blind eye for a season to ivy and brambles, and you'd rue it. On the other hand, blast a dell of enchanter's nightshade with herbicide and you'd imperil not only the soul of the wood, but a bit of your own too. The trick is, of course, to let none of this show, neither the commissions nor the omissions, while never losing sight of that overall vision: everything is work-in-progress, nothing is ever finished or final, nothing ever can be.

On the fringes of the wood – those liminal areas where wildness meets the garden (which is really the zone where the heart and soul of gardening lies philosophically, anyway) – there are more woodland carpeters: ferns of course, and trilliums, meconopsis, arisaemas, spring-flowering erythroniums, as well as spruce and pine gradually giving way to magnolias and species rhododendrons. Gloom gives way to shade, shade gives way to light.

There is an avenue of young rhododendrons between the discreet car park and the garden, but out of their flowering season this is a quiet enough overture and it doesn't prepare you for the deep, steep beds behind the gates (fabulous gates actually – sculptures in their own right). These beds utterly refresh that tired old cliché of garden writing, the 'riot of colour'. It's the swell of indiscipline – the seething tendency to 'riot', if you like – which characterises and then, frankly, thrills. That, and the sheer generosity of the planting.

There's an excitement, an unbuttoned elan about it, that makes you smile, then grin, then laugh out loud. Like a Grayson Perry pot, there's an unstudied, artless naivety about it … in thrumming tension with a plot in which it has designs upon your peace of mind. There are colours – sometimes subtle, sometimes bold nursery primary colours – chuckling in a good light, keeping secrets in the shade, the playfulness developed through eye-snaring sculptural flowers planted here and there. They *could* be proteas; they *could* be aloes or puyas; but actually they're metal and painted, made cunningly by a blacksmith named Dainius Varneli, and planted quite liberally by Jimi Blake to amuse, and then to poke fun at and destabilise received ideas: so what *do* we mean when we talk about art, artifice and the artificial?

Certain themes emerge: freedom and looseness, graduated seamlessness – whether it be between groups of plants, zones of the garden (woodland and cultivated border) or between the structured and the anarchic – then there's leafiness, thorns and thorniness, grasses and a spirit of playfulness: for example, classy pink angelicas at chest height but down below that lovely (lowly) pink cow parsley, *Chaerophyllum hirsutum roseum*. Apart from the splendid gates there are really no boundaries, or even edges: as another, earlier Blake had it in his Proverbs of *The Marriage of Heaven and Hell*, 'Damn braces: Bless relaxes.' All the beds and borders are mixed; there's no rigid demarcation of the herbaceous and the shrubby, the bulbous and the annual, the grassy and the flowery – just a simple discipline, as in a school photograph: tallest at the back, titches in front. The cheekiness of some of the juxtapositions, the surges of greenness and of things almost audibly growing, the innocence and naivety of the nursery colours on the verandah (the furniture, etc.), the pre-lapsarian candour and primitiveness of some of the plants, the sense of freedoms everywhere – these are what constitute the sense of place here.

Then there's leafiness, and *big* leafiness. Palmate rodgersias, frosted-leaved brunneras, fatsias and silver-leaved lungworts, the lovely pleated leaves of veratrums, maples, their leaves spinning in a breeze like showers of pieces from a broken jigsaw. And then the leaves get bigger (*Paulownia tomentosa*), and bigger (*Inula magnifica*), and

bigger still (*Musa* - bananas). Some leaves are sensuously tactile –
Hydrangea sargentiana, and the downy paddiness of *Senecio petasites*
(in flower rather like a computer-enhanced ragwort, but giddily
handsome in leaf). There's a sort of rhythm of leafiness too: finger-
leafed *Acer serrulatum* – small and refined – blurs into much larger
finger-leafed fatsias and rodgersias, and then into really big palmate
aralias. Some are edible (*Persicaria virginiana* 'Compton's Form'),
some are fragrant (lemon balm). Other kindred shapes set up other
rhythms, leaves webbed and ribbed like goose-feet, for example: that
senecio (again) has it perfectly, but the same thing, in different sizes
and different greens, comes again in the foliage of the climbing cape
gooseberry on the house, the middle-sized kirengeshoma and the
lowly, poppy-like hylomecon.

There are lots of bamboos and even more grasses. Lots of ferns
and fern-like foliage – witty associations of glossy, ferny angelica
foliage (the rich mauve *A. gigas* here) with some pink-tinged hog-
weed allowed in from the hedgerows (*Heracleum sphondylium*
– cow-mumbles, lumperscrump, humpy-scrumples, kecks, call it
what you will, but it's the pinkish variant, not the ordinary dirty-
white one that makes the point here ... and is it a natural hybrid

with the angelica anyway?). It's a witty but thought-provoking play upon the nature/culture, wild/cultivated theme.

Jimi Blake was a member of one of Seamus O'Brien's several Chinese expeditions, retracing the work and journeys of the Irish plant hunter, Augustine Henry, a century ago. The bamboos strongly attest to this, but stronger still is the frequency of (Chinese) members of the araliaceae. By and large, you wouldn't be surprised by spotting *Aralia elata* in Western gardens, and you'd occasionally be notably impressed by *A.* albomarginata: it looks like a similarly layered, similarly airy, but more baroque *Cornus controversa*, especially if you keep it to two or three stems only – quite a stunner. Here, however, are well over a dozen different, rarer aralias – *A. echinocaulis*, *A. chinensis*, for example – and more still of their relatives – fatsia, for example, and *Pseudopanax crassifolius*. Take *Tetrapanax papyrifer* 'Rex'. Something about the slight stooping of the leaves of this – and all these plants share this tendency to a greater or lesser extent – makes them both characterful in their melancholy and beautiful in their modesty. But most are fiercely thorny … which is why they associate here so much and so well with another of the signature plants, members of the rubus clan, the ornamental brambles – dusty, silver barks, feathery foliage, and vicious thorns!

Just one of those aralia relatives must serve to convey something of the character and stature of them all, *Neopanax laetus*. Six feet tall here, and still growing, it has a single stem at the moment, but will make a thicket in due course if it's given its head. It branches only at the top and from these hang fingers of leaves which are very handsome indeed – quite narrow, long, systematically ribbed like the geometry of a Victorian glasshouse roof, light green at first, then darkening and thickening, pointed at the tip, cleft like a heart at the top where leaf meets pedicle, the slim, stiff connecting shaft. In winter it's deciduous. Not only the leaves but the whole apparatus of stalks will fall, and that produces the fabulous patterning of chevron scars on the main stem – the nave columns of Durham Cathedral gracefully slimmed down, perfectly formed. *Laetus* is the Latin for light-hearted; but it isn't, or not here. Much better would have been *gravissimus*, or *architectoricus*.

Looking closely at plants like these, and then standing back and taking in the whole, urges a revision of conventional canons of beauty, but Jimi Blake has his critics. 'Jurassic', I've heard somewhere, and it was meant scornfully, in the sense of primitive, uncouth, barbarian. To a degree I can imagine him revelling in that obloquy, but there's an element of (pejorative) truth in it. So many of the plants here are strangers that, being literally aliens, they could provoke a sense of alienation. But people used to say similar things about plantations of tree ferns before they became fashionable. Now – as, indeed, here at Hunting Brook – those same dicksonias are frost-blighted, struggling or dead, and they look sad, but it was our fault for planting them in an alien climate and context, not something intrinsically alien in the plants themselves.

'A scrap yard' is another jibe I've heard (from a doyen of the Dublin garden world), and if you're of the fussy inclination, it's true here and there: the polytunnels were weedy, pots and trays topsy-turvy, a limbo of lost botanical souls. Or perhaps not; perhaps their proprietor knew where things were, knew what plants were what. If you would find this visually offensive, then the sight of acres of factory-farmed, mechanically fed and watered, chemically weeded, robot-handled infant rhododendrons in a state-of-the-art factory-nursery is pretty offensive too, I think – but, though we are entitled to our opinion, neither is really our business and nobody is under any obligation to take notice of us anyway.

At least some of Jimi Blake's untidiness (remember 'Damn braces') is amusing. I think of a wicker armchair, abandoned in the garden apparently (or was it placed there?) and where once was a cushion there's now a surprisingly neat, chair-sized mound of fresh green grass. Intentional? I wouldn't be surprised if there were a bit of Dada in Mr Blake. Another piece of slightly edgy *Alice in Wonderland* imagery? Or homage to a tutelary William Blake? Here's another and it's probably serendipitous (but one wonders): one of Jimi's cats dangerously abseiling the wobbling trunk of a dead dicksonia. Not so much *Untidy Gardening* as a bit of *Real Circus*, I thought.

These two gardens diverge extremely in terms of style but converge massively in terms of substance over appearance, of respect for plants, and – most subtly of all – in their Irishness: the largesse of the planting, the sheer generosity, in both gardens, reflects the temperaments of the gardeners, of course, but also the generosity of the climate and something of a generosity of spirit, an openness to adventure, and a resistance – witty sometimes, almost confessional at others – to the braces and belts which constitute (and constrict) canons of conventional 'good taste' and received opinion about 'good design'. There's that quiet tell-tale of Irishness, the (relative) absence of roses. There's that Irish hallmark: an unusually strong tendency towards an integrity of the landscape outside with the garden inside.

June Blake's garden makes of modernism a classic on its own terms, but without any sort of divorce from the past – a very, very moving experience. Jimi Blake privileges laughter and elan, puzzlement and poetry in a way that revises what we think a garden is anyway.

Envoi: Ireland as a Place in the Mind

Joyce's precise, dust-dry, super-meticulously detailed itemising of the journey of water from the Roundwood Reservoir (see the opening of the preceding chapter where, briefly, we encountered both Joyce and the reservoir) to the tap of No. 7 Eccles Street, Dublin, the house of Leopold Bloom, is an example – but only one of the countless available – that illustrates what Bernard McCabe calls Joyce's 'meticulous, almost superstitious attention to topographical exactitude'. If Joyce didn't matter, we would dismiss it as some minor piece of a neurotic obsessive, and leave it – and *Ulysses* – at that. But – like him or not; read him or not – Joyce does matter, so we should not.

Joyce's principal source was the 1904 edition of *Thom's Dublin Post Office Directory*, which was first published in 1886, but he must also have been relying on memory, fallible memory, because he gets some of his facts ever so slightly wrong. He began *Ulysses* in 1914, and more or less finished it by 1918, but the last time he had been in Ireland – and then only briefly – was in 1912, and the last time he had lived there properly (so had known it intimately) was prior to 1904 when he went into voluntary exile. The water in the Dublin Water Works' aqueduct does not exactly go 'by way of the Dargle' (a tributary of the Liffey), it goes *over* it, and the two-hundred-and-fifty-foot gradient does not run from Stillorgan 'to the city boundary' but from Stillorgan to the quays in central Dublin, a distance of another mile or two at least.

How exasperatingly petty to correct him on such fine points! But both the fallibility and the creativity of memory are, in fact, very much to the point for a number of interesting reasons. Firstly, Ireland has the distinction of being the only country in the world (with the telling exception, of course, of Israel) the majority of whose citizens don't live in it. I use the word 'citizens' in the loose but legitimate sense of people who regard themselves as Irish, though they may be several generations removed (forty million of them in the USA, millions more worldwide). These are people for whom Ireland – the Old Country – is far more a place in the mind than a place of flesh and blood, stone and concrete, grass-clad earth, rain-dripping trees, and the shit-stained rumps of cows. Secondly, Joyce, more than any other writer (except Proust, I suppose), makes memory – its loss and recovery, its propensity to edit experience, its role in making the inchoate present make sense – both his central theme and his proteanly shaping method. Thirdly, there is something about Ireland which provokes again and again those who have visited it to construct, with selective hindsight, their own versions of it in their minds. The Irish themselves, the ones who do actually live there, laugh and sigh about it – all this dewy-eyed sentimentalising, all the romanticising – and then they adroitly exploit the commercial opportunities it offers. And there are many of them: everything from tourism to marketing Kerrygold butter. Nowhere else on earth has so very many books in print about itself. Nowhere else has copious shelves in bookshops and libraries labelled *Irish Interest* (or whatever is its equivalent wherever else in the world you may be). Nowhere else is there so much national navel-gazing. Which – as it happens – would not surprise Joyce, whose most frequently used bit of geographical signage is the word *omphalos* – navel, world-axis, original-mother-connector, etc. But the geography in question here belongs to a place in the mind, a place *called* Ireland, it is true, but imaginatively rather than topographically configured. Ireland *is* – even for those who really do live there – at least partly, a place in the mind, a mental construct rather than a place on the ground. And as often as not, the people engaged in this construction take their cues from writers. *Inventing Ireland*, as the literary critic Declan Kiberd demonstrates in his book of that name, is what Irish writers have been doing for a very long time now. Less imaginatively, probably, but no less powerfully, it is also what all those millions of second, third, fourth generation Irish exiles *hungry for home* do in their heads … or in their gardens, when they plant a bit of shamrock in the soil of their alien dwellings.

It – the process of constructing in your head a place you'd like to live in – is also the essence of gardens: the recovery, or reconstruction, or the making of a stylised version of, or just nostalgia for something lost, something real but out of reach. If the coincidence of Ireland and gardens – Ireland *as* a garden – hadn't occurred naturally, it would have been necessary – indeed, it would have been inevitable – for people to have begun to invent it anyway. In an Irish context – which is to say, by and large, from the point of view of the exile – it is that primitive, visceral *hunger for home*. In a more cross-cultural, timeless, more universal sense, it is simply a nostalgia for an Eden. But for an Irish person, to plant a piece of the shamrock – to begin a garden, wherever you were – would be to assuage a bit of that hunger. It generally worked (works). It put you in mind of home. It located a home in your head. But it wasn't modelled just upon Eden, upon a lost garden. Generally speaking, the place-in-the-mind the Irish exile built – and still does build – was a cross between a garden on the one hand and the sort of haven/heaven represented by islands and islandness on the other (see again the opening of the chapter for

Ilnacullin for a discussion of *islandness*). For more than two hundred years now, they have called it The Emerald Isle. They emphatically do not need to know that that very term was itself an invention, an artifice, a piece of imaginative creation. It was coined (in a dreadfully bad poem called *Erin*) by a certain William Drennan in 1795:

> When Eire first rose from the dark-swelling flood,
> God blessed the green island, and saw it was good;
> The emerald of Europe, it sparkled and shone,
> In the ring of the world, the most precious stone.

If people *did* come to know that – people such as a prosperous but constitutionally homesick fifth-generation Irish immigrant family in New York now, for example – they might prefer not to. Its being an artifice might seem somehow to cheapen something that should enjoy an almost sacred status in their minds: the place itself, of course, but also the form of words so familiarly used to configure that place.

Probably it was Francis Bacon – the Elizabethan essayist, rather than the twentieth-century Irish painter – who blazed the modern trail to impossible islands. It had been done before, of course. Atlantis had always been offshore *somewhere*. Thomas More's Utopia had begun as a peninsular appendix to a mainland, connected to it by an isthmus, but quickly the land-bridge had been breached and the place rendered an island. All these places, however, had been social ideals rather than material loci. They were good to live in because the folk there behaved themselves and worked together for the common good, but it still rained too much sometimes, and life was still tough. Fairness rendered it bearable, but it could still be hard. However, Bacon's *New Atlantis* (of 1625) was subtly different. This island was in a fastness of ocean 'somewhere off Peru'. On it, an enlightened ruler, Salomon, was leading and inspiring an enlightened race to achieve a technological nirvana. These people could fly; they had conquered disease; they could harness winds and waves; they milled beautiful papers, wove beautiful cloths and enjoyed the beautiful sense of security that comes from knowing that you have mastered the science of gunpowder and high explosives. When he wrote it, Bacon was an old man, a disappointed man. He had spent his life in the pursuit of high office, and often he had been successful, but so little had actually been achieved. This fable of his old age seems to be saying that perfection – or even more tenuously, the possibility of perfection – is only ever really achieved by a very few people, creative people, imaginative people, and even then only in their own heads. The Good Life belongs to the imagination, not to the factual.

Swift, with characteristically uncharitable honesty, thought these literary caprices – Bacon's particularly – not only unrealistic but absurd. So much so that it became the model for the third of Lemuel Gulliver's *Travels*. This is the one that takes him to Laputa, an island (but it floats on air, not water) infested with mad scientists. They are engaged in projects such as extruding sunbeams from combustible cucumbers, trapping them in glass cylinders, and storing them for use

later as central heating units. Another scientist was working on returning human excrement to its original forms in ingestible foodstuffs ...
minus the smell. Yet another had been devising methods of building
houses from the top downwards, starting with the roof. Possibly the
most ingenious of all these schemes, which, its author declared – like
a politician on the hustings – would be of incalculable benefit to mankind, would preempt totally the need for the plough, would probably
Save the World! You planted an acre of land, at six-inch centres, and
at a depth of eight inches, with acorns, dates, chestnuts and any other
sweet-tasting goodies. Then you herded six hundred hogs into the
field. Effortlessly, they would dig it all up for you.

Swift, the Irishman, had only to look up from the book he was
reading (Bacon's *Works*, perhaps) and look out of the Deanery window
into the Dublin street to sense not just an impossible island, but an
impossible Ireland. In his jaundiced but truthful imagination, it's as
if he generated his own prototype of an emerald island. He'd read his
Bacon, he'd read his Voltaire, he'd know a Cockaigne if he saw one.
He'd read Shakespeare's *Tempest*. In Voltaire's *Candide*, in the land of
Eldorado, there is so much gold that the kids play skittles with nuggets
of it, but somewhere at the back of the fable is the ghost of the fact
that, come hard times and famine, all that gold wouldn't suffice a jot to
assuage your hunger. Prospero on his island wields enormous power,
and it's got nothing to do with money for a change, but in the end it's
only a means to an end, and that goal is the province of something
in the heart, inaccessible and impermeable to whatever you might
have stashed away in the vaults of a bank or to whatever pressures
and big sticks you could muster from the arsenals of field marshals.
Swift would have snorted upon that trope: 'the emerald island'. Like
gold in Eldorado, you couldn't eat emeralds in Ireland (even in the
unlikely event that there were any there to eat anyway) ... except that,
a hundred years on from *Gulliver's Travels*, people *were* eating the
emeraldness, the grass, the greenness of Ireland, because – in a crazy
world where fungal disease could strike at random, and what passed
for fiscal and social policy (which could have alleviated famine) was
about as morally developed as larval growths in the rotting crops –

precisely that was the way of the world. Swift had had the measure of absurdity even before its worst happened.

It is that same sense of the absurd – our helplessness in the face of it, but also the profound benefaction to mankind of laughter – that runs through so much of Irish writing. It amounts to a national speciality: Swift's Laputa, Sterne's *Tristram Shandy*, Flann O'Brien's *At Swim-Two-Birds*, Samuel Beckett's *Godot*. And it goes into the pollinating of quite a lot of Joyce's vision in *Ulysses* too, where the incontrovertibly ordinary is so often transubstantiated into something extraordinary, and you find yourself snorting with (albeit a possibly forbidden) laughter. Or else deeply moved by some strain of pathos.

Joyce's Water Works moment occurs in the Ithaca episode of *Ulysses*, the last-but-one chapter of the book. It is two o'clock in the morning. Bloom, a small-time advertising-space salesman, is almost at the end of a long day, almost home (just as Homer's Odysseus – the eponymous *Ulysses* – is almost at the end of his ten-year journey home from Troy, his odyssey, when his island kingdom, Ithaca, comes into sight). Upstairs is Molly, Bloom's unfaithful wife. He is nervous, his mind and fingers fidgety. Putting on the kettle serves to distract him from the thought of the dishevelled bed, from the forgiveness he must feel before he can speak it, from the sense of his own unworthiness to occupy that warm, sensual place – unworthy not least because it is not only she who has been unfaithful, but he too. But putting on the kettle is also, of course, part of the process of preparing two cups of Epps's Soluble Cocoa, one for himself and one for Stephen Dedalus, the young man he has spent the latter part of the day with, the boy who he hopes might become the son he never had (son-in-law, if Stephen makes it up with Milly, Bloom's daughter). A domestic moment, then, like a painting by Joyce's near contemporary, Walter Osborne. But actually, the tap (water) that we have observed him interrogating will supply, in another moment's time, not only the liquid for the cocoa, but also the water with which he will wash his hands, as if he were engaged not just in the imbibing of cocoa, but were also someone preparing to be the celebrant in a rite about to be performed.

The two torn betting stubs on the dresser – left behind by Molly's lover Blazes Boylan – haunt the scene. Of course, Epps's is only a 'massproduct' of grocery, only a household commodity, a commonplace. So is water. So sometimes is adultery. And ordinary enough, too, is the uncertain soul of Leopold Bloom. But a rite *is* to be performed and it is in the nature of the sacramental to transform and transcend anything, however ordinary, even a rackety marriage, even a cup of Epps's Soluble Cocoa, a transubstantiated *Mass*-product indeed.

Water – from the Roundwood Reservoir, in this only adumbrated, reconfigured rite – cleanses and purifies. But water also destroys. Conventionally, the sacrament of baptism destroys the old Adam, and washes clean the soul of the initiate. The neophyte is given a new name, inaudible to the Devil and the powers of evil because the doors of the baptismal chamber are shut against them. This is the power of words vanquishing the forces of darkness, just as – in the form of metaphor – language transforms and transcends quotidian experience and makes poetry out of the dross of the commonplace. In this tiny vignette of Joyce's book, the merely *mass*-product assumes its true character as *Theobroma cacao*, the Latin name for the plant which gives us cocoa beans. Did it grow in the tropical house at Glasnevin in the first decade of the twentieth century? Yes, it did, and Joyce must have noticed it and its Latin (Greek) scientific name. Of course he did, just as he noticed the source of the water coming out of the tap in Eccles Street. The name means (but I expect you have guessed it) *God-food Cocoa*.

Joyce was not much of a gardener, a gardener on the ground, that is; he did most of his garden-making, his mythopoesis, in his head. Nevertheless, if Ireland hadn't been in some sense a garden already, it would have been necessary to invent it as such, and Joyce would have understood that. Joyce-the-exile invented Bloom-the-Jew – the exile, the outsider twice-over – to enact his metaphor of modern man in search of a home, somewhere he belongs, somewhere there's someone and something to welcome him.

Joyce's Bloom began his day (16 June – *Bloomsday*, we all know it as now) with a hankering for grilled kidneys. He slipped round the corner to the butcher's in Dorset Street Upper and spent 3*d* on said 'bloodgouts'. On the way he passed the open windows of St Joseph's National School and caught the sing-song voices of the boys reciting their alphabets, and then a snatch of a geography lesson. It's a litany of the names of islands off Ireland's west coast: Inishturk, Inishark, Inishbofin. More precisely than merely 'islands in the west', these are actually situated off Connemara. And it just so happens that the central region of Connemara has been known as Joyce's Country since time immemorial. Bloom is alert to the psycho-geography bearing upon the name of his creator, Mr Joyce. Alert too to the psycho-geography of himself: 'Inishturk. Inishark. Inishboffin.' (Bloom hears them recite.) 'At their joggerfry. Mine. Slieve Bloom.'

Slieve Bloom is actually in County Offaly, quite a way inland from Connemara, but psycho-geography is no respecter of space and place plotted merely mechanically. After all, the most meaningful places – especially if you are in any sense an exile, a placeless person – are places-of-the-mind. And the most meaningful, the most important, of them all – the place each of us calls *home* – is not to be found in any published atlas anywhere. Walking down this early morning Dublin street, Leopold Bloom feels the magnetic pull of the word that intimates *his* home. Slieve is the anglicised version of the Irish *sliabh*. It means 'mountain'. Bloom is a pretty un-Irish word with undertones of German-Jewishness – a misfit of linguistics to match a homeless wanderer. Almost at the end of the book, and hundreds of pages later, Molly affectionately recalls Bloom dubbing her his 'mountain flower'. Psycho-botany.

But the point of all this is mostly to draw attention to what was on the butcher's counter that morning when Bloom called in to buy his kidneys: it was a pile of paper – newspaper, trade papers, paper to wrap up the meat for the customer to carry away. And the uppermost sheet was a flyer for a 'model farm at Kinnereth on the lakeshore of Tiberias'. At precisely that time, enterprising Zionists were trying to set up quite a number of these pioneering communes, to make the desert of the British Protectorate of Palestine bloom again, as it had done so long ago (in history perhaps; in the imaginations of exiled

Jews certainly) before the Romans had finally lost patience with the province of Judea and sacked Jerusalem, precipitating two thousand years of Jewish diaspora.

Exile, in other words, but on a scale unprecedented before and unrepeated in such a relentlessly serial form anywhere else. I suspect that the very word *diaspora* (it's a new word, as recent as the late nineteenth century, and precisely it means 'dispersal of Jews among Gentiles') may have been invented to throw dust in our eyes, as if a new word were denoting a new phenomenon. But, of course, the Jews had experienced exile twice already before the Romans initiated a third round of it in AD 70. The first was as slaves in Egypt (which is what occasioned God's promise to give them a safe haven, a Promised Land, in the first place). The second as captives in Babylon. For history to record exile three times over begins to look like systematic persecution – hence, perhaps, the new, cod-Greek, slightly sanitised word *diaspora*. Language reflecting uneasy consciences, I think we reasonably may infer.

However that may be, the flyer that Bloom spotted at the top of the butcher's pile of papers was for the sort of place that we would call now a kibbutz. Thus named, there were a great many of them set up in the 1950s – kibbutzim – and they were popular in the 1960s and 1970s with idealistic young beatniks (a Russian-Yiddish word, this time), Jewish and Gentile. Kibbutzim: gardens in the desert, recoveries of mythic places presumed lost. The flyer which caught his eye and which Bloom stuffed into his pocket, where it remained until almost the end of the book, was for an early prototype of precisely this sort of place. When he was getting undressed and was on the point of climbing at last into bed, nine hundred pages and eighteen hours later, his attention (ours too) is drawn to it again. It reappears. Only in passing, it is true, but nothing in *Ulysses* is ever gratuitous. And the point here? Tucked into his pocket for the entirety of this day-in-the-life of Leopold Bloom was a little atlas of psycho-geography, a blueprint of a mythic place, presumed lost, now promised anew, and its form is that of a sort of garden … in other words, it's the map-in-the-mind of the entire book, the book which (some might not unreasonably argue) is also a sort of mind-map of who and where we are now – ourselves, us: intelligent, alert, vulnerable, disabled somehow by a sort of shame – cultural, historical – but we don't quite understand why, bookish perhaps (but not ashamed of *that*), we modern and postmodern Europeans.

Joyce was not much of a gardener; he did most of his gardening in his head. But sometimes, he stepped out of the study, out of the mind, and set a foot on the terrestrial, the real soil – to do a bit of fieldwork, as it were. The obsessively topographical, evinced here by that tediously exact logging of the journey of Dublin's water from Roundwood, serves exactly that process: the fixing of the imaginative in the terrestrial and the material. And it really isn't that much of an exaggeration to say – as all the tourist guide-books do – that if Dublin were destroyed tomorrow, you could reconstruct it from the pages of *Ulysses*.

Shortly after one o'clock in the afternoon – so, much earlier in the day – in the bar of Davy Byrne's pub in Duke Street (the Lestrygonians chapter) Bloom is wistfully, impressionistically, slightly boozily, remembering the erotic rapture of The Song of Solomon in the Old Testament, then the salad days of his own courtship, remembering Molly's breasts and Molly's lips and Molly's eyes. Joyce has Bloom conflating the garden of Eros with the garden of Eden, blurring it with the place, the 'beds of spices', wherein Solomon, the lover, has gone 'to feed in the gardens, and to gather lilies', and then decanting the whole, half-remembered, half-created scene onto the Hill of Howth, the narrow peninsula just north of Dublin, where there do indeed grow heathers and rhododendrons in abundance:

> … memory. Touched his sense moistened remembered. Hidden under wild ferns on Howth. Below us bay sleeping sky. No sound. The sky … Pillowed on my coat she had her hair, earwigs in the heather scrub my hand under her nape, you'll toss me all. O wonder! Coolsoft with ointments her hand touched me, caressed: her eyes upon me did not turn away. Ravished over her I lay, full lips full open, kissed her mouth. Yum … Flowers her eyes were, take me, willing eyes. Pebbles fell. She lay still. A goat. No-one. High on Ben Howth rhododendrons

a nannygoat walking surefooted, dropping currants. Screened under ferns she laughed warmfolded. Wildly I lay on her, kissed her; eyes, her lips, her stretched neck, beating, woman's breasts full in her blouse of nun's veiling, fat-nipples upright. Hot I tongued her. She kissed me. I was kissed. All yielding she tossed my hair. Kissed, she kissed me.

Me. And me now.

Fieldwork. And so is this really:

Three days imagine on a bed with a vinegared handkerchief round her forehead, her belly swollen out! Phew! Dreadful simply! Child's head too big: forceps. Doubled up inside her trying to butt its way out blindly, groping for the way out. Kill me that would. Lucky Molly got over hers lightly. They ought to invent something to stop that. Life with hard labour …

because in the pattern of all gardens, Eden itself, pre-lapsarian Eve would have had no need of a stupefying narcotic to ease the pain of childbirth. There *was* no pain of childbirth then, labour was not work. That's one of the things that came of expulsion from The Garden: 'In pain shall you bring forth children', thunders the punitive God. But Joyce – of all modern authors – is the most incapable of crying over spilt milk. Of course he remembers the story of Paradise, but it's too late to cry over Paradise Lost; we must patch up things as best we may. Like Queen Victoria, make the best of the bad job, take chloroform against the pain: 'Twilightsleep idea: queen Victoria was given that. Nine she had. A good layer.'

Fieldwork. Eden-archaeology, but with the nostalgia wrung out of it.

In the vast Circe chapter (Circe is Homer's enchantress), Stephen and Bloom are in Bella Cohen's brothel in Tyrone Street Lower (now – in the interests of topographical precision, you understand – Railway Street). The time is midnight. This is the part of the book that marks the human race's graduation to adulthood. People must always have *thought* this sort of thing because, constitutionally, we are dreaming animals, we cannot help it; and probably some people – quite a lot of them? – have been *writing* this sort of thing; but only with the (much contested, frustrated, challenged) publication of *Ulysses* have we been allowed to *read* it. It marks the coming of age, at last, of our race – which, of course, is not necessarily something to be proud of, but there we are (unless, that is, you rate honesty itself as a grown-up achievement). But it does just so happen that respect for honesty, along with an absolute respect for myth, is the cornerstone of the world according to James Joyce. Stephen and Bloom are in the brothel, the latter lacerating his soul with thoughts of parallel goings-on at No. 7 Eccles Street where Boylan, at this very same time, is likely disporting himself with Molly; the former gloomily making

connections between Hamlet's mother's perfidy and his own towards *his* mother on her deathbed when he refused to commit himself to the church, her church, the Roman Catholic Church. But this is a brothel as well as a soul-house, and there is other stuff going on too, of course. The scene is not edifying (but there you are):

> (*Halcyon Days, high school boys in blue and white football jerseys and shorts, Master Donald Turnbull, Master Abraham Chatterton, Master Owen Goldberg, Master Jack Meredith, Master Percy Apjohn, stand in a clearing of the trees and shout to Master Leopold Bloom.*)
> THE HALCYON DAYS: Mackerel! Live us again. Hurray!
> (*They cheer.*)
> BLOOM: (*Hobbledehoy, warmgloved, mammamufflered, stunned with spent snowballs, struggles to rise.*) Again! I feel sixteen! What a lark! Let's ring all the bells in Montague Street. (*He cheers feebly.*) Hurray for the High School!
> THE ECHO: Fool!
> THE YEWS: (*Rustling.*) She is right, our sister. Whisper. (*Whispered kisses are heard in all the wood. Faces of hamadryads peep out from the boles and among the leaves and break blossoming into bloom.*) Who profaned our silent shade?
> THE NYMPH: (*Coyly through parting fingers.*) There! In the open air?
> THE YEWS: (*Sweeping downward.*) Sister, yes. And on our virgin sward.
> THE WATERFALL:
> Poulaphouca Poulaphouca
> Phoucaphouca Phoucaphouca

All through *Ulysses*, Joyce has been very careful of the word *bloom*, the common noun, the verb, rather than the proper noun borne by the book's protagonist. The dictionary provides not many paraphrases and synonyms for the word *bloom*, but assiduously Joyce has employed them all – blossom, break, flower, bud-burst – because the word *bloom*, in its ur-form, has been requisitioned from the impersonal science of botany and quarantined, so that when eventually it is used, it will belong personally and peculiarly to Molly and Leopold (Bloom), it will reflect very precisely their states of mind (and conceivably their bodily functions as well). Joyce judges this almost epiphanic moment very, very carefully. The alert, patient, but now rewarded reader will have been galvanised at last by the word's appearance, nearly seven hundred pages into the book. The Yews rustle, their fronds are gingerly parted as the wood-spirits, the hamadryads (they're nymphs who live and die with and within their host-trees), hardly able to keep to a whisper the cumulative bubbling of their b's, peep out from the *boles* of the yews, and then *break, blossom* and finally *bloom*. Strictly speaking, their theatre of operations should be the Poulaphouca Falls on the upper Liffey (another supply of water for Dublin actually, but this time we are spared details of gradients, distances, water pressures, etc.) ... to which beauty-spot Bloom is recalling a school outing years earlier. The *Poula* part of the Irish name simply means 'pool'. But, if you look again, you see that its second half is the word *Phouca*. Or *Pooka*, as it's written sometimes (and in Irish that's spelt *Púca*). The Pooka is the Irish Puck, the Lord of Mischief. So this is all happening in 'another part of the wood', as Shakespeare has it when he is preoccupied with his version of another rackety marriage in need of repairs, magical or otherwise, that of Titania and Oberon. The Pooka in Ireland is mischievous like England's Puck, but probably more so, and with a markedly earthier, not to say ribald tendency. He is a shape-shifter. His favourite borrowed forms are those of the horse and (you guessed) the goat. Goats are notoriously randy (though in the Howth episode you'll have noticed that it's a nanny, and she confines her bodily functions merely to the quite decorous dropping of 'currants'). Dryads (ordinary dryads, that is, as opposed to hamadryads who are bonded to their trees!), on the other hand, are quite chaste and live unseen in secret groves of the wildwood; nymphs live by secret waters and bathe naked. Watery, remote, unvisited woodlands on the margins of the human world ... this is the realm of the Great God Pan, who is, you'll remember, man from the waist up but goat from the waist down, he who chased the nymph Syrinx and precipitated her metamorphosis into reeds, then into incorruptible, incorporeal sound, and finally into pan pipes. But it was yews (and oaks) that were the preferred – indeed sacred – trees of the Druids, the priestly magicians of ancient Ireland, whereas Pan is universal rather than local and he is always crowned with ivy, not yew. Has Joyce suffered, therefore, a lapse of concentration here?

Pan had muscled his way into the literature of the early twentieth century well before Joyce began writing. He is found there so frequently that you could be forgiven for thinking a new (old) cult had sprung up. The best known of his appearances is in the central chapter of *The Wind in the Willows*. It's called 'Piper at the Gates of Dawn' and in it the errant Little Portly, whom his parents feared drowned, is found by Ratty and Mole safely asleep at the feet of the Great God Pan. *Willows* was published in 1908.

J.M. Barrie's *Peter Pan* – the least godly of all Pan's latter-day appearances – was published in 1904. E.M. Forster is rather vague about the date of *his* first short story, but it seems to have been somewhere around 1903. It is called 'A Story of Panic' and, as you'd expect with that title, it revolves around an epiphany of the god. Arthur Machen's *The Great God Pan* was written in 1894, but much more widely read was his *The Hill of Dreams*. Let drop your guard on the rational, waking mind, and the gods of the old world will appear, Pan among them, both books warn. *The Hill of Dreams* was published in 1907. Kenneth Grahame's own *Pagan Papers* appeared in 1893, but the sequel *Dream Days* was published five years later. The poet Swinburne, the last of the Victorian linguistic sybarites and the first of modern pagans, was obsessed with Pan. And so on.

How serious was all this? Probably the vogue, or cult, or whatever it was, reflected a state of exhaustion in the high culture in Europe rather than a new chapter of religious or literary thinking and, whimsy apart, all of it evaporated in due course anyway under pressure from the fallout of the Great War. However, Spiritualism – attempts to make contact in particular with the multitudinous dead of that war – began to attract a very great following indeed. One of its most famous adepts was the poet Yeats (but he had been deeply involved in matters occult long before war broke out); one of its most discreet, but nonetheless ardent, had been the old Queen Victoria twenty years earlier, still searching for her Albert; a more recent convert – and contemporary again with Joyce – was Arthur Balfour. Conan Doyle was a very seri-ous follower (and perhaps that accounts for some of Holmes' almost supernatural powers of intelligence). But wishful thinking, of the whimsically neo-pagan kind embodied in quite a lot of these books and poems, was never going to survive the gunfire and the grief. Nevertheless, Pan is an idea that refuses to lie down and die, even now. He embodies too faithfully our own divided natures for him to give in and vanish without a fight. That pivotal chapter in *The Wind in the Willows* is frequently missed out in later editions – censored, in effect – and at first you wonder why, but once you begin to think about it, caution, even trepidation, makes sense. Pan represents uncomfort-able truths about ourselves. And despite the passage of time, he *won't* go away. Thirty years on, there he is, the *éminence grise*, in George Allen's *Picnic at Wittenham* (now in the Tate). In a sense this was the picture that even Manet dared not paint with his *Déjeuner*. Far more unsettling than a naked woman of the *demi-monde* insinuated into your picnic is this sinister, god-suggesting figure, standing at the very edge of the liminal woodland where Nature has to connect with Culture and, equally magisterial as he is mysterious, he is overseeing the *plein-air* party taking place a hundred yards away below him. Unseen, his presence is nevertheless unmistakable, and emphatically unnerving. And the picnic not quite just another piece of English flummery pastorale. Because of Pan's tutelary oversight, the scene and its subject are not comfortably benign any more. Pan was with us again in 1967 with Pink Floyd's classic *Piper at the Gates of Dawn* album. Perhaps further epiphanies will occur as time goes on.

Did Joyce take it at all seriously? Is he poking fun at it, or shyly leaving his prayer card at the temple's threshold? Both, I think.

Look again closely at Joyce's magic wood, though, and you prob-ably won't be able to make up your mind whether it is the faces of the hamadryads which are *blooming*, or the yews, whose leaves and eve-rything else have been brought to a pitch of such excitement by what they are witnessing. So much so that *they* too are blooming. Of course, yews *do* bloom, but so modestly that no one ever remarks upon the flowers (though the berries in due course are plain enough). So is

Joyce playing fast and loose with his botanical experience? Here too, the answer is both yes and no. This is, after all, a magical wood and he is entitled to tease us with improbabilities. What we do need to notice, however, before we lose patience with him, is that the wallpaper of this room in Bella Cohen's stew is (did you guess?) *ivy* leaves, so everything is approximately alright after all. The master was *not* nodding off.

By way of Celtic myth, crossed with Greek myth, crossed with Shakespeare's Forest of Arden, and probably with the memory of strolls through Glasnevin too, Joyce deconstructs the ancient and the modern, and constructs a new Ireland. Along the way he opens yet another (queasily guilty) window upon Bloom's mind, but the manner in which he does so is in the form of a virtuosically clever parody of the typical periphrases (for sex and orgasm) that you find by the dozen in the not quite audibly panting pages of Victorian fiction. Dear Reader, in the case of those lines from the Circe chapter, I'd blush to provide an exegesis, blow by blow, of what is actually going on. I leave it to you to do it for yourself or, indeed, not, if you prefer. Suffice it to say that the episode is very funny, very sad for Bloom, and it climaxes in the very eponymous word *bloom*.

Fieldwork. If Irishmen were not naturally the makers and denizens of gardens – Bloomeries, let's say – it would have been necessary to invent them as such.

Ireland being the sort of place it is, we should not be surprised to be reminded that the crust of the present is permeable to interventions by the past, nor should we be too slow to spot where the past is lurking, neither very far nor very invisibly, beneath the surface. Those precautions taken, we are in a position to have our minds stretched sufficiently to cope – equally and simultaneously – with a past as recent (in this instance) as Parnell or with things as mythically timeless as the *Púca* and Druidic rites. (Parnell's death on 6 October 1891 was remembered as Ivy Day ... thus generating for Joyce another ramification of the theme of infidelity, Parnell's heart having been broken by Catholic Ireland expressing revulsion towards him once he was unmasked as an adulterer ... and another botanical trope, of course.)

Classical Christianity evolved between two trees intensely stylised, almost from the start, into symbols, the tree at the heart of the Garden of Eden on the one hand, and on the other, the 'tree', the Cross, that was in the very long term the consequence of Adam's fall when the great scheme of atonement came full circle in the Garden of Gethsemane and at Golgotha. In the first place, classical Christianity demonised trees – woods and forests – probably because its parent, and in some respects its prototype, Judaism, had set an example in its own relentless execrations (in the books of the Prophets) of the Groves of Baal. And prototype became stereotype: first Baal-worshippers, then Druids, and then eventually every deviant cult – whether it was Polynesian cannibals or devil-worshippers in Salem, Massachusetts – were reckoned to assemble and conduct their business in 'groves', or 'woods' or just impenetrable forest: impenetrable and impermeable to the light of truer religions, that is. Christianity itself – you can see it in the pages of the Gospels – grows up in a shadowy ambivalence towards this same idea. Christ has an ancestry claimed for him via the Tree of Jesse. But other trees, more literal ones, are quite often the objects of execration: a fig tree is to be 'dug up and dunged', shysters climb up and hide in sycamores when they should face the honest light of day, olives and vines are metaphors for things that must earn their keep by delivering bounty: simply being a tree is not enough; they – and you too, of course – you must bear fruit. Latterly, the metaphor of the forest as the zone of evil – originally Judaic – served the new religion in its own right, not least because it fitted what evolved into the new religion's historical circumstances. The north-eastern frontier of the Roman Empire (a name which itself became, after the conversion of Constantine in AD 312, coterminous with Christendom) was precisely that: a wild, forested region, ungovernable, volatile, dangerous and resolutely pagan. Germania, Roman historians called it, and by the time of the fall of the empire it had already done four hundred years' service as a synonym for wilderness: political, cultural and moral. There in the forest, went the warnings to Christians both early and late, were the barbarians, the godless, waiting their moment, like the wolves, to prey upon the bodies and souls of the god-fearing. This wildness and imperviousness to civilisation was perceived – correctly, as it turned out – to be the worst threat to the Roman imperium, and thus to Christendom itself. From the pretty innocuous Latin *silva* (wood), it was no distance linguistically to the French *sauvage* ('in a state of nature'), and then – in the thirteenth century, and possibly earlier still – to the English *savage* ('ferocious; untameable; amoral'). Occasionally – as in Eliot's *The Dry Salvages* – the *l* of *silva* survives, and it reminds us of *salvage*: what remains when nature ungoverned has wrecked our ships, the instruments of our endeavours towards civilisation and commerce, culture and colonisation. Though it seems unlikely now in an age of tree-huggers, the excoriation of trees and woods and forests still permeates deeply into both our language and our culture. On the evidence of the savagery of the continuing commercial exploitation of trees the world over, and in the spinelessness of contemporary attempts to resist it, I would think that those cultural memes hold as much sway now as ever.

Crudely binary though it was – good versus evil, the city versus the wildwood, the citizen versus the barbarian – there was something compellingly simple and powerful about both the metaphor (of the wickedness of forests) and the fact of the increasingly frequent, increasingly destabilising incursions by these warring northmen into the empire. After all, the eternal city *was* a city, not a rural retreat: Jerusalem was a city; Rome was a city. The very word *civilisation* began its rapid evolution from the Latin *civis* – citizen, city-dweller. St Augustine mapped out Christendom as the hinterlands of *The City of God*. Thus understood, the term *to clear a forest* expressed exactly what it took to make way for civilisation. In modern parlance, we'd read a policy of *scorched earth*. The words – whether we imagine Roman legionaries wielding axes more than one thousand years ago or the bombed and chemically defoliated forests of south-east Asia in the 1960s and 1970s – are intrinsically violent, so violent that it is hard to avoid concluding that they are actually fuelled by barely suppressed fear of that most fearful thing of all: that which is unknown and perhaps unknowable. And hard, too, not to see that familiar compensating mechanism – in the presumption of moral superiority over the perceived enemy – of people with a grudge to nurse and a corner to defend … except that the enemy here was nature. It was a short step then to personify and reify that abstract threat into the forms of wyverns, witches, wolves and ogres, denizens of the wildwood, all of them. As late as the seventeenth century (we are told), witches danced in woods. Arthur Miller (in the Preface to *The Crucible*) reminds twentieth-century theatregoers that, for the people in his play, these insecure, early-Massachusetts settlers, the forest 'stood, dark and threatening', so much so that 'the Salem folk believed that the virgin forest was the Devil's last preserve … the citadel of his final stand'. It's what the play hinges upon. At the end of the eighteenth century – and so much anthologised now that the image is not only reified but almost canonised – William Blake has his tyger – his incarnation of elemental, naked power, the generative imagination liberated into some god-fuelled frenzy of creation or destruction – stalking 'the forests of the night'. More or less contemporaneously with Blake – and almost definitively to us even now, because of the way it has permeated our consciousness through popular representations of the myth of the colonisation of the New World – the Founding Fathers of America were avid gardeners at the same time as they demonised the 'dismal Wilderness' (as John Adams had it) of all those new territories brought into the fold of the Union by the Louisiana Purchase in 1803. And that vision of wilderness was not confined to vegetation: the indigenous people who were already there, living in these uncharted regions, were not people at all but 'savages'. (The word *savage*, we remember, is cognate with *silva* – woodland – by way of *silvaggio, salvage,* etc.) The War of 1812 – the more or less systematic elimination of the native Americans who resisted the theft of their land – was seen, and is often represented still, as an almost religious cleansing … which is, self-evidently, to be preferred to the word 'genocide', which too violent a shaking of the kaleidoscope of language would otherwise – and perhaps more honestly – throw up.

Language, we know (Joyce knew), both reflects and shapes the way we see things: it may have been an accident in the first place – in the salad days of language itself perhaps, millennia ago – that someone stumbled upon a metaphor whereby a problem did not have an origin or a source so much as a *root*, and that to mend a situation would require social or political or religious surgery to eradicate (*radix* – Latin, *root*) the evil not merely piecemeal but *root and branch*. Accident it may have been, but the consequences have been incalculably great. Forests became so deeply seeded into our minds and into the patterns of our speech, so reflexively institutionalised and epitomised, as the definitive zones of darkness, of inchoate, unbridled energy, that it's doubtful if we could ever completely emerge from the shadows those tree-like words have cast and indeed still do cast. It would take poets rather than social reformers or linguistic hygienists to unpick the knots of a metaphor so deeply embedded. We would probably have to depend upon a William Blake and upon his progenous ilk to know where we really stand: trees and forests are generative or degenerative depending on what poems you know by heart (metaphorically rather than literally, but the metaphor is, in any case, always more potent than the literal anyway), as well as – in a much broader, much more popular sense – on how you view them (or indeed upon how you view tygers).

Inventing bogeys, credible or simply fantastic, has long served as a means of chilling and chastening wayward children, just as – in the public realm – it has so often been put into service as remedial, makeshift glue to repair many a fraying and insecure society. The Brothers Grimm and sci-fi novels such as John Wyndham's *The Day of the Triffid*s share some common ground of imagery, and some-thing too of technique (if very little else), with that long gallery of demagogues in history disturbing our collective peace of mind by bogeyfying 'enemies of the state'. And as often as not, the 'enemy' is located in the dark, dangerous (Blakean) 'forests' of our own insecuri-ties because whether it be tool for rabble-rousing, stock-in-trade of fairy tales, or stick to beat errant infants, what the (bogeyfied) forest represents would seem to be an archetype of our sleeping minds: the threat to innocence from wilderness. Babes-in-the-wood are always at risk, whatever the era. And – in the context of our studies – Irish rebels (*wood-kerns*, Edmund Spenser tellingly calls them in his report to Queen Elizabeth I, *A View of the Present State of Ireland* of 1596) exhibited precisely that same *soi-disant* wicked, ungovernable wildness of behaviour. They would harry the English coloniser and then vanish into the forests, first exasperating, and then leaving the English (in Spenser's view) with no choice but to combine genocide with total forest clearances in the form of fire: the razing of Ireland; the cleansing and purifying by flame and by sword. For the Irishman C.S. Lewis in the twentieth century – in the *Chronicles of Narnia* – forests were still as primitively and powerfully dangerous as ever they were in the Old Testament. Fifty years on, and miles down the road towards a better educated view of why actually we need trees, the anathematising of them is still as deeply at work perhaps in our *sub-conscious* as when – while chainsawing plane trees in Sheffield's or London's or indeed Dublin's streets, for example (because they mess the place

up with leaves falling or they hinder satellite TV reception) – it is actively at work in our *conscious* mind, in the flimsiness of our public policies towards woodland, and in our insatiable appetite for hardwood timber felled in irreplaceable rainforests.

Developed Christianity (in the form of the Roman Catholic Church) had it both ways: the tree remained the vile gibbet upon which the God had been immolated, but the (almost entirely unbiblical) Cult of the Virgin espoused gardens in abundance: the *hortus conclusus*, the rosary and the rose garden, *the Rose of Such Virtue*, indeed, *that it bore Jesu Christ*. And there grew up a language of flowers, sentimental and Victorian now, but Marian in origin. Gardens were alright … sort of, but the church had to be vigilant because the whole thing could so easily revert to a pre-Christian nature cult, as if the metaphors we used to denote these Other Worlds – heavens, paradises, gardens even – needed in essence only the simplest of keys to unlock them: the *Other* was really *Mother*. How real that risk was can be seen quickly and incontestably in a visit to virtually any Gothic church. Southwell Minster's Chapter House, with its more than forty images of the Green Man/Jack-in-the-Green (call him what you will) peeping out through the stone leaves on the capitals and ceiling bosses, is as good a place to look as any. The arcades and nave of a great Gothic cathedral, where the floor blossoms underfoot with plants and flowers in the encaustic tiles; where the piers rise like the stylised trunks of the trees in a great forest, and then branch out into a traceried canopy of boscage overhead, occasionally breaking into leaf or blossoming into flowers in the carving of the bosses; where – to reach the high altar – you must pass beneath the Rood, the Great Tree; where (if you're lucky) the pew-ends blossom in poppy-heads; where the great window in the west wall is a Rose Window, and so on. It's about as 'pagan' as can be, *if* pagan means taking forms and metaphors from the natural world.

Until recently, Ireland was a very (Roman) Catholic place but, at the same time that almost every parish had its officially sanctioned grotto where the Virgin smiled down upon a flowery turf and us, there was (is?) also the unofficial, out-of-the-way holy well where the chthonic presences of something much older, much harder to catechise, come into play. The priests railed against them. Sometimes they succeeded in having them shut down. Quite often, though, they had to compromise and agree to permit, or even themselves to attend and be the celebrants there at one open-air Mass a year. Now these strange, undeniably cultic places, *grounded* in the actualities of the raw materials and processes of life, have almost all gone *under*ground to a greater or lesser extent, but they don't wither away, and we should wonder why.

I think it's likely that these places – and the very telluric rounds, the patterns, the pilgrimages, the rites of passage round and through water, the prayer clooties, etc., which yet survive – are really the very heart of religion as they are also the heart of gardening, however crudely and clumsily expressed, no matter how scruffy the horticulture, or how improvisatory might be the rites of spring celebrated there (and the rites of Lughnasa, and Bealtaine, but probably above all of Samhain – Christianised as All Hallows and All Souls – when the walls between the worlds of the natural and the supernatural were traditionally reckoned to be at their most penetrably thin). These places – despised though they are by the Church and by modern sophisticates alike – are the very pattern of that so-hard-to-articulate yearning to recover, discover Eden.

That's what the Irish mind once upon a time – upon a historical and not just mythic time – would have thought, anticipated, expected, and then been in aweful respect of. But probably not now. Or not in the form of one that you'd want to stand up and be counted for. Some sense of a fourth dimension, is it? Or just whimsical Lepre-Corn? It sounds improbably fantastic, or gothic, or computer-enhanced.

But perhaps not necessarily so. Perhaps you don't have to blush, after all, at this morganatic marriage between twenty-first and eleventh-century minds. You don't have to be New-Ageist, or attend psychic fairs, or become a born-again pagan ... or even a conventional Christian, for that matter, to identify with some of this: imagination and received imagery working synthetically together. What follows is the American novelist William Maxwell writing from Ireland to Sylvia Townsend Warner in 1968. It's July. He's a fresh-eyed stranger (yet again), seeing both more and less of Ireland than the habituated indigenous Irish might see for themselves ... if it were not for the likes of Joyce and Beckett, Yeats (both Willy and Jack), Flann O'Brien, James Stephens, and so on and on ...

> The long twilights were even more satisfactory ... it was like having everything you had ever lost given back to you. You are used to this phenomenon, probably, but I simply couldn't get over it. Twilight, and then the half light that comes after that, and then the quarter light, and the eighth light, and then the almost darkness that is still somehow a kind of light, in which the shapes of things emerge in all their solidity, and people are doing very odd things – such as fishing at eleven thirty at night – and the supernatural is not at all implausible.

Ulysses apart, there is only one other modern Irish novel (of real stature) in which a garden is the central metaphor. It distils the melancholy – its mythic paradigm more Gethsemane than Eden, I suppose – to which its author, William Trevor, almost always inclines. It is a version of a *Paradise Lost*, but not without intimations of some sort of recovery in the end. It is called, appropriately, *The Silence in the Garden*. Joyce – the urban writer – also taps into the myth of Eden, but in a less visible, less obviously explicated way, though probably more deeply than any other modern author, deeper than William Trevor certainly, though Trevor's work too will last and last.

Ireland, if it hadn't already existed, would have had to have been invented, but the myth of paradise as a garden was already there, and both – an idealised place and a beautiful garden, fused, confused, married teasingly or even divorced uneasily sometimes, and only hinting at a reconciliation – constitute that primary place which we either construct in our minds for ourselves or look to poets, painters and novelists to construct/reconstruct for us.

For mankind, growing things to eat is imperative. The fact that virtually all governments and most of the people they govern have lost sight of that – the primacy of agriculture – is perhaps the defining feature of modern life, and also the silliest thing humans have ever done.

It is an oversight which helps to cast gardening – ornamental agriculture, as it were – as merely a whim indulged in by neo-romantic ruralists, a luxury, a caprice, something gratuitous.

I doubt, however, if that is the truth of the matter at all. The making of gardens is as compulsive still, at least to some humans, as migration is to some birds. And it is as compulsory as agriculture, but not to satisfy the hunger of the stomach – rather, to feed some hunger in the soul, to mend some deep, nagging dislocation in the way we live.

What we see in the primitive, ungroomed, secretive *ur*-gardens that go with the holy wells of Ireland is far older than Christianity, and it represents the unreformed (pre-patrician) compulsion to connect with earth (and with sky and water, with rocks, and with trees). Joyce, the most sophisticated writer of the modern age, locates the minds of his characters sometimes in these primitive, primal regions of human compulsion. Myth. Joined-up lives where the material is not entirely disconnected from the spiritual.

Lots of other places have more or less the equivalent of these holy wells, but Joyce is Irish. And so is the creative tension within an Irish culture which, while apparently moving away now from conventional religion, and still labouring, as it seems, under a post-colonial stigmatising of gardens, nevertheless shows no sign of losing a grip upon the great, primal metaphors – earth and motherhood, generation and gardens – as the defining zones of those very things. These are indeed the bricks that myths are made of. And one of the contributing factors to this is the legacy of the blurred gender of the divinity, the person being worshipped, which Catholicism (and especially the cult of Mary) has conferred – not quite exclusively, but nevertheless very formatively – upon Ireland's cultural genes. But questions of gender predicate questions also of identity, irrespective of gender. A Martian beamed down now into a church would surely be very much at a loss to work out who, or even what (in a putative *mono*-theism) was really being *worshipped* … or *adored*, or *venerated*, or *receiving devotions*, or *being supplicated to* – be there never so many theological/semiotic hairs split. Was it Father? Was it Son? Was it Mother? Was it not also some of these Saints whose

chapels are ubiquitous, even when they are architecturally periph-
eral? Was it the ancestors even, especially in the forms of those
images of deceased prelates and patrons that the larger churches
boasted of? Or was the deity a compound of elements of all of these?
In sum, was this not really a polytheistic religion?

None of this ought to be all that surprising in view of the legacy of
aboriginal Celtic religion – archeologically almost invisible as it is,
but deeply informing all the same. When its time came, the Catholic
Church did not really *confer* a legacy of a blurred gender in divinity,
it *confirmed* it. Our understanding of Celtic religion – and, indeed,
of the north-European religions that predated it – is provisional: we
don't understand it all that clearly; and we should be even more than
usually careful of jumping to conclusions, because of the temptation
on the one hand to back-read into history elements of the character of
modern, resurgent Celtic Christianity, and on the other of the received
and beguiling simplicity of the story of the Patrician conversion of
pagan Ireland, fabulous though it often is. Nevertheless, however
cautious, there *is* a scholarly consensus now in perceiving Celtic
religion in terms of at least some contrast with the religions of the
ancient Near and Middle East: the cults of Kronos, Yahweh, Zeus,
Shiva (and, in due course, of Christ and of Allah) – religions whose
origins would seem to have been at least in part matriarchal but in
which the male principle progressively has ousted (as in Islam), or
at least relegated (as in Christianity), the female. What we know of
Celtic society – particularly the evidence for matrilinear succession
in leading families, and then for laws governing the inheritance of
property through the female line – seems to support this provisional
view of Celtic religion as fundamentally divergent from those later
and earlier, but more geographically penetrating religions.

This pre-history we do not understand clearly. History, however –
and specifically Irish history – we may see at least somewhat more
clearly and, though it doesn't always correspond perfectly with fact, it
is hard not to notice the ways in which Ireland has often characterised
its own story in terms of polarised genders. On the one hand, there is
an Ireland personified as the girl-goddess Erin, as Shan Van Vocht –

the Poor Old Woman – as Kathleen Ni Houlihan, as Mother Ireland, and so on; and on the other, there is the narrative of imperialism – cultural, even sexual sometimes: the invading, usurping (male) stranger, often but not always, with an eventual concomitant of rape. That blurred gender in the divine that we (or the Martian) may perceive even now in Irish religion has roots in both history and pre-history, and it has analogues in the national narratives, but above all in those liminal regions where *story* bleeds into *his-story*. Irish resistance to invasions – cultural, political, religious, linguistic, economic – has always taken as many forms as were available, but it is one of them in particular that concerns us here: a persistent, even conscientious unwillingness to conform to that part of the prevailing modes of the conqueror which would erase the female, and making that resistance most intense of all – at least symbolically – at the very place of initial penetration: first the beach, the strand, where the invaders' ships make landfall, then the land, the earth itself.

> Speaking broad Devonshire,
> Ralegh has backed the maid to a tree
> As Ireland is backed to England
> …
> She fades from their somnolent clasp
> Into ringlet-breath and dew,
> The ground possessed and repossessed.

That's Seamus Heaney in his poem 'Ocean's Love to Ireland', fascinated, horrified, indeed almost complicit in the fact that Ralegh, also a poet, could have done this rapacious, nonchalant thing … and then gone on to write a poem called 'Ocean's Love to Cynthia'.

Analogues in Irish writing are, in fact, legion. The ruins of a way of life evoked in Goldsmith's *The Deserted Village* in the eighteenth century is essentially the pattern still of Heaney's desecrated, raped Ireland in the twentieth. But analogues of the same in the Irish (historical) national narrative are much more contentiously slippery, though not impossible for all that, even when they seem to appear just as readily as they do in the poetry and prose of the country's creative writers. Here is a sample – and, if it works, one that is strangely germane to our theme – just one, contentious to be sure, in some respects conjectural too, but possible. Pádraic Pearse, a man whom some see as both a begetter and godfather of the Irish Free State, was the man who read the Proclamation of the Republic to the small, unenthusiastic, Easter 1916 crowd outside the General Post Office, the person who embodied so much of what Yeats identified as the 'terrible beauty' in Ireland's birth pangs once he became one of those sixteen men the English shot by way of reprisal for the Easter Rising. A man of action, then, but he was also – and perhaps essentially – a poet, a schoolmaster, a polemicist and an ascetic. St Enda's, the school he founded (in 1908) and ran first in the family house in Ranelagh and then in Rathfarnham – the latter now a national shrine really – was a seedbed for Irish patriots, for Irish-speaking, green-wearing, priest-fearing and, if necessary, blood-sacrificing boys. The place was (still is) pretty austere. At first sight, you'd take this sparseness to evince a militaristic ethos on the Spartan model. Indeed, there was quite a lot about St Enda's which was overtly paramilitary (ironically, like an English public school, in fact). But looking again, you might see something not necessarily so militaristic as monastic about it, particularly in that very (Spartan-lookalike) air of asceticism. If you go on with the monastic analogy, then it could lead you to see behind the surface of St Enda's the shadow particularly of Cistercian models, those monastic houses famous indeed for their austerity. There were upwards of thirty-five Cistercian houses in Ireland – a remarkable number – almost all of them founded in an extraordinary blaze of religious enthusiasm beginning in the 1140s. There is a case for seeing Cistercian devotion – silent, celibate, a conscientious exposing of the body to extremes of physical privation, gruelling work on the land, these things generating a tension between the material and the spiritual, engendering perhaps in the end an ecstasy of contemplation – you *could* see this as not by any means exclusively Irish, of course, but nevertheless as a frame of mind curiously attractive to some elements of Irish temperament. The order has always seen itself as subject to the peculiar aegis of the Virgin Mary. Alone among monastic orders, the *Salve Regina* is an integral part of Cistercian liturgy: these monks lived (live) and worked not just *sub specie aeternitatis*, as they see it, but also in the special shadow cast by Mary's cloak. Pearse lived – in his cottage in Connemara and in Dublin – somewhat monastically, and his bond with his mother was, by almost any standards short of the religious, fierce. When he opened his school in Dublin, the premises were never going to be large enough, so he was looking out for somewhere more suitable, somewhere with more space but also with what he would have deemed to have been the right mood, the right ambience. He found it – in Rathfarnum, then a rural outpost of south Dublin – in a house called, perhaps significantly, The Hermitage. He renamed it St Enda's, but the original Enda (Éanna of Inishmore) himself enjoyed some part of his fame from the fact that his cell on Aran was famously a 'hard narrow prison of stone'. None of this is by any means sufficient to support conclusively a picture of Pearse as a monk manqué. To use the word *monastic* to describe his lifestyle remains figurative: he was never in holy orders, still less a Cistercian monk. No analogy, perfectly fitting, is offering itself. Nevertheless, is it really an accident that his most famous poem – the poem so often asked for, even now, when favourite poems are canvassed – should be 'The Mother'? It is really a sort of secular *Stabat Mater*. This mother – like Mary at the foot of the Cross – speaks for all mothers whose sons have died (as they see it) in a righteous cause, just as Pearse's own mother would come to mourn, celebrate, and then almost sanctify the deaths of her own two sons – as Pearse must have known she would when he wrote his poem – right up to her own death in 1932:

> I do not grudge them: Lord, I do not grudge
> My two strong sons that I have seen go out
> To break their strength and die ...
> We suffer in their coming and their going;
> And tho' I grudge them not, I weary, weary
> Of the long sorrow – And yet I have my joy:
> My sons were faithful and they fought.

Be that as it may, what can perhaps be seen as a pattern in Irish historiography (*pre*-historiography too) – history and ethnography feeding upon mythography – is certainly active in literary cartography, Irish writers mapping their own origins. The scholarly consensus in respect of *ur*-Celtic religion is matched by a consensus of poets (and painters, and sculptors, and indeed prose writers such as Joyce). Whether it is based upon a 'truth' or not, current perceptions lean pretty consensually towards crediting what Seamus Heaney has identified as an 'ancient feminine religion of Northern Europe', which is to say Celtic, and most particularly Irish, though among the moderns Heaney et al must have been taking their lead in the first place not so much from James Frazer and *The Golden Bough* (1880–1915), must have taken their cues not so much from an anthropologically persuasive argument as from a powerful *poetical* polemic, one that was written quite a lot later, in 1948. Robert Graves is usually co-opted as an Englishman but actually his immediate origins were Irish, his grandfather a bishop of Limerick. This shows, both in the central thesis of *The White Goddess* (that the muse of poetry is a goddess, not a god, and certainly not a mortal) but also in the Irish dimensions of quite a lot of his references in the course of the book. Heaney's position (it's in the essay 'A Sense of Place' in the volume *Preoccupations*) is bold. Not everyone would go so far as to support and to use it as comprehensively as he has. However, it certainly convinces *poetically* when it fuels poems such as 'Ocean's Love to Ireland'.

So much for that, but there is yet another factor – and the one towards which Joyce most often nods, both in his art and in his life of self-imposed exile. It is the powerful, primitive compulsion on the part of those exiled to see Ireland as their own Paradise Lost: the visceral longing of those no longer sensing themselves really as *belonging*, anywhere. As deracinated Irish-Americans, or third-generation Irish families in Liverpool or Wandsworth, or Irish expats in Australia, Canada or New Zealand, they are surely entitled – or even to be expected – to do so.

And they have as their model, should they need one, James Joyce. Joyce who expresses wittily, infinitely ingeniously (and actually very compassionately) not just that age-old heartache of the physically exiled, but also more modern inflexions of the sense of loss, whether it be to do with loss of paradise or loss of home and – perhaps most contemporary of all – simply loss of peace of mind. All of them conditions of the exiled, in one way or another. It is some years now since George Steiner wrote about 'the privilege of exile' – and a long time before the currently fashionable Diaspora Studies, with its attention to displaced writers such as Derek Walcott and Joseph Brodsky, began to strut its stuff in our universities, a long time before the Irish government would establish a Ministry for Diaspora Affairs (in 2014) to wait upon those estimated eighty million Irish worldwide: the 'Fifth Province', people began then to call it (Munster, Connaught, Leinster, Ulster, and … the world at large). At the time of writing his book (1997) that was probably to go a long way out along a limb, but Steiner knew what he was talking about: the mindset, as he saw it, of people like himself, exiled Jews. In the event, what he meant spilled out to include *any* exile, *any*where: and then to embrace the way those exiles value so much more both what they have and, of course, what they have not, so that even to be alive brings with it a sense of privilege. 'Privilege' – however dangerously or recklessly expressed – is what Steiner called it, but he was not speaking glibly because in almost the same breath he spoke of the 'price' of that privilege … and the awful facts of history, ancient as well as modern, supply the rest of what he meant. Joyce's own exile was voluntary (more or less) and, though he knew privation, it fell far short of what so many Jews experienced. Nevertheless, his identification of Bloom as a Jew was a very bold move. Joyce's only play – in part a rehearsal for *A Portrait of the Artist as a Young Man* (1918) – is called *Exiles*. This from the same author who casually planted a rose into the description of Molly's hair that day on the Hill of Howth before they were married, before his (Bloom's) father, a hotelier in Ennis, had given up on life and killed himself, before his son Rudolf had died, aged eleven days, and he and Molly had buried him in the knitted jumper she was making. Eleven years on, Molly is there musing in bed and sleepily, mistily she remembers that rose, *and* it reappears – 'rose … red' – on the very last page of the book. Molly indeed was almost asleep, but the writer was not. That metaphor – the garden, the rose – like the flyer in Bloom's pocket, had been shaping the book off and on throughout its nine hundred and thirty pages.

But you don't have to read Joyce to understand Irish gardens. Bookless, you could simply follow and trust the experience of your own eyes. And the Poulaphuca Falls – in the best once-upon-a-time tradition of all fictions – is no more anyway. It has shrunk to a trickle. It has been superseded by a new, larger reservoir: the Blessington Lakes.

This envoi – this last chapter – is for those who feel a need to try to understand Irish gardens in the wider context of Ireland itself, its history, its cultures, its countercultures and its literature. In a sense, the whole of the book has been doing that anyway. And this closing chapter just complicates the issue ... for those who enjoy a bit of complication perhaps, or for those who need no further demonstration of the thesis that the Irish garden is a complicated, contested territory anyway – contested culturally, historically, politically – and all the more interesting because of it.

But as Gerard Manley Hopkins put it – he essentially an Englishman, but whose last poems were written in Ireland – these gardens are also 'heaven-havens', places where beauty speaks for itself. That being so, books – this or any other – become an impertinence. Not a bad conundrum, that.

Bibliography

John Adair, *Hints on the Culture of Ornamental Plants in Ireland*. Dublin. 1878.

John Akeroyd (ed.), *The Wild Plants of Sherkin, Cape Clear and Adjacent Islands of West Cork*. Sherkin Island, Co. Cork. 1996.

Anon, *The Voyage of Saint Brendan* (trans. John O'Meara). Dublin. 1978.

Toby Barnard, *A New Anatomy of Ireland: The Irish Protestants, 1649–1770*. New Haven & London. 2004.

Mark Bence-Jones, *Twilight of the Ascendancy*. London. 1987.

John Bew, *Castlereagh*. London. 2011.

Heinrich Böll, *Irish Journal* (trans. Leila Vennewitz). London. 1983.

Pat Boran & Gerard Smyth (eds), *If Ever You Go: A Map of Dublin in Poetry and Song*. Dublin. 2014.

Patrick Bowe and Keith Lamb, *A History of Gardening in Ireland*. Dublin. 1995.

Patrick Bowe, 'The Traditional Irish Farmhouse and Cottage Garden' in *Irish Architectural & Decorative Studies*. Vol. III. Dublin. 2000.

Patrick Bowe & Michael George, *The Gardens of Ireland*. London. 1986.

William Bulfin, *Rambles in Eirinn*. Dublin. 1907.

Jeremy Burchardt, *Paradise Lost: Rural Idyll and Social Change since 1800*. London. 2002.

Edmund Burke, *A Philosophical Enquiry into the Origins of Our Ideas of the Sublime and Beautiful*. London. 1757.

Paddy Bushe (ed.), *Voices at The World's Edge*. Dublin. 2010.

Michael P. Carroll, *Irish Pilgrimage: Holy Wells and Popular Catholic Devotion*. Baltimore, MD. 1999.

Charles Castle, *Oliver Messel*. London. 1986.

Sybil Connolly & Helen Dillon, *In an Irish Garden*. London. 1986.

Maurice Craig & Michael Craig, *Mausolea Hibernica*. Dublin. 1999.

Patrick Crotty (ed.), *The Penguin Book of Irish Poetry*. London. 2010.

John Crowley, William J. Smyth, & Mike Murphy (eds), *Atlas of the Great Famine*. Cork. 2012.

Michael Dames, *Mythic Ireland*. London. 1996.

Wes Davis (ed.), *An Anthology of Modern Irish Poetry*. Cambridge, MA. 2010.

Annabel Davis-Goff, *Walled Gardens: Scenes from an Anglo-Irish Childhood*. New York. 1989.

Angélique Day (ed.), *Letters from Georgian Ireland: The Correspondence of Mary Delany, 1731–1768*. Belfast, 1991.

Roger Deakin, *Notes from Walnut Tree Farm*. London. 2008.

——— *Wildwood: A Journey Through Trees*. London. 2007.

Terry Eagleton, *Heathcliff and the Great Hunger: Studies in Irish Culture*. London. 1995.

Evan Eisenberg, *The Ecology of Eden*. New York. 1998.

Damien Enright, *A Place Near Heaven*. Dublin. 2004.

——— *The Kindness of Place*. Dublin. 2012.

Nigel Everett, *A Landlord's Garden: Derreen Demesne, County Kerry*. Borlin. 2001.

——— *Wild Gardens: The Lost Demesnes of Bantry Bay*. Borlin. 2000.

——— *The Woods of Ireland: A History, 700–1800*. Dublin. 2014.

J.G. Farrell, *Troubles*. London. 1970.

Deirdre Flanagan & Laurence Flanagan, *Irish Place Names*. Dublin. 2002.

Olda Fitzgerald, *Irish Gardens*. London. 1999.

Lavinia Greacen, *J.G. Farrell: The Making of a Writer*. London. 1999.

Miranda Green, *The Gods of the Celts*. Godalming. 1986.

Peter Harbison, *Pilgrimage in Ireland: The Monuments and the People*. London. 1991.

——— *Guide to the National Monument in the Republic of Ireland*. Dublin. 1982.

Robert Pogue Harrison, *Gardens: An Essay on the Human Condition*. Chicago. 2008.

Marie Heaney, *The Names Upon the Harp*. London. 2000.

Seamus Heaney, 'The God in the Tree' in *The Pleasures of Gaelic Poetry*. Ed. Seán Mac Réamoinn. London. 1982.

——— *Preoccupations*. London. 1980.

——— *North*. London. 1975.

——— *Wintering Out*. London. 1972.

Pauline Henley, *Spenser in Ireland*. Cork. 1928.

Marianne Heron, *The Hidden Gardens of Ireland*. Dublin. 1993.

James Howley, *The Follies and Garden Buildings of Ireland*. New Haven & London. 1993.

Edward Hyams, *Irish Gardens*. London. 1967.

Douglas Hyde (trans.), *The Love Songs of Connacht*. Dundrum. 1904.

James Joyce, *Ulysses*. London. 1922.

Richard Kearney, *The Irish Mind*. Dublin. 1985.

Ian Kershaw, *Making Friends with Hitler: Lord Londonderry and Britain's Road to War*. London. 2004.

Declan Kiberd, *Inventing Ireland: The Literature of a Modern Nation*. London. 1995.

Brian Lalor (general ed.), *The Encyclopaedia of Ireland*. Dublin. 2003.

Winifred Letts, *Songs From Leinster*. London. 1913.

Colm Lincoln, *Dublin as a Work of Art*. Dublin. 1992.

Mary Low, *Celtic Christianity and Nature: Early Irish and Hebridean Traditions*. Edinburgh. 1996.

Niall Mac Coitir, *Ireland's Trees: Myths, Legends and Folklore*. Cork. 2003.

—— *Ireland's Wild Plants: Myths, Legends and Folklore*. Cork. 2006.

Alen MacWeeney & Richard Conniff, *The Stone Walls of Ireland*. London. 1986.

Sean McMahon & Jo Donoghue (eds), *Brewer's Dictionary of Irish Phrase and Fable*. London. 2004.

Edward Malins & the Knight of Glin, *Lost Demesnes: Irish Landscape Gardening 1660–1845*. London. 1976.

J.P. Mallory, *In Search of the Irish Dreamtime*. London. 2016.

Thomas Mason, *The Islands of Ireland*. London. 1938.

Bernard McCabe & Alain le Garsmeur, *James Joyce: Reflections of Ireland*. London. 1993.

Alan Mitchell, *Champion Trees in the British Isles*. London. 1994.

Alberto Manguel & Gianni Guadalupi, *The Dictionary of Imaginary Places*. London. 1999.

E. Charles Nelson, *A Heritage of Beauty*. Dublin. 2000.

—— *An Irish Flower Garden*. Kilkenny. 1984.

—— *The Wild Plants of the Burren and the Aran Islands*. Cork. 2008.

E. Charles Nelson & Eileen McCracken, *The Brightest Jewel: A History of the National Botanic Gardens, Glasnevin, Dublin*. Kilkenny. 1987.

—— *An Irishman's Cuttings*. Cork. 2009.

Seamus O'Brien, *In the Footsteps of Augustine Henry*. Woodbridge, Suffolk. 2011.

James O'Connell, *The Meaning of Irish Place Names*. Belfast. 1979.

Dáithí Ó hÓgáin, *The Sacred Isle: Belief and Religion in Pre-Christian Ireland*. Cork. 1999.

Finola O'Kane, *Ireland and the Picturesque*. New Haven & London. 2013.

—— *Landscape Design in Eighteenth-Century Ireland: Mixing Foreign Trees with the Natives*. London. 2011.

Thomas Pakenham, *Meetings with Remarkable Trees*. London. 1996.

Valerie Pakenham, *The Big House in Ireland*. London. 2000.

Anna Rackard & Liam O'Callaghan, *Fish – Stone – Water: Holy Wells of Ireland*. Cork. 2001.

Claude Rawson, *God, Gulliver and Genocide: Barbarism and the European Imagination, 1492–1945*. Oxford. 2001.

Chet Raymo, *Climbing Brandon*. Dingle. 2004.

Tim Robinson, *Stones of Aran: Labyrinth*. Dublin. 1995.

Yvonne Scott, *The West as Metaphor*. Dublin. 2005.

Sean Sheehan, *Jack's World: Farming on the Sheep's Head Peninsula, 1920–2003*. Cork. 2007.

George Steiner, *My Unwritten Books*. New York. 2008.

Caleb Threlkeld, *Synopsis Stirpium Hibernicarum*. Dublin. 1726. Reprinted in facsimile in 1988, Kilkenny.

William Trevor, *The Silence in the Garden*. London. 1988.

Colin Tudge, *The Secret Life of Trees*. London. 2006.

Wendy Walsh, *An Irish Florilegium*. London. 1983.

Marina Warner, *Alone of All Her Sex: The Myth & the Cult of the Virgin Mary*. London. 1976.

D.A. Webb, *Fifty Trees of Distinction in the Birr Castle Demesne*. 1992.

Eithne Wilkins, *The Rose-Garden Game: The Symbolic Background to the European Prayer Beads*. London. 1969.

Christine Zucchelli, *Trees of Inspiration: Sacred Trees and Bushes of Ireland*. Cork. 2009.

Index of Plants

Bamboo 59, 60, 96,
   161–4, 214, 218,
   233, 267, 328–9
Baptisia australis 257
Begonia 142, 144, 152,
   232
   augustinei 193
Berberis 35, 230
Bergenia 35, 306
   'Ballawley' 262
Beschorneria yuccoides 98
Betula (Birch) 100, 149,
   233, 273, 275
Blechnum tabulare 217
Bowkeria gerrardiana 112
   verticillata 112
Brunnera 327
Buddleia 35, 190, 275
Bulbinella 260
Buxus (Box) 64, 80,
   125, 154, 183,
   202, 230, 250,
   287–8, 306

Callistemon 142, 230
   'Murdo MacKenzie' 144
Calocedrus decurrens 112
Camellia 95, 110, 141–3,
   179–80, 214–5,
   218, 230
Campanula 223, 225,
   257, 290
   lactiflora 257
   'Pritchard's Variety' 195
   rotundifolia (Harebell)
   12
Cardiocrinum giganteum
   231, 306
Carpinus (Hornbeam) 80,
   124, 288
Carrierea calycina 75
Castanea variegata 97
Ceanothus 222
Celmisia 254, 258, 275
Centaurea 256
   cyanus 257
   macrocephala 306
Cephalaria gigantea 306
Cercis siliquastrum (Judas
   Tree) 119, 319
Cestrum roseum
   'Ilnacullin' 144
Chaenomeles x superba

'Rowallane
   Seedling' 309
*Chaerophyllum hirsutum
   roseum* 327
Chamaecyparis lawsoniana
   'Kilmacurragh'
   299
Cinnamomum camphora
   110
Circaea lutetiana
   (Enchanter's
   Nightshade)
   121, 326
Cladrastis sinensis 309
Clematis 151, 183, 185,
   193, 194, 199,
   231, 278–9
   durandii 257
   'Perle d'Azur' 257
   recta 'Purpurea' 305
*Clerodendrum
   trichotomum*
   125, 198
Convallaria majalis (Lily
   of the Valley)
   64, 231
Cornus (Dogwood)
   controversa 329
   var. 60, 312
   kousa 319
Correa lawrenceana 186
Cortaderia selloana
   (Pampas Grass)
   50, 305
Cosmos 320
Cotinus coggygria (Smoke
   Bush) 194
Crambe cordifolia 290, 306
Crataegus monogyna
   (Hawthorn)
   89–91, 195–6,
   250
   'Birr-bi-Rosea' 76
Crinodendron hookerianum
   (Lantern Tree)
   61, 98, 125, 148,
   164
   patagua 186, 210, 219
Crinum x powellii 125,
   140, 165, 217,
   306
   x powellii album 217
   moorei 50, 217, 296

Crocosmia 50, 195, 212,
   250, 278, 287
   x crocosmiiflora 20
   'Lucifer' 212, 230
   masonorum 278
   'Mount Usher' 115
   'Mrs Geoffrey Howard'
   199
Cryptomeria japonica
   'Elegans' 153,
   164
Cunninghamia lanceolata
   110
*x Cupressocyparis
   leylandii* 55
   'Castlewellan Gold' 304
Cymbalaria muralis
   (see Toadflax;
   Killarney Ivy)
Cymbidium mooreanum 50

Dacrydium franklinii
   148–9
Dahlia 29, 98, 151, 195,
   254, 255, 321
   'Negligée Mauve' 258
Davidia involucrata var.
   vilmoriniana
   (Handkerchief
   Tree) 34, 110,
   123, 190, 197
Delphinium 35, 80, 115,
   185, 195, 222,
   255, 257, 290
Desfontainia spinosa 96
Desmodium elegans 254
Dianella caerulea 278
Dianthus 35
   barbatus (Sweet
   William) 16
   'Mrs Sinkins' 190
Dicksonia antarctica (Tree
   Fern) 77, 95,
   101, 110, 113,
   123, 163, 218,
   267, 330
Dierama 35, 50, 115,
   212, 257, 305
Digitalis purpurea
   (Foxglove) 53,
   93, 121, 199,
   212, 231, 250,
   257, 290

Index of People, Places, Ideas and Events